Duck and Cover: Things Learned Waiting for The Bomb
A Memoir in Essays
By Mark Munger

Cloquet River Press
Publishing Stories from the Lake Superior Basin
www.cloquetriverpress.com

First Edition
Copyright 2021 © Mark Munger

ISBN 978-1-7324434-2-6
Library of Congress Control No.: 2021907454
Published by: Cloquet River Press

Edited by Betsey Norgard
Cover Design by René Munger
Visit the publisher at www.cloquetriverpress.com
Email the author at cloquetriverpress@yahoo.com

Printed in the United States

ACKNOWLEDGMENTS

I would like to thank the following individuals who served as readers for this project: Ken Hubert, Wayne Rikala, Polly John, Sharon Howard, Kim Buncich, Dave "Eddie" Salveson, Steve Cordes, Jeff Tynjala, Judy Infelise Bonovetz, Mark Rubin, Bruce and Jan Larson, Larry and Dode Paasch, Gordy Mesedahl, Dave Michelson, Mike Town, John McLoughlin, Gerry Henkel, Scott Burnes, Tim Thorp, Carolyn Gunderson, Vicky Pufall, and Ron McVean. A special shout-out to Wayne Rikala who scoured his basement archives for evidence of our adolescent depravity.

Without these dedicated friends devoting their time and effort to reading the manuscript, the content and flow of these stories might be vastly different—and more than likely—vastly inferior.

A word of thanks to my wife, René. Many days and nights have been lost to family while I type away at the keyboard, struggle with revisions, or sleep in my chair because I've been up at five in the morning working on this book. Her patience through the duration of this project is much appreciated.

Finally, this collection was written over a considerable period of time. A handful of stories in this memoir appeared in previously-released essay collections *River Stories* or *Doc the Bunny*. When I began writing the story of my upbringing, essays from those earlier collections that fit the timeframe of this book were excised and not included in *Black Water*, the ultimate compilation of my published essays. "The Old 300" made its debut on the *Great Northern Radio Show* where I read the story live—from the Lincoln Junior High stage—on KAXE radio. "Hunting the Ore Docks" was written for and broadcast on Wisconsin Public Radio as part of a celebration of the St. Louis River. The rest of the tales you are about to encounter have, with the exception of the kind folks listed above, never been read by anyone.

Mark Munger
2020
Duluth, Minnesota

In memory of John McLoughlin, Roni Seger Town, Pat Pufall, Dode Komalainen Paasch, and Russ Ditman who experienced many of these tales. A special "thank you" to Randy McCarty, who believed in my words.

I do like men who come out frankly and own that they are not gods.

—Louisa May Alcott—

A WORD ABOUT PROCESS

RIGHT or wrong, the process used in creating this string of vignettes from childhood and early adulthood, from birth to wooing my bride, is one of memory. I have not, in the writing of these essays about my life, checked dates and occurrences and events drawn from personal recollection against the historical record. I have not, for example, sat down at the microfiche machine in the Duluth Public Library to discern if a person depicted in a story was at a particular place on a particular date, stayed at this hotel or that hotel, lived here or there, or said this or that. What you will read are pure, unadulterated visions of the past drawn, as best as could be, from my own memory. Others who were present at the events and circumstances and incidents chronicled in these stories may disagree with my rendition. That's just fine. They're free to write their own memoirs; embellishing them, editing them, and birthing them on the unsuspecting public as they so choose. If folks who grew up with me or experienced the incidents reported on these pages feel so inclined, they can argue with my version of history by writing scathing letters, posting criticisms online, or leaving me irate voicemails.

My goal in sharing my perceptions of my life is to preserve a sense of where I came from, the boy I was, what I experienced, the times I grew up in, and the man I've become. That's it. Anything else a reader assigns as a motive or reason for the writing of this book is on the reader. I'll accept such assignations as the unencumbered right of a reader to understand things in his or her own way but I won't engage in a debate as a means to ferret out "truth." In the end, I'll consult my childhood scrapbooks, photographs, family, and friends to ensure I'm getting things close in terms of reality. This is the written and created memory of one man's past. It is not an autobiography.

Mark

TABLE OF CONTENTS

BEGINNINGS

I am a St. Paulite who considers himself a lifelong Duluthian. I was born on October 30, 1954 in Miller Hospital in downtown St. Paul because Mom and Dad were living in a two-bedroom flat off Grand Avenue in Minnesota's capital city. Dad worked days as an insurance adjuster and went to night school at the St. Paul College of Law. Mom, who had graduated from The Villa (now known as the College of St. Scholastica) in Duluth with a degree in medical technology, spent her days drawing blood and doing other mysterious stuff at a St. Paul clinic while waiting to give birth to me.

1954, the year I emerged onto the scene, was also the year my uncle Willard Munger won a seat in the Minnesota House of Representatives. Uncle Willard, who was nearly seventeen years older than Dad, ran a little ma and pa motel back home in Duluth—the Willard Motel (named after the famed hotel in Washington, D.C. where politicians chewed the fat and made the <u>real</u> decisions of government). The motel never made much money and Willard, needing a place to stay while the legislature was in session, ended up living with us. I don't remember this part because I was a newborn. But I can imagine how much fun it must have been for my youthful parents to have a snoring, neophyte, Liberal politician sleeping in the next room while I screamed for food and attention. If you learn anything about me from these stories it's that I've always demanded an unusual (and my family would say, unfair) amount of attention.

I don't remember much about the four years we spent in St. Paul. The few memories I *think* I have may be mine or they may be scenes I've imagined because I've studied a handful of old black-and-white photographs in scrapbooks. My mother—Barbara Jean Kobe Munger Tourville—is a saver. I doubt, in the entirety of Mom's life, she's ever thrown out anything including her old underwear. There's good and there's bad that comes from such an obsessive/compulsive (OCD) nature: Her closets are perpetually overrun with out-of-style shoes and dresses and skirts that, while she'll never wear them again, are somehow too precious to discard. That's the bad. Mom's not inclined to generosity when it comes to her stuff. She has no urge to donate things that are in good shape to charity. Those need to be stockpiled, to be stored, even if they will never be worn or used again. It's as if Mom's signed on to that old Egyptian notion you need to haul all your stuff into the grave with you for the afterlife. That's the bad part of Mom's OCD affliction, which she passed on—in no small measure—to her eldest child.

The good part of Mom's obsessive saving? She made sure milestones of my life were preserved for posterity; you know, in case I ever became president. More about that little weight on my shoulders later. For now, understand that the early flotsam of my life was cut and pasted into scrapbooks for future reflection. I have a few photographs of school picnics and family vacations and Little League baseball and such; some class pictures from elementary school; assorted baptismal and birthday and confirmation and graduation cards from family and friends; and a smattering of other bits of paper from which I can try to reconstruct my life. For this archive, I have to thank Mom.

Dad—Harry Leonard Munger—wasn't much of a saver. That might be because he was blessed with a nearly photographic memory. Though experts dispute adults can possess an eidetic memory (picture perfect recall), I'm here to tell you that, at least up until Dad hit his late eighties, he was one of the rare adults who was endowed with that gift. But Dad was more interested in the political heritage of the Munger Family, the family's Liberal leanings and background that made him a dogged member of the Minnesota DFL (Democratic Farmer Labor) party than he was about personal trivia. Dad was oblivious to what was going on at home while he built his law practice, hobnobbed with politicians and party officials, and rubbed elbows with the elite of Duluth (which is odd because Dad was like a bull in a china shop when it came to social functions). He was also more concerned about enjoying his two favorite pastimes away from the law—hunting and fishing—than preserving family history. I'm certain Dad never really understood Mom's passion for archiving the past, at least in terms of his children's lives.

My parents were products of the Great Depression. For Mom, this meant moving from place to place with her father, a traveling salesman for Berwind Coal Company; and her mother, a former elementary school teacher; and Mom's only sibling—her younger sister and my aunt—Susanne Kobe Pederson Schuler ("Sukie"). My maternal grandfather—John "Jack" Kobe—moved the family from Aurora on Minnesota's Iron Range to Wadena to Iowa to the Twin Cities before finally settling in Duluth. In Duluth Jack and Marie (my maternal grandmother) moved from the Congdon neighborhood in Duluth's East End to Riverside to West Duluth. The Kobe family never had much money but they got by. And Grandpa and Grandma Kobe had dreams even in the midst of the worst economy in our nation's history. One of those dreams was building, owning, and operating a family resort on Bear Island Lake between Babbitt and Ely in northern St. Louis County.

Before you get the idea that the Kobe side of my family "made it big," you need to understand something. The 160-acre parcel that made up the Buena Vista Resort property was purchased by my grandparents for a thousand bucks from the widow of a Finn who'd been killed in a logging accident. Granted, a thousand dollars was a considerable sum in 1939 but not unreachable for a guy with steady employment who was industrious and frugal. The resort itself was a collection of handcrafted cottages, a fish house (for cleaning fish), a small store, an ice-house (for storing blocks of ice), and a shed housing a gasoline powered light plant (though most often, the cabins were illumed by kerosene lamps). The buildings were built of white pine logged and milled on site. The interiors were finished in varnished white pine. Though sturdy (and still standing today) the cabins were uninsulated. Heat was provided for guests by small stoves capable of burning either wood or coal. The spartan structures were crafted by Finnish carpenters hired and supervised by Grandpa Jack. Grandma Marie oversaw the marketing of the place, the cleaning of the cabins and grounds, the laundry, and the registration of guests. In addition to coordinating the construction of the cabins and outbuildings Grandpa Jack was the fishing guide, on-site repairman (when his job as a coal salesman allowed), wood splitter, fish cleaner, and, not to be too cute about it, Buena Vista's Jack-of-all-trades. Mom and Sukie were the labor, charged with toting buckets of drinking water and coal and firewood to each cabin, sweeping the privies, scouring floors, putting fresh linens on the beds, and stocking the cabins with clean towels and washcloths. After their chores were done, the Kobe girls enjoyed idyllic summer life in the Minnesota bush. The only winter activity at the resort was the one January weekend the family headed north from Duluth to meet friends and relatives to cut and put up ice sawed from Bear

Island Lake, ice that would last an entire summer when covered with sawdust in the ice-house.

This is a long-winded way of telling you that Mom and Aunt Sukie, while not hailing from a well-to-do family, experienced childhoods few children of the Great Depression enjoyed. Grandma Marie—an ex-schoolteacher and silent movie house pianist—loved the North Woods and was the impetus behind Buena Vista though Marie had a somewhat unrealistic and romantic notion of the out-of-doors. I have journals of her finely crafted verse tucked away, odes reminiscent of Service and Whitman. For a seemingly patrician gal from the suburbs of Chicago (Oak Park), Grandma Marie was resilient and tough. She died when I was three and a half years old so my memory of her is limited. From family history, she appears to have been the perfect match for Jack, an immigrant from Austria-controlled Slovenia who left school in the eighth grade to work in the iron ore mines around Aurora. Despite his lack of education, Grandpa Jack was a wise, dapper, well-mannered man who loved to hunt and fish, a man of the out-of-doors fully capable of assisting Marie in finding the wilderness Shangri-La she longed for. He passed away the year I met my wife, René. Though René and Grandpa Jack never met, I'm sure he would have loved René as I do.

Dad's story was markedly different. His parents, Harry and Elsie Munger were poor. Dirt poor. Literally. They began their lives in Pockerbrush, the hardscrabble landscape memorialized by novelist Herbert Krause in stories about the Germanic settlers of Otter Tail County, Minnesota. Grandpa Harry tried to emulate his own father by farming a forty-acre tract adjacent to the ancestral homestead in Friberg Township. Didn't work. Grandpa Harry apparently took after his own father—Great Grandpa Lyman Munger—which meant Grandpa Harry was a terrible farmer.

Dad was the youngest of five children born to Grandpa Harry and Grandma Elsie Zuehlsdorf Munger; Bob, Willard, Barney, Elsie, and "Little" Harry. The span between Uncle Bob and Dad was nearly twenty years. Grandma Munger was done bearing children until Barney died of scarlet fever. She had "Little Harry"—after Barney passed—when she was in her forties. Dad often remarked he was a replacement child; a stand-in for the well-loved, tow-headed Barney whose tragic death haunted the family.

Given the advanced ages of his folks when Dad was born, it fell upon Aunt Elsie to keep an eye on Little Harry, or "Baby" as he was sometimes called. But Elsie was a teenager when Dad was toddling around Fergus Falls (the Depression was on; Grandpa Harry lost the farm, moved to town, and took a job as a game warden despite having only a fourth-grade education) so Dad was pretty much a free-range kid. Which meant he skipped a lot of school to hitch rides to farms owned by his paternal and maternal grandparents where he spent his days fishing and hunting instead of attending class. To say Dad was a wild child would be an understatement. As I look back upon my life with Harry, I'm reminded of this singular truth: Like every fourteen-year-old boy I've ever known (including me), my father was egocentric, self-centered, and on the lookout for a good time. This aspect of Dad's character never changed and his stunted emotional development is likely one reason Dad was married and divorced twice and lived with three different women.

Dad grew up in poverty. He never owned a bicycle, not even a used one. Grandpa Harry kept his game warden job, obtained through political patronage as a loyal Farmer Laborite (FL'er), only as long as Governors Floyd Olson and Elmer Benson held office. The Munger family had little savings or assets or spending money despite Grandpa being steadily employed throughout the Great Depression. The family's meager paycheck-to-paycheck existence was supplemented by fresh vegetables, meat, and canned goods provided from the larders of extended family. Even with such support, the Depression was a time of constant want and worry for the Mungers. I'm fairly certain that the threat of financial ruin formed Dad's belief that enjoying life—having fun, something his parents were unable to do given their life-long economic struggles—was the only thing that mattered when traveling life's veil of tears.

There came a time during Dad's childhood when things got so bad the Mungers were forced to leave Pockerbrush. Dad's older brother Willard, also an FL'er and newly married with a young daughter, saw little opportunity for advancement in Otter Tail County and accepted a series of political patronage jobs in Duluth. With the election of Republican Harold Stassen to the governorship in 1938, both Uncle Willard and Grandpa Harry lost their jobs. After struggling to find work, Willard turned a couple of university extension courses in marine drafting into an opportunity: He was appointed foreman in the Butler Shipyard in Superior, Wisconsin where he also secured employment for Grandpa Harry.

In 1941, Grandpa Harry went to work in the shipyard, Grandma Elsie began keeping house in a ramshackle two-story in Riverside, and Dad enrolled in Duluth Denfeld High School. Dad met Mom at Denfeld and that's where my story begins.

BOOK ONE: 2402
CHAMBERSBURG

I had a deep sense of ownership of the Woods behind my house. They were <u>my</u> woods.
—Richard Louv—

PIEDMONT

THERE is no question about it: I was a blessed child. The neighborhood where Dad and Mom chose to raise me (and later, my brother Dave and my sister Anne) was and is a magical place, a protected place, a bit of heaven on earth. I'm not talking about my first four years of life spent in a cramped two-bedroom walkup in the Grand Avenue neighborhood of St. Paul. I'm talking about the Piedmont Heights neighborhood of Duluth.

My memory of early childhood, as it would be for anyone trying to recall events taking place sixty years ago, is sketchy. This truth is magnified when trying to summon images stored in my brain from birth to age four, the age I was when Dad, and Mom, and I left St. Paul and moved back "home," Dad having finished law school and anxious to begin work as a personal injury attorney.

How it was that Harry Munger decided to open up his own law office, first with a guy by the name of Don Mehrman, then with Milan Balach, and then finally, for nearly forty years, with Canadian-born attorney A. Blake MacDonald, as his partners, is lost with Dad's passing. Other than citing Dad's independent personality and his love of gambling (cards, dice, sports—it didn't matter), I can only speculate about why he chose to become a Personal Injury (PI) lawyer. I'm pretty sure if Dad had asked Mom, she would have preferred that he join an established firm representing corporations and insurance companies. After all, PI lawyers only get paid their one-third contingency fee if they settle a case or win at trial. Such speculative work is a difficult premise upon which to raise a family. However, I am convinced several things in Dad's personal history and persona likely led him to hang out his own shingle and become a plaintiff's trial lawyer.

First, there's the fact that, in the most important of ways, Dad reared himself. Saying he was raised by wolves would be doing a disservice to wolves! Because of his—shall we say— "casual" upbringing, Dad made most of his childhood choices for himself. Consequently, he was not risk averse. In fact, Dad loved taking chances, such that turning <u>that</u> personality trait into a profession seemed, I'm sure to him, a natural progression.

27

Then there was the lure of a big payday. Even in the late '50s and early '60s when Dad was getting started in Duluth as a lawyer, a PI attorney could—if he snagged the right case—generate a fee equal to an entire year's salary. To a gambler, the possibility, however remote, of such a bonanza could overcome a lot of fears and uncertainties including the uncertainty of whether the mortgage gets paid.

Finally, as a trial lawyer, Dad saw himself on the side of virtue against the dark lords controlling commerce and industry. Looking back on Dad's vocational decision, it seems only natural that the son of Populists (as members of the Nonpartisan League) and FL'ers would cast his lot with "The People." Having lived with the man for over twenty years, known him for sixty-three, and worked alongside him in his law firm for more than a decade, I'm pretty sure Dad saw himself as a knight in shining armor fighting evil capitalist dragons set upon devouring the powerless, the indigent, and the unfortunate. I also believe that my prim and proper mother, while pleased with the lifestyle Dad's vocation afforded, would've been far happier if Dad had chosen probate or real estate law for his line of work.

With our move north, I became a child of Piedmont, growing up atop the hills overlooking Duluth's harbor and the city's industrial base, completely sheltered from the poverty that formed Dad's world view. I don't know where Mom, Dad, and I lived between the time we returned to Duluth and when our new rambler on Chambersburg Avenue was ready for occupancy. Maybe with grandparents on one side or the other. Maybe in an apartment. I haven't a clue. I have no memory of it. Likewise, I have no memory of moving day. But I do recall something of living in Bob Huseby's housing development.

Most of the fathers living in our new neighborhood were veterans. Some kids—like my best friend growing up, Dave "Eddie" Salveson—had fathers who'd been in uniform during WW II or who'd served in Korea.

Dad was only 17 when he graduated from Denfeld. Too young for WW II, Dad, who wanted to be the first Munger to be a college graduate, enlisted, served two years in the Army Air Corps (the Air Force's predecessor), was honorably discharged, and missed being recalled for the Korean conflict by a week.

The point of this isn't to tell you I grew up amongst heroes, men who served and, according to Tom Brokow, make up "The Greatest Generation." My recollection of the collective history of the men who lived in my neighborhood—many of whom served as mentors—is more pedestrian than recounting their wartime exploits. Piedmont Heights sprouted new homes due to those veterans' ready access to VA loans, the inexpensive mortgages that fueled Mr. Huseby's vision. Dad took advantage of the GI Bill to fund college and law school and then used his own VA benefits to build a bungalow on Chambersburg Avenue.

From what I was told by Eddie's father—Ed Salveson—most of Piedmont Heights had been farmland prior to Bob Huseby's bulldozers arriving. Evidence of that history could be found in the forest adjacent to Hutchinson Road at the bottom of Chambersburg. When we were old enough to safely explore "the Woods" we found rotting fence posts hidden amongst aspen and birch reclaiming land that had once been pasture. We also encountered old bottles and rusted cans—abandoned household dumps evidencing farmhouses long since demolished, leveled, and reduced to memory. Occasionally, we'd stumble into strands of barbed wire (sometimes with unfortunate results, requiring us to undergo the most feared of all doctor's tortures—a tetanus shot). A few blocks north of Piedmont Elementary School, a truck farm still grew vegetables for the innumerable corner grocery stores located throughout Duluth. That last remaining, working farm in Piedmont succumbed to development around the time I entered high school.

Ed Salveson was a rare bird. He was a native of Piedmont Heights, having grown up on top of the hill before Huseby's homes were constructed; before the Piedmont Shopping Center was built; before two gas stations and a hardware store and a barber salon and a dentist office and a greasy spoon and a Catholic school were added to the landscape he called home. I took what Ed passed on about the history of his old stomping grounds as gospel. I had to: He was an Eagle Scout, a Navy veteran, an engineer, and the father of my best friend.

For whatever reason, Dad and Mom didn't select Huseby as our builder. I'm not sure why. I mean, if you drive around my old neighborhood, you'll see Huseby homes in a handful of designs replicated up and down Chambersburg Avenue,

Hutchinson Road, Robert Court, and Morris Thomas Road. Our house was built by another Duluth contractor. It's true the lot was purchased from Huseby since he controlled most of the land in Piedmont Heights. But our house was built by one of Huseby's competitors, which might be why—shortly after we moved in—the basement walls began weeping water and the garage developed a noticeable downhill list. Having one contractor prepare the site and another build the house probably wasn't the wisest of decisions.

As a toddler, I tended to roam. Maybe roam is too passive a term: I liked to escape. We lived on the downslope of a big hill, where Chambersburg Avenue plummets to intersect Hutchinson Road. Our neighborhood was still being developed, which meant the landscape was pockmarked with excavations awaiting foundations. Those digs filled up with rainwater and Mom tried to prevent my drowning by tethering me to our back porch. I'm no rocket scientist but at four years old I was smart enough to unhook a leash. I have a vague memory of standing in the lot next to our house, a lot that became the Sundins' home, looking at a big hole. What I was thinking, what I was considering while staring at the muddy water pooled below me, I have no idea. Before anything untoward occurred, Mom found me, grabbed me up, and trundled me to safety. After another escape—where I ended up standing at the edge of a similar yawning, artificial canyon of death (the excavation for Kingo Olson's house)—Mom gave up tying me to the railing like a dog.

That's about as much as I can remember from my first few years in the neighborhood. Somewhere along the line, I met that blond-headed kid I mentioned. I've known Eddie Salveson, both of us now grandfathers, for over sixty years. In some ways, this memoir is as much Eddie's story—and the story of hundreds of other children who grew up in Piedmont Heights during the late '50s, '60s, and early '70s—as it is mine.

CONFLICT

I never saw Dad hit Mom. Even so, their marriage wasn't rosy. There was a brief period where they got on just fine though I never—even in the good times—saw my parents express overt affection towards each other in the nature of spontaneous hugs or kisses. I also never heard (even though my bedroom was right next to theirs) proof of lovemaking. Obviously, that happened at least once. But beyond my procreation, I have no evidence my parents engaged in such antics after I darkened their door—or brightened their lives—however my arrival is to be interpreted.

Dad could be intimidating. Towards Mom, towards me, towards other folks, though not in a physical sense. The one and only time he took after me with a belt was because I zoomed down Chambersburg Avenue in a little blue pedal car; a car Grandpa Jack purchased for me with Green Stamps. I was five years old. When I returned to our driveway exhilarated from the rush of adrenaline caused by defying traffic and exhausted from pushing the heavy, pressed tin car up the steep hill, Dad was waiting for me.

"Get over here!" Dad yelled.

I hesitated.

"Now!" he screamed, removing his belt from his trousers.

The leather belt stung when it connected and I cried. After it was over, I'm guessing Dad regretted whipping my bare bottom with his belt: He never used one on me again.

Dad rarely laid hands on me; not because I didn't need discipline but because he wasn't around. Unless we were on a family outing, or fishing together, or taking a ride somewhere as a family, I was either on my own, hanging with friends, or Mom was supervising me. When I misbehaved, Mom was the one who redirected my wayward path. If I bit someone, Mom's response was to grab hold of my arm and bite down, never drawing blood but leaving a deep impression of her teeth in my skin. If I used a bad word she'd drag me into the bathroom, grab a bar of soap, pry my mouth open, and rake the bar across my teeth. The residual taste of Ivory—which took time to rinse out—was one hell of a reminder to watch what I said.

I spent hours sitting on a three-legged milk stool in a corner of my bedroom staring at the bumpy plaster wall. Mom didn't shorten my punishment or acknowledge my protests, which often took the form of yelling, screaming, and kicking the wall with tennis shoes. She was patient that way, letting me vent without intervention.

When I wasn't listening or I talked back or I got into mischief (like stealing matches to make a campfire at the shack Eddie and I built behind his house), Mom was there with her weapon of choice.

"Pull down your jeans and underwear," she'd command.

I'd shrink from Mom's ire and plead my case. But, given both my parents had severe streaks of stubborn resolve as part of their countenances (it was, given my father's brashness and temper obvious in Dad; it was far more subtle but equally present in Mom), urging Mom to reconsider the yardstick never worked.

"Pull down your jeans and your underwear!" she'd repeat.

After I complied, Mom would wind up and whack, whack, whack me with the wooden yardstick; raising welts on my tender buttocks as reminders that disobedience to Barbara Jean Kobe Munger would not be tolerated.

As I grew older, Mom's attempts at corporal punishment became less effective. Around age eleven, I did something untoward and she commanded me to pull down my pants and drawers, bend over, and receive the benefit of her favored, supple wooden reminder. I refused and a chase ensued. Wearing pedal pushers and running in bare feet, her hair extensions up in a Laura Petrie bun, her face without makeup, Mom pursued me through the house. I ducked behind the refrigerator and, without considering the consequences, stuck a foot out. Mom tripped and stubbed her big toe. Mom drove and I rode in the front passenger's seat of our black '64 Pontiac Grand Prix (a car that looked like the Batmobile) to the hospital. I was saddened by my conduct but happy I'd escaped punishment. An X-ray at St. Mary's confirmed Mom's big toe was broken. I'm pretty sure I said I was sorry even though I was pleased with how things turned out: That was the last time Mom tried to spank me.

Dad's verbal abuse started when I was young, maybe eight or nine years old, not long after Dave entered the picture. That said, my brother was a little kid and had nothing to do with the change that took place in our household. Dad began keeping later and later hours at the office—ostensibly "building his practice"—and became less and less able to hold civilized conversations with Mom. I'm not sure if he was having an affair early on in their marriage. I'm certain that eventually happened. In fact, I know it did because he divorced Mom and married Kay (a woman two decades younger than Mom) and told me, after introducing me to Kay in a downtown bar, they were in a "relationship." But that scene would transpire years later; after my parents staggered through thirty-plus years of matrimony.

Like I said, I never witnessed Dad engage in physical abuse. But man, the screaming and the yelling! His voice would escalate without warning, signaling it was time for me, my brother Dave, and sister Anne to clear the deck. There were times when Dad threw things and broke things, including a very expensive watch. Dad's Bulova shattered against the concrete wall of our basement after he took issue with how Mom was ironing his shirts. I was there, a foot or two away, when Dad's watch whizzed past my head, struck the wall, and exploded.

After another very loud and scary dustup, Dad stormed out the front door, muttering something about "taking a walk to clear his head." Mom packed suitcases, grabbed Dave and me, and pointed us towards the door.

"I'm not going to let him do this to us again," Mom said through tears.

Mom pulled the family's white Dodge Dart station wagon out of the driveway and into the dark night, the car's high beams pointed towards liberation. We ended up at the public landing on Pike Lake, the station wagon facing the lake, my little brother and me in the back seat, all of us staring at the moon and stars through the windshield as celestial light reflected off calm water. I was confused and frightened. I was also sad because I was too small, too puny, to defend Mom. What was Mom thinking? Was she deciding whether to drive the Dodge into Pike Lake and end the charade of family? Or was she pondering what should come next in terms of her marriage? I've never asked Mom about that night and, given her advanced age and the trauma she experienced, her mind has likely wiped away any trace of the event.

It's obvious that Mom didn't kill us off and she didn't leave Dad; at least, not then. Their breakup—as I've said—was decades away. Mom drove home, put us to bed, and somehow, a marital truce ensued. The incident was never talked about; never discussed so that Dave and I could understand that "these things happen between parents who love each other." There was no, "and we both love you and your brother" or any other reassurance. That's not how things were done. We simply went back to being a family, albeit a fractured and tenuous one.

Dad and I didn't get along. I'm sure Dad's yelling at Mom, whom I always thought was the closest thing to a saint on Earth, had something to do with creating the emotional distance between us. Then too, Dad's disinterest in me as an athlete fueled feelings of inadequacy. I remember playing catch with Dad a few times. Given my eyesight was terrible, given I closed my eyes when Dad soft-tossed a ball towards me as I batted, and given Dad's lack of patience, I'm surprised he spent any time at all trying to teach me the fundamentals of baseball.

In the end, the rift between us was built upon two simple truths: I didn't understand Dad and he didn't understand me. I also didn't understand why Dad grew distant from Mom. Years later I would learn that she was spending money faster than Dad could make it; that she skimped on groceries to buy clothes, shoes, and accessories for herself. Since Dad grew up with a mother who was an excellent, "from scratch" cook, Mom's inability to cook hearty, old-fashioned meals—resorting to hotdish experiments from the pages of *Good Housekeeping* and *Ladies Home Journal;* Banquet frozen chicken, pot pies, and TV Dinners and Totino's frozen pizzas to fill the void—only added to the stress. By the time Dad and I were walking the woods north of Duluth with our black Labrador (Deuce II) searching for ruffed grouse, me having passed gun safety and carrying a single-shot twenty gauge, my fear and upset and uncertainty concerning Dad had festered into loathing. I didn't act on my emotions. But my memory of that walk in the woods—and the evil thoughts that filled my mind as I carried a shotgun—still haunts me, as does a humiliating exchange that occurred the following winter.

We were on a family ski trip to Snowmass, Colorado. Mom and Dad went to an evening cocktail party and left me in charge of Dave, who was old enough to ski, and Anne, who wasn't. Before my parents left for the party, I'd asked to join other kids on the ski trip in the pool.

"No," Dad said, "you're watching your brother and sister."

After our parents left, I made a deal with Dave. He'd watch Anne and I'd pay him to do it. I figured *Our parents are in the bar; they'll never know.* But the party my parents were attending was poolside and when I showed up at the pool in my swimsuit, a towel draped over my shoulder, Dad spotted me. Instead of taking me aside, reprimanding me, and sending me back to the room to babysit, Dad grabbed me by the back of the neck and started cussing. That was unusual. I never heard the word "fuck" come out of Harry's mouth until I was an adult. But Dad wasn't a prude. He knew most of a sailor's vocabulary, much of which he unloaded on me as he repeatedly kicked me in the ass in front of my parents' friends and their children before marching me back to our room.

Dad's devotion to growing his law practice at the expense of family dinners, his volatile temper, his excuses as to why he couldn't be at certain events, all of them fostered a tenuous relationship. It wasn't like we didn't do things together. We made annual treks to Liston Deer Camp and to the fishing opener at the Scotts' cabin on Whiteface Lake and other inland lakes to fish; sometimes just Dad and me, sometimes as a family. I'm not saying there wasn't a parent-child bond between us. But it was buried beneath uncomfortable tension.

To complicate matters, I started going off the rails my junior year at Denfeld. Though I managed to stay out of trouble for much of high school—despite the fact eighteen-year-olds could buy booze in Superior, Wisconsin, just a stone's throw across the Arrowhead Bridge from Duluth—when I finally fell from grace my fall was widely known and notorious. And around the time I became embroiled in adolescent misadventure, my parents' marriage started to unravel.

Yelling beckoned me from the basement of our new home on Miller Creek. I was in my senior year at Denfeld. I'd planned to stay in and study. As the discord upstairs grew louder, it sounded like Mom was in trouble. I put down my pen and ran up the staircase. I opened the door to my parents' bedroom to find Dad in the midst of a tantrum and Mom sitting on the edge of their shared bed, crying.

"What's going on?"

"Your mother!" Dad yelled, "is having an affair with a doctor; a goddamned doctor from the Cities!"

I'd always suspected that Dad was the one stepping out. Even though I idolized Mom, ascribing to her a level of perfection that was humanly impossible, the anxiety on Mom's face appeared to confirm Dad's accusation.

"He's just a friend," Mom whispered.

"Bullshit!"

Dad advanced with his right hand balled in a fist. Like I said, I never witnessed Dad hit Mom but that seemed like a real possibility.

"Get back!" I warned, my voice cracking as I stepped between my parents. "Don't come any closer!"

Dad looked at me, his face flamed, his breath soured from whiskey. Dad wasn't an alcoholic but he was a consistent social drinker who, while he rarely partook of the noontime cocktails that were prevalent amongst lawyers and judges of his generation, always had a cocktail or two at a local watering hole before coming home from work. His insistence on stopping "for one" was another source of conflict in my parents' marriage.

Dad had me by a good seventy pounds and an inch or two. I wouldn't gain my full height for a few months and, when I graduated, I'd barely tip the scales at one-fifty. If blows were going to come, I'd get the worst of it. But she's my mother: I'd take whatever Dad wanted to dish out to protect the woman who gave birth to me, whatever her faults, whatever her sins.

Inexplicably, Dad lowered his fist and headed for the door.

"She's having an affair with a fancy-assed Twin Cities doctor. Believe it or not, Mark, that's the truth!"

Mom summoned up the temerity to respond, "And what about all the women you've been with? What about them?"

Dad didn't answer. He left the bedroom, exited the house, opened the garage door, fired up the Grand Prix, and roared away. After offering Mom hesitant words of consolation and a hug, I grabbed my letter jacket, exited the house, closed the garage door, and walked to my friend Vicky Stauber's house. I had a few beers with Tom—Vicky's dad—slept on a davenport in the Staubers' basement, and came home the next morning.

Dad was gone for a week.

THE BASEBALL GAME

Dazzling sunlight touched the trampled grass of a sandlot overlooking the bronze water of the St. Louis River. I was at Grandma Munger's house in Riverside, a neighborhood located at the western edge of Duluth, a development created in the late 1890s to house employees of the McDougal Shipyard.

Elsie Munger, my paternal grandmother, was a rotund woman who loved to feed anyone who happened by. She was a wonderful cook and a terrible housekeeper. A dusty piano—untuned and unplayed—crowded Grandma's living room. After Grandpa Harry died of a heart attack, Grandma took in "boarders." Single men who worked blue-collar jobs lived at Grandma's and ate breakfasts and suppers at her dining room table.

The aroma of Grandma's caramel rolls greeted me when I ambled into the kitchen.

"Hi Grandma."

"Hello Mark," Grandma replied, her hands and wrists white from flour. "I made rolls for breakfast," she added, tilting her very old head in an effort to keep her eyeglasses from sliding off her nose and falling into the bread dough she was kneading.

I grabbed a hot, gooey roll and slathered it with butter. The caramel and pecans glistened in morning light despite a film of grease coating the kitchen windows.

"What are your plans for the day?" Grandma asked, rolling and unrolling the dough, the loose skin of her upper arms wobbling from effort.

"The kids up the street wanna play baseball," I said, before gulping down a glass of cold, whole milk.

Nothing but whole milk, heavy cream, and real butter at Grandma's. At home, it was artificial whipped topping, skim milk, and oleo margarine. On reflection, I'm sure the difference between Grandma's and Mom's kitchens caused Dad untold upset.

"Be careful," Grandma warned as I stood up from the table, pulled my ball cap over my eyes, and headed toward the door.

"OK."

38

Grandma never entertained me. When I visited her place, I was left to my own devices. It was either use my imagination and play with toys I brought from home or seek out kids from the neighborhood. Grandma spent her time doing laundry, cooking, and watching soap operas on a black and white television in the living room. We didn't play board games or interact much beyond eating together but I didn't mind. I was an only child back then used to having my way.

It was late September. I'd just started kindergarten. I was five years old—almost six—and didn't own a baseball glove. I didn't know how to properly throw a ball or swing a bat. But I was an extra body to put in the field.

"Hey," one of the older boys called out as I approached. "With Munger, we've got five a side. He can be on the team that's batting."

The team in the field had a pitcher, a first baseman, a shortstop, and two outfielders. The side batting supplied the catcher. The boys playing all had gloves and wore baseball caps over neat crew-cuts. It was late morning. The day was heating up. Grasshoppers sang from weeds defining the ballfield's informal boundaries.

I'm not sure what I was thinking when I walked between the batter and the catcher. All I remember is the hollow sound of wood meeting my skull. How long I remained on my back with nine other boys clustered around me, calling my name, trying to get me to come to, I don't know.

"Munger, you OK?" someone asked as my eyes opened.

"You're bleeding like crazy," another boy added. "You better go tell your grandma."

My head throbbed. "No," I said as tears streamed down my face. "She'll call Dad and he'll be mad he has to leave his office to come and get me."

"You don't look so good."

"I can play," I said, sitting up. The sudden movement caused my head to spin. I thought I was going to puke.

"I dunno," the big kid who first greeted me interjected. "You should probably go home."

An adult voice called from across the street.

"That's my dad," the oldest boy said. "He's taking me and my little brother to Dairy Queen. You wanna come?"

"It's too hot to play anyway," another boy said. "I'll go get some money."

Everyone grabbed their gear and ran towards their houses. Danny—the boy who had extended the invitation—looked at me and whistled.

"Wow, that's one nasty cut!" he observed. "You sure you're OK?"

I stood up and wiped blood and tears from my face with the edge of my T-shirt.

"Ya. I'll go ask my grandma for money. Don't leave without me."

Danny nodded and ran off.

I stood in the living room as Grandma Munger watched *The Dottie Becker Show,* my T-shirt worn inside out to hide bloodstains. The brim of my ball cap was pulled down to conceal the cut and the bruise above my eye.

"Danny's dad is taking us to Dairy Queen."

"That's nice," Grandma replied, never taking her eyes off the television. "There's change in my coin purse. Help yourself to fifty cents."

Whenever I asked to visit the Riverside corner store, Grandma would hand me two quarters and, given you could buy a fistful of penny candy for half a buck, my sweet tooth never went wanting when I stayed with Grandma. I walked into the dining room, found her purse, and took the change.

"Don't be gone too long now," she admonished.

"I won't."

"What'll you have, Munger?" Danny's dad asked as we pulled into the parking lot of the Grand Avenue Dairy Queen.

The iconic bell tower of Denfeld High School rose behind drive-in to touch the late summer sky. I knew Denfeld was where Mom and Dad had met. I guessed—correctly—it was where I'd go to high school.

"Blueberry malt," I answered.

My headache hadn't abated. Eleven boys were crammed into the car. Three of us sat in the station wagon's cargo area on the floor.

"What's wrong with you?" Danny's dad asked when he faced me to take my order.

"Nothin'."

"You're as white as a ghost!"

"He got hit by a bat," Danny offered. "Right between the eyes."

"What? Let me see," Danny's dad said. "Take off your hat!"

I lifted my cap.

"Are you nuts?" the man whispered. "You need to see a doctor. That eye is so puffed out, who knows how bad you're hurt. I gotta get you back to your grandma's."

"Can we still get ice cream?" Danny pleaded.

Danny's dad pulled hard on his chin with his right hand and thought. "I guess. We're already here. But we're heading back as soon as you get your ice cream."

"Sorry to have to tell you this," Danny's father said to Grandma as he stood behind me on the bottom stair of the rickety old staircase leading to the front door of Grandma's house.

"Front door" is a misnomer. The stairs we were standing on led to the kitchen. The front of the house actually faced the St. Louis River and the enclosed front porch was cluttered with old furniture, dead houseplants, and inoperable household appliances. Because the main road passed by the rear of the house where a decrepit garage slanted towards collapse, the back door was the entrance everyone used.

"Mark got hit with a bat," the man continued, removing my cap.

"Oh, my word!" Grandma gasped.

Grandma called Dad. He left his law office to bring me to the doctor. "Does it hurt?" Dad asked as he slid behind the steering wheel of our big black Dodge station wagon, closed the driver's side door, and drove away from Grandma's.

I shook my head. I anticipated a lecture about the dangers of walking into baseball bats. I also figured we'd head to the Duluth Clinic where Mom worked and where the family doctored. Dad didn't lecture me and instead of heading downtown, the Dodge turned left on Commonwealth Avenue.

"Where we goin'?"

"Doc Munger's house."

41

Jim Munger was a member of our church but no relation. He worked as a physician in the Gary-New Duluth steel plant. As we entered Morgan Park—a factory town built by U.S. Steel in the early 1900s—and passed row after row of company houses, I began to cry.

"It'll be fine," Dad said.

Doc Munger greeted us in the foyer with a black leather medical bag in one hand.

"Nothing broken," Doc opined after palpating the bruise obscuring my left eye. "But he needs stitches. I'll give him a shot of Novocain before I sew him up."

The syringe Doc Munger pulled out of his bag looked to be two feet long. I bolted when I realized he intended to stick me in the face with the thing. It took the good doctor and Dad the better part of ten minutes chasing me around furniture before they trapped me in a corner so Doc Munger could administer the dreaded shot.

I wore a black eyepatch over my eye when I went back to school. When kids at Piedmont Elementary asked me what had happened, I didn't tell them I'd walked into the business end of a baseball bat. Instead, I told them I was a pirate.

ELEMENTARY SCHOOL

Miss Ness seemed to be about a hundred years old, though I'm sure she wasn't: No school board would allow a centenarian to teach little kids. But to me, a boy who turned six the October I started school, Miss Ness, a demure—yet indestructible—woman appeared ancient.

Back when I started Piedmont Elementary, there was no such thing as "all day" kindergarten. Kids were randomly assigned to "morning" or "afternoon" sessions. Miss Ness was it: She was the only kindergarten teacher. Once you made it through the elementary gauntlet, Piedmonters were bussed down the hill to Lincoln Junior High School, an ancient and imposing edifice located in Duluth's West End. The culture shock of that transition will be the fodder for other stories. For now, just understand this: Eventually nice, prim and proper, white-and blue-collar kids from Piedmont Heights would attend a junior high school that looked, felt, and operated like a juvenile reformatory.

Piedmont Elementary was nearly brand new when I first walked through the doors. A big, metal clock was affixed to the brick wall outside the school's main entrance but the clock had already stopped working by the time I started kindergarten.

Few Piedmonters rode the bus to school. Most of us walked to class through rain and sleet and snow and frigid Minnesota winters. In the spring, we'd stop along the way and play marbles, winning and losing the precious glass cat's-eyes we carried in our pockets or in little cloth bags. Boys who owned "steelies" (ball bearings) were envied. If you were able to win a steelie away from another kid, man, that really made your day!

In winter we trudged along in clutches—boys and girls together—the boys engaging in snowball fights with Catholic kids headed in the opposite direction.

Before the Catholic Diocese of Duluth decided to build St. Lawrence Catholic School, the property behind my parents' house was a vacant hayfield interspersed with crab apple and pin cherry trees and boulders left by glaciers (the largest being dubbed "Stagecoach Rock" because of its shape and size). Older boys in the neighborhood played baseball in that field until excavating machines tore up the ground.

I was seven years old when the construction of St. Lawrence began. I'd inherited Dad's penchant for wandering and spent lots of time exploring the building as it took shape. The diocese originally planned to build a parochial school and a church to replace the aging St. Clement's complex in the West End but only the school was built. For the first few decades of St. Lawrence's existence, mass was held in the gymnasium. In the early '80s St. Lawrence School closed and the gymnasium was repurposed into a permanent worship space.

I led my Episcopal priest's two sons on a subterranean tour of the new school's sewer pipes. I didn't know it at the time but the younger of the two Fenwick boys—Bobby—would become a celebrity. I was a rabid basketball fan and later watched him play guard for Anoka High School in the state tournament on television back when the tournament was a one class, big school versus small school, winner-take-all affair—like the story depicted in *Hoosiers*. Watching my former priest's kid play for the championship—after the Fenwicks moved to the Twin Cities—I took childish pride knowing Bobby was a fellow subterranean explorer. The fact he later became a major league baseball player (with the Houston Astros and the St. Louis Cardinals) was icing on the cake.

St. Lawrence got built. Catholic kids I'd started Piedmont with also walked to school, which allowed opposing sides of the religious divide to lob snowballs at each other. One such incident of tomfoolery got me in trouble. As we marched towards Piedmont I decided—since I'd missed clobbering a Papist—to pick another target. Beaning a police boy (crossing guard) holding a wooden stop sign in the middle of Piedmont Avenue with a snowball wasn't too smart. I don't remember who I hit; I do remember the kid dragging me into Principal Hollingsworth's office for the first of my many sit-downs with authority figures.

That I ended up spending time with the principal during my second year of public education shouldn't come as a surprise. Miss Ness, who was saddled with me and two other mischievous boys—Bruce Patterson and Bruce Brooks—in her afternoon kindergarten class, curbed our enthusiasm by sequestering us in disparate corners for "time outs." I don't remember all of what got me in trouble with that very patient lady, with one notable exception.

Curtis was a kid with special needs. He wasn't a bad kid or a stupid kid or a physically handicapped kid. He was just different and needed extra help. We knew we weren't supposed to tease Curtis. But kids are kids and teasing—and being teased (they'd call it bullying today)—was a right-of-passage.

Miss Ness's class had big, red, cardboard building blocks lithographed to look like bricks. One day while Curtis was playing with toy cars on the floor, I got the bright idea to wall the kid in. When Curtis looked up, he discovered he was surrounded by bricks. He panicked, went nuts, and smashed through the carboard walls like an out-of-control Hulk. Then I made a mistake: I laughed. At Curtis. So he bit me. In the face. When I showed the bite mark on my cheek to Romayne Urie—the lady across the street who babysat me after school while Mom worked—and told her what had happened, Mrs. Urie simply said, "Good. You deserved it."

I recall walking single file from Piedmont Elementary to the Kirby house for a field trip. Mark Kirby, the eldest Kirby kid, was my age. His dad had been in the military so Mark was born in Germany. Mark's dad, Dave, was a garbageman but not my family's garbageman. Bob Bjorlin—who lived at the bottom of Chambersburg—collected our garbage. Back then, Duluth had a city landfill where the neighborhood trash haulers dumped their loads. On summer evenings, Dad would pile us into the family car, drive to the dump, and hit the high beams so we could witness black bears snacking on yucky stuff.

Though watching Mrs. Kirby milk a goat was entertaining, the highlight of our class field trip for me was encountering Miller Creek, a small brook trout stream flowing behind the Kirby house. There was something magical about standing next to a gurgling creek located only a few blocks from school. In that moment, I experienced a hint of the wanderlust that compelled Dad to skip school in Otter Tail County.

I became friends with Tim Thorp, a kid who lived at the far north end of Chambersburg and whose extended family owned a chain of grocery stores. We met in Mrs. Bard's second grade class and we both became smitten with our young and pretty teacher. Thorp and I spent story time, where we sat in a circle on the floor around

Mrs. Bard while she read to us, trying to look up her skirt. I had no idea why we were trying to peek at her undies. I was years from puberty and I hadn't seen a naked female of any sort (except for the time when Cheri Urie and I pulled down our pants and compared privates). Staring up Mrs. Bard's skirt made very little sense but that's what we did.

The following year, Tim and I were assigned to a split-grade classroom. We hadn't failed second grade nor had Mrs. Bard discovered two lecherous old-men-in-the-making staring at her garters. We'd matriculated but the school decided to divide the third-grade boys and girls such that Tim and I were the only third-grade boys in our class. When Mom learned about my class assignment, she called Mrs. Thorp. Both moms raised a fuss. Mr. Hollingsworth's response was something akin to, "It is what it is," which prompted Mom to tell Mr. Hollingsworth that "if things don't get corrected, Mark will transfer to St. Lawrence." Imagine my dread: Mom, a life-long Episcopalian, threatening to turn me into a Catholic! Cooler heads prevailed and Tim and I were re-assigned to Mrs. Bard's third-grade class which had plenty of boys. When Mrs. Bard became pregnant partway through the school year, she was replaced by Mr. Stevens.

The girls at Piedmont Elementary including Annie Stortz—one of the Stortz girls who lived at the bottom of Chambersburg; girls who had horses corralled on Huseby's land; girls who tried to raise giant rabbits, rabbits that escaped and terrorized the neighborhood by eating everything in sight—were far better athletes than the boys. Our machismo was on the ropes until we heard some sweet news: We were getting another boy, a kid transferring in from St. Jean's Catholic. His arrival was as anticipated as a Mercury rocket launch. Oh, how disappointed we were! The kid was the opposite of what we'd longed for. Instead of an athlete—a boy capable of knocking smart-alecky girls on their butts during trench ball games—we got Tom. Tom was a total klutz, but Eddie and I made it our business to befriend the new kid despite his failings.

Girls wore dresses or skirts in school, though they were allowed to wear slacks when walking to and from school in cold weather. When girls arrived at school, they went into the girls' cloak room, slipped off their slacks, and hung them on hooks.

46

Boys wore jeans or dress slacks and no one, whether boy or girl, wore T-shirts or sweatshirts or hoodies to school. In winter, the girls also wore their slacks under their dresses and skirts during recess. Cold didn't deter kids from going outside after lunch. Boys would play Rebels and Yankees (capture the flag without the flag) on gigantic snowbanks surrounding the parking lot while girls stood around in clusters gossiping and making goo-goo eyes at their make-believe heroes.

One day after lunch Mr. Stevens—the third-grade teacher who'd replaced Mrs. Bard—said, very loudly, "The girls need to dress for recess." The announcement prompted a herd of young ladies to rush the girls' cloakroom. In the middle of all that chaos was Tom. He'd misunderstood our teacher and thought the boys were supposed to get dressed as well.

A Disney movie—*Thomasina*, a film about a gender-confused cat—was playing in theaters and every kid in Piedmont Heights had seen the movie. When Mr. Stevens saw Tom moving towards the cloakrooms surrounded by young ladies, he yelled, "Are you a girl, Thomasina?" Eddie and I thought it was pretty funny, our teacher calling Tom out like that. But the joke turned ugly when Mr. Stevens took a marker, a piece of cardboard, and some string from his desk and made a sign; a sign that Tom was forced to wear around his neck for the rest of the week. The sign read: *Thomasina*.

There was this girl, Dee Dee. Pretty as a rose. Dark haired, brown eyed. Italian. She and I got under each other's skin in kindergarten and, up until shortly before she died (in her fifties of ALS), that equation never changed. For me, I think the rub was that she had it all. Good looks. Smarts. Poise. More irksome, when our teachers chose kids to read aloud, Dee Dee was always selected. I prided myself on being a pretty darn good reader. Miss Ness even said so when I mastered *Tip and Mitten* in kindergarten, though along with that accolade Miss Ness shared an astute observation with Mom during a parent-teacher conference, "Mrs. Munger, keep that boy busy or he'll end up in jail!"

For whatever reason, I failed to make the highest reading group in third grade, but in Mr. Ames's fourth-grade class, things had improved and I was selected for Mrs. Zakula's "special class."

One hour every afternoon, Mrs. Zakula taught a handful of "gifted" children reading, comprehension, spelling, and writing at an advanced level. Though I caught up to Dee Dee in terms scholarship, I never got over my envy.

It was in Mrs. Zakula's class that I fell for a cute, blonde-headed, Scandinavian girl. I was immediately smitten with Sharon; so much so that Bruce Patterson—who had a "thing" for Dee Dee—and I memorialized our affection in chalk on the brick wall outside the school's office. Patterson and I wisely used only initials—ours' and the girls'—to proclaim our undying love. The deception must have worked because we were never asked to erase our graffiti.

I went so far as to give Sharon a ring I bought from Terri Hanson for fifty cents. Sharon's mother promptly made her give it back. I should have seen that coming. The locket I gave Cheryl Williams in first grade when I asked her to marry me (she was a real catch; it's not often you find a girl who likes to play with army men!) was sent back by Cheryl's mother in equally curt fashion.

Sharon's presence made gym class a torture. We'd parade into the gymnasium, the boys in their blue jeans and tennis shoes and the girls—who'd been forced to wear weird blue, one-piece gym outfits during first and second grades—in dresses or skirts and tenners, where we were assigned partners for square dancing. I hoped my teachers would pair me with my sweetie during those stupid hoedowns. When that didn't happen and I was unmercifully joined at the hip to some cootie-infested girl, I was crestfallen. The few times I was paired with the lovely, shy, blonde girl of my dreams, I'm pretty sure I stepped on her shoes.

Annie Stortz—the best girl skater in Piedmont and maybe the best skater in Piedmont <u>period</u> (Bruce Brooks was pretty fast but in a one-on-one race, I think Annie would've whooped him)—tried to get me to skate with Sharon on the Piedmont pleasure rink over Christmas vacation. When I resisted, my ankles bent, my inability to stand upright on skates obvious, Annie tossed me head-first into a snowbank.

Since I'd scrawled Sharon's initials next to mine for all the world to see, my devotion to the young lady wasn't a secret. On our sixth-grade trip—an annual rite of passage for Piedmonters where sixth-graders took a passenger train from Duluth to St. Paul and visited the State Capitol and the Como Park Zoo before returning home on the train—I enlisted the help of Gary (more about him later), a kid I met in another "special class" (also something you'll read about in a bit) to relay notes to Sharon.

Bruce Patterson and I were celebrities during the visit to St. Paul; me because Uncle Willard was a Democrat in the Minnesota House; and Bruce because his grandpa—Dwight Swanstrom—was a Republican representative in the same legislative body. When Bruce and I entered the hallowed halls of the Capitol with our classmates and teachers, our chests burst with pride at having Bruce's grandfather and my uncle function as our tour guides.

Little blondes with sparkling eyes and quiet dispositions were in short supply at Piedmont Elementary. It was only natural that Eddie took a shine to the apple of my eye. Despite Gary dutifully delivering my hastily drafted entreaties of affection, Sharon sat next to Eddie on the train ride back to Duluth. I was crushed by my best friend's betrayal. It was my first lesson, that in affairs of the heart, it's every man for himself.

Fifth and sixth-grade boys were selected to serve as "police boys," Piedmont's term for crossing guards. Originally police boys (there were no police girls at Piedmont) carried little wooden stop signs and wore white, canvas belts displaying shiny, silver badges. Police boys worked in pairs and would nod to each another, step out into the street, and stop cars so kids could cross. Somewhere along the way, the police department replaced those hand-held wooden signs with nylon orange-and-black flags affixed to galvanized steel poles. and Eddie and I were selected as police boys in fifth grade. The following year, Eddie was elected captain though he didn't have any real authority over me. Despite spending mornings of sixth grade at Lincoln Elementary in yet another "special class," I remained a police boy at Piedmont, acting as such when kids were released at the end of the school day. Being on "the force" made me feel like I was a big deal; that I was part of something special. This belief of self-importance was reinforced when crossing guards throughout the city were treated to a picnic at the Duluth Zoo at the end of the year. At the party, we were given pocketknives in appreciation of our service. We were also able to choose either a softball or a softball bat as an additional "thank you" gift from Officer Kehoe, the Duluth cop running the program. Imagine giving knives and bats to kids as part of a school-sponsored activity!

At the beginning of sixth grade, I was having a hell of a time. I'd contracted infections in both ears and my eyesight had worsened. I began my final year of elementary school sitting in the last row of Mr. Childs' classroom. With clogged ears and fuzzy vision I had trouble hearing the teacher and difficulty seeing the blackboard, so I crept forward until I was in the front row. Despite being only a few feet from Mr. Childs, I couldn't hear or see what was going on. My grades went in the toilet and I thought Mr. Hollingsworth was crazy when he asked Mom if I'd like to spend mornings at Lincoln Elementary in an enhanced learning program taught by his sister.

An eye appointment; my first set of glasses. A doctor's visit; my ears cleaned out. Then, off I went to spend mornings with classmates I'd never met (other than Jan Erickson, another Piedmont kid). The school district, while it supported accelerated learning for "gifted" kids, didn't provide transportation so Shirley (Jan's mom) and Mom worked out a schedule to drive Jan and me to and from Lincoln.

Miss Hollingsworth's "special class" included kids from Duluth's western elementary schools. Most participating schools sent two kids. Many of the students were under Miss Hollingsworth's tutelage for a second year. Jan—along with Sandy Fredrickson—had attended "special class" in fifth grade as Piedmont's representatives. For whatever reason, Sandy didn't want to return. Mr. Hollingsworth thought I could handle the work and I was selected as Sandy's replacement. Given I was failing Mr. Childs' "ordinary" class, I was nervous about attending a laboratory for the gifted.

AN INCIDENT AT GRANDMA'S HOUSE

You'd think I'd suppress memories of being targeted for molestation. Aren't such moments in a child's life supposed to be locked away and forgotten? I'm living proof that's not how it works. Nearly sixty years after the fact, some of what happened to me remains vivid in my mind's eye. Not all of it, you understand. But some of it. The important parts. The ugly parts.

The houses of Duluth's Riverside neighborhood were originally constructed by Alexander McDougall, the inventor of whaleback boats—low slung steamers also known as "Pig Boats" due to their stubby, blunt-nosed bows. By the time I arrived on the scene, the shipyard was history and the neighborhood was in decline. Though Grandma Munger's house overlooked the St. Louis River estuary, the attraction of living next to a river was illusory. In the early 1960s, the St. Louis was an open sewer, flushing untreated industrial and municipal waste from Cloquet and Carlton and Esko and Scanlon and Proctor and Duluth into Lake Superior. The one time I fished the river with Dad as a child (Harry had read an article in *Outdoor Life* or *Field and Stream* proclaiming the St. Louis to be a "hotbed for walleye") the fish we caught were not fit for the frying pan: The white underbellies of the walleye had been stained yellow by a mixture of sewage and poison.

This ugly depiction of the St. Louis as it flowed past Grandma Munger's house also applied to swimming in the river. I didn't swim in the St. Louis until Uncle Willard passed legislation to clean up Minnesota's polluted waters. When Dad reminisced about his youth, he recalled the river's toxic stew. No matter how hot the summer, no matter how desperate the times, no kid wanted to exit a swimming hole smelling like a turd. Willard's cleanup efforts were in the future; and at the time of this story, Duluth was still a manufacturing town, a place that made steel and cement and wire and carpeting and refrigerators and aviation equipment and fiberboard and industrial cranes and built ships. Byproducts of industry flowed directly into the river or were deposited on its banks and allowed to leach into the St. Louis, making the river a cauldron of ugliness you could smell standing on Grandma's front porch.

Most times when I visited Grandma Munger, it was just me and her and, occasionally, one of her boarders hanging out. The boarders—single guys who rented upstairs bedrooms—ate their meals with Grandma. Grandpa Munger had passed away. At the time of his death, Grandma had no savings and no investments upon which to live—only Grandpa's small Social Security retirement, so she had little choice but to rent bedrooms to strangers.

Cousin Samuel and his mom and I were at Grandma's. All the boarders were gone. Samuel is ten years older than me. Pudgy, effeminate, and prone to grandiosity, Samuel wasn't, to my mind, a bad kid. Because Dad was much younger than his siblings, Samuel and my other first cousins who lived in Duluth—Willard Junior and Patsy—are decades older than me.

It happened when Samuel and I were alone. I don't remember where my aunt and Grandma had gone off to. Perhaps they were outside picking vegetables from the weed-choked garden Grandpa Harry once tended on the hillside above the river. As I've said before, Grandpa Munger gave up farming in Otter Tail County because he, like his father (Great Grandpa Lyman Munger), wasn't a man of the soil. But old habits die hard and Grandpa Harry had continued to try his hand at gardening, planting a small vegetable plot behind the house in Riverside, a garden Grandma Munger maintained after Grandpa's passing. I'm guessing that's where Grandma and my aunt were when it happened.

It was midday when Samuel asked me to follow him upstairs. I didn't hear anything alarming in my cousin's voice and, at six years old, had no idea what puberty could do to a boy. I had no concept of sex or reproduction or what use one could make of a penis beyond peeing. Sure, I'd experienced the occasional "stiffy" when my immature maleness became as hard as a lead pencil. But sex? I had no mile markers, no roadmaps in my young mind as to what the hell that meant.

I don't remember what transpired in Grandma Munger's bedroom. I do recall that something, some behavior by Samuel, made me flee the room. I can't swear he touched me. I can't testify that he did something untoward. I just know I ran from whatever was going on. Unfortunately, leaving Grandma's bedroom did not end the matter.

This part is as real today as it was when it occurred. I was sitting on the stairs leading from the second floor to the first level of the house pondering whatever it was that had just happened when Samuel came up behind me and said, "Wanna see something?"

I don't think I answered him right off. The way I remember things is that when I turned my head to reply, there was a fully erect, adolescent penis in my face. Samuel was standing over me, his hands holding his very hard thing next to my mouth, asking, "Why don't you kiss it?" I'm pretty sure I didn't say anything, which caused my cousin to lower his voice, jab his junk at me, and ask pleadingly, "Won't you just lick it? It won't hurt you."

I jumped up and ran outside. I didn't say a word to my grandmother or my aunt when I found them. I also remained silent about what had happened when Dad picked me up. There was something about reporting such an awful thing to Dad that made me hold my tongue. But that night I told Mom everything even though I knew she'd tell Dad. I intuitively understood what Dad's reaction would be. Sure enough, he didn't believe me. Something to do with protecting the reputation of the males of the Munger line. Mom—bless her heart—did believe me. Her only child had told her something horrific and that was enough to convince her of the truth.

Mom didn't try to explain Samuel's actions. I was too young to understand. But she relayed the incident to Sally— Cousin Willard Junior's wife, and Cousin Patsy so that their children were never left alone with Samuel. The males in the Munger family universally dismissed my story. But the Munger women? They went about the business of protecting their children.

It was a different time, a different age. I had not been exposed to nudity or sex or other exemplars that could form the basis for a false report of abuse. I didn't have any of that as part of my understanding of the world. I was truly, up until that encounter on the staircase, an innocent. Part of my childhood was stolen by Cousin Samuel that day, but Mom made sure it never happened again.

SLAYING DRAGONS

I am standing on a fortress wall, sword in hand. There's a dragon
on the loose menacing the kingdom. I am not a monarch charged
with protecting his subjects but a knight holding a crude wooden
sword. I am seven years old and already, I am hailed as a great
warrior.

I remember little of my maternal grandmother, Edna
Marie Kobe. I never heard her called by her first name; she was
always addressed by her middle name. Grandma Marie died when
I was three-and-a-half years old, so what I recall of her is now over
sixty years distant. Memory, as the writing of this collection has
proven, is a tricky thing. One minute, you believe you recall an
incident, a place, a person in a certain way. You're positive in your
recollection. Then a friend or relative or reader peruses your story
and finds a flaw, a memory that is artifice and not based upon
actual circumstances. The few memories I have of Grandma
Marie are like that. I do recall—when she was deathly ill—crawling
beneath her bed in my grandparents' house in West Duluth and
banging away on the bed springs with a toy hammer. I was trying
to "fix" Grandma. I'm pretty sure I didn't attend my
grandmother's funeral. In fact, I don't recall attending any funerals
until I was an adult. Repressed trauma perhaps? But one day,
Marie was my grandmother and, seemingly, the next day Nancy
was.

Grandpa Jack married widower Nancy Krantz when I was
in first or second grade. That's the timeframe for this story.
Before they married, I spent time at Nancy's place in downtown
Duluth. Nancy's apartment was in a fourplex she'd inherited from
her late husband. Built of brick and slanting towards St. Louis Bay
on one of Duluth's vertically challenged avenues, the rent from
the place was Nancy's main source of income outside a modest
social security check and the meager stipend she earned fixing
dead people's hair at Crawford's Mortuary. Nancy had a parakeet,
a bird that squawked loudly and pooped a lot and kicked bird
feed out of its cage and onto the kitchen floor but didn't say or do
anything profound. Due to traffic, I never played outside Nancy's
apartment though I remember Nancy making me the best old-
fashioned oatmeal I've ever eaten.

After they married, Nancy sold her apartment building and my grandparents bought a small two-story Tudor in Duluth's East End. Their house on Vermillion Road is where I became legendary as a knight of the realm.

Up the block from Jack and Nancy's new house, a stone castle—its tower soaring to the sky and overlooking Lake Superior, its walls solid and demonstrative of great authority—awaited investigation. While my grandparents scraped wallpaper off the walls of their new house, I was free to explore the neighborhood. During one such excursion I earned my knighthood and the self-appointed title of "Sir Mark."

"Grandma," I said breathlessly, having just returned from an epic journey, "I killed a mountain lion."

Grandma Nancy smiled and nodded as she made me a peanut butter and jelly sandwich. "That's nice, Dear."

"Really, Grandma. It was big and growling and trying to break into the castle when I wrestled it and snapped its neck."

"Uh huh," Nancy said, sipping hot coffee. "And where is the lion's body now?"

I thought for a moment between bites of sandwich hoping against hope that she wasn't asking me to produce proof of my kill. "At the castle."

Grandma pondered my disclosure. "Don't you think you should bury it?"

The idea had never occurred to me. "Sure," I replied. Having never attended funerals as a child (including the ceremony laying Brice—a four-year-old cousin who drowned on Minnesota Point—to rest) I was clueless as to what the funerary process entailed. Grandma noticed me pondering her suggestion.

"You'll need a shovel to dig the grave. And a cross to mark it," she said, playing along. "Grandpa can help you with that."

My maternal grandfather was a lot like Uncle Willard in that both men were handy with tools. But whereas Willard had a complete woodshop located in the basement of his motel, a retreat that included joiners and planers and band saws and drill presses, Grandpa Jack—an immigrant from Slovenia—was more of an Old World craftsman. I remember him building a doghouse for Deuce I—my first dog—in the basement of his West Duluth house before Grandma Marie died. He cut all the lumber with a hand saw, used a hand drill to make holes for bolts and screws, and never, so far as I know, used power tools during the process. That doghouse lasted through four or five dogs, a testament to Grandpa's handiwork. Grandpa Jack's workshop in the basement of the house on Vermillion Road was like something you'd expect Geppetto to labor in. There were jars filled with screws and nuts and bolts and other hardware lining a shelf above a wooden bench tucked into a corner. Saws and hammers and wrenches and plyers and screwdrivers and other hand tools—all neatly organized and arranged—hung from hooks on pegboard above the workbench.

I found Grandpa Jack working in his basement shop.

"Grandpa," I said with seriousness, "I need to borrow a shovel. I also need to make a cross. For a grave."

"Oh?"

My grandfather wasn't one to pry too deeply.

"I killed a mountain lion," I explained, "at the castle. Grandma says I need to bury it."

Grandpa nodded, left whatever project he was working on (likely yet another birdhouse for the backyard), found some scrap lumber and, in short order, nailed together a crude wooden cross. "How's that?"

"Great. I'll need a shovel. For the grave."

He smiled, exposing teeth yellowed by age, coffee, and the hand-rolled cigarettes he smoked away from Grandma Nancy's scrutiny. "There's one in the garage you can use, next to the service door."

I don't think I dug a grave. But I do remember walking back up the hill towards the castle, cross in hand, finding a soft spot on the fortress's lawn, and sinking the wooden shaft of the marker into the ground to memorialize the mountain lion's final resting place.

Sometime later, Grandpa made me a wooden sword to fend off the dragon I reported was threatening the castle. "You were lucky with the mountain lion," he said as he screwed two pieces of pine together, the wood painted white and the sword's handle wrapped with black friction tape to improve grip. "You'll need this if you encounter any other creatures or monsters."

I nodded, accepted the sword with solemnity, climbed the basement stairs, and wandered out the back door in search of adventure. I don't remember if a dragon challenged me as I stood on the steps of Holy Rosary Catholic Cathedral, my eyes fixed on the bluebird sky cloaking the Kingdom of Duluth. I do recall priests and nuns eyeing me with curiosity as they made their way to confer with the Almighty. I'm pretty sure those men and women of God felt safer knowing Sir Mark was keeping watch.

THE WOODS

All the real timber had been logged off. What was left in the forest between Hutchinson Road and Skyline Parkway was scrub; aspen, birch, black alder with a mix of balsam, spruce, and the occasional maple and white or red pine tossed in for good measure. That being said, the forest of my childhood was mostly aspen and birch and—in the low, swampy places—alder; trees that last a few decades and are eventually replaced by more serious foliage.

We called it the Woods and every kid in the neighborhood knew what that meant. When alluvial ponds dotting the Woods filled with snow melt and adult amphibians laid eggs, tadpoles—the beginnings of frogs and toads and salamanders—would emerge from clusters of caviar and seek places to hide from kids with nets and jars. The Woods was also where tree forts were built by neighborhood boys, allowing them to escape real life and fulfill their dreams; fantasies enlarged by watching *Swiss Family Robinson* on the big screen at the NorShor or the Granada or the West theaters.

My first interaction with the Woods was as a second or third grader. Some of the older kids in the neighborhood, Mike Urie, Eddie Rauvola, the Milich boys, the Moe brothers, and others got it in their heads to "borrow" some of Mr. Huseby's form lumber (piles of plywood and planks stacked next to the Woods for easy access when Huseby started another house) and build tree forts. These youthful creations were not sophisticated; just two-by-twelves spiked to aspen trees with plywood sheeting for the floors and roofs and sometimes—if a boy had made money mowing lawns or shoveling snow—blessed with tar paper purchased from the local Coast to Coast hardware store. Such forts were crude but pretty darn cool if you were into playing "guns" and emulating the combat dads in the neighborhood had experienced in WW II and Korea.

Toddlers started out with Western style cap guns, replicas of the six-shooters Wyatt Earp, Matt Dillon, Bat Masterson, and Paladin carried holstered at their sides. I'm only talking about the boys here: I never saw a girl strap on a pair of six-guns.

As boys aged, cap pistols of early childhood were supplanted by more sophisticated weaponry. You could buy any manner of toy gun at the Ben Franklin five-and-dime in the Piedmont Shopping Center. Replica guns were also gifted to us on our birthdays and at Christmas. No pacifist, Saint Nick managed to leave the Salveson boys two Johnny Sevens one Christmas morning. The Johnny Seven had seven different functions. The envy of every boy, the gun fired plastic bullets, anti-tank missiles, and grenades. It also morphed into a rifle, a machine gun, and a pistol. How is that not cool? Ads running between Saturday morning cartoons declared, "(T)here's no other gun like it!"

The point of the shacks Eddie and I helped older boys in the neighborhood build wasn't to construct havens where we could study *Playboy* or other dirty magazines. Our forts served as outposts against incursions by the Germans or the Japs or the Sioux. Even after Mr. Huseby tore down our erstwhile fortifications—using a backhoe to rip the plywood and tar paper and lumber from the trees—the boys of the neighborhood continued to war. The two network television stations broadcasting in Duluth (before ABC came to town in the late '60s) were replete with Westerns, WW II shows, Civil War dramas, and *Swamp Fox*—a fictional rendition of colonial freedom fighter Francis Marion. Though the men of the neighborhood who'd seen the horrors of combat revealed little about their wartime experiences—not to their wives, their children, their pastors or their priests or their rabbis—we knew heroes lived amongst us and we wanted to be heroes too.

Writing about early television shows reminds me of something else. Every morning like clockwork when my parents were done watching the forecast scroll across the bottom of our black-and-white television—a regular part of *The Today Show* on the local NBC affiliate (Channel 6)—I'd switch channels to watch *Captain Kangaroo* on Channel 3, the CBS station. I loved watching Tom Terrific cartoons, listening to the Captain read books to the audience, and following the antics of Mr. Green Jeans, Bunny Rabbit, and Mr. Moose.

When my little brother Dave came along, *Romper Room* was popular on PBS. Dave was invited—at age four—to be on the show. He was on the set, got nervous, and started to barf.

Thankfully, the WDSE staff whisked him off-camera before he puked on live television!

As soon as I got home from elementary school I'd tune into Channel 6 and watch locally produced shows. In the late '50s and early '60s, I watched *Captain Q* religiously. The program featured a Lake Superior ship captain (played by local weatherman Jack McKenna). His sidekick, Sparx the radioman, was played by Ray Paulson, another Twin Ports broadcasting legend. The show interspersed cartoons and re-runs of the marionette show *Fireball XL-5* with live hijinks. I sat in our den watching the family's black- and-white TV, eating cookies or a bowl of cereal, drinking cold skim milk, and following the Captain's antics after a hard day at Piedmont Elementary.

Ray Paulson later donned makeup to portray clowns Bozo and Mr. Toot on the small screen. I won a pair of tickets to the Ice Follies at the Duluth Curling Club after entering a *Bozo* coloring contest. As a sixth grader—at the upper age limit of Mr. Toots' viewer demographic—I won a road race set for my drawing of Duluth's iconic Lift Bridge. To claim my prize, I was forced to attend a live broadcast of *Mr. Toot*. My appearance on a little kids' clown show led to no end of teasing from my fellow sixth-graders. Susie LeGarde—one of fourteen LeGarde kids—told me years later (when we attended Denfeld together) that she was still pissed at me because my drawing had bested hers.

When ABC finally came to town as Duluth's third network affiliate (WDIO, Channel 10), the world of afternoon television changed. WDIO had a program, *Afternoon Movie Matinee*, in the same time slot as the insufferable *Mr. Toot*. The *Matinee* ran WW II flicks, Tarzan movies, Greek and Roman and Viking epics, and Western shoot-em-ups, all of which stirred my imagination and convinced me to abandon clowns as role models.

In addition to making war in the Woods—engaging in battles that involved dozens of kids, one side playing the Germans, the other, the Americans; all of us reenacting D-Day in summer or the Battle of the Bulge in winter—I became an ardent fan of toy soldiers. On the basement floor. In my sandbox. With or without Eddie or his brother Jerry, I would set up plastic soldiers and engage in hours of mock conflict.

Buying packs of bubble gum at Torgersons' Store, the Rexall Pharmacy, or the local Ben Franklin, we collected trading cards depicting scenes from the Civil War, the Revolutionary War, and WW II. I don't recall buying cards honoring the Korean Conflict. Maybe because the good guys didn't really win; they just fought to a truce. And I surely never bought any bubble gum cards memorializing Vietnam.

In the spring, Eddie and I would gather up scraps of wood and craft miniature Civil War vessels to launch in water-filled ditches. Snowmelt pouring off the hillside would create a torrent of clean, cold water rushing alongside the Woods towards Lake Superior. Flat pieces of pine became decks upon which to glue turrets (rounded wooden caps from Tinker Toy sets) re-creating the North's hero of Hampton Roads, the ironclad *Monitor*. Quarter-rounds became the *Merrimac* and other Rebel ironclads. We'd embed finishing nails in our tiny models to mimic cannons and carve frigates and brigs from pine—complete with toothpick masts—to do battle. It was great fun watching our little ships scoot down the ditch, enter a culvert and reappear at the far end of the tunnel.

The Woods also figured prominently in plans made by older girls living in the neighborhood. One summer, Carolyn Granley, Dee Dee and Lori Ramfjord, Marie Jentoft, and Michelle Huard approached our moms with a proposal: "Pay us ten cents a day and we'll keep your kids busy at day camp." Since the young ladies in the mix were responsible (and already babysat for the same families) our moms were all "in."

Weekday mornings, ten or twelve kids would gather at the Ramfjords' house and march into the Woods. At the direction of our counselors, we built huts of aspen sticks and ferns—a village as it were—to serve as a basecamp. We carved a garden from jungle and planted seeds in hopes of growing vegetables and flowers. We pulled segmented weeds ("Chinese puzzles") from the ground, broke them apart, put the pieces on a blanket, and tried to reassemble them in the order God intended. The spot our caretakers—who would later become some of the cutest girls at Denfeld—selected for "the village" was near Merritt Creek. The basecamp was dry enough so we weren't traipsing through swamp and eaten alive by mosquitoes but near enough to the stream to provide a ready source of water for art projects.

Day camp's demise was Eddie's fault. That's not quite true: The camp's abrupt ending was Eddie's <u>and</u> Wendy Sundin's fault. During a game of hide-and-seek, long after the rest of the campers had been found, Eddie and Wendy remained unfound. Our counselors organized a search party. We tromped about, looking in rocky nooks and brushy glades, shouting the missing kids' names, all in vain.

"We better tell their moms," Carolyn finally said.

The other counselors agreed. When the bad news was relayed to Eddie's and Wendy's mothers, the police were called. Cops combed the Woods and I remember being concerned, as concerned as a ten-year-old boy can be, for my friends. Though this was decades before the disappearance of Jacob Wetterling, ominous dread caused me to fear something untoward had happened.

"Where did you two go?" Liz Salveson—Eddie's mom— asked when the missing kids finally turned up.

"We got lost," Eddie explained. "We just kept walking until we heard the Mister Softee bell and followed it."

Saved by a soft-serve ice cream truck. Go figure.

The Woods was large enough and wild enough for me to lead my Scout patrol on a campout.

"You need a permission slip signed by a parent," Ed Salveson—one of my Boy Scout leaders—advised.

Troop 67 didn't do a lot of overnight camping beyond weekends at Camp Horace Johnson north of Duluth and Camp Newman in Wisconsin, though we did spend a week at Camp Jamar near Danbury, Wisconsin every summer. This dearth of camping opportunities was problematic since Scouts need time out-of-doors and under canvas to earn merit badges.

A handful of boys were authorized by their parents to spend the weekend in the Woods with me. It was pretty heady stuff, being fourteen years old and responsible for a half-dozen Scouts. I was hopeful I'd do a better job of keeping track of my boys than the girls running Day Camp did of keeping track of Eddie and Wendy!

I drew two-man canvas tents and cooking gear from supplies stored at the Piedmont Community Center where the troop met. Then Eagle Patrol traipsed into the forest, found a glade adjacent to Merritt Creek, built a fire ring with stones hauled from the stream, and set up camp.

For the most part, the campout went as planned. There was only one glitch. My neighborhood nemesis, Patrick Osbourne, showed up with a couple of hooligan pals. My patrol and I endured taunting and teasing until the bullies grew bored of torturing us and wandered off. We then went back to learning knots and how to build a fire and how to cook a meal in tinfoil covered with hot coals; checking off each completed task in the bible of Scouting; the Boy Scout Handbook. By Sunday morning, I was exhausted and the boys were tired of my bossiness, but we'd survived.

Though we were Scouts, Bruce Patterson and I started something called "The Adventure Club," an informal gang of would-be explorers consisting of Patterson, the Granmoe brothers, Tom Kubiak, Mark Olson (from Harvey Street), and me. For one of its outings, the Adventure Club decided to traipse around the Woods. We were climbing bluffs above Skyline Drive when guys plinking tin cans with .22s *seemed* to point their rifles at us and send a few rounds our way. We scrambled like hell to get out of there. I'm still unsure whether the teenaged boys were shooting at us or simply didn't appreciate we were in their line of fire. In any event, I thought enough of the event to write a story and submit it to *Outdoor Life* and *Boys Life* and *Reader's Digest*. The neatly typed rejection letters I received from those magazines introduced me to the world of authorial disappointment.

On another Adventure Club outing—climbing those same cliffs and bluffs overlooking the city—I lost my grip, tumbled fifteen feet, and landed on unyielding gabbro. I think that's when my spinal problems—eventually requiring fusion surgery—began.

There was also the afternoon when the Adventure Club crawled up the storm sewer in front of my family's new house on Miller Creek. We managed, flashlights in hand, to navigate the sewer to the intersection of 22nd Avenue West and Leonard Street before claustrophobia, fear, and the chirping of rats forced us to back out of the pipe.

I once tried to chop down an aspen sapling with a rusty hatchet while exploring the Woods with Jerry Salveson. The hatchet's dull blade glanced off the tree and slashed through my blue jeans and into my shin. The wound was deep and ugly. I removed my T-shirt, tied it around my leg to stop the bleeding, and leaned on Jerry—who helped me home. Mom was hosting a bridge club luncheon. Eight mothers from the neighborhood sat around two card tables on folding chairs, sipping tea or coffee, chattering about kids and life and men and the cost of things while playing bridge.

"What happened to you?" Liz Salveson asked as I limped into the living room, my chest bare, my bloody shirt wrapped around my leg.

"Hit my leg with a hatchet."

"Maybe you should get that looked at," Romayne Urie suggested.

"Mom?"

Mom glanced up from her hand. "You really should wear a shirt when we have company over."

I didn't see a doctor. The bleeding stopped without stitches but my right leg still bears a nasty scar as a reminder of that day.

Bruce Patterson and I were afflicted with boredom. We must have been fifteen or so when we packed bag lunches, filled our canteens, and headed for the Woods. There was no intentionality behind our walkabout. We came to a clearing—the same open spot where I'd held the Scout campout, collected dry wood and birchbark and stacked it inside the fire ring my Scout patrol had left behind. Patterson pulled out a farmer's match, struck it on the zipper of his jeans, and touched flame to bark. Fire crackled as we sat on dry grass, sipping Kool-Aid from canteens, eating sandwiches under the brilliant sun, talking about girls and sports and life. After lunch, we plucked hollow reeds from the creek bed, lit them, and smoked, emulating scenes from movies, scenes where the cool guys, the tough guys—the soldiers and cowboys and mobsters—smoked and cast lustful eyes at sultry women. We laid back in the grass, the two of us trying to blow smoke rings but coughing uncontrollably from the burning weeds clamped between our teeth. It was a perfect day until the wind ramped up, grabbed embers from the fire, and carried them into the grass.

"Shit," Patterson said.

"What?"

"The field's burning!"

We tossed our would-be Marlboros into the fire ring and tried to extinguish the grassfire by stomping on it with our tennis shoes but the blaze continued to grow.

"Let's get some water!"

We raced to the creek—empty canteens in hand—filled them, and ran back to the fire.

"Shit," Patterson muttered.

The fire had spread.

"We need to get out of here," I said.

"Roger that."

We ran through the glade. Behind us, sparks settled in trees and thick gray smoke wafted skyward. By the time we emerged from the Woods, our malfeasance hung over the Merritt Creek valley like a shroud.

"Let's go to Eddie's," I said. "We can hide out there."

"OK."

We sprinted up Chambersburg. Eddie was sitting on his front porch mesmerized by a pillar of smoke billowing above forest. "You see that? The Woods is on fire!"

"We know. We started it," I replied. "Can we go inside, maybe get a better view from upstairs?"

Eddie nodded and opened the front door. We ran to the second floor where the older kids' bedrooms were located and stopped in front of a south-facing window.

"What happened?" Eddie asked.

"Campfire got away from us," Patterson admitted.

Sirens wailed. Hook and ladder and pumper trucks careened into position. A phalanx of firefighters in yellow turnout gear emerged from the vehicles carrying axes and wearing portable water tanks on their broad, strong backs. Patterson and I had been too scared to do the right thing. Someone else had seen the smoke, dialed the fire department, and saved the Woods.

LOW CRIMES AND MISDEMEANORS

You'll learn from this memoir that I'm far from perfect and that my arc towards criminality began early.

I'm not sure why I turned into a petty thief. In retrospect, my urge to commit crimes might have been an attention-seeking device. I was pretty much the bomb in both the Munger and Kobe families. I was adored by relatives who had high expectations of me. My fourth-grade teacher (Mr. Ames) once proclaimed I'd become President of the United States. That wasn't something Mr. Ames revealed in confidence: It was something he announced in class. I'm certain his handicapping my future was based upon the fact that Gary Ames was a Democrat—as were all the members of my family (save Grandpa Jack; an Eisenhower Republican)—and that Uncle Willard and Dad were big wheels in the Democratic Party. Truth is, despite all the love and kindness and praise heaped upon me during childhood, I'm the sort of human being who needs <u>all</u> the attention. When my parents brought Dave into the family, I think jealousy pushed me over the edge.

Torgersons' Store—a neighborhood ma and pa grocery— was our "go to" for buying candy and soda and Popsicles. Beginning at seven or eight years old, Mom would let me walk to Torgersons' with Eddie or Patterson or other kids from the block, a few coins in my pocket, to buy a treat.

I'd asked Mom for money to buy a Lunch Bar. Lunch Bars were chocolate bars filled with peanuts. They came in a green and red wrapper and were a bargain at three cents (versus five cents for the competition). But Mom said, "No—supper's almost ready. You'll ruin your appetite."

I wasn't yet trimming crabby Mrs. Swanson's lawn to earn spending money. My allowance was paltry. If Mom wouldn't open up her coin purse and hand me a dime, well, I was out of luck in terms of getting the Lunch Bar I wanted.

Like I said, I'm sure Dave was part of our family when my thievery began. He was likely a year or two old, smiling his cute little boy smile, his big ears and shaved head far more endearing than my gangly awkwardness, when I started breaking the law. That afternoon, I made up my mind I'd get myself a Lunch Bar whether Mom gave me the cash or not.

That was easy, I thought, the stolen candy bar hidden in the front pocket of my jeans as I headed home. When I was certain no one was following me, I pulled out my treasure, opened the wrapper, and gobbled chocolate. When I was done eating the candy bar, I shoved the wrapper in my back pocket; cocky and self-assured I'd gotten away with a crime.

"What did you do?" Mom asked when I entered the house.

"Huh?"

"Mrs. Torgerson called. She's very upset."

Crap.

Mom grabbed me by the ear and pulled me into the kitchen. "Give it to me!"

I started to wail.

"I said, give it to me!"

"I already ate it," I confessed, handing Mom the empty wrapper through tears.

"You're going to march right back up there," Mom ordered, "and pay for what you took." She handed me a dime. "You'll also apologize. Do you know how embarrassing this is?"

I opened my hand and accepted the coin. I didn't know what to say. I'd let Mom down. I ended up dealing with Oscar Torgerson, the gruff, matter-of-fact owner of the store. I offered Mom's dime in my outstretched hand at the end of a hurried apology. He accepted both without a word, handed me my change, and I shuffled away.

Mom brought me with to visit Betty Strum at the Strum home on Pike Lake. I played in the sandbox with Betty's kids while our mothers talked and drank iced tea. I was enthralled with the plastic Disney figurines we were playing with in the sandbox. When our moms called us inside for lunch, I dawdled long enough to pocket Mickey and a few of his friends. If the Strum kids told their parents "Munger kidnaped Dumbo," I never heard about it.

Something similar happened at the Liston's house in Morgan Park. Jim and Pauline Liston were close friends of my parents. They were also my godparents. One year, Jimber—the youngest Liston kid, received the coolest Christmas present ever.

We were sitting in his bedroom playing with his new Tudor football game; the kind you plug into the wall and the tin surface vibrates causing little plastic football players to move up and down the field. I was enthralled by the thing and when we said our goodbyes, half the yellow team and half the white team went home in my jean pockets.

"Your godmother called," Mom said sternly.

I began crying.

"Where are they?"

I sobbed all the way to my room and back, opened my hands, and dumped the stolen figurines onto the kitchen table.

"What were you thinking? Jimber is heartbroken that a friend would do such a thing."

I shook my head.

"I'm seeing Pauline tomorrow. You'll write an apology and I'll return these to Jimber with your letter."

I wrote the letter. Pauline read it to Jimber, gave it back, and Mom pasted it in my scrapbook. I came across it years later. The shame was too much: I ripped the letter from the scrapbook and threw it away.

Dave Forsyth, a friend who didn't have a whole hell of a lot, brought his brand-new Viewmaster to class for Show and Tell. Viewmasters are plastic devices where you place a circular reel containing a dozen or so photos into a viewer, click a lever, and view the images in 3D. Mom and Aunt Sukie had one when they were children. I inherited that Viewmaster and kept it in my room along with vintage reels from the 1930s and '40s. Which begs the question: Why would I need to steal Dave's Viewmaster when I already had one? I'm unable to answer that question except to say: I did the crime. Once again, I ended up returning my ill-gotten gains and apologizing.

My urge to take things eventually evaporated. Whether I'd become more comfortable sharing familial love with my brother and little sister, whether I'd overcome evil urges, or whether I'd simply grown tired of getting caught and having to apologize, I have no idea. But around sixth grade, my thievery stopped: I never again took someone's property without permission. Wait. That's not entirely true. In high school and college, I'd "liberate" beer glasses and pitchers and furniture from local tippling establishments to stock a log cabin I helped construct. But there was at least a reason—perhaps insufficient in the eyes of the law—but a reason, nonetheless, why I took things that didn't belong to me on behalf of the Cabin. There was also one time, drunk at Frankie's Pizza in the West End, when I got the bright idea to break into a candy machine and steal a Snickers bar. Problem was, the candy bar I stole was an exemplar; one that had been on display under glass for a decade. That candy bar was so stale, I almost broke a tooth when I bit into it!

I've fessed up: Not all of my urge to take things evaporated at age twelve. And I certainly don't want to leave you with the impression I suddenly became a saint.

When Grandpa Jack retired from Watkin's Spices and no longer needed his leather briefcase and other items related to working as a salesman, he gave me the briefcase and a book of receipts. Handing a young boy blank receipts might seem innocuous but Grandpa handing me those receipts was like giving a pyromaniac a box of matches.

"I've got a summer job selling candy," I bragged to other kids while playing in front of Jentoft's house.

"Really?" Jerry Salveson replied. "That's cool."

Jerry was, like his older brother, skinny, gangly, and blond-headed. He and I spent a lot of time together despite there being a three-year age difference because Jerry had a more active imagination than Eddie; meaning he was more likely to assist me in putting on marionette shows for the neighborhood or playing army men or cowboys and Indians in my backyard sandbox. Eddie would do those things but only for snippets of time. He was easily bored whereas Jerry had staying power. Jerry was also impressionable and well-liked. Once I had Jerry hooked, I knew other kids would follow his lead.

I made a great show of printing kids' names and scribbling quantities of assorted candies on the blank receipts Grandpa Jack had given me before signing my name with a flourish. While handing the receipts to unsuspecting marks (including my brother) I told a whopper: "Take these to Torgersons' Store. They'll give you the candy listed on the checks. For free!"

Lie upon lie. I was handing the kids *receipts*, not checks. I didn't have a summer job working for a candy company (unless selling chocolate bars door-to-door to raise money for Little

League counts). And the Torgersons—nice people—certainly weren't expecting a herd of neighborhood children to show up at their tiny market demanding free candy.

Dad got a call from Oscar Torgerson and I got a scolding. Despite Dad's warning to "Never pull a stunt like that again," I detected a grin on Dad's face as he confiscated the receipt book and ended my career as a grifter.

PIANO LESSONS

Eddie convinced his mom that piano lessons wouldn't take and she released him from keyboard bondage. I wasn't so lucky. I was forced to plunk away—a half-hour a day—on the Munger family piano for years. We had two different pianos during my childhood. The first, an old rickety upright Mom painted lime green, lasted through junior high. That ugly, frog-colored thing was then replaced by a stately, black walnut upright-grand.

I started lessons in second grade. My first instructor was a neighbor—Mrs. Carlson. When I knocked on the Carlsons' door, I was ushered into the living room by their only child, Elaine. I always thought Elaine was a dwarf, like the ones in *Snow White*. Turns out she was born with Down Syndrome but I didn't realize that until later in life. During lessons, Mrs. Carlson would fart and leave me plunking away while she excused herself, whereupon Elaine would manifest and stare at me. I tried, as best I could, to hit the notes depicted in my Thompson piano exercise book (Mrs. Carlson didn't believe in using contemporary music to teach: No Bee Gees or Beatles or Stones allowed) while holding my breath as an odd, square, and squat young woman leered at me.

I hated taking lessons but I hated practicing even more. While my friends played outside I was stuck in our basement—a drab and unfinished concrete bunker of a space—playing the piano in disbelief that my mother actually thought I enjoyed the ordeal.

No, Mom, I'd think as practice time dragged on, *I'd rather take guitar lessons.*

It's unlikely I would have done better trying to emulate Keith Richards or Eric Clapton or Jimmy Page. But at least it would have been *my* choice. Time spent with Mrs. Carlson and in the basement practicing (or, in some cases, pretending to practice) wasn't my idea.

I switched from Mrs. Carlson to a new teacher in seventh grade. Miss Eck lived a few blocks from Lincoln Junior—on West 4th Street—meaning I could walk to my lesson after school and Mom would pick me up when the lesson was over. Miss Eck had been Cousin Samuel's piano teacher. Based upon a recommendation from the kid who tried to molest me, Mom changed teachers. What the hell was she thinking?

"Play that new piece, Mark. I'll be right back."

I'd start on a Simon and Garfunkel number or a Three Dog Night song (Miss Eck was fine with contemporary music), and Miss Eck would get up from the piano bench, smooth the wrinkles in her house dress, adjust her glasses, and wander off to make a sandwich. Her mouth full of bread and liverwurst and onions, Miss Eck would return to the bench, sit next to me, and munch away.

"No, not a flat, Mark, a sharp," she'd say. "Use your left index finger like this," she'd add, holding the sandwich between her teeth as she demonstrated. It also wasn't unheard of for Miss Eck to leave to answer the phone and spend most of my half-hour lesson talking to a friend. At least she didn't fart.

The best part about time spent with Miss Eck was that I met John McLoughlin and Bruce Larson—two West Enders also taking lessons. Those guys are real cut-ups who—like me—gave our piano teacher a run for her money. More about John later. For now, just know that Bruce attended sex education classes (at the suggestion of another mutual friend, Mike Town) with me at Holy Apostles Episcopal church. Bruce's mom, a devout Baptist, apparently decided Bruce needed more guidance concerning fornication than Baptists could provide. Why Miss Eck scheduled the three of us back to back to back, I'll never understand. But her poor timing allowed John, Bruce, and me to become lifelong friends.

By the summer of ninth grade, I'd had enough. We'd moved from Chambersburg to our new house on the creek and Mom didn't need the added burden of dropping everything to pick me up from the West End. She'd enrolled Dave in lessons and I was able to convince her it was time for me to quit. The big, black walnut upright? That piano followed us to the new house where Dave practiced on it and I occasionally banged away on its keys without nostalgia.

A dartboard hung near the door leading from the utility room into the hallway where the upright-grand was located. If you were playing darts—and the door to the utility room was open—it was a straight shot to the piano.

My version of events is that, while Dave sat at the piano in a half-hearted attempt to practice, I was throwing darts in the utility room. The door was open. I think you can see where this is headed. I threw a dart—a steel tipped, very dangerous projectile—with my eyes closed. I just *happened* to miss the dart board and the wall behind the board and the dart just *happened* to stick in Dave's forehead. My brother ran upstairs, screaming and bleeding, the dart protruding from his skull. Mom pulled the dart out, consoled Dave, and sent him back to practicing. An interrogation followed. I must have been convincing because I don't remember any consequences flowing from my miscue.

Dave doesn't buy it.

"Impossible," he said recently. "It was intentional."

Dave's emphatic when it comes to this piece of familial history. "There's no way you'd miss the target and the wall and hit me between the eyes without trying."

I disagree. But it wasn't long after the dart throwing incident that Dave convinced Mom he'd had enough. Mom let my baby brother quit piano lessons without any arguing or handwringing. In hindsight, maybe I did him a favor.

ALWAYS TRUST YOUR CAPE

Though Jerry Salveson was three years my junior, whenever
Eddie would get in one of his moods or moved on to his new best
friend of the moment (which happened with some regularity),
Jerry and I would spend time together. That was alright by me
because Jerry had a vivid imagination, one he would later turn into
a vocation as an interior designer for restaurants. Like his mom,
Jerry would also excel at painting and drawing. I don't remember
Eddie expressing an interest in art. Music, sure: He was a rabid
fan of the Beatles though his aim at collecting the band's work
wasn't always spot on. After a trip to a local record shop Eddie
came home with an album by some group called "The Beats"
thinking he was buying the Beatles' latest masterpiece. Talk about
disappointment!

    I was given an allowance for doing chores around the
house. When I was too young to operate our Toro mower I
trimmed around trees and Mom's flower gardens with hand
clippers. I started mowing the lawn around age ten and my net
worth increased. I think my weekly allowance started at a quarter
and by the time I was in high school, I was getting five bucks a
week, money I sorely needed to put gas in the family Jeep
Wagoneer whenever I was able to snatch it away from Mom. But
early on, when I was being paid a quarter a week for doing chores
and I needed extra cash, I came up with a legal and ingenious way
of fattening my wallet: I sponsored backyard carnivals. Mom was
OK with me dabbling in commerce. She had no problem having a
dozen kids visiting our backyard to take in the Not So Greatest
Show on Earth or if the weather was nasty, letting me stage an
event in the basement or the garage.

    I'd rehearse puppet shows with Eddie or Jerry as the
highlight of these impromptu gatherings. I'd write a ten to fifteen
minute play incorporating a half-dozen or so of the Pelham
marionettes in my stable. I'd cast Donald Duck, Pinocchio, Mike
Mercury (from the British television show, *Supercar*, a show we
didn't get but one similar to *Fire Ball XL5*), the Wicked Witch,
the Big Bad Wolf, and the Beatles (I had three of the four) along
with Mom's puppets—ones I was allowed to use from her
childhood—in performances that sometimes caused laughter but

more often engendered only silence. The puppet show was supposed to be the climax of the carnivals; festive occasions that included games of chance (kids would win toys I no longer valued, or penny candy or Bazooka bubble gum bought from Torgersons' Store as prizes), and a Kool-Aid stand. Whether it was Eddie or Jerry helping out, I'd split the take fifty-fifty. I never deducted my costs from the gross receipts. To me, every dime received was profit; an accounting approach that still bedevils me as a self-published author.

Other than occasionally storing Dad's fishing boat, the garage on Chambersburg rarely, if ever, was used as anything more than an oversized shed. An unimpressive structure detached from the house, the garage was built into the hill between our lot and Swansons', which meant the north wall of the garage also served as a retaining wall. That wall—constructed of concrete block—leaked and was in constant danger of collapse.

"Mark, bring in some kindling and firewood," Dad said one winter evening. "I'll make us a fire."

Every home in our neighborhood had a wood-burning, brick fireplace. This was long before anyone cared about global warming. Our fireplace didn't have airtight glass doors to ensure it burned efficiently and there was only a chain screen between the firebox and the living room carpeting to prevent catastrophe.

"OK, Dad," I replied, dressing for weather. Ski jacket. Stocking hat. Leather choppers with wool liners. Dad's old Army surplus felt boots (with the slipperiest soles ever conceived). Ready for the cold, I headed out the back door where Deuce I was chained to the doorknob.

I should say this: Deuce was so wild (Dad loved his Labs but didn't have the patience to train them) he'd wag his tail with enthusiasm—the tip beating cadence against plaster—that the skin would open up and spew blood all over the kitchen. He was the only Labrador I've come across with a docked tail—shortened a good five inches by the local vet to stop the carnage. All winter long, snow piled higher and higher inside the dog kennel attached to the garage. The snow would drift and invariably cover the doghouse Grandpa Jack had built. Deuce spent most of his life in that kennel. It was my job to feed Deuce, take him for an occasional walk, and bring him in at night. He slept on a rug in the back entry tied to the doorknob. One morning, I approached the kennel with Deuce's dish filled with Vet's canned dog food (man, did that crap stink!) only to find my dog as stiff as a board.

While alive, Deuce made a lot of shit. Excrement would pile up inside the kennel all winter long. In the spring, as shit was exposed by melting snow, it was my job to wade into the mess, shovel dung into a wheelbarrow, and haul it to an incinerator at the back of our lot. I'd unload all that wet, smelly, and disgusting crap into the metal stove. Dad would lug a gasoline can across the lawn, dump a prodigious amount of "incentive" onto the mess, and light it up. The odiferous smoke Dad's shit burns created wouldn't be tolerated today. But in the '60s and early '70s, even grocery stores had incinerators they used to burn trash and paper and cardboard. There was no recycling of packaging and certainly no recycling of dog shit.

During one of his shit burns, newspaper Dad used to assist ignition wafted into the sky, landed in the St. Lawrence Memorial Forest, and caused a blaze so large, Duluth firefighters were dispatched to put it out. Dad never received a ticket or a talking to concerning his little mistake in judgment. In retrospect, I doubt a fine or a lecture would have done much good.

Back to carrying firewood.

I loaded my arms with birch, exited the garage, waddled down the sidewalk, entered the house, repeating the process until I had one, final load of firewood left to carry. *How do I turn off the light?* The answer was succinct and immediate: *I'll flick the light switch with my tongue!* You're thinking, *That's a stupid idea: A wet tongue should <u>never</u> be applied to an electrical fixture.* But that wasn't the half of it.

Unlike the plastic light switches and switch plates we're all familiar with, the switch plate in the garage was metal. When I leaned over and flicked my tongue, I immediately knew it was one of the stupidest things I'd ever done. It was below zero outside and not much warmer in the garage. I stood there, my arms full of firewood, my tongue frozen to metal, pondering how in the hell I was going to break free. I yelled but my cries in a muffled, Elmer Fudd-like voice brought no savior. Finally, I gathered up courage and yanked my tongue away from the switch plate. Bleeding like a stuck pig, I ran into the house and tossed the firewood into the wood bin. Mom, who was sitting in front of the fireplace knitting, nearly fainted. I don't remember how she stopped the bleeding but she did. Every time I went into the garage over the next week, frozen pieces of tongue stuck to the switch plate reminded me of what a ninny I was.

I'd start off summer vacations happy to be free of teachers and homework. That giddy feeling lasted until early August when I'd start wondering what teacher (or teachers) I'd draw for the upcoming year and what kids would be in my class or classes. The joy I felt in early June at being free from educational bondage was usurped by the anticipation of beginning anew.

Unlike Benson, Minnesota—where my Uncle Paul and Aunt Sukie (and later, my cousins Julie and Heidi) lived—there is no public outdoor swimming pool in Duluth. I spent several weeks in Benson over a couple of summers (including when my parents attended the 1968 Democratic National Convention) and though I loved golfing with Uncle Paul, it was the trips to the Benson public pool that saved me from boredom and sweltering heat and thick humidity of summer on the prairie. Diving into the public pool is as good as it gets in Benson when the mercury tops eighty-five with humidity to match. Because Duluth has no outdoor public pool, the best we could hope for was to earn the quarter needed to gain entry to the Welch Center on Central Avenue in West Duluth. In truth, Piedmont kids needed more than a quarter to swim at the Welsh Center: We needed fifty cents because it cost a quarter to ride the bus from Piedmont to West Duluth <u>and</u> a quarter for admission to the pool.

Over summer vacation, and on weekends during the school year, we'd also take the bus from Piedmont to the NorShor or the Granada movie theaters in downtown Duluth. The Lyceum, a big, old, palatial, opera house also located downtown, ran double and triple matinees of B-movies on Saturdays. I only patronized the Lyceum a few times before the place was shuttered and its architectural splendor reduced to rubble. Another option was catching the bus to West Duluth to see flicks at the West Theater. But such trips were infrequent; the norm was riding the bus downtown to the NorShor or the Granada to see first-run movies. Given Dad was never around, I had to ask Mom's permission to go. More than once she said "no" because I needed to finish trimming the grass or practice piano. It grated me to see Eddie, the Osbournes, and other neighborhood boys wandering off to see *How the West Was Won* or some other epic while I was stuck at home.

One time I received Mom's blessing but my brother Dave—who was supposed to tag along—didn't make the trip. Here again there are divergent versions of what happened. My take on it is that we were playing H-O-R-S-E. Dave must have been about eight; I was thirteen or fourteen. The basketball got stuck behind the plywood backboard. Dave and I agree on these basic facts. I remember that my brother, on his own, decided to climb a wooden trellis next to the garage to retrieve the ball. Dave says I told him to climb the trellis. In any event, the trellis broke and Dave fell and fractured his arm. After presenting my bawling brother to Mom, I went to the movies and Dave went to the ER.

There was a city beach complete with a water slide and a lifeguard at Twin Ponds; two pools of murky water fed by Coffee Creek located a short drive (or a long bike ride) from Piedmont Heights. Park Point, a spit of sand that separates St. Louis Bay from Lake Superior also has a beach manned by lifeguards. I passed a YMCA lifesaving course as part of Boy Scouts and applied for my dream job—protecting scantily-clad girls from drowning in Lake Superior—but wasn't hired. Though the city still operates the beach on Park Point, Twin Ponds is no longer open for swimming.

Which is to say that opportunities for Piedmont kids to cool off during summer were limited. Consequently, I bought an above-ground wading pool with money I'd saved from mowing lawns, grifting kids at carnivals, and my allowance. It wasn't much of a pool; just ten feet in diameter and waist deep but it was a great place to beat the heat.

Summers on Chambersburg Avenue were also filled with bike riding, playing trench ball, four square, tag, engaging in Western gun fights and mythical WW II battles, and playing army men and cowboys and Indians in the sandbox. When all those activities failed to fill up the time, we got creative.

The late Texas folksinger Guy Clark must've grown up in a neighborhood like mine. How else could Guy replicate what transpired on the roof of Salvesons' garage with the exactitude depicted in his song, "The Cape."

I wasn't stupid enough to attempt flight with a flour sack tied *all around my neck*. Neither was Eddie. But Jerry? Gullible, fun-loving Jerry? That seems right, doesn't it; a ten-year-old being talked into near-suicide by his older brother and his older brother's sometime-best-friend?

"You think it's safe?" Jerry asked.

The heat of midday was disbursing as the sun moseyed west. Eddie and Jerry and I stood in the window of a second-floor bedroom surveying the flat roof of the Salvesons' garage.

"It's like a parachute," I said. "You're pretty skinny and if you run fast and jump high, it should work."

Eddie nodded. He was holding a contraption we'd pieced together. We'd found an old sheet in the basement, some rope in the garage and, not to make a pun here, jerry-rigged a crude parachute we wanted Eddie's kid brother to slip on and prove our genius. "It's not that far from the roof to the ground," Eddie observed. "What's the worst that can happen?"

Jerry agreed to be our test pilot. The three of us slid out the window and stood on the garage roof. Eddie fitted the makeshift harness around his brother's chest. We gave Jerry the thumbs up and watched him scamper across hot tar before taking a running leap into humid summer air.

Jerry didn't break any bones in his attempt to become a bird. But his brief flight did prove one thing: Eddie and I didn't know squat about physics.

HARRY AND THE SKEE HORSE

Dad was the least mechanically inclined human ever created by God. That's the truth. So, while this story seems to be about the first snowmobile in our neighborhood, it's really much more than that. It's an indictment of Harry's disinterest in anything requiring industrial intellect. As an example, I can only recall one instance of my father mowing the lawn before his children grew up and moved out of the house. That's an appropriate place, I think, to start this story.

Dad bought a new Toro mower from Daugherty's Hardware, brought it home, filled it up with gasoline, and started it up. This must have been sometime in 1961 or 1962, I'd guess. I'm dating this part of the story based upon the fact that one of the other kids involved in this tale was Mike Urie. Mike was fully capable of pushing a lawnmower without lopping off his toes. For those of you who think *that* caution is just fearmongering spawned by overly protective parents, you're dead wrong. One summer not long after Dad bought the Toro, Mr. Sundin, our next-door-neighbor (and the father of Wendy, the girl who got lost in the Woods with Eddie) mowed over his toes, necessitating a trip to the ER. So don't discount what your parents told you about being careful when mowing, OK?

"This thing isn't worth a damn," I heard Dad mutter.

Up to that point, Dad had cut most of the yard without incident. Looking back, I'm not sure what my folks did for lawn care before Dad bought the Toro. Maybe Dad hired one of the Milich boys—Dave or Gary—to mow, using the Milich family lawnmower. Or maybe Mike Urie mowed our lawn with the Urie family mower. I just don't remember. But the day Dad tried to mow, well, that memory is as clear as the water in Lake Superior.

When I went outside to see what Dad was complaining about, the source of his upset was obvious. The Toro's blades had struck a rock; a rock that whoever had been mowing our lawn up to that point had avoided. Dad was incapable of such diligence. As I've said, in all things, he was pretty much hell-bent-for-leather.

"The damn mower quit working," Dad said as I approached. "It hit a rock and now it won't start."

"Rock" would be an understatement. Small rocks get kicked out by a mower's spinning blade, becoming dangerous missiles that can take out a window or an eye. After we moved to our new house on Miller Creek, Dad learned that truth. Not by operating a lawn mower: He bought a snowblower, intent upon clearing the driveway after a snowstorm. But the new driveway was gravel—not concrete or asphalt. It took Dad one pass down the driveway, the snowblower tossing gravel—breaking windows and the panes of streetlamps lining the driveway—to realize his mistake. The snowblower went back to Daugherty's hardware store and Dad hired a guy to plow.

The Toro got fixed. Mike Urie got hired to mow and Mom paid me to trim around her gardens and the trees in our yard with hand clippers. I would have rather mowed. Trimming was a crummy task. Crawling around on your hands and knees cutting weeds and grass and dandelions with a hand trimmer sucks. But I was too young to push a power mower so trim I did. Mike made a couple of bucks for his half-hour of work, money I could've used to buy cool stuff at the Ben Franklin store in the Piedmont Shopping Center or comics at the adjacent Rexall drug store (we never called it a "pharmacy"). In any case, Dad didn't attempt lawn care again until after his kids left home.

One autumn, Dad and I drove to Goldfine's department store on Duluth's waterfront to check out snow machines. Dad loved to ice fish so buying a snowmobile made practical sense. He rarely took me with on his Nanook of the North excursions. Ice fishing wasn't something I enjoyed as a child—or frankly, ever. That's beside the point—my aversion to sitting in a tent or a dark house freezing my ass off, staring into a hole, waiting for fish to swim by. Our trip to Goldfine's was focused on Dad's obsession. He figured a snowmobile would make getting on and off a snow-covered lake a hell of a lot easier than dragging a toboggan full of gear behind him while he trudged along on snowshoes. We looked at Fox Tracs at Goldfine's, machines painted bright orange with the engine not under a cowling in the front—as most snowmobiles are designed--but fully exposed and located behind the driver. Ultimately, Dad came home with a green and orange Johnson Skee Horse, an underpowered, heavy-as-a-tank rig.

Until the Osbourne family moved into the neighborhood, the Skee Horse was the only sled on the block. After big snows, you know, those monster winter storms we seemed to get every year before global warming messed things up, Dad would don a one-piece, black snowmobile suit, snowmobile boots, put on a stocking hat (he never wore a helmet) and leather choppers, go outside, tie a wooden toboggan to the machine, and fire that sucker up. What followed was pure joy. He'd pick up kids and adults who wanted rides, zooming over plowed streets at the machine's top speed (thirty miles per hour), whipping around turns, dodging traffic, and scaring the hell out of anyone trying to hang on to the toboggan for dear life.

Shit happened when Harry drove his snowmobile. During one wild ride, the throttle on the Skee Horse froze wide open. Dad tried to stop the out-of-control iron sled from crashing into a neighbor's house at the bottom of Chambersburg but couldn't. He surveyed the damage done to the front porch, checked on the kids being towed (no serious injuries had occurred), loaded the machine onto a trailer, and hauled it back to the dealer where he used—I'm quite certain—colorful language to indicate just what was wrong with "their stupid machine."

Another time, Dad took the corner at the bottom of Chambersburg too fast and launched a young mother off the toboggan and into the ditch, breaking her arm.

But the most memorable episode of Dad's operation of the Skee Horse wasn't related to porches or passengers.

A snowdrift covered Salvesons' backyard. Eddie, Jerry, and I decided the drift was the perfect place to build a snow cave. We worked for hours digging a narrow tunnel into the heart of the drift before carving out a chamber spacious enough for three or four of us (boys only; Eddie's sister Diane, was not, I repeat, not allowed to enter our domain!) to sit in, chew the fat, read *Superman, Batman, Haunted Tank,* and *Sgt. Rock* comic books, and eat sandwiches and snacks by candlelight. Eddie, Jerry, and I were inside our hideaway when the roof started to shake.

"Oh, Oh."

"What?" Eddie asked.

"My dad."

Harry had decided the new snowfall was too glorious to ignore. He'd pulled the Johnson out of the garage, filled it with gas, fired it up, and was topside pulling a toboggan load of kids. Not once. Not twice. But three times Harry's Skee Horse zoomed overhead. We were pretty sure we were going to die but it's pretty obvious we didn't.

The Johnson eventually gave up the ghost and was carted off to wherever old snow machines go to die. The few times I tried to use the thing—I was a small, skinny kid who didn't hit puberty until eighth grade—I managed to bury it. Which meant trudging back to the house to get Dad. Who would, after a few choice words, slip into his snowmobile suit and boots, follow me into the field behind the house, dig the Johnson out, ride it home, and pretty much make it clear that my time on the snowmobile was over for the day.

Dad's disinterest in mechanical things, working around the house, and doing chores continued. I never saw the man lift a paint brush. I never saw him change a light bulb. I never saw him use a tool. I never saw him split wood for the fireplace. In truth, I rarely witnessed him doing physical work. This next story is an exception to that general observation.

After we moved to our new home on Miller Creek, Mom got the bright idea she wanted a rock garden—complete with a pump and a fountain—installed in the backyard. There was a low spot near the creek where rain and snow melt pooled, a natural breeding place for mosquitoes. Mom thought that swampy area would be perfect for her garden. Dad borrowed a small John Deere bulldozer from a client—Jim Robertson—who owned a local cement company. Jim dropped the dozer off at the house and gave Dad a crash course in its operation. Within minutes of Jim's departure, Dad got the dozer stuck. The thing was so completely buried, even Dad's civil engineering pal, Rudy Monson, who came over to survey the damage, couldn't free it. Dad called Jim Robertson and Jim trucked over the biggest bulldozer he owned. To reach the buried John Deere without destroying our lawn, Jim drove his ginormous machine up the bed of Miller Creek (likely without the DNR's knowledge), attached a steel cable to the sunken dozer, and rescued it from its mucky grave. The hole the dozer left behind? Mom had me line it with boulders from Miller Creek and install a submersible pump. Then she planted forget-me-nots and lilies and other wildflowers in terraces around the gurgling, artificial cascade. Dad's part in all this? Other than creating a deep hole by burying Robertson's dozer, he didn't have anything to do with the project.

I inherited Dad's uncanny ability to mess up machinery.

I was learning to drive. I only had my learner's permit when I decided to take the family Jeep Wagoneer for a spin. Knowing it was illegal to drive a car on a public roadway without adult supervision, I drove the Jeep across Miller Creek, followed a path to Vo Tech (now Lake Superior College), and tooled around the school's parking lot for practice. Things went well until, on my way back across the creek, the Jeep stopped smack dab in the middle of the stream.

I tried and tried and tried to get the car to move. The engine was on and the car was only in a few inches of water but it wouldn't budge.

Dad's gonna kill me.

I ran home crying, found Mom, and confessed my sin. Mom called our local gas jockey and mechanic, Al Hansen, whose daughter Nancy was a classmate and a friend. Al dropped everything and, after spending a moment under the Wagoneer, his shirt and trousers soaked by Miller Creek, emerged, wrench in hand, smiling.

"All fixed."

"What was wrong?" Mom asked, her cowardly fifteen-year-old son hiding in her shadow.

"Hit a rock and jammed the emergency brake. I released it."

If Al charged for his time and expertise, I never heard about it.

"Let's just keep this to ourselves," Mom said as Al drove away in his tow truck.

I was fine with that.

If there were chores that needed doing, one of us kids did them or Mom paid for help, including hiring my pal Wayne Rikala to do yard work. Mom borrowed an antiquated Chev pickup to haul wood and leaves and brush to the city dump. Because I didn't have a license, Wayne drove. He knew how to operate a manual transmission and taught me—when no one else was around—how to drive a three-on-the-tree.

One of the more endearing characters who worked for us was Arthur. Art was a pokey worker but a very nice man who became part of the family once we moved into the new house. When I'd come home from Denfeld and later, from UMD, he'd be planting flowers or raking or fixing things that needed repair, a little battery-powered AM radio whispering the play-by-play of the Minnesota Twins as he puttered away. After supper, I'd drive Art back to his room at the old St. Louis County poor farm where he lived for most of his life. He'd been born a twin but because of a pronounced stutter, his parents kept his brother but gave Art up for adoption. Art was deemed unadoptable and became a ward of the state. During the Great Depression, he worked for FDR's Civilian Conservation Corps before enduring the hardscrabble life of a day laborer. I always felt sorry for Arthur; especially after Mom stopped hiring him due to his advanced age and dwindling physicality. He was replaced by Jack Crooks, a kindly, retired neighbor whose wife, Dolly, cleaned house for us. Jack didn't do yard work. He was strictly a fix-it guy. The Munger kids were tasked with doing the outdoor jobs Art once did. Years later I was at St. Mary's Hospital waiting for the birth of my second son. I wandered over to Jim's Hamburger's and spotted Arthur sitting at the lunch counter eating the daily special. I walked up and said hello. Art looked at me, dementia clear in his milky, unfocused gaze and shook his head as if he'd never met me. It was the last time I saw him before he passed away. The fact that Arthur likely died without family or friends by his side still haunts me.

Dad's primary interests in life were fishing and hunting, sipping Canadian whiskey, smoking stinky cigars, and having a good time. His older brother Willard—a guy who built a gas station, two homes, and a motel—usurped all the Munger family's mechanical ability. I think Dad was OK with that. There were fish to be caught, deer to be stalked, grouse and ducks and pheasants to be hunted, and poker and dice games to be played. It took time for a fellow to pursue such interests, time Dad didn't want to waste puttering around the house.

BACKYARD SPORTS AND OTHER DELIGHTS

Dad's University of Minnesota-Duluth (UMD) letter sweater, the one he earned as an undersized varsity punter and reserve quarterback, hung in a closet of our house as a constant reminder that Dad managed to beat the odds and play college ball. Long before I sat on the bench or my brother Dave became a starting offensive guard for the Denfeld Hunters, my parents—who graduated from Denfeld High in 1945 (Dad) and 1946 (Mom)—kept tradition alive by braving autumn's chill and attending football games at Public Schools Stadium (PSS). Their "dinner club"—a group of high school friends that got together periodically to break bread, drink booze, smoke cigarettes, and tell tall tales—was a constant presence at Denfeld sporting events. The group's loyalty towards their high school was legendary, unequaled, and the envy of outsiders. A backdrop of rabid fandom for the maroon and gold is what pushed me to try my hand at backyard athletics in hopes I'd find a sport I could excel at.

As I've related, older boys in the neighborhood played baseball on land that eventually became St. Lawrence School. When the old field was torn up, those same boys constructed the Field of Unfulfilled Dreams. I never played hardball with the older boys; I only played softball, a game the Osbournes excelled at, a game for which I was almost always the last kid picked.

We played softball on the gravel of the St. Lawrence parking lot or at the base of Chambersburg's steep hill. This latter "field" was problematic: Foul balls headed over third base ended up in the Bjorlins' front yard, a dangerous scenario if Mrs. Bjorlin—a chain-smoker and the only neighborhood mom who wore a bikini—was on her lawn chair soaking up rays. Or worse yet, a well-struck foul might hit the house, causing Bob Bjorlin to come outside and ask us, very nicely, not to break his windows. Bob had two boys, Scott and Mark, who would later play on a neighborhood football team I coached against teams made up of the Huard Gang and boys from Plymouth Street. But when I played softball at the intersection of Chambersburg and Hutchinson, the Bjorlin boys were too young to join our fun and, because no girls were allowed, their older sister, Stephanie, never joined us. Since young ladies were excluded from athletic activities in the neighborhood except trench, tag, and four-square, one would have expected them to form their own teams and play their own games of softball or boot hockey or the like. To my knowledge that never happened.

In the late summer and fall, we played football, but there was no real place to hold games other than the Osbournes' swampy backyard. The lack of a serviceable field caused us to wander over to Huards' Field. Games played on the vacant lot next to Jeff Huard's house were hotly contested. I always played on the line. I never got a chance to run with or catch the ball, mostly because Patrick Osbourne's view of things was that he was the second coming of OJ Simpson. Not the hero-turned-murdering-bastard OJ but the OJ who starred for USC. Truth is Patrick was never all that great though he was plenty fast, much faster than I was. Playing pick-up games at Huards'—a grassy, empty lot lacking goal posts, goal lines, or any sort of markings but well-mown by Jeff's dad, Herb Huard, my barber at the Piedmont Barber Shop—it didn't matter if I was fast or not. The Osbournes determined I was a lineman and so I was.

We usually got our butts kicked by the Huard Gang, a team consisting of Tom Kubiak, the Granmoe brothers, Jeff Huard, the Flood boys (both of whom became pretty fair athletes at Duluth Cathedral), John Holt, Mark Olson, Ricky Hendrickson, Packy Pederson, Rod Peltoma, Kevin Dahl, Scott Burnes, the Luczaks and others. Packy Pederson was built for football. He ended up starting both ways on the line for Denfeld. But on Huard Field, Packy's low center of gravity and churning legs were utilized by his pals as the type of fullback defenders dread. Tackling Packy was like taking on a dump truck.

Eventually, I got eyeglasses and discovered I had decent hands. Kubiak and I were tossing the ball in Olsons' front yard before a game when Tom commented, as he spiraled the ball high, low, and everywhere in between—all of which I caught—"Munger, you'd make a decent end." Given the Osbournes' dim view of my abilities, I never played wide-out during games, though Kubiak's observation made me feel a tad better about myself.

Our best hope to beat the Huard Gang was when we brought in ringers like Billy Erickson, a friend of Carson

Osbourne. Billy was fearless. He had no problem tackling Packy. Billy was also a delinquent who caused no end of problems for his mom, a widow who went to the same church my family did. Despite his legal troubles, Billy was a genuinely nice kid and one hell of an athlete who sadly, when it came to organized ball, never realized his potential. Without Billy or some other ringer lining up on our side of the ball, we rarely won.

The Harrises were the only poor family I knew. They lived in an old farmhouse, a remnant from the days when Piedmont Heights was all hayfields and cows. Though the house had running water and plumbing, an artifactual outhouse stood in the backyard, making the Harris kids targets of ridicule. When Devin, the oldest Harris, showed up to play football for the Huard Gang one Saturday morning, his attire also became an issue.

"You can't play in those," Carson Osbourne said, pointing to Devin's shoes.

"Can too," Devin replied.

"No way," Paul Ebert chimed in. "You'll cut someone up."

"They're just spikes."

"They're golf spikes, you moron!" Patrick Osbourne chided.

"He's right, Dev," Tom Flood, the oldest Flood brother, said. "Go get some other shoes."

Anguish was clear in Devin's gait as he shuffled home, his helmet dangling from one hand, his shoulder pads shifting beneath his sweatshirt, his dad's metal golf cleats clacking against blacktop. Sadly, the kid never came back, likely because he had no other shoes to wear.

Dad only had a few songs in his repertoire. He'd learned "The Weatherman's Song" in the Army Air Corps. He'd learned "Porky, Porky, Porcupine" growing up in Pockerbrush. He'd sing a single line of that stupid song over and over and over again in his out-of-tune voice until you wanted to run away. Then there was "I scream, you scream, we all scream for ice cream ..." a song, like the one about Porky, that never reached conclusion. Still, the ice cream song made my brother Dave and me perk up when Dad started in. That song meant Mister Softee was in the neighborhood. When the ice cream truck's bell rang, kids around the block held out their collective hands, begged for change from their parents, closed their fingers around borrowed coins, and ran for the door. Parked at the top of the hill was salvation in the form of a blue-and-white truck. The engine kept the truck refrigerated as the owner took orders through an open window, plucked money from sweaty hands, made change, received completed orders from his wife, and disbursed frozen treats to impatient kids. It was a big deal when I saved enough from doing chores to buy a Mister Softee soft-serve sundae. Fifty cents bought you a bus trip to the Lyceum and a triple feature matinee: Forking over half a buck for soft-serve ice cream was an extravagance.

October is my favorite month. Not only does October mark the beginning of serious grouse hunting (the season starts in September but it takes the October winds to shake leaves free of trees to make hunting decent), it includes my birthday and Halloween. Halloween denotes the last bit of fun before winter cloaks northeastern Minnesota in perpetual gloom. Given my birthday is but a day before All Hallows Eve, many of my first "kid" birthday parties included friends—boys and girls—attending the celebration of my blessed arrival in their Halloween costumes. Around age ten, that protocol changed in a number of ways.

First, girls were no longer invited. The affairs became boys-only celebrations. Additionally, Mom decided that having a half-dozen kids cavorting about her house was traumatizing. Instead of partying in our cinder block basement, she'd take us to a movie and then, once we'd calmed down, back to the house for cake and ice cream. Problem was, Mom had no idea what sort of movie might entertain pre-teen boys. Instead of seeing *The Battle of the Bulge* (as Eddie and I did for Dave Hendrich's birthday) or *20,000 Leagues Under the Sea* (Jimber Liston's eleventh birthday at the West theater), Mom picked films like *Heidi* for me and my pals to endure. Imagine my horror at age twelve, the age when kid birthday parties ended in our family, sitting with my buddies and watching an insipid story about a little girl in some godforsaken mountain village. No bombs exploding. No arrows flying. No bodies falling. *Heidi* was the most embarrassing cinematic choice Mom could've made.

That said, Mom couldn't completely ruin October. Because our neighborhood was filled with pre-teen boys and girls, unless it was raining cats and dogs on Halloween, Piedmont's streets became clogged with costumed kids going door to door for "treats." Illumined by golden light from streetlamps, with autumnal cold chilling our bones, we'd walk in groups—boys and girls together—filling paper sacks or plastic jack-o'-lanterns with edible treasures. We praised folks who gave us full-sized Hershey or Mars bars instead of the miniature candy bars most homes gave out. We lamented "healthy" offerings such as shiny red apples or homemade cookies or Rice Krispy bars; not because we were worried about poison or razorblades embedded in those handcrafted treats but because such offerings were lame.

I remember one Halloween, shortly after *The Great Pumpkin* became a holiday classic on TV (a story where Linus from the Peanuts crew waits and waits and waits for the mythical Great Pumpkin) when my brother channeled his inner Charlie Brown. In the show, Charlie, always downtrodden and on the cusp of psychiatric collapse, looks into his paper bag and bemoans "I got a rock." Dave, who actually got the same candy as the rest of us, repeated that phrase after every house until I finally found a handful of gravel and dumped it in his bag, fulfilling his wish and shutting him up.

Occasionally, delinquents would create a spectacle at the water tower next to the community club at the top of Piedmont Avenue. Under cover of night, teenaged boys (I'm pretty sure no girls were involved) climbed the ladder affixed to the tower and hung a straw-filled scarecrow from a rope. As trick-or-treating kids swarmed past the swinging effigy, someone would put a match to the scarecrow and the resulting blaze would illuminate the dark, eerie, night like a macabre beacon.

We played a few hockey games on a rink Doug Osbourne flooded behind the Osbourne house but Eddie and I were clueless when it came to ice skating, which meant that boot hockey—played on a level stretch of Hutchinson Road—became our winter sport of choice. We used chunks of snow placed at either end of our makeshift "rink" as goals and tennis balls instead of pucks. Boot hockey games were played at night, after supper and before homework. Though the games were heated affairs involving body checks and inadvertent sticks to the face, no one got seriously hurt. Our biggest fear wasn't injury but that when cars came upon us—we were, after all, playing hockey at night in the middle of a busy road—our makeshift goal posts would get smushed.

I was playing goalie when a sedan approached and we all scrambled up the snowbanks lining Hutchinson. Whenever a car avoided our goals, we'd raise our hockey sticks in salute. I was holding my stick in the air and, as the sedan passed by, lost my grip and the stick slammed down on the car's trunk.

"What the hell do you think you're doing?" a very irate, fat man said after he stopped the car, opened the driver's door, and stepped out into night.

I was scared: It wasn't often that an adult directed his or her ire at me. I gulped and whispered, "I'm sorry."

The man advanced. I retreated to the top of the snowbank. Given the man's bulk and the fact he was already huffing and puffing, I figured I was safe. The guy pivoted and walked back to his car to inspect the trunk. "You're lucky. I don't see any damage. But you kids need to find another place to play," he said, anger firm in his voice.

"And where would that be, Mister?" Carson Osbourne asked with attitude. "There's not a rink for five blocks. We're not causing trouble. It was an accident. Munger apologized. Maybe it's time you moved on."

The guy's face reddened. "You're kind of a smart ass, aren't you?" he asked, sizing up Osbourne. "I can't get into it with a kid," the guy fumed. "But I'll bring my nephew back here and when he lands, man, you'll be in a world of hurt!"

"Oh, he'll land, will he?" Ricky Plys quipped. "What is he—a Martian?"

The guy started for Ricky but common sense kicked in. He muttered something as he headed towards his car. Carson Osbourne sniggered.

"Someday, you're going to jail," the guy said, turning around and pointing a finger at Carson. "And you," he added, singling me out as I stood on the snowbank. "And you," he continued, pointing at Ricky.

Paul Ebert chimed in. "Hey, I've got an idea. My dad owns a station wagon that'll carry us all. Let's all go to jail!"

The fat guy's face flashed menace as he muttered, got in his car, slammed the door, and backed over the goal I was defending. After the sedan roared away, I replaced the snow chunks, and we went back to our game.

The 1968 Winter Olympics concluded with American Billy Kidd—a tough, no nonsense skier from Steamboat Springs—bringing home silver and Frenchman Jean-Claude Killy collecting gold in three alpine events. Inspired, I decided to stage a neighborhood version of the Games. I set up a slalom course (with poles cut from aspen saplings) behind the picket fences defining our backyards. A discarded Christmas tree covered with snow became a ski jump. A sled race was held on Chambersburg Avenue. Fastest time in the alpine and sledding contests—using the second hand of my Timex as a crude stopwatch—was the winner. Ski jumping distances were measured with pine boughs stuck in the snow. I crafted awards: gold, silver and bronze medals cut from construction paper affixed to ribbon Mom donated to the cause.

In winter, boys zoomed down Chambersburg on Flexible Flyers after city plows cleared the street. The trick was to get on the hill before the sanding truck came by and contaminated our makeshift bobsled run. Boys pretended their sleds were fighter planes engaged in dogfights with the hated Germans and Japs. Girls sledded too but I have no idea what was in their heads as they plummeted down the steeps.

Each winter, Mr. Stocke—a neighbor across the street—built a flying saucer run behind his house. He iced the track with a garden hose and welcomed kids to test their mettle on his ridiculously fast track.

The snowbanks those city plows left behind? They became our fortresses. We'd carve out rooms and tunnels and build ramparts in preparation for battle and battle we did. During one snowball fight in Bruce Patterson's front yard, Doug Wait, a kid visiting Patterson from the West End, hit me in the mouth with an ice chunk and I lost two front teeth. Mom took one look at my empty smile and hauled me off to see Doc Deadon, the family dentist. There was no cause for alarm: The missing teeth were only baby teeth.

When it snowed and the winds whipped up, snowdrifts—like the drift involved in the Skee Horse incident—nearly covered our houses. Folks carved steps into the snowdrifts and walked onto the roofs of their bungalows after those old timey blizzards roared in from Canada. In the early '60s, a blizzard to end all blizzards knocked out the power in Piedmont. With no electricity and no heat, Mom bundled Dave and me in our winter clothes and Dad drove us to Uncle Willard's because the motel still had power. It didn't take long for our parents to grow tired of Dave and me jumping from bed to bed to stave off boredom in our motel room. Dad and Mom were thankful when the electricity was restored and we went home.

Much of my time wasn't spent with other kids: It was spent alone, in the imaginary world inside my head. I was never fond of playing cars and trucks, though I had a fine collection of Match Box cars I bought at Carr's Hobby in the West End. I also had a few larger trucks, one of which, a blue Buddy L pickup with a plastic camper, was a beloved Christmas present from Santa. Sadly, Brother Dave sat on the camper before Christmas Day was over, leaving behind a stupid blue pickup truck and shards of blue plastic.

An inquisitive child, I became an admirer of George Armstrong Custer. I know, I know. It's politically incorrect to glorify a guy who made his mark killing Indians. With apologies to my Native American friends, I was raised on Errol Flynn, John Wayne, Roy Rogers, and Sky King. Cowboys and pony soldiers were the good guys and Indians (except for Tonto) were the enemy. I became enthralled with Custer and when I was seven, my parents and I joined the Lundeen family on a camping trip out West. For me, the highlight of that trip was visiting the Little Big Horn Battlefield in Montana.

This is not to say that I didn't appreciate the heroes on the other side of the equation, especially Crazy Horse and Sitting Bull. When I learned from Doc Deadon (another Custerphile) that a Dakota chief—a man who'd been a child at the time of Custer's death and who'd visited the Little Big Horn battlefield and seen the dead bodies, was visiting Duluth—I convinced Mom I had to go see Chief Red Fox. I met the Chief at Wrazidlo's Meats at the top of Piedmont Avenue where Mom took our picture and I asked Red Fox a shitload of questions. Talk about being on the top of the world! Turns out, even though Chief Red Fox made numerous appearances on television (including *The Tonight Show* with Johnny Carson) as a sponsor for Wilson's

Meats, regaling audiences with his experiences as a nephew of Crazy Horse, a survivor of Wounded Knee, and a member of Buffalo Bill's Wild West Show, it was all bullshit. The guy who claimed to be a Sioux chief? His real name was William Humes. He was a white dude—born eight years after the Battle of the Little Big Horn took place—who was just really good at impersonating an Indian!

Even though I had solid childhood friends, in some very basic way, I was lonely. Maybe it was having been an only child for the first six years of my life. Maybe it was because the adults in my life saddled me with high expectations, causing me to experience early maturation. In any event, I spent a lot of time on my own, playing in my own world, on my own terms.

It was below zero. I was bundled up—stocking cap, snow pants, ski jacket, winter boots, and leather choppers with wool inserts— standing sentinel on a snowbank adjacent to St. Lawrence School with a toy flintlock in my mittened hands. My eyes were clear and dutiful as I scanned the wintery landscape. I was, at that moment, not a shivering, lonely, ten-year-old boy trying to understand his family, his little brother, or his world: I was one of General Washington's patriots guarding the Delaware River. Dusk approached. The sky darkened. I held my ground until Mom called me in for supper.

DEAD LETTER

Davy Crockett stood tall in the midst of the Mexican horde. His musket was useless; there was no more powder, no more shot. He raised his heavy rifle by its barrel like an ax. Gunfire rang out. Travis was already dead. Bowie would not live more than a minute or two. Santa Anna was poised to enter the old mission at the head of his triumphant army.

I sat on a braided rug in our basement, my knees curled beneath me in the flexibility of youth. I was absorbed in reliving the heroism of the Alamo. Pale blue figurines of molded plastic, historically accurate and detailed, surrounded the pressed tin walls of the fortress. Few Texans remained alive. I was a small boy of nine, talking softly to myself, carefully advancing Mexican soldiers towards destiny.

Mom stood at the ironing board watching *As the World Turns* on an old black-and-white cabinet-style Admiral television. Her thin, blue-veined hands pushed and pulled the hot iron in no particular pattern as she tried to follow the parade of simulated domestic problems portrayed in front of her.

It was a school day. I shouldn't have been home. But it was November. I always get strep in November. That year was no exception. I stayed home, nursing my sore throat and the bruise on my butt from where Mom gave me a shot of penicillin.

"What're you doing?" Mom asked.

"Playin' Alamo," I replied without looking up.

"Who's winning?"

"Mexicans. Rotten old Santa Anna wins every time."

"Can't you change it so the other side wins?"

"Mom, that's not what happened. That'd be cheating," I said as dragoons galloped toward the beleaguered mission.

"We interrupt our regular programming to bring you a special report," a male voice said. The seriousness of the TV announcer's tone forced Mom to focus on the flickering screen.

"This morning in downtown Dallas, President Kennedy and Governor Connally of Texas were shot. Eyewitnesses say that both the President and the Governor were rushed to a Dallas hospital. The conditions of both men are unknown. Stay tuned to this station for further details."

"Oh my God!" Mom murmured, placing the iron on edge and cradling her face in her hands.

"Is the President hurt bad, Mom?" As I spoke, I placed the figure of Santa Anna next to Davy Crockett. The tip of the Mexican's saber nudged the frontiersman's chest, foreshadowing Crockett's demise.

"We don't know yet, Mark. Just pray it's not bad. He's such a good man. Remember seeing him at UMD?"

I remembered. President Kennedy had been in town a month or two before the shooting to give a speech. My father was an official in the local Democratic party and I'd attended the historic event with my parents. I fell asleep in the bleachers of UMD's gymnasium and didn't hear the President's address. Still, because the man was the President (his photo hung in our den like that of a saint) there wasn't any need to remember his words: Whatever John Fitzgerald Kennedy said was gospel.

As the afternoon lingered on, the news grew worse. Mom and I sat together on the braided rug listening raptly as reporters talked about bullets to the head and blood staining Mrs. Kennedy's dress. Mom held me, embracing my sickly body, taking solace in the life she'd brought into the world. And then, we watched Walter Cronkite—his velvety voice cracking with grief—announce to the world that the President of the United States was dead.

Mom rocked me in her arms. She did not speculate why the President had been shot. She did not contemplate whether the assassin would be found. Her thoughts were singular and were devoted to the brutal fact that the First Lady had been widowed and left alone to care for two small children.

"What a horrible thing for those children," Mom whispered, tears sliding down her young cheeks as she spoke.

"Do you think I should write Mrs. Kennedy a letter 'bout not being too sad?" I asked, pulling away to look at Mom's troubled face.

"That would be very comforting," Mom encouraged, her voice soft and tender.

Leaving the defenders of the Alamo to their fate, I climbed the crude wooden staircase from the basement to the kitchen. Mom remained behind, immobilized by shock from the most horrific event she'd witnessed in her lifetime.

I wrote a letter of condolence to the First Lady. After finishing the message, I lost the nerve to send it. Mom tucked the letter away, saving it for when I was older, for when I would understand.

In the intervening decades, through the tumult of the Vietnam War and the deception of Watergate, that unsent letter remained in my scrapbook. Years later, I happened upon the letter and considered mailing it to Jackie (who'd remarried to become Mrs. Onassis). I thought it might serve some purpose for her to know that the children who witnessed her anguish had not forgotten. Instead, I did nothing.

Then Jackie Onassis died. After reading about her funeral, I searched for the letter. My childhood missive to the First Lady was gone. It had disappeared, leaving me to ponder whether it's possible to retrieve what has been lost.

FIELD OF UNFULFILLED DREAMS

There were a lot of kids in Piedmont Heights. Eddie and his dad once calculated that, in the three blocks considered to be "our neighborhood"—Chambersburg Avenue, Hutchinson Road, Morris Thomas Road, and Robert Court—nearly two hundred children—from infancy to high school age—called that little pie-shaped piece of the world "home." This meant plenty of boys available for tackle football games against the Huard Gang or for ball hockey on Hutchinson Road or for playing baseball.

When I was very young, older boys played ball on the grassy field beyond our backyard fence. Then the Catholic Diocese of Duluth decided to build St. Lawrence school and church. Though the church never got built, the school was constructed, destroying the neighborhood's impromptu baseball diamond.

Bob Huseby realized the pent-up desire of WW II and Korean War veterans to own their own homes was an urge he could satisfy. He acquired land at the top of Piedmont Avenue and set about building houses. Even though Huseby constructed hundreds of homes on the knoll overlooking Lake Superior, acres of his land—land that had been logged off at the beginning of the 20th century and converted into vegetable and dairy farms by Scandinavian immigrants—remained undisturbed. There were no signs prohibiting kids from using this vacant land. And so, the Field of Unfulfilled Dreams was born.

We should have seen it coming. Despite the lack of "No Trespassing" signs posted along the Woods bordering Hutchinson Road, we knew Bob Huseby wasn't fond of kids. Despite this truth, older boys in the neighborhood believed Huseby's undeveloped land was open to their use.

Eddie and I were younger than the guys we hung out with, serving as batboys for baseball games and as fans for surf music jams that took place on steamy summer nights in the Milich garage. When Dee Dee and Lori Ramfjord and Carolyn Granley taught neighborhood kids the Twist, Eddie and Ronny Granley and I learned Chubby Checker's moves alongside our teen idols.

Given our past experiences with Mr. Huseby, we should have anticipated the man's displeasure when we decided to build a baseball field. We'd stood by helplessly as our shacks—crudely constructed tree houses—were ripped apart by Huseby's backhoe. Destruction of that handiwork occurred even though Bob Huseby never warned us about trespassing. He simply removed the offending structures and went about the business of building houses and making money, as if all of us—all the children living in his subdivisions—didn't matter.

When Mike Urie, the Moes, Eddie Rauvola, Denny McClain, and the Miliches decided to build a ballfield in a meadow surrounded by second growth aspen and birch on land owned by Mr. Huseby—Piedmont's version of Mr. Potter—the longevity of a ball field should have been obvious.

Eddie and I joined the older boys under the intense sunlight of high summer chopping down trees and clearing brush. Insects buzzed the sultry air. We sweated bullets working in the heat. The supports for the field's dugouts, log backstop, and homerun fence came from aspen trees felled by ax. Chain saws were virtually unknown and no father in his right mind would have let any of us use one had one been available. After a weekend of labor, the ballfield was ready. Pennants made from old pillowcases—one labeled "Home" another labeled "Visitor"—flapped in the breeze. Nomenclature really didn't matter since all the players lived in the neighborhood. The sides were selected—one boy at a time—by team captains, the captains alternating picks to ensure teams of equal talent. Eddie and I were designated "ball boys" and charged with shagging balls hit into the Woods.

I don't remember the outcomes of the games played on the new field but I do recall the thrill of being part of something created entirely by kids. I remember searching for lost baseballs in the alder swamps behind the backstop and beyond the outfield fence. I also recall that the older boys played to win. They dove for ground balls hit across perilous ground. They ran after pop flies and line drives, disregarding stumps dotting the outfield as they sprinted. They wore baseball caps displaying the insignias of the Twins, the Yankees, and the Duluth-Superior Dukes—our local minor league team—and were serious about America's game.

One summer morning, we arrived at the ballfield and found that a bulldozer had made short work of things. The fences and dugouts had been plowed into a heap. The carefully mowed infield had been defiled by the dozer's steel tracks.

A guy from the old neighborhood once told me that Bob Huseby wasn't a bad person—that he helped down-on-their-luck families in unsung ways. That may be true. But I never, during the years I lived in Piedmont Heights, heard anyone sing the man's praises. It's possible Bob Huseby changed as he aged and that, like Scrooge in *A Christmas Carol*, he repented his sins. If such a transformation occurred, I didn't witness it.

Here's what I know: As the boys from the neighborhood stared at the carnage left behind by Huseby's bulldozer, a lesson—a lesson repeated throughout history regarding powerful men and their tendencies—was revealed.

DUCK AND COVER

I'm pretty sure it wasn't the intention of the adults in charge of the United States of America to scare the shit out of their kids, but that's exactly what they did.

One of my earliest memories of elementary school is being part of regular drills that were supposed to prepare us for Armageddon. Those exercises took place during the Cold War, when the Soviet Union tried to place missiles tipped with nuclear warheads ninety miles from Florida. At the time, Duluth was supposedly in the "top ten" of targets slated for holocaust. I'm not sure where that pronouncement came from but that's what we were told. The reasons for a city of just over 100,000 folks supposedly being so high up on the Kremlin's "hit list?" Duluth allegedly made the cut because of iron mines being nearby, a steel plant being located in town, and because of our seaport. If the Russkies could take out the source of iron that made steel—almost all of which came from northeastern Minnesota—America would be brought to its knees. Thinking it through (after I became educated as to geography and politics) I realized it'd be far easier to bomb the Sault St. Marie locks—where Lake Superior flows into the lower Great Lakes—to block shipments of Minnesota iron ore to eastern steel mills. But that wasn't what we were told. We were told "They're coming for Duluth."

Newsreel footage of Hiroshima and Nagasaki and atomic testing on the Bikini Atoll played during the evening news, convincing us we were destined for vaporization. Such fears compelled America to send young men to Vietnam to stop the Commies from taking over yet another country.

"These barrels," our principal—Mr. Hollingsworth—would say as we toured the Piedmont Elementary School basement, "will save lives." Mr. Hollingsworth made his proclamations in the hallway leading to Piedmont's rudimentary auditorium (used for the occasional choir or musical performance or stage play or for the annual Halloween carnival) the dank, dreary corridor crammed with drums filled with fresh water and round cardboard cartons labeled "Biscuits." I don't remember our principal opening a carton, removing supposed life-giving nourishment, and allowing us a taste. But we were told that what was in those barrels and cartons would sustain us <u>when</u>—not <u>if</u>—the Soviet Union dropped the Big One. They drop an atomic bomb on Duluth to wipe out the ore docks, or at the airport where the Air Force had a full contingent of interceptors, or out at French River where there was a Nike missile base, and we survive to eat moldy crackers and drink stale water? I didn't buy it then and I don't buy it now.

We periodically crouched beneath desks in our classrooms, heads between our knees, hands behind our heads in the "duck and cover" position in anticipation of the blast that would send us to Jesus. Really? Cowering under desks like sitting ducks was going to save us? It was stupid, frightening, and asinine. But we did as we were told, ever hopeful the Russians would drop the Bomb on someplace more deserving—like Minneapolis.

It was no better, no less scary, at home. My parents received a brochure detailing the construction of a personal fallout shelter. Dad kept that pamphlet on an end table in the living room where I read it multiple times.

"We gonna build one of these, Dad?"

"Too expensive," Dad replied.

Uncle Willard—if he believed he needed such a thing— would have built his own bunker stocked with a generator, food, water, medical supplies, ham radio, clothing, and whatever else needed to survive nuclear annihilation. But my uncle never fell for the ruse. Consider: If the Russkies were actually gunning for Duluth, do you think a homemade shelter would make a difference? I'm no genius, and at six or seven I had a very limited understanding of Soviet nuclear capabilities. But even at that tender age, I was pretty sure a hole in our backyard (with Mom and Dad and Dave and I crammed inside) would end up being our final resting place—not our salvation—if the Reds attacked.

During the Cuban Missile Crisis, Dad—who was the Chairman of the Democratic Party of St. Louis County—invited me to tag along for breakfast with Senator Hubert Humphrey. I'm not sure of the year or the exact nature of where the U.S. and the U.S.S.R. stood with respect to their standoff but I know that during breakfast, Senator Humphrey left to take a phone call.

"I need to get to the airport," the senator said when he came back. "There's something brewing with the Soviets."

"Alright, Senator. Mark, drink your milk and we'll head out."

We drove Senator Humphrey to the airport where he caught a North Central flight to the Cities, and from there, flew on to D.C. On the ride home, Dad filled me in regarding how important a man Hubert Humphrey was, how vital his input would be to President Kennedy. Despite the explanation, I was disappointed: The call disrupted a rare treat for me—eating breakfast with Dad.

All of the fear mongering and anxiety and practicing for the End Times had a deep and lasting impact on American children. Then too, around the time we were being instructed to duck and cover, American kids were told God was no longer welcome in school.

Before the Supreme Court issued its edict, "No more school-led prayer" there were two reminders of God every school day. First, we said the Pledge of Allegiance before morning announcements were read by Mr. Hollingsworth over the P.A. The Pledge affirms that America's "one nation under God." And before eating lunch in the gymnasium, we'd sit at tables with hands folded while an adult led us in grace, which, if I remember right, was very Christian in sentiment. We had, despite the fear of being instantly turned into dust by the Russians, the power of faith to steady our nerves. Until we didn't.

After the "no prayer in school" edict was issued by the Supreme Court, Christ Lutheran Church started a weekly Bible study. The class was held every Wednesday morning and Mom made sure I attended those sessions—despite the fact it was held in a Lutheran church—because the Big One was imminent and my soul needed preparation.

As tensions with the Soviet Union lessened, one might think the trepidation instilled by the "duck and cover" routine dissipated. That's mostly true, though an undercurrent of unsettling fear lingered.

The sun was high and glorious. Miller Creek bubbled towards the Bay. I was fishing for brook trout when all I'd learned in elementary school about nuclear holocaust overcame me. Standing in cool water, enjoying what can only be described as a bucolic outing—fishing an urban trout stream just a stone's throw

103

from our new house—I heard an explosion. The sound was ominous and untoward and caused me to look heavenward. As I stood there gawking, I was convinced I saw a mushroom cloud; evidence that the Soviet Union had finally done the unspeakable. Stark, unnatural dread gripped me, caused me to pull in my line, and run for home.

Of course, there'd been no attack. It was only an illusion—a naturally occurring sleight of hand—that led me to the darkest corner of my bedroom to duck and cover.

SPEED DEMONS

"Wanna build a go-cart?" Eddie asked, sipping on a glass of cherry Kool-Aid.

"Sure," I answered. "Got any wheels?"

We sat on a weathered redwood bench of a picnic table, gazing intently across the green grass of Eddie's backyard. A mechanical push mower leaned against the baby blue siding of the house. Ed Salveson, Eddie's dad, didn't believe in gasoline-powered mowers; retrograde thinking that forced his eldest son to push an artifact from the Great Depression across the Salveson lawn once a week. As we talked, the smell of freshly cut grass wafted on a warm summer breeze.

"You bet," Eddie said. "My dad's got an old garden cart in the garage with two good wheels an' we can take two more off my sister's doll buggy."

I didn't bother to ask whether Ed would object to us dismantling his garden cart. And it wouldn't make any sense to ask whether Diane cared we were about to destroy her buggy. After all, she was a year younger, a brat, and a girl. As we talked, a bumblebee avoided my attempts to swat it as it circled my glass. I didn't want to make the mistake Eddie's little brother Ronny had made by drinking a glass of Kool-Aid with a bee in it. Ronny's tongue had swelled up after being stung; the kid talked like Daffy Duck for a week. No way was I gonna swallow a bee.

Chambersburg Avenue was blacktopped and very steep. Most of the houses in our neighborhood had at least two or three kids. A few childless couples made the mistake of buying homes in Piedmont with an unreasonable expectation of quietude. Those folks tended towards crankiness when kids ran through their lawns or darted into their flower beds to retrieve rogue balls.

"These are some pretty nice wheels, eh Mark?" Eddie said as he pried the cap off one end of an axle holding the wheels on Ed's garden cart.

"Yep. Should really go if we put them on the back," I replied as I nailed 2x4s together to form the vehicle's chassis.

Eddie let a wheel drop onto the garage floor and pulled the axle free. We'd learned the craft of cart building from older boys; boys who no longer built pretend cars but drove real Fords and

Chevrolets and Dodges; boys who listened to Gary Puckett and the Beach Boys and Donovan and the Ventures, went out on dates, and ignored us; boys who'd very shortly go off to college or find jobs or get drafted into the Army or the Marine Corps and end up fighting in Vietnam.

The carts we learned to build were not sleek, sophisticated vehicles. Of the myriad go-carts built on our block, only one was built to compete in the local Soapbox Derby. Despite our jealousy at Ronny Granley's expertly constructed go-cart—a vehicle Ronny's dad spent inordinate amounts of time perfecting—the thing was a bust. Ronny's cart was a heavy, foolish thing that didn't do well in the Derby race at Hartley Field, which pretty much ended any other boys setting their sights so high.

Our go-carts used 16-penny spikes placed through the wheels as axles. The frames were constructed in the shape of a triangle with the narrow end facing downhill. Using a hand drill (no father in his right mind allowed his son to use power tools) we'd drill a hole through the side pieces and the front cross member. A single bolt, secured with a nut and washers, served as the pivot point for steering. Shorter 2x4s covered with a piece of plywood or hardboard formed the seat.

Eddie grunted as he pulled the wheels off his sister's doll stroller.

"Ouch, that hurts!" I yelped.

I'd hit my thumb with a hammer. A blood blister formed. Pain throbbed. Eddie smiled.

"Ssshhh. Diane'll hear us and go runnin' to my mom."

"Easy for you to say. You didn't just smack your thumb."

Eddie passed a bolt through wood. By nailing rope to the ends of the crosspiece, the cart could be steered. To turn left, you pulled the rope left. To turn right, you pulled the rope right.

The advantage to using the wheels and axle from Ed's garden cart was that we hoped to avoid the most common mechanical defect in go-cart design; nail-axle failure. Using spikes as axles allowed two or three trips down the hill before the nails bent and needed replacing. Because we only had one axle from Ed's garden cart, I hammered two 16-penny spikes through the centers of the stroller wheels and into the front cross member.

"It's sure low to the ground," Eddie observed, sitting in the driver's seat, tugging on the rope to turn the front wheels. "Let's try 'er out!"

It was just before nightfall. Fresh tar and rocks loomed beneath the chassis as we pushed the cart up the hill. The city had just resurfaced Chambersburg with a mixture of tar and gravel, leaving the once smooth roadway bumpy and brutal. Fresh scabs on my knees bore witness to that painful truth.

"You go first," I told Eddie. "They're your wheels."

My buddy grinned, his dimpled cheeks and fair skin framed by clean, blond bangs that evoked jealousy because he was a dead ringer for David McCallum, one of the stars of *The Man from U.N.C.L.E.* "Actually, they're my dad's and my sister's wheels," he quipped.

Eddie braced his tenners against wood. I positioned myself behind the cart.

"Ready?" I asked.

"Yep. Let her go!"

I pushed the rickety contraption until gravity took over. The cart bounced over tar and rocks as it raced down the hill. Neighborhood kids stopped playing to watch Eddie's ride. Panting and wheezing, I caught up to my pal as the go-cart coasted to a stop in front of Bjorlins' house.

"You gotta try it, Mark. It's super-fast!"

Dad met us as we pulled the cart back up the hill. I expected a lecture about zooming down the middle of a busy thoroughfare. Dad's crewcut—his black hair shiny from tonic—caught the last rays of daylight as he surprised me with a request: "Mind if I try 'er?"

"You bet Mr. Munger," Eddie replied.

"You sure you want to do this, Dad?" I asked. My old man was fun-loving in an adult sort of way but didn't usually join kids at play.

"Looks safe enough," Dad said, cramming himself into the cart. His thick fingers grabbed the rope. The frame creaked under his weight.

"Give me a push."

Eddie and I took up positions behind the cart and started running. At Jentofts' driveway, we stopped to watch the go-cart plunge over the crest of the hill.

"Where're the brakes?" Dad yelled.

"There aren't any. You use your shoes to stop!" I yelled back.

I couldn't see Dad's face as the go-cart plummeted down Chambersburg Avenue. I can only imagine what his thoughts were as he considered the fresh tar and jagged rocks passing beneath his stockinged feet.

LITTLE LEAGUE

Baseball was the only organized sport other than ice hockey available for boys. That's not quite accurate. Some elementary schools sponsored basketball. And pony league football was also an option, though I didn't know anyone who played. There were no organized sports for girls. Even when I entered Denfeld High School in 1970, athletic options for young women were limited. It wasn't until Title IX that girls received their athletic due. My lack of skating prowess meant hockey was out. I was too small and timid for organized football. Since basketball didn't start until sixth grade, my only opportunity to play a team sport was through Little League.

Dad and I spent a few evenings playing catch. Harry didn't play baseball growing up in Fergus Falls but after graduating from Denfeld he joined pals to play fastpitch softball on bar-sponsored teams. He was still playing softball with his buddy George Stoyanoff at the Buffalo House when I entered high school, meaning there was history of a Munger successfully throwing a ball and swinging a bat. Whether it was my timidity or lack of coordination or poor eyesight, Dad gave up trying to make me into a ballplayer. He did, however, let me sign up for Little League. Which is how Eddie and I became the youngest members of the Yanks. Minor leaguers, we wore team T-shirts and matching ball caps for games but weren't provided baseball pants or fancy jerseys or stockings. Such finery was reserved for boys who made the majors.

Eddie and I biked to the ballfield behind Christ Lutheran's new brick church building. The ballfield, also new, featured concrete block dugouts, chain link fencing, and a scoreboard. We thought we were pretty cool in our game T-shirts and ball caps despite being affiliated with the Minnesota Twins' perpetual nemesis—the New York Yankees. We figured our coach, a DJ on a local Christian radio station and a youth pastor, would give us a fair shake.

Coach Jason never put us in a game. Not an at bat. Not an inning in the field. I was downhearted after attending every single practice and never playing. Eddie was in the same boat. In high school, we encountered Jason again at Westminster Presbyterian. He was the church's youth pastor and had organized a basketball league for high schoolers. Playing pick-up ball against Jason at

Westminster, I learned the true mettle of the man. Jason, despite his claimed piety, was a cheater who bent the rules to suit his purposes; a failed athlete trying to prove himself. The fact he never let his two youngest players play in a game was based on an insatiable need to be a winner, which, in my book, he never was.

Dad coached older boys from the neighborhood in Babe Ruth, the age group above Little League. I hung around practices and games as the team's bat boy. When Dad piled his ballplayers into the Munger family's white Dodge Dart station wagon, drove to the A&W in Hermantown, opened his wallet, and treated the team to root beer floats and soft serve cones and sundaes and shakes, I was in the back of the car squished between players.

The summer between fourth and fifth grades, Dad agreed to coach my Little League team. That season, he also did a stint as the president of the Skyline Little League. I'm pretty sure he assumed the office because no one else wanted it. I begged Dad to let me pitch in a game even though my skills were suspect. I could catch a routine fly and hit a single every once in a blue moon but my arm was as weak as a wet noodle. Why I thought I could pitch, I have no idea. Dad said, "OK," likely his way of letting me try something new in a safe setting. Or perhaps, since Dad knew my ability, he figured he'd hand me the ball, watch disaster unfold, and never have to listen to such a stupid request again.

Mark Carlson is two years older than me. He later became the golf pro at Nemadji Golf Course in Superior. During the game in question—the game where Dad let me pitch—Mark was my catcher. His take on my performance is succinct:

"You set the Skyline Little League record for most walks issued in a game!"

That's my pitching legacy and though I'm not proud of my single-game ERA, I'm glad I gave it a try.

In sixth grade, I was finally fitted with eyeglasses. The summer between sixth and seventh grades, I had the notion to try out for the majors. Eddie had tried out the year before and ended up becoming an all-star. My parents were too busy to drive me to tryouts so I stuck it out in the minors where Bruce Rudd and I were the only twelve-year-olds on our team. Coach put me at second base. I batted near the top of the order, even hitting a pair of doubles in a game played on an old cow pasture known as Stebner Field in neighboring Hermantown. During another game, I filled in for Karl Erickson at catcher and pegged out a kid stealing second. Though I missed one contest because I was sunburned from swimming at the Listons' cabin on Rose Lake, my final season in Little League was a success. My teammates liked me. My coach had faith in me. And though I wasn't a star, my presence in the universe seemed to mean something.

THE OSBOURNES

We heard the rumors months before they moved in.

"There's a new family—the dad's a lawyer like yours—building a house on Hutchinson," Ricky Plys said.

"I hear there's five boys," Phil Rolle added.

I don't remember where we were when this conversation took place. Maybe it was in the gravel parking lot of St. Lawrence during a lull in a softball game. The school parking lot was about as good as it got in our neighborhood in terms of a place to play ball given we lived at the top of a hill where everything pitched towards the St. Louis River. In any event, we were talking, a group of pre-teen boys, salivating at the prospect of five more bodies to make up sides.

This was before I got glasses. I have no idea if my vision was already shot or not. As I've said, I wasn't much of an athlete growing up. That equation improved in sixth grade, when I started wearing glasses. As soon as I got home from the eye doctor, I ran up the hill to Eddie's house. The first person other than Mom to see me wearing those ugly, thick-lensed, heavy-framed eyeglasses wasn't Eddie but his mom, Liz, who remarked "how smart" they made me look as I waited for Eddie at the back door.

What a world opened up to me once I could see! To be fair, I don't know that I would have been any better at hitting a baseball or catching a football or smacking a tennis ball in boot hockey if I'd have been fitted for glasses earlier. I'd like to think it would have made a difference. But I have no proof that it would have. When picking sides for our neighborhood games, Eddie was usually picked second to last and I was nearly always the last boy standing—unless Duane Linski was playing (which was rare). It hurt deeply, being considered the worst. That would change after I got glasses, grew some, developed muscle, and gained coordination. I'd never be the first guy picked but by the time I was playing competitive slow pitch softball and touch football and broomball as an adult, I was no longer mired at the bottom of the athletic heap. That was in the future. At the time the Osbourne boys were bandied about as the saviors of the neighborhood, I was the worst athlete of the lot in the eyes of my peers.

Doug Osbourne was a criminal defense lawyer who hunted and fished with Dad. From Dad I learned the Osbournes were building a new house because the family needed more room. There were no houses next to the lot where the Osbourne rambler went up. Behind the Osbourne place, the Woods spread out for miles. That second-growth forest, now home to the Piedmont Ski Trail—loved and used by mountain bikers, hikers, and cross-country skiers—was bounded by Hutchinson Road, Skyline Parkway, and Morris Thomas Road. As you've already learned, the Woods was the source of endless childhood adventure and the low-lying land abutting the Osbourne place held some of the best pollywog-hunting water around. I remember bringing back a gallon jug from that swamp—the container filled with swarming tadpoles—and dumping the would-be frogs into our basement utility sink. My intention was for the tadpoles to transform into their adult selves in the safety of our house. Mom put an end to such nonsense by pulling the plug and draining the mess into the sewer. It was a major disappointment, losing all those frogs-in-the-making, especially since I'd paid Mike Urie fifty cents for the amphibian treasure Mom flushed away.

The Osbourne home was completed. The family moved in. Given Mr. Osbourne was a lawyer and Mrs. Osbourne was a nurse, we had high expectations of what sort of kids were coming to Piedmont Heights.

"I'm Mark, this is Dave," I said, pointing to Eddie.

"I'm Carson," the eldest Osbourne kid said.

We chit-chatted in the Osbournes' basement for a bit. Our "welcome to the neighborhood" mission completed, Eddie slid open a patio door and we left. The Osbourne house was an anomaly, the first on the block with a walk-out basement. Every other home, whether built by Huseby or someone else, was a traditional rambler. The basements of the other houses in the neighborhood didn't have direct access to the outside. But the Osbourne house had bedrooms in the basement that required egress. There we were, two fourth-graders looking over the Osbourne backyard when Carson opened the sliding glass door, took aim, and promptly shot me in the ass. Not, mind you with a BB from a Daisy BB gun—where you pump air into the chamber and launch a little copper ball out of the barrel—but with a pellet propelled by compressed gas.

"Ouch!" I screamed, crumpling to the ground.

"What happened?" Eddie asked, whipping his head around to determine what had laid me low.

"Just wanted to see what this thing could do," Carson said through a wide grin as he closed the door, leaving me with tears, pain, and a bruise that eventually rose like Mount McKinley on my tender young ass.

Still, though Carson Osbourne was clearly a bully, it was his younger brother Patrick who caused me the most grief.

I don't know where it came from. Maybe their dad had a temper and took it out on his brood—though I never witnessed Doug Osbourne hit his kids. Maybe Doug was mad at the world and that anger infected his children. Maybe, with Doug working full time as a trial lawyer and Mrs. Osbourne working as a nurse, the Osbourne kids raised themselves and the pecking order (as to the boys) was that Carson punished Patrick, and Patrick punished Evan, and Evan punished Lonnie, and Lonnie punished Buddy, the youngest boy. Growing up with the Osbournes, having daily contact with them from fourth through eighth grade (when my family moved across Piedmont Avenue to our new house on Miller Creek), I never saw bullying or viciousness or unkindness from the younger boys; only from Carson and Patrick. I really don't have a good explanation for where things went wrong. I just know that for five years I endured the teasing and taunting and physical abuse Patrick Osbourne thought I deserved.

It's also possible the rage Patrick expressed had something to do with race. Piedmont was largely devoid of minorities. Only a few families in Piedmont had Hispanic or Native American roots. None, to my knowledge, came from African American ancestry. We didn't ask our few darker-skinned friends what was up, what their family stories were. Discussions about race were limited to exploring European ancestries, not delving into exotic bloodlines. A kid was an oddity in our neighborhood if he or she wasn't Scandinavian. When we talked ethnicity, we zeroed in on unusual *European* backgrounds. In my case, that was the Slovenian blood on Mom's side. In the case of other kids, it was their Italian or Polish or Irish heritage. I can't recall being regaled by a kid discussing his or her non-European roots except once and that very short conversation.

114

"You guys are Indian (meaning Native American), right?" someone once asked Carson Osbourne.

"No. We're Syrian."

That was it. The question had been asked and answered so we moved on.

I'd eventually graduate from Denfeld High School in a class of over four hundred and thirty young men and women. Less than a handful of the Class of '73 had African American roots. A couple had Asian ancestry. A few claimed Native American heritage, including my pal, Pete Senerighi, who later asked me to be godfather to his son, Pete, Jr. Then there was Tina, a lovely, brown-eyed, black-haired girl who I thought had a Hispanic mother, one of the many reasons I fell hard for her in junior high. Turns out, Tina's mom was a dark complected Croatian. Exotic for Piedmont for sure, though not as ethnically intriguing as if she'd been from Puerto Rico.

That was about it in terms of diversity. Maybe the older Osbourne boys fought the anxiety of being immersed in the lily-white culture of Piedmont Heights because they were Ojibwe (which, we later found out, they were). Carson and Patrick might have resorted to bullying little white dweebs in response to racism. I'm not sure about that but it's about the only explanation I have for the anger and unkindness Patrick Osbourne displayed towards me.

I don't remember every instance Patrick went off on me. But if I looked sideways at him or said something he took offense at he was on top of me—egged on by Carson—punching me in the face. I tried to fight back but was no match for my antagonist. I was an easy target for someone who'd learned pugilism first-hand. After these "lessons," I'd leave whatever game or sport or activity we were engaged in, run home crying, enter my bedroom, close the door, hunker down, and ponder why the kid was such a jerk. Patrick never picked on Eddie even though Eddie wasn't much of a fighter. Maybe Patrick knew my best friend would eventually tower over us. Or maybe it was that, when I turned twelve and got those eyeglasses, I was a more enticing target. I'll never knew the "why." I just remember the "what."

In junior high a new brand of toothpaste—Vote—was introduced to the world. One of the Osbournes (Carson, I think,

115

through his paper route with the *Duluth News Tribune*) was charged with hanging bags containing sample-size tubes of Vote on mailboxes. The majority of the bags containing Vote were placed as instructed, but for those families who didn't get along with the Osbourne boys, well, let's just say that the messages written in toothpaste on their homes and garages and cars included words one doesn't utter in polite company. There was even a rumor— one I can't personally vouch for—that the gas tank of Mr. Stocke's car ended up with a squirt or two of Vote in it. I don't know what that did to Mr. Stocke's engine if the story's true but I'm pretty sure toothpaste doesn't improve fuel economy!

The fall of seventh grade, a memorable episode of Osbourne-inspired shenanigans took place. Paul Ebert, Carson and Patrick Osbourne, Eddie, Ricky Plys, and I decided to pilfer tomatoes and apples from Peterson's garden at the bottom of Hoover Street. Our sweatshirts loaded with would-be projectiles, we set up camp at the intersection of Morris Thomas Road and Piedmont Avenue. After dark, tomatoes and apples began raining down on traffic from our makeshift bunkers.

I'll stop here to explain something about the participants in this mischief. Only the two older Osbourne boys were true delinquents. Eddie was a good kid. So was Ricky Plys. And Paul Ebert was a studious, serious boy. He was also a mentor, in terms of intellect, and in Boy Scouts—where he was my patrol leader. Paul would become an Eagle Scout and, following Paul's example, I too earned Scouting's highest rank. You have to ask yourself: Why would good kids engage in such nonsense? I can't explain it other than to suggest that teenaged boys, when drawn collectively to a bad idea, don't consider the consequences.

Towards the end of the night, a Volkswagen beetle came chugging up Piedmont. On Carson's signal, we unloaded. We hit that bug so many times I thought it was going to tip over. Little did we know we'd pummeled a car full of UMD football players. The Volkswagen pulled around the block and parked. Moments later Ebert's high pitched, "They're on to us, run for it!" tipped us off that we'd been had. In a split second, I was sprinting up Harvey Street, flying past Patrick Osbourne as if his shoes were filled with cement—a feat I couldn't duplicate without fear as fuel. I turned onto Chambersburg and slowed to a walk. "That was close," I muttered. Somewhere during the chaos, I'd lost Eddie. I had no idea whether he'd been grabbed up by the college boys or made it home. Given my own close call, I wasn't about to start looking for him.

Later that evening, I was sitting in the den watching TV with Dad. Mom was off dealing with my brother and sister. The doorbell rang and Dad answered the door.

"Mark, get out here!"

I entered the foyer, the front door open to October's bracing touch, to find four huge guys wearing UMD letter jackets standing on our front porch. The biggest guy was holding Paul Ebert by the scruff of his neck so that Paul's shoes barely touched concrete.

The next day, most of us (Eddie was absent) got up early, buckets of sudsy water and washrags and towels in hand, and met at the corner. We walked to the Volkswagen owner's house and spent the better part of Saturday morning erasing the evidence of our crime. Eddie? Ebert had ratted out the rest of us but hadn't fingered Eddie. After that escapade, my buddy developed an uncanny ability to steer clear of notorious behavior. I, however, wanted to be liked, wanted to fit in, wanted like hell not to feel the brunt of Patrick Osbourne's fists. I continued to hang out with the new kids on the block in hopes my acquiescence would end my suffering. Sadly, my "go along to get along" approach didn't work.

SKATING

I was one of a handful of boys in Piedmont Heights—a hotbed of hockey that produced the Stauber brothers (all six played college hockey)—who didn't know how to skate. How I ended up so inept at something nearly every boy in Piedmont Heights mastered isn't a mystery. It was Mom's fault. How's that, you ask? How could a boy's inability to skate be blamed on his loving, doting, attentive mother? Well, it's pretty simple. You buy a boy black figure skates—you know, the kind male Olympic skaters use to do triple axels—when every other boy in the neighborhood is wearing hockey skates, and failure on ice is pretty much assured.

My godmother, Pauline Liston, a woman who ended up living with Dad at the end of his life (that's a whole 'nother story, as they say) had a son, Jimber; a big, raw-boned, athletically talented kid a year younger than me. When I was six and Jimber was five, our mothers decided to teach us how to skate. That's when this whole mistake, Mom's insistence on buying me figure skates, came to fruition. We were in Morgan Park, where Jim and Pauline Liston and their three kids lived, skating on a pleasure rink when my failed legacy on ice began.

I always thought that my ineptitude was due to weak ankles. That might be partially true. But in hindsight, having finally mastered the fundamentals of ice skating well enough to play games of pick-up hockey later in life, I'm pretty sure my failure on the Morgan Park rink wasn't completely due to my unathletic nature or lack of ankle strength. In some part, my dismal showing was attributable to those damned figure skates.

It isn't easy to balance on figure skates. The blades are narrow and rounded; not at all like the blades of hockey skates. Then there are the toe picks for stopping. Learning to use those cursed picks proved to be a skill impossible to master. As Jimber waddled across the ice on his wide-bladed, manly hockey skates learning balance and the ability to push off, I fell on my face. I never made it more than two or three hesitant steps before crashing onto the hard, cold, cruel surface of the rink.

Mom and Pauline skated brilliantly. Their ability to turn, stop, and skate backwards on their white figure skates, the only skates women and girls wore back in the day, made things look easy. It wasn't. Consequently, that was the only time I ever wore those awful skates. From then on, the figure skates sat in a cardboard box on a shelf in the garage—unused and unwanted.

A pair of borrowed men's hockey skates ended up hanging from a nail in our garage. The few times Eddie and I walked to the rink behind Piedmont Elementary to skate, I wore those hand-me-downs. Despite avoiding the embarrassment of wearing black figure skates, which would have resulted in being called untoward names impugning my masculinity (things were different in terms of orientation sensitivity back then), the hockey skates didn't help. Try as I might, I couldn't do much more than stagger across the rink like a drunken sailor on leave. I had no ability to make the graceful, swirling, turns Rod Peltoma and Bruce Brooks and Bruce Patterson and Scott Carlson and the other boys who were hockey players made effortlessly. Hands down, I was one of the worst skaters in the history of Piedmont Heights.

"There'll be a race tomorrow at the hockey rink," Miss Johnson, my fifth-grade teacher announced in class. "Both boys and girls."

It was pretty much a given that Brooks would win the boys' race. Peltoma and Patterson and Carlson and Beardsley were all fast, but they couldn't catch Brooks unless he fell. Which we knew he wouldn't. And it was equally certain that Annie Stortz would beat any girl who challenged her. But here's the weird part of this tale: Despite being barely able to stumble from one side of the rink to the other, I decided, right then and there, to enter the big race.

Brooks lapped me twice in a four-lap race. I didn't just come in dead last: I crossed the finish line a week late. The old joke, that I should've been timed by a sundial, is fitting. Still, that race taught me a valuable life lesson. There are things a person is good at naturally. There are things a person can practice and become proficient at. And then there are things that, no matter how hard a person tries, one should abstain from. Pratfalling my way around the Piedmont hockey rink to the bemusement of my classmates convinced me of these truths. That said, I'd like to think things would've been different if Mom had bought me hockey skates. You want proof?

119

Jimber Liston played four years of varsity hockey at Harvard.

SWORDS

Despite my affinity for Robin Hood, The Three Musketeers, and pirates, I never touched the swords hanging over our fireplace until Bruce Patterson came over.

"What are those?" Patterson asked.

"Fencing swords," I replied, not knowing the proper term of art is "foils."

"Cool."

Bruce was a kid Mom dreaded. He wasn't a bad kid: He was just energetic. More so than me, a kid—now a grown man—who doesn't let grass grow under his feet. I was and am anything but sedentary. Bruce? He was hyperkinetic times two. The day he came over, we played army men and diddled with my chemistry set—the one Evan Osbourne and I were using when I accidentally lit Mom's favorite chair on fire. We steered clear of trouble until Patterson spied the foils.

"Can we take 'em down?"

"We're not supposed to."

"Who's gonna know?"

Bruce's point was valid. Mom was off doing mom things. Dad was at work. It was summer vacation and we were unsupervised.

"I guess."

We parried and thrusted and slashed and ran each other through. I never, not a once while we were dueling, regretted my disobedience.

"Aw crap."

"What?"

"Look at the blades."

Up until that moment, I believed Patterson and I were getting away with our crime but as I stared at the foil in my hand, I knew there was trouble ahead.

"They're scratched," Bruce said.

"Yup."

"Your mom's gonna know."

"Yup."

"Do you know where she keeps the paint?"

I shook my head.

The swords were returned to their place of prominence. Mom eventually noticed the damage, confronted me, and pulled a confession from my trembling lips. I was grounded, the foils were repainted, and I forgot about them.

"Let's play a trick on Anne," I said to Dave when I was in my teens. Dave was ten or so and Anne was maybe five or six. We'd moved to the new house on Miller Creek and the fencing foils made the move as well.

"Like what?"

I wanted to pull one over on our baby sister. I wanted a gag that would have an immediate impact and screw her up for a good long while. "Let me think."

As I cooked a Totino's frozen pizza for the three of us, I thought and thought: *What to do? What to do?*

Anne trundled off to her bedroom after eating her slice of pizza. The kids' bedrooms were in the basement. The lower level also had a full bath and a fireplaced recreation room where late-night poker games with friends would be the norm once I entered Denfeld High School.

My brother and I sat at the kitchen table munching pizza and drinking milk. I'm not sure what Dave was thinking. I know I was hard at it in terms of figuring out a stunt to pull. Then it dawned on me. I went to a drawer, found a plastic bag, walked to the fridge, opened the door, removed a bottle of Heinz, unscrewed the cap, squeezed catsup into the baggie, held the pouch of red goo up for Dave to see, and smiled. "The swords."

"I'll get you, you little bastard," I screamed, using language Anne had not yet learned, shouting in a tone of voice sure to bring her running. Dave stood across the living room with a foil in his right hand. I was a few feet away, my sword at the ready. "That's the last time you mess around in my room without permission, you little jerk!" I yelled.

Anne scampered into view.

"Take that," I said, thrusting the foil at Dave.

Dave parried my blow and swung his blade at my head. "You're not long for this world," I said, winking at Dave. I forced Dave into the kitchen before burying the foil's tip in his chest.

Dave cried out, clutched his side, fell to his knees, dropped his sword, and collapsed.

"You stabbed David!" Anne screamed in horror when she saw the "blood" on his sweatshirt. "Why did you do that?"

I raised my blade in salute. "He had it coming. He was snooping around in my room."

Dave moaned, groaned, and thrashed about on the linoleum floor.

"Is he dying?" Anne asked.

"If he is, it'll serve him right."

Dave started giggling.

"Well done, little brother. Well done."

Dave sat up, reached under his shirt, and pulled out the punctured baggie.

Anne has never forgiven us. She's the kind of gal who, even fifty years later, holds a grudge.

SPECIAL CLASS

I was ostracized. The girls in "special class" weren't unkind. It was the boys in Miss Hollingworth's class—a laboratory for the gifted—who gave me the cold shoulder. I was at a complete loss as to what I'd done to incur their disdain.

"It's your cousin," whispered Jeff Tynjala, a blond-headed Finn who wore the same nerdy black rimmed specs I did, as we worked on a writing assignment.

"Huh?"

"You have a cousin named Willard, right?"

The question caught me off guard. "An uncle. State Representative. Owns a motel by the zoo."

"Ya, I know. But he's got a son named 'Willard' too, right?"

"Oh, you mean 'Butch.' That's how I know him. But his real name is Willard Junior."

"Rikala's got it in for you because of him."

"Why?"

Jeff glanced towards the front of the room, noted that Miss Hollingsworth was busy, and continued. "Your cousin hired Rikala's brother, John—he plays cornet in the Denfeld band—to play music on a float carrying your uncle in a parade."

"What's that got to do with me?"

"Your cousin never paid Wayne's brother."

"Oh."

Later that morning (our special class only met in the morning; in the afternoon, Jan Erickson and I returned to Piedmont Elementary for math, gym, science, art, and music), I approached Wayne, apologized for my cousin's behavior, and made a new friend.

Miss Hollingsworth was a taskmaster, which is to say she sought perfection. Her assignments included three massive reports. Our first writing project was to profile a foreign country. I chose Costa Rica because I was intrigued that it had no standing army. Unlike the other kids—who typed their own reports—I had the luxury of having Dad's legal secretary type up my narrative though I was charged with the researching, writing, editing, and collating my work.

Completing a report wasn't the end of the assignment. We were also required to give a fifteen-minute talk about our chosen subject. And while Miss Hollingsworth graded our written submissions, it was our peers—the other Brainiacs in the class—who scored our oral presentations. I did OK: I never got the highest score for my talks, but I also never got chastised like Kathy S. did (there was also a Kathy M., a strikingly pretty, blue-eyed, blonde Finnish girl, in the class). With her mom in the audience, Kathy S., a goody-two-shoes who liked to hear her own voice, went overboard. Instead of a fifteen-minute talk, we endured a half-hour of Kathy S. blathering on and on and on about Mexico.

Our second writing project was a biography. I profiled not one but three ancient heroes; Alexander the Great, Hannibal, and Xenophon.

The final report was student's choice. Given my love of space, I wrote a history of NASA, ending with a preview of the impending Apollo project. I called it "A Smattering of Space Exploration." My report was exactly what Miss Hollingsworth was looking for, though again, my oral presentation received only middling approval from fellow students. Still, I learned more about researching and writing and editing in that sixth-grade class than I did in high school or college. Miss Hollingsworth could be a stern, no-nonsense taskmaster but man, could she teach!

Dean Cox was our class treasurer. He collected a dime a week from each student as dues—money dedicated towards an end-of-the-year party. Somewhere along the way, Dean's bookkeeping went awry.

"I don't know what happened, Miss Hollingsworth," Dean lamented, looking into the bottom of the coffee can that served as the class vault. "There was ten dollars and forty cents in here yesterday. Now, it's all gone."

Miss Hollingsworth scrunched her face. "Are you sure?" Dean nodded.

"Seems like someone in this class is a thief," Miss Hollingsworth said aloud, scrutinizing the boys; making it clear she had no inclination a girl could have itchy fingers. "If that person doesn't come clean by the end of the week, there'll be no end-of-the-year party."

Tynjala and I had taken the money but never intended to keep it. We'd lifted the cash to drive Dean nuts. Our plan

125

worked. Dean was so distraught over being labeled an embezzler, he went around, his head down, and his spirit bruised for the better part of a week.

"We'd better put the money back," I finally said to Jeff. "You still have it?"

He nodded. "I'll slip it back in the can when I have a chance."

The money reappeared, Dean was off the hook, and Miss Hollingsworth ended her investigation.

We'd walk to the West End branch of the Duluth Public Library or ride a big yellow school bus to the old Carnegie library downtown to borrow books. We also made field trips to the Aerial Lift Bridge (where we got to ride in the bridge's control room as the span rose to accommodate a ship), the Duluth police station, and Duluth's new fire department headquarters. During our visit to the firehall, a second scandal erupted.

There were two Kennys in special class: Kenny Hubert and Kenny from Bryant Elementary. This story involves Kenny from Bryant.

Touring the new firehall, we climbed in and out of firetrucks, studied turnout gear, and slid down the firepole from the crew's living quarters into the truck bay. We only learned there was a problem when the fire chief stopped our school bus in the parking lot as we were leaving.

"Miss Hollingsworth, a word," the chief said after climbing onto the bus.

Our teacher left her seat to confer with the chief. "That's completely unacceptable!" she exclaimed.

A tall, intimidating woman, Miss Hollingsworth put her hands on her hips, screwed up her face, and scrutinized her petrified charges. "This bus is not moving until you hand it over!" Only one fool in special class knew what the hell Miss Hollingsworth was talking about. "I'll say it again: We're not leaving, and, in fact, if the person who took it doesn't come forward right now, the chief's going to call the police and every last one of you will be searched."

Kenny from Bryant stood up—his head hung in shame—approached Miss Hollingsworth, opened his hand, and gave our teacher the jackknife he'd stolen from the firehall.

Later that week a message appeared, scrawled in black marker across the mirror hanging above the sink at the rear of our classroom:

There's a pig in this room and her name is Miss Hollingsworth.
K.B.

Though Miss Hollingsworth was outraged, she was unconvinced Kenny from Bryant was the culprit. "If the person who did this doesn't confess, the Christmas skating party will be canceled!"

The message was wiped away and Miss Hollingsworth must have decided it wasn't worth denying the entire class its fun because of one idiot. The party went on as planned even though the offender never confessed.

Years later, Jeff Tynjala disclosed he'd scribbled the graffiti on the mirror in hopes of framing Kenny.

"He should've been kicked out of class for that shit," was Jeff's take on the Great Jackknife Heist.

Despite Jeff's misguided attempt at justice, Kenny from Bryant remained in special class and that was that.

SIBLINGS

My parents didn't procreate after me. The exact reasons are a bit murky though I remember racing to the hospital with Mom—blood gushing down her leg—my father driving like a madman. Dad snuck me into Mom's hospital room despite the scrutiny of the stern Benedictine nuns who worked at St. Mary's. I was six. You had to be twelve to visit patients. Dad lied to the nuns about my age and I got in to see Mom. I know she eventually had a hysterectomy and I think the car ride was a prelude to the operation. Something happened. I likely caused it (or at the very least, the trauma of birthing me did) and Mom couldn't have any more babies.

Shortly thereafter, I was told a brother was coming to live with us. We drove to Detroit Lakes: Dad, Mom, and me in the 1959 black Dodge station wagon Dad bought from Monson Motors, a dealership owned by the father of his high school and college boozing buddy, Rudy Monson.

We drove to northwestern Minnesota in the Dodge, pulled up to a dilapidated farmhouse, and parked amongst raucous chickens pecking gravel. I don't remember going into the house. I recall being introduced to my new brother—Dave was ten months' old—when Mom brought him out to the car. Dave's dark hair touched his shoulders; something that was unheard of in the days before the Beatles invaded America. Whatever paperwork was needed to whisk a kid away from his foster home must've already been signed because we didn't appear in front of a judge. One minute, we were a family of three. An instant later, we were a family of four.

Mom held Dave in her lap in the front passenger's seat (there were no seatbelts in cars back then and certainly no car seats) while I read *Mad* magazines on the rear bench seat and Dad smoked cigarettes (he'd eventually replace them with cheap, dime-store cigars, and finally, a pipe) for the trip back to Duluth. We took a detour to see Great Aunt Linda (Grandma Munger's sister) and her husband, Pete Clambey, as well as Dad's first cousin Ken Clambey, Ken's wife Margaret, and their kids Gary and Kathy on the Clambey Farm outside Fergus Falls, where the Clambeys welcomed Dave into the extended family.

Dave was happy and quiet all the way to Duluth. But—and I think this was Mom's doing—before we returned home, we had one last stop to make. When a West Duluth barber started his electric shears and began hacking away at Dave's hair, the poor kid screamed bloody murder. There wasn't any *physical* pain involved; the barber didn't nick the kid or anything like that. It was simply, I think, the very first time Dave had his hair cut and the experience terrified him.

Things were OK between my brother and me until he was old enough to speak up for himself. Dave was a genteel kid who adapted to life in our house and fit in; at least until he started telling me "No" whenever I asked him to get me a bottle of soda, or a box of crackers, or perform some other menial task. The fact my kid brother started denying me my authority caused me to be less than kind. Not all the time, you understand. Just sometimes. This change in our dynamic may have been related to the Osbournes moving into the neighborhood and me facing, for the very first time, serious bullying. I'm not making excuses here. I'm just trying to understand, fifty-plus years later, why things went sour. Most days Dave and I got along and did things together—as brothers do—without conflict. But I could turn mean without warning and torment Dave in ways I won't detail here. He can tell that part of our story if he wants to.

Not long after Dave came to live with us, the family went on a long road trip. Dad rented a StarCraft pop-up camper, packed the rear of our 1962 white Dodge wagon with camping gear and luggage and food, and we joined Dad's pal Red Lundeen, Red's wife, Carol, and their two kids, David and Barbie, on a three-week journey from Duluth to Vancouver and back. The Lundeen kids were older than me, cool, and taught me how to swear. I'm relating this because, as we traveled cross-country in a two-car caravan, Dave stayed with Grandpa Jack and Grandma Nancy. While it was a fun trip for me (I got to visit the Little Big Horn Battlefield, Yellowstone National Park, the aftermath of an earthquake, the '62 World's Fair in Seattle, Vancouver, Banff, the International Peace Garden, and a host of other cool places) I never considered how that trip impacted Dave. He'd been whisked away from the only place he'd ever lived, had his hair chopped off, been thrust into a loud and obnoxious family, and then, less than a year later, spent a month with old people he barely knew. In retrospect, that had to be pretty scary.

My parents always claimed Dave was one hundred percent Norwegian. I mean, that's what I was told, and that's what Dave believed until he was in his thirties and learned he was part Ojibwe. As I look back it makes so much sense; the long hair Mom had lopped off and the horror Dave exhibited in the barber's chair. His trauma was not unlike the experience of Native kids sent off to boarding schools. First thing the schools did was cut off the boys' hair, eliminating an important aspect of Indian culture. Leaving Dave behind, when he'd endured so much inexplicable trauma in his young life—some before he came to live with us, some afterward—didn't make things easier for the kid.

I wasn't always a jerk. From age ten or so to age thirteen is the period where I bullied and belittled Dave. At least, that's what I remember. Like I said, maybe it had to do with the crap I was being forced to eat at the hands of neighborhood bullies (there would be more of that sort of thing once I entered junior high). Or maybe I was just angry that a cute, brown-eyed, brown-headed kid was crowding my comfy nest. For whatever reason, I was a jerk, but only for a while.

My relationship with my sister Anne wasn't as problematic. She came to live with us "on approval"; for what I now know was a "trial home visit." Anne was placed in our family through St. Louis County Health and Human Services, and the agency made periodic inspections to ensure things were going well. Anne was eight months old when Mom and Dad adopted her. I was twelve and Dave was six when that blonde-headed, brown-eyed little girl became our sister. I can honestly say I never tortured Anne the way I tortured Dave. There was something about her vulnerability, her small stature, and her innocence that forbade such conduct.

Somewhere between adopting Dave and adopting Anne, a weird thing happened to us and other families in our neighborhood. I'm not sure where or how it all started but nearly every kid on our block came down with parasites known as pinworms. I remember we could still play—while taking medicine to rid us of those nasty little buggers—with other infected kids, meaning Eddie and I got to hang out since the entire Salveson family was also stricken.

During early childhood, I also contracted German measles. I remember being listless, languid, and burning up with fever. I could tell Mom was worried given her only child might not survive. The fever relented, the marks of the disease disappeared, and I recovered because Mom was attentive to my needs and nursed me back to health.

Then there was the time Dave, Anne, and I all came down with chicken pox, which while itchy and annoying, wasn't so bad since Dad paid Dave and me (Anne was too little and didn't know how to count) a penny for each pox we found on our bodies. Dave later developed the mumps, an illness that laid him low but gave me a few laughs given how his throat swelled up and made him sound like an old man.

One thing that frosted me about Anne joining our family wasn't her fault. The day Anne's adoption was to be finalized, Dad pulled me out of Lincoln Junior (I was in seventh grade) and Dad, Mom, Dave, Anne, and I drove to the St. Louis County Courthouse for a hearing in front of a probate judge.

When I returned to school after Anne's adoption, my homeroom teacher, Miss Hanson—a stern old witch and a teacher I thank the Lord I never had for math (her chosen subject of expertise)—took me aside and interrogated me as to why I'd been absent. I explained I'd been at my baby sister's adoption. I figured that was a pretty good excuse for missing homeroom.

When report cards came out, I had high enough marks to make the "A" honor roll, but Miss Hanson decided that I should be penalized for my "unexcused absence." She gave me a "U" (Unsatisfactory) in conduct, which meant I wasn't eligible for the honor roll. When Dad saw the "U" on my report card, he marched me down to Miss Hanson's classroom and had it out with the spinster. Dad had a bit of a temper and while he sometimes appeared to not care about his children, one thing that drew Dad's ire was injustice. Despite Dad's dander being up and him making poignant arguments on my behalf, Miss Hanson wouldn't budge.

"Your son did not present a written note <u>before</u> missing homeroom," Miss Hanson said with precision, clearly establishing that "the rules are the rules." "I cannot change a "U" once it's written in <u>my</u> grade book."

Dad couldn't sway the teacher. A sit-down with the principal, Mr. Card, went nowhere, and to this day, I blame Anne for keeping me off the honor roll.

SWIMMING NAKED

I first experienced the inexplicable at the Duluth YMCA. This was at the old "Y" before a modern edifice on First Street was built.

I'd taught myself to swim in a naturally warmed, mineral water pool near Yellowstone on our camping trip with the Lundeens. Dad—who rarely donned swimming trunks—didn't teach me. Mom—who occasionally entered the water in her bathing suit and unflattering rubber swim cap—grew up swimming at her family's resort on Bear Island Lake. You'd have thought she had a hand in teaching me the fundamentals. That wasn't the case. I simply, as unathletic as I was, figured it out on my own.

I was never a Cub Scout. I joined Boy Scouts because Eddie's dad was an Eagle Scout and insisted that Eddie join Scouting. That said, Eddie and I were never Cub Scouts. Following Ed Salveson's lead, we joined a YMCA organization known as Indian Guides. Indian Guides functioned like Cub Scouts in that weekly meetings were held in boys' homes. During these weekly gatherings, we'd work on craft projects (involving birchbark or other locally sourced materials so as to mimic Native American handiwork) all led by that week's "Chief"—one of the fathers. Dads were expected to participate, "guiding," as it were, their sons. Unlike Cub Scouts, which took place right after school, Indian Guide meetings occurred after supper. Dad rarely attended the sessions of our tribe—the Sioux—except when meetings were held at our house. In Dad's absence, I was mentored and guided by Ed Salveson, Mr. Dahl, and Mr. Prayman. With the exception of Kelly Prayman's house, all of the tribal members' homes were within walking distance so I didn't have to ask for a ride. Though Dad missed most meetings, when the Sioux visited the old "Y" for swim night, he made it a point to attend.

Up to the moment I stood in the Y's shower room stark-ass naked with my fellow Indian Guides and our fathers, I'd never seen an adult penis. That group shower was a shocker. The difference between my pert, little nub of circumcised dick and Dad's impressive, uncircumcised penis was unsettling.

Showering wasn't something the Munger kids did even though the tub in the house on Chambersburg had a shower head and a shower curtain. Perhaps—I don't really recall this for certain—our parents took showers. But Dave, Anne, and I—up until we moved into the new house on Miller Creek—took baths. Why were we prohibited from using the shower? Mom was worried we'd make a mess. Worse yet, because we couldn't use the shower when our hair needed washing; Mom insisted on scrubbing our scalps with a hard-bristled rubber brush under scalding hot water in the kitchen sink. There was, to my mind, an element of sadism in the delight Mom evinced while abusing our heads until we bled.

I'd packed my bathing suit for the Indian Guide swim session, but when I went to put on my suit, Ed Salveson kindly said, "Mr. Munger, you won't be needing that."

Our tribe lasted a year or two before fading away. The demise of the Sioux made perfect sense given the weirdness of swimming naked, which I was certain, once Indian Guides was in the rearview mirror, would be the end of such insanity. I was wrong about that as I've been wrong about so many things in life.

After Eddie and I "graduated" from elementary school, we learned some important truths about Lincoln Junior High.

"Don't wear shirts with fairy loops," Carson Osbourne warned as Eddie and I sat on Ricky Plys' front stoop.

"Why?" Eddie asked.

"Kids rip them off your shirts," Ricky advised.

Dress shirts, required attire at Lincoln, were equipped with a little piece of cloth stitched to the shirt between the shoulder blades. What purpose fairy loops served, I don't know. But given we weren't allowed to wear T-shirts or hoodies or sweatshirts (a dress code strictly enforced by Miss Hanson and her pal, Miss Gilmore) and given every dress shirt has a fairy loop, we felt doomed.

"What're we supposed to do?" I asked.

"Cut 'em off."

Which is what our mothers did.

The second truth learned from the less-than-reliable mouth of Carson Osbourne was that we were required to take swim classes taught by Coach Nelson. We'd learn—soon enough—

that Richard Nelson was an ex-Marine who looked and acted the part. To a kid barely tipping the ruler at five foot nothin' and the scale at ninety-five pounds, Coach's reputation caused concern. But that wasn't the half of it.

"You know you swim naked; right, Cigar?" Carson Osbourne asked.

The nickname referred to a boast I'd made. We'd been sitting around a campfire behind Ricky's house when the topic of girls and "fucking" (I had no idea what the word meant) and the size of things came up. That's when I told a lie about my personal anatomy. Carson would toss the "Cigar" label out whenever he wanted to point out my failings. The truth was, I was a year away from puberty. Nothing had changed down there. My eyes widened at the prospect of being forced to swim in the nude with thirty other boys, some of whom were as developed as Dad.

"You're kidding."

"'Fraid not, Cigar. You all shower together in one big room and then march to the pool single file, one naked ass after another."

"It's true," Ricky confirmed.

Trepidation came to a head during the first week of seventh grade but my fears quickly dissipated. No one made fun of my bald, turkey-skin balls and pecker. Everyone, even the guys with hair growing all over their bodies like gorillas, kept their comments to themselves. Why? Coach Nelson made it clear he'd deal with anyone saying anything or doing anything untoward with a heavy hand. Consequently, when we were required to jump off the diving board, our Johnsons flapping in the breeze, our balls shriveled from chill, all that collective, exposed maleness never bothered me though, to this day I've never been able to figure out the "why" behind boys being required to swim naked.

Maybe that weirdness had something to do with turning boys into men. I mean, that makes sense. Girls didn't swim naked; though their school-supplied, moth-eaten, unattractive one-piece suits (handed out by Miss Wilson—the girls' phy ed teacher) weren't much better than swimming nude. Then too, girls had another issue to deal with. In every gym class, a few young ladies were experiencing their monthlies. Indisposed girls had access to private stalls for showering. Not so the boys. We stood in one big room under spigots fully exposed to each other in all our glory every single day. For whatever reason, be it their periods or Puritanical thinking or modesty, junior high girls didn't swim naked and were afforded occasional respite from group showering.

I was in ninth grade when Dave Olson, a guy with a fully developed body, decided I deserved to die. I was swimming along, minding my own business, when Olson jumped in the pool, put me in a choke hold, and dragged me under. As I struggled and kicked and tried to free myself, panic set in. I was headed towards unconsciousness when Joe Misiura—a big Polish kid who'd come over to Lincoln from St. Peter and Paul Catholic—dove in, grabbed hold of Olson, forced the bully to let go, and saved my life. Over the years, I've thanked Joe any number of times for his intervention, but I think such heroism deserves a mention here.

Talking in the locker room after ninth grade swim class, Rod Peltoma and I got the bright idea to audition as MCs for the school variety show. Rod and I were in choir and vocal small group so we could sing a bit. We put together a Smothers Brothers-style routine, one that included my clumsy attempts to play the Beatles' "Something" on piano with Rod singing harmony to my falsetto, followed by an insinuation of ballet. While we weren't selected to MC, the adults auditioning us rolled in the aisles when we broke into our tortured dance. I played the guy and Rod, who was physically mature and a head taller than me, played the girl our disjointed version of Swan Lake. Despite not being selected to MC, the faculty asked us to reprise our dance routine for the big show.

To hone our moves, Rod and I approached Miss Wilson. The girls' gym teacher consented to work with us, and Rod and I spent time after school with her. The evening of the big show, I was dressed in a tuxedo and Rod wore a pink blouse, tutu, hose, and slippers. We killed it. Because of Miss Wilson's tutelage, we were the most beloved act of the evening and were chosen "Best Dancers" by the "unofficial" Lincoln Junior High newspaper.

No one of the female persuasion was supposed to enter boys' swim class. I've been told by reliable sources—guys who have nothing to gain by inventing tall tales—that Miss Wilson once came into a boys' swim class unannounced. I haven't called her up, fifty years later, to verify the tale: I'm just conveying what I was told. The story goes something like this.

136

Miss Wilson had a key to the pool. The door to the pool was always locked. Smack dab in the middle of a boys' swim class, Miss Wilson—a very attractive, athletic young lady with immense poise—opened the door and walked in, causing every boy in the class to hug the pool wall for dear life. Miss Wilson was immediately intercepted by Coach Nelson. As Coach escorted Miss Wilson across the room, she reportedly noticed the consternation she'd caused and, without missing a beat, remarked, "Don't worry boys; I've seen real men," before continuing on her way.

GOLFING WITH HARRY

You'll learn soon enough that this story has nothing to do with golfing with Dad. I just thought the title was catchy and fit a story that is, well, about golf and Harry but not necessarily in the way the title implies.

My pals and I golfed at Enger, a public golf course not far from Five Corners, the intersection of Skyline Drive, Piedmont Avenue, Trinity Road, and 24th Avenue West. Why it was called Five Corners when the intersection was the convergence of four roadways, I'll leave to someone else to explain. Just know that until the highway department reconfigured the intersection (and gave us Mondale Drive in the revamp), that's what it was called. To get to the golf course, our tattered golf bags full of hand-me-down clubs slung over our shoulders, we gathered at Ricky Plys' house, trekked along the gravel shoulder of Hutchinson until it hit Five Corners, scampered across Piedmont to Skyline, and walked the gravel shoulder of Skyline Parkway to arrive at Enger.

I started playing golf with the Osbournes and Plys and Eddie and Ebert and Phil Rolle when I was eleven years old. The clubs I carried were a birthday gift from Dad to Mom. What's noteworthy about Dad's present is that Mom didn't play golf—she played tennis—lots of tennis with lady friends. In addition, Mom never expressed an interest in golf. Finally, Mom's left-handed. The clubs Dad gave Mom were right-handed. I remember the look on Mom's face when Dad gave her those right-handed Gene Sarazen men's clubs. The set went into storage until Dad decided, "What the hell" and started using them. I'm suspicious as to whether those clubs were *really* intended for Mom. I'll let you judge Harry's conduct. Eventually, Dad broke down and bought himself a set of Jack Nicklaus clubs and I inherited "Mom's" clubs.

We'd arrive at Enger, pay the green fee, get a number from the starter, and golf (or, as we renamed the game, "Flog"). There was no honesty on the course. Everyone cheated. We wanted scores lower than one-twenty for eighteen, which, if our actual strokes were counted, never happened. Sometimes, we'd arrive before the course opened but we never played without paying. Most of us were Boy Scouts and were bound to be "trustworthy" according to Scout Law.

To practice, I'd whack whiffle balls around our backyard. When Dad was gone, I'd pull out his nice, shiny, new Jack Nicholas clubs and use them, hoping fancier, more expensive clubs might do the trick. They didn't. But the fact I borrowed Dad's clubs is the gist of this story.

"Where's my sand wedge?"

I was sitting in the den watching Saturday morning cartoons and cowboy shows, maybe the *Jetsons* or *Rin Tin Tin* or *Roy Rogers* in my flannel jammies when Dad entered the room.

"Huh?"

"You heard me. My sand wedge. I golfed with Red yesterday at Lester and when I needed my sand wedge, it was missing."

"I dunno."

Dad's face turned crimson. "I know you used it! My seven iron is covered with grass and there are divots all over the backyard!"

"I used 'em but I put 'em all back."

"No you didn't. The sand wedge isn't in my bag!"

I stopped and thought. "I didn't use your sand wedge."

Dad lifted me off the couch, marched me barefooted to the garage, and had me pull every club out of my bag. No sand wedge.

"Where is it?" Dad's face was red and his voice cracked.

I shook my head. "I never ..."

Dad dragged me into the house, shoved me into the bedroom I shared with Dave, slammed my butt down on the three-legged stool reserved for "timeouts," shut the door, and muttered: "Don't come out until I tell you to come out."

It felt like a day. I'm sure it was only a matter of a couple of hours that I sat, forlorn, upset, in my pajamas, on the milk stool contemplating the plaster of the bedroom wall. When the door opened, it was Mom, not Dad, who granted me parole.

"Get dressed," Mom said quietly.

"What about Dad? He put me in here because he thinks I lost his golf club."

"Oh that. Red called. He found your father's wedge in the trunk of his car."

"Really?"

Mom nodded and left the room. I got dressed, had my breakfast, and went outside to play. I never touched Dad's clubs again and Dad never apologized for labeling me a liar and a thief.

A QUIET EVENING AT HOME

"What's in this casserole?"

Though I was only twelve years old, I knew Dad's question would cause trouble.

Dave—six years old and terrified of loud noises, Dad, and I sat on steel and plastic chairs pulled up to the Formica top of our kitchen table contemplating the hotdish Mom had placed in front of us.

"Ya, what's in this?" I knew better than to chime in but something caused me to live dangerously that summer evening.

Mom was at a disadvantage. She had a hard time competing with the Munger women when it came to cooking. Grandma Munger and Aunt Elsie made everything—including bread and pies—from scratch. They used real whipped cream stirred to fluffy perfection by their thick wrists, and real butter—creamy and rich—in and on everything. Mom's response to such competition rang hollow. When Dream Whip came out as the first non-dairy artificial whipped topping, she latched onto it like the Holy Grail. When Cool Whip emerged from the atomic test site where it'd been concocted, it became the new craze in our home. Cool Whip pies. Cool Whip and Jell-O. Cool Whip and Jell-O with pickled beets.

With each issue of *Good Housekeeping* magazine, Mom's efforts to amaze us with her culinary skills reared up like an ugly domestic rumor. Hotdishes? Mom insisted on attempting every possible rendition of the most Scandinavian of meals even though the closest her ancestors had ever been to Norway was England. Mom's maternal kin were not Norwegian purveyors of fine casseroles but weak-kneed Celts who offered their virgin daughters to Viking raiders in hopes of saving their sheep and their heads.

"It's something I thought you'd like."

The males of the household stared at a serving bowl of steaming vegetables, suspect meat, and pulpy noodles while Anne sat in a wooden high chair, cooing contentedly and pressing strained Gerber's vegetables into her hair.

"I can't eat this ...," Dad mumbled, careful not to utter <u>that</u> word.

Dad spoke as if reporting a scientific reality. In our family, he was the loud one, the one who could raise and lower his voice at will. Mom—thin, quiet, and demure—never yelled back though she rarely yielded ground. I knew I should keep my mouth shut and just eat the stuff. There was a big bottle of skim milk (Dad preferred whole milk but had lost that battle of wills to Mom as well) to wash the mixture down. Or I could jam casserole into my paper napkin when Mom wasn't looking and toss it to Deuce I—our black Labrador—who was tied to the doorknob of the back door and within reach. I didn't need to speak my mind to escape Mom's latest gastronomical experiment.

"I'm not gonna eat it," Dave said.

"It smells gross," I added.

I watched Dad push himself away from the table. It was a hot, steamy, uncomfortable night. An approaching thunderstorm thickened the air and caused Dad's ribbed undershirt to cling to his skin. Mom stood across the table from Dad, a serving spoon trembling in her left hand.

"Fine."

Mom appeared to accept the unanimous verdict of the men of the house. I chanced a sidelong glance at Dad. He wasn't smiling.

Mom set the spoon on the table and picked up the bowl of hotdish. I figured Deuce would be eating fine tonight and, if we were lucky, Dad would drive us to Mr. Nick's for a Charburger basket.

The serving bowl shattered into a million pieces when it hit the floor. Dave's face evinced horror as he watched Mom launch dishware. Mandarin orange Jell-O hit the wall behind Dad and showered him with gelatin and fruit. Our daily dishes were made of Melmac, a supposedly unbreakable substance. Though Melmac was created with the intent of surviving a Soviet missile strike, it didn't stand a chance in the hands of a suburban mother on a rampage.

When it was over, when Mom had emptied the table of every dish and every utensil, she snatched Anne from the high chair and walked out the back door. Dad and I gaped at each other. Then I looked at Dave. My little brother was so awestruck, he didn't even cry.

Most of the hotdish ended up on the floor though a few random noodles hung from the ceiling like impotent stalactites. Shards of broken dishware littered the place. Milk and orange Jell-O stained the plaster walls as we listened to the family Jeep Wagoneer peel out of the driveway.

The kitchen was spic and span when Mom and Anne came home.

THE FISHING BUG

Dad is to blame. Or should be praised. Take your pick. I was five years old and in nursery school while Dad worked as a lawyer in his cramped downtown office and Mom saw to her duties at the Duluth Clinic as a medical technologist. I don't remember a whole lot about nursery school other than I loved my teacher and sessions were held in an old downtown building that had a gymnasium on the top floor where we rode tricycles and scooters and pedal cars across a distressed and scuffed hardwood floor. In truth, the most memorable thing that happened in nursery school was Dad stealing me away from nap time to go fishing.

We went to the Brule River, Wisconsin's iconic trout stream, where Dad worked his way into frigid water wearing chest waders with a fly rod in hand and I sat on a mossy bank playing with a cowboy and Indian set Dad bought at a dime store on the ride over. Near dusk, Dad latched onto a real prize, a seven-pound German brown. Uncharacteristically, Dad handed me his rod and let me fight the trout. The fish stayed on despite my best efforts to screw things up, and we took it home for dinner, impressing Mom but enduring no end of interrogation as to how I'd skipped school.

The first place I fished on my own was Engwall's Pond in Hermantown. I heard about the man-made pond from older boys in the neighborhood. I asked Dad if I could use an old spin cast rod and reel collecting dust in the garage. He smiled, likely remembering his own treks across Otter Tail County in search of fish and game, and said, "Sure."

I dug earthworms from the backyard, plopped a baseball cap on my head, tied the rod to my single-speed Columbia, stuffed my pockets with lead sinkers and number 8 hooks and a bobber, filled Dad's metal worm box with worms, and pedaled to Engwall's.

The Roed brothers—fraternal twins—also fished Engwall's. They were a few years older than me but helpful to a young guy just starting out. As I sat there, unable to react fast enough to set the hook on a trout nibbling my worm, the bobber bouncing but never quite going under, one of the twins would yell out, "I got one. Munger, you want to bring it in?" and I'd jump at the offer. When a tiny palette of color was laid in the cool morning grass, its sleek

144

body glistening, its red gills opening and closing in desperation, I was smitten.

To this day, fishing North Shore streams—the serenity of walking a pristine river, cool, artifactual water gurgling over ancient stones and past my waders exudes sanctuary. Ducks quacking, blue jays squawking, bald eagles crying, and deer rustling surround me as I chase trout in wilderness. Such interludes in the daily cacophony of life allow me to experience inner peace.

I'd occasionally hook and land brookies at Engwall's. I'd take them home, gut them, and Mom would fry them up. All you need to do to make brookies ready for the frying pan is to remove their innards. The meat is sweet and tasty, and they remain my favorite fish to eat.

When the sun cleared the tree line and the day began to heat up, I'd fish the rivulet emptying the Engwall's Pond. I'd walk undulating, marshy terrain surrounding that stream—Keene's Creek—in hopes of tricking trout. I wore the typical garb for a suburban boy at play; tenners, white gym socks, blue jeans, sweatshirt, and ball cap. No waders were needed to fish Keene's. It was rudimentary fishing; perfect for a child.

Most times, I fished alone. It seemed to me then (and now) that's how one should fish for brook trout. There were other streams in Piedmont and Hermantown I explored though I often came home empty-handed. That was OK. Even as a child, I knew fishing was about more than catching trout. I fished every nook and cranny of Keene's Creek. I caught a few. I missed a few. But most often, I fished Keene's by myself. Brook trout fishing isn't a social event but a reflective, peaceful, Zen exercise involving a rod in your hand and fast-flowing water swirling around your legs.

One summer morning, Eddie and I biked to the Midway River. Whoever decreed the Midway a "river" was either in need of eyeglasses or overly optimistic. The Midway was and is a glorified creek. But it did and does hold both native brook and planted brown trout. There were rumors, as there always are when trout fisherman whisper to each other after a day on the water, of twelve and fourteen inchers being caught in the Midway. Considering most of what we pulled out of Keene's, and later, when I moved to live on its banks, Miller Creek, were six-inch trout, with an eight-incher being a real prize, a foot-long or better brookie or brown is a trophy. And so, like Ahab in search of his white whale, Eddie and I set out on our bikes—me on my Schwinn five-speed Varsity and Eddie on his three-speed Raleigh—for the Midway.

I don't remember catching anything other than pesky chubs, native minnows that delight in nibbling away at a worm until it's used up. When the day grew hot, even the minnows grew lazy so Eddie and I decided to take a dip. Which meant stripping down to the altogether since we didn't have swimming trunks with us. The place we chose to enter the river was next to a pasture where black-and-white cows grazed. The bovines nibbled grass with scant curiosity evident in their big, brown, eyes as we slipped into cold water. Recovering from the Midway's embrace, we kicked and dove and giggled and laughed in delight. My downfall came when, climbing the riverbank to retrieve my clothes, I latched onto a wire fence for balance. With one foot in the Midway and my right hand grasping barbed wire, I was hit with a pulse of electricity so brutal, it knocked me on my ass.

"Yeow! The fence is electric!"

"Barbed wire? I never knew barbed wire could be electric," Eddie said.

"Me neither," I replied, rubbing the palm of my hand. "But I do now!"

Another kid who loved trout fishing—Johnny Ray—and I fished Miller Creek a few times together. We even dragged Wayne Rikala away from his beloved West End and handed him a rod, a reel, some hooks, and some worms, whereupon the Finlander out-fished us.

Upstream from the house on Miller Creek there's a shallow, sandy-bottomed pool. A nameless tributary joins the creek just above that pool. Johnny and I were exploring—no fishing on the agenda—when we noticed the tiny rivulet was full of trout. The water was so clear, it wasn't hard to spot oodles of four- and five- and six-inch brookies suspended above the gravel bottom.

"They're spawning," Johnny said.

We hid behind cedars to watch female trout lay their eggs and witness males release their cloudy milt. October air settled over the valley as the brookies did their business.

"I thought trout spawned in the spring."

That tidbit of fish sexuality was something I'd gleaned from fishing steelhead, migratory rainbow trout that spend most of their lives in Lake Superior before returning to the rivers of the North Shore to spawn in the spring.

"Not browns and brookies," Johnny replied. "They're fall spawners."

We set about creating places for the trout to hide from predators. We moved logs and rocks to form pools that offered trout respite and protection in a youthful attempt at wildlife conservation.

I never really took to steelheading. Even in its heyday, when the legendary Knife on Minnesota's North Shore rivaled the renowned Betsie River in Michigan as a place to catch steelies, when Dad fished the Knife and the Lester and the Sucker and every other creek, stream, and river from Duluth to the Canadian border, coming home with big, fine looking trout nearly every time, I didn't catch steelhead fever.

Dad tried. He had me up at four in the morning pulling on my long underwear, winter jacket, gloves, stocking cap, and hunting boots for the short ride up U.S. Highway 61 to the Knife. We'd park in the gravel lot near the falls, pull off our hunting boots, slip into chest waders, and amble towards the stream with fly rods in hand. As dawn peeked over Lake Superior, we'd work opposite banks of the frothing river, tossing yarn and spawn bags into the murky, melt-clouded water in hopes a migratory rainbow trout would strike. I never caught a one. I don't remember having one on. Dad? He was a rock star when it came to steelhead fishing. He was a persistent angler—a quality, when the fish aren't biting—that everyone from his kids to his grandkids to his longtime fishing partner, Fritz Mondale, found irritating. Very simply, the man did not know when to quit.

Though I never caught or hooked a steelie during my excursions with Dad, we made memories. Once, while fishing the Gooseberry River with Dad, Jim Liston, and his son Jimber, the entire river turned silver. There was no warning, no inkling that the day we fished the Gooseberry would be the day that smelt (small Atlantic Ocean fish that originally entered Lake Superior through the St. Mary's River) would begin their spawning run.

With the onslaught of smelt came the ruination of trout fishing. Jimber and I were headed toward the Jeep to put away our gear when a car pulled into the parking lot. A guy got out of the

147

sedan, opened the trunk, and pulled out a smelting net. From the looks of his togs (he was dressed in street clothes and dress shoes) he seemed intent upon smelting from shore, an iffy proposition given the smelt were clogging the middle of the Gooseberry.

"You want us to get you some?" Jimber asked.

"I was fixin' to do it myself," the guy replied, eyeballing us.

"We can do it," I said. "You'll have a tough time reaching them from shore."

The guy looked at the river. "I guess it couldn't hurt to have some help."

I thought the stranger would hand us a bucket or a pail to fill. Instead, he gave me his net, reached into the trunk of his sedan, and pulled out a thirty-gallon trash can. Jimber and I filled that steel garbage can with smelt in less than twenty minutes.

The last time I fished the Knife wasn't with Dad. I was attending UMD. By then, the Minnesota DNR had stocked Chinook (King) salmon, pink salmon, and Coho salmon in Lake Superior. Lake trout, a native species, had made a comeback after being nearly wiped out by invasive sea lamprey (which got into the Great Lakes from the Atlantic Ocean through the Welland Canal). West Coast rainbows had been introduced into Lake Superior in the 1890s to enhance sportfishing opportunities but didn't fare well until the lamprey decimated the lake trout, which is when the steelhead took off. The lake trout eventually rebounded after the DNR began controlling the invasive lamprey through poisoning and electric barriers. In sterile Lake Superior—a place that's tough on game fish given its sparse forage—something had to give and that something were the steelhead.

Pat Pufall ("Poof") a guy I met playing B-team football at Denfeld (and who died far too young of Alzheimer's) and Larry Paasch spent the night at my house on the creek. The alarm went off while it was still dark. We got dressed, loaded Poof's Olds Cutlass with gear, and drove to Sambo's Restaurant at the Miller Hill Mall.

Remember the illustrated children's book about Little Black Sambo? Originally, Sambo's restaurants weren't affiliated with that offensive caricature. The franchise's name was actually an amalgamation of the founders' surnames. But some bright light at Sambo's corporate decided that since the public *informally* associated the restaurant with a racially insensitive children's story, well, Sambo's should cash in on that untoward affiliation. Which is to say that the morning three tired, goggle-eyed fishermen walked into Sambo's for breakfast, the place was adorned with pejorative cartoons of Black Sambo and all his friends. I'm pretty sure the depictions only raised mild alarm in me at the time but after reconsidering the matter, I have to ask: "What the hell was Sambo's thinking?"

It turned out I hadn't missed much by taking a hiatus from steehead fishing. None of us had a bite, though there was a plus side to our expedition. After Larry, Poof, and I worked our way onto the gravel bar at the mouth of the Knife and the day warmed, we found places to curl up, nap, and dream about the girls we were dating, girls who, without exception, would become our wives.

BULLIES AND SCOUNDRELS

The first bully I encountered lived half a continent away. I was seven years old and on the only extended road trip we ever took as a family, towing a rental tent camper behind our Dodge Dart station wagon, with the Lundeen family in their own car towing their own rental camper, making the westward journey with us—when I confronted ugliness.

We arrived in Seattle and briefly split off from the Lundeens. Grandma Nancy had two daughters, Kay and Corrine. Kay lived in Seattle, and we spent time visiting Kay and her family before reuniting with the Lundeens. I thought the visit would be a dull, uninteresting diversion. But Kay had a son, Dean, a year younger than me. Dean and I explored his suburban neighborhood and ended up swinging and teeter-tottering and sliding at a local playground when some older boys showed up. During the "getting to know you" phase, one of the boys started teasing Dean. I don't remember what it was all about—that detail is lost to time—but, eventually, the kid put hands on Dean.

When it came to fisticuffs with Patrick Osbourne, I invariably lost. The few times Bruce Patterson and I squared off—not because Bruce was bullying me, simply as a rite of passage—he ensured I knew that his head was a hell of a lot harder than mine. Though Eddie and I never exchanged blows, I had plenty of dustups with other boys that I ended up losing. When the bigger, older kid started pushing Dean around—Dean being someone I barely knew, a shirttail relative through Grandpa's second marriage—history wasn't on my side.

The bully tossed Dean to the ground and the injustice of the assault (something I recognized as wrong thanks to Dad) compelled me to speak up.

"You stop that!" I said.

"Or what, Kid?" the bully replied.

There's a key to winning a fistfight, something I didn't know at the time but learned very quickly: If you strike first you have a decent chance of winning. I grabbed the kid's shirt with my left hand and hit him with a solid right. One punch, and it was over.

"My son's nose is broken," the bully's irate father said a short time later while standing on the front porch of Dean's house, the injured boy hiding behind his father. Bill—Dean's dad—and Harry were shielding Dean and me from the guy. "He's gonna have to go to the hospital!"

"The way my son tells it," Bill said evenly, "your boy attacked Dean. He had no business doing that. He's three years older than Dean; two years older than Mark." Bill paused to stare down the guy. "Your boy got what he deserved. Now, if you don't mind, get the hell off my porch!"

Dad never said a word. He was only there as backup. The bully's father scrutinized his potential adversaries—two middle-aged men in T-shirts, cans of Olympia beer in their hands—pointed at me, mumbled something about "that little bastard," turned, and retreated.

Until the Osbournes moved in, Piedmont Heights was nearly devoid of bullies. The one exception was Jackie, a nephew of the Swansons. The Swansons were empty-nesters who owned the house between our house and Salvesons'. Because Jackie didn't live in Piedmont, my statement is a bit inaccurate. He wasn't a native thug: He was an import.

Playing with Eddie and Jackie in the Swanson backyard (one of the rare times we were permitted on Annie Swanson's lawn) I learned just how nasty Jackie was. He'd teased me and taunted me before but until he drove a toy knife into my right thigh, leaving a piece of plastic embedded under the skin (I was wearing shorts), I didn't know what a nutcase he was. After I barged into the kitchen, tears streaming down my face, blood dribbling down my leg, Mom had words with Mrs. Swanson and I don't remember ever playing with Jackie again.

I encountered another bully in the person of Simon—the son of my dad's second law partner. The kid was a bad seed. I remember being at his house out in Fond du Lac (a neighborhood at the far western limits of Duluth) for dinner, before Milan (Dad's partner) built a new home in the hills so—as the son of Serbian immigrants—he could run sheep. Simon and I were playing in his room when evil overcame the kid. Simon left the room, returned with a very agitated cat and tossed the critter at me. The cat landed on my face. When I ran downstairs, blood streaming down my shredded cheeks, I couldn't talk for the crying. Simon calmly related to his dad, a criminal defense lawyer raising a future criminal, "He tried to pick up the cat and she didn't like it." I told my parents the truth on the ride home.

There was an overabundance of repugnant boys at Lincoln Junior High waiting to torture smaller, meeker kids. Shop class with Mr. Skinner was replete with boys of evil, nasty dispositions. One of the baddest of the lot, Albert Johnson, a tall, lanky boy who'd failed seventh grade twice, was a man-child you didn't look at, smile at, or interact with. Dave Oman, a kid from my neighborhood who once bit me for no reason—prompting Romayne Urie, who was babysitting me while Mom worked, to march me into the Jentofts' backyard where she instructed me to "bite him back" (which I did)—wasn't a bad seed. I'd later end up pummeling Dave at Denfeld High School, where we shared a locker, because he was riding me about something. After I beat Oman silly in tenth grade, he never bothered me again. And like so many encounters between testosterone-driven boys, we remained friends. The point here is that Dave Oman wasn't a bad sort; he just wasn't astute.

"You got a cigarette?" Albert asked as Oman worked on his shop project.

"Ya but I'm not giving you one."

The next thing Oman knew, Albert was pressing Oman's head into the spinning wheel of a buffer.

"In my shirt pocket! Take whatever you need!" Oman squealed.

I later ended up sitting next to Albert in Mrs. Severance's eighth-grade social studies class. I steered clear of Albert until he leaned over during a test and whispered, "Hey Munger, what's the answer to number four?"

I pretended not to hear him.

"Hey, Munger, let me see your answers," Albert whispered.

I weighed the pros and cons of cooperating. Mrs. Severance looked up from her desk, likely mindful shenanigans were afoot. I ignored Albert and figured I'd get my comeuppance after class. For whatever reason, retribution never arrived.

Lincoln Junior was a snake pit of bullies and scoundrels. The worst of the lot was Danny Cummins, a guy with a head shaped like an anvil. Even kids like Big Mike Donahue, a guy twice Danny's size with a reputation for quick fists, steered clear of Danny. Whenever Coach Nelson wasn't looking, Danny would wind up his wet towel and snap me or Doug Wait on the bare ass. The welts Danny raised hurt like hell but neither of us tattled: We knew that if Coach took measures to stop the bullying, Danny would just hunt us down after class.

Danny's abuse continued until Doug and I had endured enough. Somehow the two of us—naked after swim class—got together and jumped Danny. One of us alone couldn't have taken Danny on. But combined, we taught Danny Cummins a lesson. After that, he left us alone.

Given Lincoln was a pit of ugliness, making friends with the biggest kid in seventh grade made sense. When Big Mike Donohue asked me to carry his guitar amp from Lincoln to his house, I jumped at the chance. After that, I counted Mike as a protector: I'd purchased a wee bit of security by doing him a favor.

Being one of the smallest kids in my grade, wearing eyeglasses (which didn't help), and being forced to take piano lessons in the West End made me an obvious target for abuse as I lugged a leather briefcase full of homework and books in one hand, my piano books in the other, from school to Miss Eck's apartment. Unfortunately, my path went right by a house full of boys whose greatest joy in life was tormenting geeks. Pat Sullivan, the middle kid in that family of thugs, waited for me in front of his house. I could've crossed the street and avoided Sullivan. But that would've provided him with proof of my fear. There's one thing I learned dealing with bullies: Show them fear and their joy in tormenting you expands exponentially.

"Where you goin', Munger?"

Sullivan stood on the sidewalk, not much taller than me but appreciably more self-assured, blocking my path.

"Pi..a..no lessons," I stuttered.

"Ha! Now that's funny!"

I knew I wasn't getting past Sullivan unscathed. My hands were full. I was late for my lesson. I wasn't looking to fight. The speed with which Sullivan knocked the music books out of my hand was surprising. The fist that slammed into my cheek stung. A punch to the gut brought tears. Awaiting the next blow, it dawned on me: *I'm holding a weapon!* When my briefcase full of textbooks connected with Sullivan's head, the blow knocked him off his feet and into the middle of the street, his will to fight dispatched.

Over time, the bullying at Lincoln lessened. Some offenders dropped out after turning sixteen—the age at which students could legally quit school. Many of those boys found jobs in the factories and shops and warehouses and industries bustling Duluth. There were occasional fights at Denfeld (like my dustup with Dave Oman) but the battles between pubescent boys and occasionally, over-wrought girls—with girl fights being the highlight of any school day—diminished greatly by high school.

Tim Thorp and I both wore glasses. We were also nerds, though Tim, at five-eleven and fully mature, was the starting center on our ninth-grade basketball team and I was a fourth-string guard. We were both on student council. Tim was president; I was a member of the executive board. The day in question, we'd been at a student council conclave at West Junior and were back at Lincoln headed towards basketball practice.

In seventh grade, Lincoln's dress code required boys to wear slacks; no shorts or sweatpants or blue jeans. Button-down dress shirts only; no T-shirts or hoodies or sweatshirts. Girls were required to wear skirts or dresses or "appropriate" slacks and blouses; again, no T-shirts or sweatshirts or shorts or hot pants or blue jeans. Along the way, the student council challenged those arcane rules and by ninth grade, the dress code allowed more casual attire. But because Thorp and I had been at a student council event, we were wearing sport coats, dress shirts, dress shoes, and ties as we walked towards the gym.

I knew Joel Wheeler, a tough-as-nails West Ender. I considered him to be a friend. For some reason, as Thorp and I walked down the hallway past the art rooms, Wheeler took issue with what he apparently viewed to be my "uppity" dress. I have no idea what was said before Wheeler threw me to the ground, ripped the clip-on-tie from my neck, and started punching me. Despite Wheeler's size advantage, I got a grip on him, broke free, and we ended up going toe-to-toe in the middle of the hallway. Students from art classes gathered to watch the fracas. When I slammed Wheeler's head against the wall, Brenda Olson, a cute, tall, shapely eighth grader got her arm caught between Wheeler's head and ceramic tile. The fight ended when an art teacher, Mr. Grano, stepped in, grabbed hold of Wheeler and me and marched us to the office. For once, I didn't get in trouble. Thorp verified my story—that Wheeler had jumped me for no reason, which ended things in terms of consequences at school.

It was a different matter at home.

The Olsons lived a block away from us. That evening, Dad got a call from Don Olson, Brenda's dad. Turns out, slamming Wheeler's head into the wall broke Brenda's arm. She went to the hospital, the fracture was set, and a cast was applied. Don wasn't mad—Brenda confirmed I wasn't to blame—but Don thought my parents should know what had happened.

"You need to apologize," Dad said after hanging up the phone. "You broke Brenda Olson's arm."

"I'll say I'm sorry when I see her in school tomorrow."

"No. You'll apologize tonight."

I knocked on the Olsons' front door. Don answered, let me in, and went to retrieve his daughter. Brenda appeared, stood in the foyer, and listened as I said the words that needed saying. When I was through apologizing, Brenda smiled, handed me a permanent marker, and I was the first kid to sign her cast.

SING LIKE A BIRD

That was true before I hit puberty. In fifth and sixth grades, I was a member of the Piedmont Choir. I was a soprano with a sweet, high, tremulous voice that rivaled the best girl singers. Once puberty began to course through my veins, my voice went south. I lost the clear tremolo and the ability to hold notes and the capacity to sometimes—like when I sang tunes from *Mary Poppins* and *Oliver*—impress folks. Even so, when I entered the frightful world of bullies and naked swimming at Lincoln Junior, I signed up for seventh-grade boys' choir led by Mr. Grandahl. I also took general music with Mrs. LeNeau, a lovely, poised, confident teacher who was able to keep kids in line and interested in music.

In eighth and ninth grades, the genders came together to form a single choir and Mr. Grandahl continued on as our director. Despite my uneven voice, he found enough in the squeaking, confused, off-key noises coming out of my mouth to select me for Lincolnaires and Harmonizers; Lincoln's premier male vocal groups.

Gordy Mesedahl, another Piedmont kid, made choir a hoot. When Mr. Grandahl left the room, Gordy would open a window, slip outside, and stand on the concrete window ledge. I liked the idea of hiding in plain sight so much I joined Gordy a few times until Mr. Grandahl noticed us standing outside his window, waved us into class, and threatened to give us "U's" in conduct if we persisted.

We had no idea of homosexuality beyond innuendo. I'd never been around an outed adult male. I never heard the term "lesbian" until I was well on my way to adulthood. In high school, I'd read about such things in *Playboy* or *Penthouse*. But that was in the future. I don't think gayness was discussed during the sex-ed class I took through the Episcopal Church. I doubt the topic was broached during lectures about sex we were forced to endure during health class. When boys in choir tittered because Mr. Grandahl was wearing a green sports jacket or a green necktie or green slacks or a green shirt on a Thursday (wearing green on Thursdays supposedly denoting homosexuality) I had no idea why. If Mrs. Von Goertz, our demure, young, and vivacious typing teacher wore green on a Thursday, I'm fairly certain we never accused Mrs. Von Goertz of lesbianism.

During one choir practice, Gordy drew a cartoon guy on the blackboard in Mr. Grandahl's absence and dubbed the character "Emery Wheel." When Mrs. Infelise, my eighth-grade English teacher, challenged me to "do something worthwhile" the summer between eighth and ninth grades, I appropriated Gordy's character for a picture book entitled *Emery Goes to Sea.* I'm conveying this history here to let you know that Emery wasn't my creation.

Before choir started, Gordy would sneak up to the blackboard, retrieve erasers, tiptoe to the piano, lift the lid, and stuff erasers inside the upright. Mr. Grandahl would enter the classroom, take his seat, and begin to play. He didn't always start off with a clunker but soon enough he'd hit a key that moved a hammer that struck an eraser. Gordy was smart: He'd space out his prank—lulling our teacher into complacency until Mr. Grandahl had had enough.

"Mr. Mesedahl," Mr. Grandahl would say, "please come up and inspect my piano," whereupon Gordy would wander up, lift the piano lid, reach inside, and remove the erasers. "Thank you, Mr. Mesedahl."

In high school, my voice achieved stasis. It wasn't a great trade-off, giving up my sweet soprano for puberty. But that's maturation. The change in my voice made singing songs Mr. Baker (my high school choir director) selected a challenge. Despite such limitations, I auditioned for and made Sophomore Small Group; another select ensemble.

Junior year, I joined A Cappella, a mixed junior/senior choir. If you were a boy and auditioned for A Cappella, so long as you sang in tune, you were "in" because it was tough sledding to convince macho high school boys to sing for an audience. My junior and senior years, I had the option of also auditioning for the Ray Baker Singers, another select ensemble. I felt like I'd tempted fate, what with my precarious range and uncertain voice, by trying out for and being accepted into A Cappella so I didn't audition for the Ray Baker Singers.

We had a lot of fun in choir. The tenor section ran a year-long poker game during my junior year where Sugar Christiansen, Bob Douglas, Ed Stokes, Paul Lund, and I played nickel-ante games in the upper tier of the practice hall, our chairs drawn in a circle, coins and cards in full display. As long as we kept our banter down, Mr. Baker didn't give a damn. Being I was and am a terrible card player—and given I was playing with my lunch money—I went hungry most days.

During choir practice in the cavernous, opulent, Denfeld Auditorium, we'd sneak into the orchestra pit, disappear beneath the stage, and play five-card draw until Mr. Baker noticed his tenors were AWOL. His voice would escalate, we'd toss our cards on the table, and scurry topside. Ray never forbade our card games: He just looked really pissed-off when we were late to our appointed stations on the risers.

Someone figured out that the rubber pads on the bottom of the chairs in Ray's classroom made a loud "thunk" when tossed into the air vents above Ray's head. When rubber hit tin in the middle of a rehearsal, Ray would mutter words teachers aren't supposed to say. No one went to visit Mr. Samskar, the Denfeld principal, over such tomfoolery and eventually we stopped antagonizing our choir director.

I met Roni Seger (who later married my friend, Mike Town), a tiny, perky, bundle of energy and brains (Roni was one of the smartest kids in my class) in sophomore choir. Later, Roni and her friend Val would offer guys in A Cappella stress-relieving massages; though we kidded the girls that their offer of a "massage" carried untoward connotations. I never thought about asking Roni out. She was smart enough to see through me and would've likely provided a kind rejection if I'd done so. Remembering Roni (she died far too young after a long, brave fight with cancer) on the Denfeld stage reprising Lilly Tomlin's Edith Ann from *Laugh In* still brings a smile to my face.

A Cappella is also where I befriended upperclassmen and upperclasswomen who threw some pretty wild parties. After indulging in alcohol for the very first time, Eddie (who wasn't in choir) and I ended up on separate bunks in my bedroom, Dad having retrieved us from Jeff Tynjala's house in West Duluth, both of us drunk as skunks.

The evening started at Jan Schisler's house where two events of note took place. First, I ended up dancing on top of a console television in a basement recreation room. I don't know if I danced well or not but dance I did. And Eddie got so smashed he wandered outside without his jacket and passed out in a snowbank. Thankfully, John Blankush and Jeff Nelson—conscientious seniors—retrieved Eddie before he froze to death. When the party broke up, Vicky Stauber drove us to Tynjala's house in my Jeep so we could lay low. When I called Mom to let her know I was staying at Jeff's, she handed the phone to Dad who detected the slur in my voice, and Eddie and I were toast.

Not long after that first experience with booze, I was slated to be part of Denfeld's annual variety show. Since I'd had such a grand time dancing on the Schisler television, I convinced myself the way to improve my performance was to get drunk before going on stage. Vicky stopped me from making a fool of myself and got me home without incident. My gal pal saved me from public embarrassment but she wasn't my babysitter.

She couldn't protect me from myself.

PHEASANT HUNT

Across a frozen field, wind whipped corn stalks. Thick, gray clouds hung low over prairie. Shadowy trees stood sentinel at the edge of rattling corn. Hundred-year-old cottonwoods marked the end of plowed earth and the beginning of a creek bottom.

Dad's Jeep, its blue paint coated with dust, lurched to a stop. The doors of the Wagoneer opened. Three men exited the SUV while I remained inside.

"Come on, Mark," Dad said.

Dad slid his Browning semi-auto twelve-gauge out of its case as he spoke. Uncle Paul and Grandpa Jack stood at the rear of the Jeep holding shotguns. The vehicle's tailgate was down. My eyes remained heavy. I felt sluggish as I exited warmth. Outside, the hostile wind reminded me it was near the end of hunting season. I zipped up my canvas hunting jacket—a hand-me-down from Dad—and pulled the drawstring tight to keep nature at bay. The sleeves of the oversized jacket hung below the tips of my gloved fingers.

"Harry, is it OK if I give it to him now?" Uncle Paul asked.

Paul was a favorite uncle, a relative by marriage. Paul Pederson, the offspring of a long line of Lutheran pastors, was a man's man, a hunter, an adventurer, and an aviator who taught Marines to fly during World War II.

I knew Paul's question was about me. I didn't know what gift was in the offing.

"Just make sure he understands his limits," Dad replied.

Paul was a dark-skinned Norwegian, with inky black hair and a Clark Gable mustache. Prior to his marriage to my mom's only sibling, Aunt Sukie, Paul had been a legendary bachelor in and around the little farming community of Benson, Minnesota he called home. His voice was coarse and rough, the product of too many cigarettes. I watched Paul unzip a gun case and remove a rifle.

"This is for you," Paul said quietly as he handed me a Stevens semi-automatic .22.

"Thanks."

"Your dad says you've had firearms safety. I thought it was time you had your own gun."

I admired the weapon's weight. The stock was light oak. The barrel was blue steel.

"You can't use it for birds, but I thought you'd enjoy carrying it while we hunt."

Grandpa Jack walked up.

"That's a nice .22, Paul. Where'd you find it?"

"It's left over from the fire. It was just sitting in the garage, taking up space. Might as well put it to use."

I knew that before Paul married Sukie he owned a variety store on Benson's main street. A fire ruined the store but not everything inside. The fire was the first of many streaks of bad luck that would befall Paul during his lifetime.

Deuce II, my black Labrador, and Flaps, my uncle's Springer Spaniel, barked inside the Wagoneer. I reached into the station wagon and unlatched the doors to the dogs' wire crates. The Lab and the Springer dove out of the car. Flaps danced across the ditch bank in unbridled enthusiasm. Deuce sniffed the air with an aspect of aloof maturity.

Morning cold made the men's fingers clumsy as they loaded their shotguns. When the hunters were ready, Dad and I entered standing corn. Terrified I might make a mistake, I fingered the safety of the unloaded .22. Dad's admonition, repeated hundreds of times before that day, ran over and over in my head:

"How do you know a gun is loaded?"

"It's always loaded, Dad."

"When do you point a gun at something?"

"Only if you're gonna shoot it."

The dogs worked hard. The Labrador used his physical strength to plow through corn. The Springer dodged around stalks, his tail beating cold air like a dragonfly's wings.

"Hen!"

A female pheasant burst from cover, its monochromatic wings flapping furiously against the wind. The bird turned, set a course for the creek bottom, and landed in thick underbrush. All three shotguns followed the hen's path. No one shot. The dogs dove back into the corn in search of roosters.

I began to tire from carrying an unloaded rifle over uneven ground. A thin mist began to fall, turning hard-packed soil into slime. I had a hard time keeping up with the men. Ahead of us, the Springer started turning in urgent circles. The dog's nose dipped to the ground and he locked up.

"Flaps is awful birdy. Watch him, Harry."

161

Grandpa Jack's voice was edged with excitement. The old man crouched low, waiting for the bird to flush. Dad raised his Browning.

"Get him, Flaps."

Paul's voice fueled the dog's inclination to roust the bird. The Springer poked his nose into a tangle of standing corn.

Caack ... Caack ...

A rooster burst from cover, nearly knocking Grandpa's hat off his head. In contrast to the erratic flight of the hen, the rooster immediately found the wind.

Crack.

The bird crumpled, folded into itself, and plummeted.

"Good shot Harry!" Paul yelled.

Deuce raced after the fallen bird. Flaps followed the Labrador, intent on stealing the rooster from the larger dog.

"Come, Flaps," Paul called.

The Springer obeyed. Deuce emerged from the cornfield with the dead rooster hanging from his mouth.

"Good boy," Dad praised.

We gathered around the Lab. A quarter-mile away, another nervous rooster cackled and exploded from its roost.

"Beautiful bird," Paul observed as Dad removed the male pheasant from Deuce's mouth.

Grandpa Jack leaned on his Winchester pump and nodded. My father held the bird so I could admire it. I removed a glove and stroked the fading warmth of the rooster's breast.

In the distance, blackbirds gathered and swung south. I looked up from the dead bird to consider the faces of the men who'd brought me hunting. I felt as if the hunt, their love of me, would last forever.

What did I know? I was only a boy. That day, there seemed to be so much time. The sky was endless; the cornfields rolled on forever. To a boy of twelve, the future was far, far away.

SNAKES AND OTHER CRITTERS

There were plenty of 'em. Snakes, I mean. Black and yellow garter snakes. If you walked into the field behind the houses on Chambersburg Avenue, you'd find exposed gabbro, rock undergirding much of Duluth's hillside—ancient, volcanic stone as hard as iron and as gray as a winter sky. In spring, as the sun sought to reassert its power, garter snakes would leave hibernation to warm themselves on the rocks. That's where Eddie and I and Ronny Granley would find them behind Ronny's house; dozens of snakes huddled together, trying to stay warm and getting ready to mate. It wasn't a big deal to scoop the snakes up—grabbing them by their tails, keeping their snapping jaws away from bare skin—and drop them in a steel minnow bucket (the kind with a hinged hatch) borrowed from Salvesons' garage.

Eddie and I created a miniature village from plastic buildings that were accessories to various playsets. We set up the town, posed army men we didn't value, dosed the buildings with Boy Scout water (our first Scoutmaster, Jim Pappas wasn't afraid to give campfires an assist from a gasoline can), released captured snakes, struck kitchen matches against zippers, and set the town ablaze, causing the snakes to slither through fiery destruction like miniature Godzillas.

If there were girls around, we'd seek them out and, after telling the unsuspecting young ladies we had frogs in our bucket, scare the hell out of them by opening the lid and exposing the snakes. The girls would run off screaming bloody murder. Our mothers would get calls about our bad behavior but it was worth a scolding to see girls run.

One morning, I had a ton of garter snakes in the bucket and noticed Mom working in her flower garden. She was a proud member of the Piedmont Garden Club, winning awards for her flower arrangement and advancing in the artform to become a judge of contests around Duluth. Along came her oldest kid and she made the mistake of needing a break. That seemed like God sending me a signal. Mom returned, a glass of iced tea in hand, knelt on the ground, placed the glass on warm, black soil, and began to weed.

"Oh my! There's a snake in my garden!" Mom screamed.

163

"Really?" I said coyly. "I'm sure it's harmless."

"Maybe ..." Mom stopped mid-thought. "There's another one! And another! There's a whole family of garter snakes in my garden!" she squealed, jumping up and scampering as fast she could for the house. Standing on our back stoop Mom came to a realization: "Mark, did you put those snakes in my garden?"

Now, as you've learned, I'm a bit of a charlatan. I've done and said things in my life I'm not proud of. But I was and am the world's worst liar. I think I get that trait from Dad. He had, as I've revealed, faults. But the one constant in Dad's code of conduct was his firm belief in honesty. "A man's word is all he has," Dad told me hundreds of times from my childhood to his death. Dad's steadfast veracity was the moral compass he gifted me. So, when it came to answering Mom, I had to come clean.

"Yes."

"Why would you do such a thing?"

She had me there. I mean, I love and respect Mom. She's been a mentor regarding many facets of my life. Though she has—as I've written in other stories—her own quirks, I've always known that she loves me. To lie to Mom is an impossibility. "I thought it would be funny," I admitted.

Mom shook her head. "Well, it's not. And it's not a very nice thing to do to your mother!"

I cringed at the rebuke. "I'll get rid of them."

Another summer afternoon, Eddie and I came back from the rocky outcroppings behind Granleys' house with a bucket full of snakes. Mom was raking leaves when we crept up behind her and draped a dozen or so garter snakes in the branches of a birch tree. When Mom turned to ask what we were up to, her scream was everything we'd hoped for.

Copper-bellied snakes (northern scarlet-bellied snakes) were a much rarer find. The small, grey-backed snakes with reddish bellies don't bite and were a great discovery whenever you lifted up a board or rolled over a rock. I don't remember finding more than a single copper-bellied snake at a time and I certainly never used them to torment Mom.

Miss Johnson, my fifth-grade teacher, wanted some garter snakes to display in the classroom. Eddie and I volunteered to play Marlin Perkins—you know, from *Wild Kingdom*—and capture some reptiles. Wait. That exemplar is flawed. Marlin

Perkins never did the grunt work on his Mutual of Omaha television show. Marlin's take on securing dangerous animals was far less hands' on. Each episode you'd hear Marlin say something like, "Jim, see that crocodile over there? The Cincinnati Zoo needs one. Go wrestle it!" At which point Jim Fowler would wade into the muck and do battle. Eddie and I came through and delivered snakes to Miss Johnson just like Jim Fowler would have.

"Where are the snakes?" Miss Johnson asked one afternoon after lunch. She was standing next to the terrarium looking distressed. "Someone forgot to put the screen back on the habitat."

Since I'd brought the critters to school, I felt responsible for their well-being. "I'll see if I can find them."

"Take a few other boys with you."

We searched and searched the classroom; the girls either seated at their desks with their shoes off the floor or—with Miss Johnson's permission—standing on their desk seats.

"Here's one," a boy said, pointing to a garter snake coiled behind a trash can.

I apprehended the wayfaring serpent but of the four snakes Eddie and I brought to school, only one was recovered.

Troop 67 spent a weekend tenting at the U.S. Forest campground on Whiteface Lake north of Duluth. During free time Eddie and I explored a rocky point—a narrowing in the Whiteface River—and discovered a plethora of crayfish. The miniature lobsters scuttled backwards at our approach. Despite their speed, we collected a minnow bucket full of crustaceans. The crayfish made their way into the Salveson basement. When Eddie went to check on them, he found the lid to the minnow bucket unlatched and the crayfish, absent.

"Who left the lid open?" Eddie asked Jerry and Ronny.

Eddie's brothers didn't fess up and for the next week, Liz Salveson found dead, stinking crayfish scattered around the house. She discovered the last carcass—belly up and rotting—behind a toilet.

During childhood, I had other encounters with wildlife; creatures I captured and kept in my bedroom. There was a cute star-nosed mole that loved to eat earthworms. A salamander—a blue amphibian with yellow spots, a rarity in our neck of the woods—I found inside a tree I chopped down during a Scouting overnight also lived with me, though he or she wouldn't eat and eventually died. There were myriad frogs and toads and tadpoles by the thousands, some of which made the transformation to adulthood, many of which did not. And I can't forget the frogs Mom brought home from work. I'm not sure what those big, exotic, leopard frogs were used for at the clinic but on occasion, a laboratory frog would come home in a white cardboard carton as an unexpected gift. Why Mom encouraged my fascination with crawly things given how I tormented her with snakes I'll never understand.

I once saw a hawk circling the field next to the Osbournes' house. Without warning, the raptor dove, its plummet accompanied by an ear-piercing scream. I raced to where the hawk landed. The bird lifted away from tall grass with empty talons. The prey the hawk had attacked was a baby cottontail. The bunny was mauled and bloody but still breathing. I cradled the rabbit and ran up the hill in search of Liz Salveson because Eddie's mom had a knack for nursing wounded critters. Liz once raised a family of orphaned tree swallows by feeding them with an eyedropper. The birds loved human contact so much, they would—after learning to fly—land on our outstretched arms like tiny falcons. Given Liz's mastery over wildlife, I thought she could save the bunny.

Eddie's mom answered when I knocked on the back door. I lifted a bloody ball of matted fur towards her. Liz triaged the failing rabbit and shook her head. "It's not going to make it, Mark."

She was right.

SCOUTS

Eddie's dad was an inspiration. He was the only father in our neighborhood I knew had attained the rank of Eagle Scout. I'm guessing other neighborhood dads made Eagle though I have no idea who they were.

I remember walking towards the Piedmont Community Center after Eddie and I signed up for Boy Scouts. There was a gaggle of five or six of us, some who'd been in Troop 67 awhile, others like Eddie and me were newbies. It was a Monday evening in September. Scout meetings were suspended over the summer to allow boys to play baseball, take family trips, and attend Camp Jamar—a summer camp located in Danbury, Wisconsin.

Some of the boys walking to Boy Scouts had been Cubs. Others—like Eddie and me—had been Indian Guides. But we all knew the score. You started as a Scout, earned the Tenderfoot rank, worked up to Second Class, and then made First Class—where you began earning merit badges, showing prowess in various skills and specialties from swimming to camping to space exploration to citizenship. You needed five merit badges to make Star, ten to make Life, and twenty-one merit badges plus time in leadership positions and the completion of a service project to become an Eagle Scout. The literature suggests three to five percent of all Boy Scouts make Eagle. As my career in Scouting began, it was far from clear I'd be one of the chosen few.

Troop 67 was working in the shadow of the green water tower that supplied drinking water to Piedmont Heights. Bruce Patterson and I and a dozen or so other boys were collecting litter. Each Scout was equipped with a stick tipped with a finishing nail. The nail's head was embedded in the stick, leaving the point exposed to stab trash.

Scoutmaster Jim Pappas was keeping an eye on the younger Scouts. He should have been paying attention to Patterson and me—two boys Miss Ness, our kindergarten teacher, never allowed to be unsupervised. But Mr. Pappas was oblivious to our mischief, which included Patterson and me tossing our sticks like javelins.

"Hey, I bet you can't hit Smith," Patterson said, pointing to another Scout.

167

"Bet I can."

I launched my stick. It was a lucky throw. I hit the kid in the calf. Smith danced around like a maniac, crying, and yelling, and carrying on like he was dying. Which, given the nail only went in about half an inch, he wasn't. Patterson ran to Smith, yanked the nail out of the kid's leg, and handed my stick back to me. Smith sat on the ground, rubbing his wound and looking at me like I'd tried to kill him.

"It was an accident," I lied. "I was trying to hit the hockey boards."

Patterson nodded. "That's right, Smith. Munger just missed. Are we good?"

Smith stood up, wiped away tears, and pulled down his jeans. "I guess."

"What's going on here?" Ed Salveson—one of our adult leaders—asked as he approached.

Patterson glared at Smith.

"I just tripped. I'll be fine," Smith lied.

That night I vowed I'd follow the Scout Oath and Law and avoid further instances of bad behavior. I was nearly as good as my word, though it turned out I wasn't the only Scout who lacked sound judgment.

There was a tall, beanpole of a kid in our troop—Scott Nace—whose brother Dave, a year behind me in school, was also a Scout. Scott was a real piece of work. By high school, he'd grow to six-eight and would be taller than everyone at Denfeld High School save Don Brandt—a kid who became the starting center on the varsity basketball team. But unlike Brandt—who had skill on the court and ran cross-country—Scott Nace was completely unathletic. A tough place to find yourself if you tower above your contemporaries. Maybe Nace's difficulties arose not just from his unnatural height but also from his hair-trigger temper. Maybe he was slightly deranged. Or maybe Nace's issues in Scouting, in school, and, in life (he ended up a guest of the Minnesota penal system) were caused by a combination of all of those circumstances. In any event, when I encountered Scott Nace in Boy Scouts, I was in fifth grade, he was in seventh, and it was pretty clear he had a screw loose.

"Knock it off, Patterson," Nace said during a weekend campout at Horace Johnson. Nace was angry because after "lights out," a pea fight had erupted in the bunkroom where Scouts who'd planned ahead ("Be Prepared," right?) retrieved peas and pea shooters from their packs to do battle.

Patterson and I were side by side in our top bunks, pummeling Nace with peas whenever he popped his head out of his sleeping bag to breathe.

"Can't take it, Nace?" Patterson asked.

We stopped to reload. Nace saw his opening, slipped out of his bag, and scooted out the door. After a brief absence, Nace climbed back into his bunk. I took aim at his head but before I could fire, heavy artillery was brought to bear. Patterson was sitting on top of his sleeping bag, doing battle with Peltoma, Carlson, or Salveson when a can of baked beans toppled him to the floor. Nace launched a second can at me but having seen the effect of the first can of Bushnell's, I ducked. The second can clattered to the floor where Patterson sat, stunned and holding his head. Drawn to the bunkroom by all the commotion, Ed Salveson flicked on the light and ended the Great Pea Shooter War.

Nace brought a *Playboy* to Camp Jamar the following summer, hiding the skin mag under his gear along with cigarettes and a six pack of Old Style he bought at the Hillcrest Market. I'd later learn that the old couple who ran Hillcrest would sell 3.2 beer to just about anyone. But when Nace pulled out his cigs, his soft porn, and the beer after our troop's evening campfire, I was years away from trying alcohol.

Cigarettes? Egged on by Eddie, who cryptically said he was into O.G.'s—a code I later realized meant he was buying Old Golds from the cigarette machine located in the Piedmont Shopping Center—I tried smoking. I was thirteen when I ignored the warning label on the cigarette dispenser, a line drawing of a cop with his right hand poised in the air, the caption reading, "Stop! It's illegal to buy tobacco unless you're 18." It was expected kids would read the label and follow the law. Ha! I bought True cigarettes from the machine, tried smoking, hated it, and gave it up before my fourteenth birthday. But Scott Nace? He was a chain smoker who couldn't countenance leaving his cigs behind.

I had no objection to Nace sharing glimpses of bare breasts illumined by a flashlight in his tent, smoking, or drinking shitty 3.2 beer. That was perfectly fine with me and with every other Scout in our troop; though quite clearly, Nace wasn't living

169

his life according to the Boy Scout Law. He was not "clean and reverent." But it would have all been good, his sins unexposed, had he not wanted a second piece of watermelon.

Ed Salveson, Dale Rapp, Leo Ebert, and Mr. Nace (Scott and Dave's father)—were driving us home from Camp Jamar and decided to picnic alongside the St. Croix River. Things went smoothly until Nace decided one piece of watermelon wasn't enough. Instead of asking for a second slice, Nace—who was seated across the table from Mark Olson (Brenda's older brother) and Craig Rapp—reached for Rapp's watermelon. Rapp grabbed Nace's wrist and despite Craig's diminutive size (a trait shared by all the Rapps) a battle of wills ensued. The two Scouts ended up on the ground, rolling in the dirt, fighting over a piece of fruit. Mr. Nace left the adult table and in a loud and commanding voice, said, "Scott, stop this right now. Give Craig his watermelon!"

Mr. Nace was nowhere near the size nor the temperament of his eldest child. He was a slender, quiet, reserved man who seldom raised his voice. When Scott refused to give up the struggle, Mr. Nace reached in and grabbed his son. How Scott went from being on the ground wrestling with Rapp to being on top of his father, hands around his dad's neck, screaming expletives and choking the life out of his old man, I have no idea. It took the other dads and some older Scouts to pry Scott away from his father. That was the last time I saw Scott Nace at Boy Scouts.

During another summer camp, a kid with significant disabilities, born with what was once called "mental retardation" but would now be designated "developmentally disabled," caused quite a stir. His name was Robert Ranta. He went to Lincoln Junior and was in a special needs class, a place where the school district warehoused kids like Robert (low functioning children) with students who had physical impairments. I knew Robert, knew the torments other kids put him through. Like when Bruce Brooks threw dimes into the first-floor girls' lavatory and urged Robert to chase the coins—which Robert did—causing a herd of screaming, adolescent girls to stampede from the latrine.

Jamar had the worst lake of any organized camp. Its fetid pond was terrible for swimming beyond the camp's developed beach—where truckload after truckload of sand had been hauled in to make footing tolerable. Outside the designated swimming area, the lake's bottom oozed loon shit, which proved problematic since many Scouts attempted their mile swim at Jamar. The mile swim was an element of the swimming merit badge—one of the Eagle required badges. I remember floating amongst weeds in the middle of Lake Jamar struggling to complete my mile swim, two Scouts paddling alongside me in a canoe, supposedly spotting me as I poked along. Truth is, I doubt those Scouts could've rescued me given the water was the color of root beer. More likely, my body would've been found by the local sheriff dragging the lake following my demise. Eddie's failure to complete the mile swim is one reason he never attained Eagle. He could swim but not well enough to earn the swimming or the lifesaving merit badges, both of which were required to make Scouting's highest rank.

After Vespers—where all Scouts in camp gathered to sing songs and pray around a campfire—we headed back to our floorless, netless, Army surplus tents, the evening's dose of DDT having been sprayed into our tents and around our campsite to kill mosquitoes.

As we stumbled toward sleep on weary legs, a distant bell tolled.

"Someone's in trouble," Ed Salveson said.

Troop 67 dutifully followed its adult leaders to the dining hall where all the Scouts in camp assembled in less-than-perfect formation.

"Robert Ranta is missing," a camp official said. "Last time he was seen was near the beach. Get with your swim buddy and fan out along the waterfront."

No one had to impress upon us how serious the situation was. Scouts from the Piedmont and West End Troops knew Robert, knew his limitations. I found my swim buddy—Bernie Thompson—and the two of us walked towards the waterfront.

Bernie was a square-built, powerful kid two years older than me, who, if you got on his bad side, could pulverize you. Bernie was a legend at Lincoln Junior for his ability to stare down bigger boys and beat the living daylights out of any takers. He was fearless, and when he picked me to be his "rider" for a "chicken fight" tournament at Jamar, I was thrilled. I didn't do much other than hang onto Bernie's shoulders for dear life while we battled other Scouts in the water. Given Bernie's ability to cheat (by tripping the opposing "horse"), we bested all comers and were crowned champions. Later in the week, Bernie ended up fighting a kid from Cloquet. The guy was in high school and supposedly an all-conference linebacker. In a midafternoon bout, Bernie pummeled the Lumberjack football star.

Bernie and I walked and walked and walked, shining flashlights in the water, looking under docks, and searching brush at the water's edge. Someone found footprints leading into the lake. Robert's tennis shoes were located at the end of the tracks. He'd apparently taken off his shoes and walked into the water, but there was no evidence he'd exited.

Like I've said before, I'd lost a cousin—Brice Grinden—to drowning when he snuck out the back door of his family's house on Park Point, stepped onto fragile ice, and broke through. Memories of Brice's death disquieted me as we looked for Robert. After a half-hour of searching, the camp bell pealed and I feared the worst.

Because no one was paying attention to him, Robert had decided to play a trick on us. While hundreds of Scouts and their adult leaders and camp staff scoured the waterfront and the lake looking for his dead body, Robert was in his tent, contentedly munching candy he'd bought from the camp store.

After the incident with the make-shift javelin, I kept my nose clean. Eddie and I were even selected as honor guards for King Olav's visit to Duluth. Given Eddie is full-blooded Norwegian, it was a pretty big deal for him to be part of the King of Norway's security detail. Even for me—someone who's negligible Norse heritage is likely based upon a Viking marauder impregnating a far distant Irish, Welsh, English, or Scots ancestor—standing at parade rest in my Boy Scout uniform as the Norwegian monarch addressed Duluthians was quite an honor.

Despite a few altercations during my Scouting journey—wrestling matches with Carl Nelson (a chubby kid a year older than me) and Rod Peltoma (a good friend, classmate, and a heck of a lot tougher and stronger than me) come to mind—I earned Scouting's highest rank. My patrol and I cleaned up garbage and refuse and debris (two pickup-truck loads worth) along Skyline Parkway for my Eagle service project, the last requirement I needed to complete before enduring an Eagle Scout Board of

Review. After being grilled by adults in the basement of the Piedmont Community Center for the better part of an hour, I passed muster. I'd earned my twenty-one merit badges, held leadership positions, finished my service project, and satisfied the Board I was Eagle material.

I wasn't a perfect Scout. But experiences from Scouting—like taking refuge under a canoe with Tim Luczak during a rainstorm as lightning slashed and thunder cracked above Brule Lake in the Boundary Waters Canoe Area (BWCA) wilderness, rain pelting the Grumman's aluminum skin as mosquitoes swarmed us—made me a better man.

Evidence of how Scouting changed me can best be summed up by relating this final vignette. During my last summer camp, I helped run Scoutmaster Arne Erickson's underwear up Troop 67's flagpole. Arne's white boxers flapping proudly in the breeze over Camp Jamar is one of my fondest memories of Scouting.

COACH NELSON

He was a man's man. Square-jawed. Crew-cutted. Clear-eyed. He wore a whistle around his sinewy neck on a lanyard. Coach Richard Nelson got thirty boys to strip in full view of each other and swim naked in the Lincoln Junior High pool. In the gym, he shepherded adolescents with the stern confidence of the Marine he'd once been. Even when we were playing touch football or softball or running track on the dirt of the Lincoln Park athletic field, "Coach," as we addressed him, kept things orderly and safe.

If, during our group showers, Coach caught Danny Cummings or one of the other hellions snapping towels, he addressed it. Coach wouldn't scream or holler or otherwise let the evildoer know he'd seen the transgression. He'd simply pick up a towel, wet the tip, twist it, sneak up on the perpetrator, and unload a wicked snap. Bullies whose bare asses met Coach's ire didn't repeat their bad behavior. Granted, Coach's methods could be a bit extreme. But his punishments were never, even when they went astray, fueled by bad intent. Coach Nelson's actions were always grounded in the need to control chaos. Lincoln, especially in gym and shop classes could, if left to hooligans, be a dangerous place. Coach tried his best to corral evil, though—at times—he went too far. Like when he chased Irv Stovern—who'd just pummeled a special needs kid in the head with a basketball—around the gym.

"Stovern," Coach yelled after witnessing Irv's transgression, "get your ass over here!"

Stovern pretended he'd done nothing wrong and joined a group of boys practicing layups. Coach moved out with purpose, clipboard in hand, to deal with Stovern. The special needs kid? He was crumpled on the floor, bawling, unable to comprehend why he'd been pegged. The answer was simple: Lincoln was a place where survival of the fittest was the rule of the day, and a special needs kid, a kid normally confined to 209J or 309J—classrooms designated for the blind, the lame, and the mentally infirm—was at the bottom of the food chain. Stovern spotted Coach coming his way and began jogging around the gym's perimeter. Coach caught on and quickened his pace. It was obvious Stovern was heading for the exit when Coach reached out for the kid. It was a solid grab but as Irv pulled away, his hair, along with a tangle of root and scalp, ripped from his head. Lord, the blood! And the tears. Gym class was over for the day. So far as I know, Coach was never disciplined for his error in judgment, an offense that today would result in his dismissal and a sizeable payout by the school's insurer. Back then, the incident ended with Coach bandaging Stovern and sending the kid to his next class.

Coach was not only my gym teacher: He was also the ninth-grade basketball coach. I started playing roundball in sixth grade as a Piedmont Panther under Mr. Childs's watchful eye. Our team sucked and I was one of the suckier players. I could dribble with my right hand like crazy, so much so, Mr. Childs labeled me the "Dribbling Fool." But I couldn't make a lay-up to save my life. My left hand was useless. I was short, slow, easily winded, lacked vertical, and had no shot. Despite these inadequacies, Dad filled my head with wild notions and paid someone to erect plywood backboards and steel hoops with nylon netting on our garages to encourage my hoop dreams. Eddie and I spent hour after hour in front of his or my garage, shooting, rebounding, dribbling, playing H-O-R-S-E and one-on-one until sweat dripped from us like rain. Eventually, Eddie became tall enough and savvy enough to make varsity, though before his transformation, we were both cut from Denfeld's B-team. Dispirited, we formed a team of similarly rejected players that played in a church league at Westminster Presbyterian. After a marginal season playing rec ball, I took the hint. Eddie? His Nordic resolve pushed him to spend more time perfecting his jump shot until—in our junior year—he managed to stick on the Denfeld varsity.

In seventh and eighth grades, if you went out for basketball, you made the team. The best five guys played most of the game. The remaining players split time and if you were an end-of-the-bencher like me, you saw a few minutes in the fourth quarter, tops. I don't remember much about those contests except I do remember playing at West Junior, getting in when West still had its starters on the floor. I found myself—at five-foot nothin' (sorry, Rudy)—guarding Don Brandt who already stood six-three. Gangly and skinny and uncoordinated as he was, Don would make a name for himself at Denfeld, garnering interest from Tulane—where he turned down a full ride, deciding instead to enlist in the Army after telling Eddie (his best friend in high school), "I hate basketball."

175

When I got inserted into the game to guard Brandt, it must have been my coach's idea of a joke.

As inglorious and humbling as that debacle was, when ninth grade rolled around, the grade when Coach Nelson took charge and selected players based upon ability, I still tried out.

"I need new shoes," I told Mom.

"OK. I'll pick up some Keds at JC Penney."

That wasn't going to cut it. Keds weren't serious basketball shoes: Keds were for bike riding and running through backyards.

"I need Converse All Stars."

Mom had no idea why I wanted All Stars. She couldn't know, having zero interest in basketball, that showing up in Keds, no matter how I may or may not have improved my prowess the summer between eighth and ninth grade, the summer we moved from 2402 Chambersburg to 2921 North 22nd Avenue West, would have made me a laughingstock. Dad intervened and I got my All Stars.

Despite hours of lobbing a basketball at the hoop affixed to our new garage, dribbling in circles on the concrete apron, and seeking to will my weak left hand to do something, anything, when I tried out for Coach Nelson's team, a team that (Did I mention this?) would be cheered to victory by Sue and Vicky and Jody and other cute cheerleaders, I was the first kid cut.

I was despondent. Tommy Jones, a boy from the West End who showed up barefoot (his family was very poor) made the team after Coach snagged Tommy a pair of All Stars from the school's lost and found. The day the team's roster was tacked up on the bulletin board outside Coach's office (my name being noticeably absent) I was so upset, I didn't take the bus home. I had a good cry as I walked uphill to Piedmont, lamenting what a raw deal I'd gotten from Coach.

Sometime during my inglorious trek, truth interceded.

Time to grow up, I told myself. *It's not Coach Nelson's fault. If I want to play at Denfeld, I need to get better. Maybe Coach has some ideas.*

"What can I do for you?"

It took a lot for a small, timid, spectacled kid who'd just been told he sucked to knock on Coach's door.

"I thought maybe you could tell me what I need to do to make the Denfeld B-team next year."

Coach looked at me, I'm pretty sure thinking: *For starters, maybe find some athletic genes and grow a foot or two.* But that's not what he said. "You have a lot of areas to work on," was the gentle way he put it.

I swallowed hard, bit my lip, and blurted out an outlandish request. "Maybe I could practice with the team to get better."

Coach eyeballed me. "Oh?"

"I'm not asking to play. Just practice."

The wizened former Marine studied me. "Oh, what the hell. But during games, you'll sit in the stands."

I nodded, thanked Coach, and flew out the door.

Two weeks later, after running lines during practice until I was ready to puke, Coach called to me as I headed for the locker room: "Munger. My office."

Crap. He's seen enough.

Coach's door was open. He was sitting behind his desk reading paperwork when I rapped on the wall.

"Come in."

I entered and stood in front of Coach's desk.

"Have a seat."

I sat.

Coach smiled. "How's it going?"

I expected the guillotine blade to drop and remained mute.

"Do you think you're learning anything?"

I nodded but couldn't speak.

"Cat got your tongue, eh?" Coach Nelson reached behind his chair and pulled out a red and black Lincoln Vikings jersey, shorts, and socks. "I guess you made the team after all. Keep working hard," he said, tossing the uniform at me, "and maybe you'll get in a game."

I caught the clothing and cleared my throat. "Thanks, Coach."

"No promises, Munger. It's all up to you."

I played in a few games including one where Coach assigned me to guard George Kenezovich, Stowe Junior High's star. I only got in for the last few minutes but playing at home in front of my friends—some of whom didn't even realize I was on the team—was really something. Though I was a full head shorter than George, I held him scoreless. With a minute left on the clock, I managed to get free for a cross-court pass. I caught the ball, dribbled like mad with my right hand, switched to my always weak left, and drove the lane. George caught up to me as I started my lay-up and batted the ball away. In the process, he slapped my wrist and because I was in the act of shooting, the ref awarded me two free-throws. I'm pretty sure the game wasn't tied or anything. I wasn't a guy, like in the movies, in line for fame. Still, I'd never scored and was given the opportunity to prove to the crowd (and to myself) that Coach's faith in me wasn't misplaced. I stood at the foul line and received the ball from the ref as kids in the stands shouted, "Make 'em Willard"—a nickname coined by friends as a bow to my famous uncle.

I missed both shots.

The next year I was cut by Denfeld B-team Coach Doug McIver and endured another tearful walk home. Decades later, Coach McIver and I happened to be sitting next to each other on the Denfeld auditorium stage as inductees into Denfeld's Hall of Fame. I was being honored for things that have nothing to do with athletics. Doug was being inducted for his years of service as a coach and activities director. As we waited for the program to begin, I reminded Doug he'd cut me. His eyebrows twitched and his face tightened. Sensing I'd made him uncomfortable, I smiled, patted Doug on the shoulder, channeled Richard Nelson, and whispered: "Relax Coach. You made the right call."

SUNDAYS

Dad had his faults but he also had his positive attributes. Honesty. Integrity. Steadfastness in friendship. Fierce loyalty to his children bordering on parental love. He also bestowed upon Dave and me an appreciation for the out-of-doors. While I likely experienced more time in the woods and on rivers and in a fishing boat or canoe with Dad than Dave—and certainly more than Anne—he tried his best to instill the wanderlust he'd experienced as a boy hunting and fishing rural Otter Tail County in his kids.

When I was in elementary school, Dad lugged Grandpa Jack's heavy cedar strip and canvas Old Town canoe to the headwaters of the Lester River. Sundays after church, Dad and I would gather our gear and head to our "secret spot." We'd drive down a rutted logging trail, park the car, walk over a questionable timber-and-tie bridge, and open a gate. On the other side of the gate, Dad would flip the heavy Old Town over, lift it from its resting place, and portage it to a beaver pond fed by the Lester. I'd follow Dad carrying our rods, his tackle box, a landing net, our bag lunch, and cans of soda and beer. We'd paddle around the pond—Dad in the stern, me in the bow—until Dad found a place that seemed "trouty." We'd stop, cast our hooks, sinkers, and dew worms into the brackish water, and wait.

When beaver dam a stream, trout end up confined unless and until nature or the DNR (using chainsaws or dynamite) eliminate the impediment. While the water remains pooled, the fish eat and eat and eat, growing larger than they would if they were swimming free, which is why my father kept the pond a secret. While we fished, Dad would sip Hamm's beer and I'd drink Hire's root beer or Nesbit's orange soda. We fished, drank, talked, and ate sandwiches and chips and candy bars. We did well fishing that spot—so well, Dad decided to share our secret with Aunt Sukie's first husband, Cliff.

I previously wrote a brief reflection of Sukie's second husband, Paul Pederson. Whereas Paul was a sincerely great guy, Sukie's first husband, Cliff—though he was nice to me and all—was an asshole. To be fair to Dad, at the time, Cliff's propensity to beat my auntie wasn't public knowledge. That little secret wouldn't come out for a few years. The Sunday Dad invited Cliff to join us at the beaver pond, the adults fished from the Old Town and filled their creels with trophies. I fished from shore, near where the Lester exited the pond, and caught trout identical in size to the puny brookies I pulled from Keene's Creek, just a stone's throw from home.

On brisk, autumnal Sundays after church, Dad would load the family and whichever dog was around into the white Dodge Dart—or later, the Jeep Wagoneer—and head north; Dad's twelve-gauge Browning semi-auto cased and stored in the back of the car near the dog. Dad was on the prowl for ruffed grouse. Finding a birdy spot, Dad would exit the car, release the dog, open his gun case, load the Browning, and walk trails that even my father—a guy who loved to get his vehicles stuck—wouldn't chance. I'd walk alongside Dad. Occasionally, he'd shoot a bird. Mom and my siblings stayed in the car listening to the Vikings game playing over the radio. I remember—after passing gun safety and Dad buying me my first shotgun (a single-shot Stevens twenty-gauge)—grouse hunting with Dad; joining him on those trails as his equal. That was a rare occurrence, one that transpired only a handful of times. But on those Sunday afternoon hunts, Dad fostered in me—and likely in my brother and sister—an appreciation for leaves bursting into color and an affection for crisp air. To this day, fall remains my favorite time of year.

I have to make a confession here. One Friday afternoon after school, Bruce Patterson and Mark Kirby and Mark Olson (from Harvey Street), and I were tooling around in Patterson's car, listening to Johnny Cash and Neil Diamond on Bruce's Lear eight-track player, bounding over backroads in rural St. Louis County. I can't remember if we'd shot any grouse but while walking a trail, we spotted a porcupine in a spruce tree methodically chewing away, minding its own business, not offending anyone or anything other than the tree.

"Bet you can't hit it," Patterson chided.

We stopped beneath the porcupine and, despite the hunting ethics ("You don't kill things you're not gonna eat") drummed into my head by Dad, I took aim with my Stevens twenty-gauge and shot. The poor critter tumbled out of the tree and landed with a "thud" at my feet. The shame I felt at that moment—taking an animal's life for no good purpose or reason—remains with me to this day.

Since Duluth had no outdoor public swimming pools, another Sunday after-church ritual in the summer was driving to Wisconsin to go swimming. When the weather was shitty in Duluth but nice across the St. Louis Bay, the Mungers would pack swimming suits and towels, climb in the family car, and head across the High Bridge (later renamed the Blatnik Bridge in honor of our Congressman). Our destination was Smitty's Supper Club in Solon Springs. Smitty's had two things going for it: great, old fashioned supper-club-style dinners and a heated pool.

Dad would park in Smitty's lot. We'd tumble out of the car, change into our suits in bathrooms adjacent to the pool, and dive in. I'm pretty sure Smitty's is where Dave, and maybe Anne, learned to swim. I know Dave didn't learn to swim when I tossed him off a dock into Caribou Lake! That's beside the point. We kids had a ball jumping and splashing, our parents joining us in the water. After they toweled off, Mom and Dad would take naps or read books in the afternoon sun on lounge chairs; Mom sipping her brandy-seven, Dad relishing his Windsor-water. When we'd had enough of the pool, we'd dress and find a table in the restaurant and order dinner.

Smitty's was one of the only places in the area that served frogs' legs. Once I was brave enough to try them, I ordered frogs' legs every time we visited. I didn't order them because of their taste. Even cooked to perfection (and Smitty's did just that), deep-fried amphibian appendages are a bit like chewing rubber chicken. But being able to tell Eddie—whose large family rarely dined out—that I'd eaten a frog; well, that made Sunday afternoons memorable!

THE BIG ONE THAT GOT AWAY

Dad rigged a dead smelt on a hook and gave the rig a toss.

Splash.

"We'll let it sit on the bottom and hope a big laker or northern swims by."

Bundled against early May's cold, I nodded and accepted the outfit rom Dad. I placed the well-worn fiberglass rod in the crotch of a pine tree and we walked back to our rented cottage in search of warmth.

My family was staying at the end of the Gunflint Trail for the Minnesota fishing opener. The cabin that Mom, Dad, Dave, Anne, and I occupied overlooked the ice-jammed shores of Seagull Lake. The sun was not yet up. As Dad and I walked, I felt the sting of retreating winter being released from the lake's decaying ice.

Inside the cottage, I fell asleep watching my old man wind spools of monofilament line onto fishing reels. I was supposed to be helping. Dad had complained about my lack of concentration when I allowed line to slide off the spool and clump on the floor. He'd muttered something untoward and took over my job before I fell asleep.

"Get up Mark," Dad said, nudging me.

"Gotta sleep," I mumbled.

"It's time to go!"

I got dressed, ate a bowl of cereal, and followed Dad out the door all the while wishing I were a six-year-old kid like Dave, or female like Mom and Anne because they got to sleep in.

"Something took the smelt," Dad said as we approached the rod we'd left in the crotch of the tree.

Dad set his tackle box and aluminum rod case down on frozen ground to pick up the bait-casting outfit.

"Holy moly!" he exclaimed. "Must be a big northern."

I watched Dad battle his monster. Our fishing partners—Dick Lee and his son—were on the dock readying their boat and came over to investigate the commotion.

"What's up Harry?" Dick asked.

"Got a big one here, Dick. It's taken all the line out. I can't budge it."

I checked the reel's open bail. There were only a couple of revolutions of line left on the reel. The fish was out deep and reluctant to come in.

"Let's use my boat and see if we can't chase it down," Dick offered.

"Sounds good. I'll hold the rod. You drive. Mark, we're gonna need your help."

Dad kept steady pressure on the fish as he entered Dick's run-a-bout. The Johnson outboard was already idling. Dick's son and I loosened ropes securing the boat to the pier as a sliver of dawn appeared in the east. Dick nudged the throttle into reverse. The run-a-bout backed into a fresh breeze as Dick eased the boat through fragile ice.

"It's trying to get under a log!" Dad shouted over the din of the engine, reeling furiously as the boat chugged towards the lunker.

"Mark, get the net," Dick said, shifting the throttle to "forward". "It's under the seat."

I found the landing net and joined Dad in the open bow.

"It's surfacing."

"Keep up the pressure. You don't want to lose it!"

"I think I know what I'm doing, Dick."

"I know you know what you're doing."

As the boat cut a swath through declining ice, Dad struggled to keep the fishing line from being severed by the sharp edges of the ice.

"It's coming up!" Dad yelled.

My family spent two Minnesota fishing openers on Seagull Lake. The incident I'm writing about took place during our second year fishing the Far North. Seagull was, at the time, the place to fish. In the spring, the Seagull River is full of big-bodied, spawning female walleye that even a so-so fisherman like me can hook and land. I did just that later in our stay, hauling in three walleye over five pounds, the biggest of which topped the scales at ten pounds thirteen ounces, a mountable trophy that Dad simply carved into fillets. The next year, Dad bowed to pressure from his high school buddies, and he and I stayed at the Scott Cabin and fished Whiteface Lake on the opener. Accepting Bob Scott's invitation began a tradition that continues to this day; fifty plus years of male bonding that has been interrupted only once; by the COVID epidemic. Over that long span of time, the Scotts, the Mungers, the Listons, the Lundeens, the Nelsons, the Nickalas, and the Tessiers have fished, argued politics, played smear, drank beer, and bonded as men and boys in a way that's a throwback to a bygone era. We've watched the Scott Cabin expand into the Scott Home where Bob and Patricia Scott spent their retirement. We've witnessed our own maturation and a similar transition of our own sons into men. We've also been blessed to bring our grandsons to the opener and introduce them to the heat of the sauna and cold dips in the Whiteface mere days after ice-out. We've witnessed the aging of our fathers, their deaths (they're all gone, Dad being the last to pass), and the dwindling of participants until only the Scotts and the Mungers make the trip. There are too many memories from such a lengthy, blessed association with a kind, giving family (especially Patricia Scott, who has allowed fishermen to invade her home for six decades) to chronicle here. Suffice it to say: Dad's acceptance of Bob Scott's offer was one of the best decisions Harry Munger ever made.

A feathered torpedo exploded from ebony water.

"It's a loon!" Dick Lee exclaimed. "Harry, you caught a loon!"

"Shit."

Too tired to take wing, the loon settled on the water's surface and swam in crazed circles.

"I'll come alongside it so Mark can scoop it up with the net," Dick said.

I leaned over the bow.

"Be careful."

"Don't worry, Dad. I'm not about to go swimming over a bird."

The boat chugged ahead. I dipped the net under the loon. As I lifted Dad's trophy, the bird shook its head with vengeance.

Snap.

The line broke. The loon pushed itself out of the net with its wings—fishing line trailing from its mouth—and plopped into Seagull Lake. Dick shifted the Johnson into neutral. As dawn broke, we watched the loon cock its head, flap its wings, release a piercing laugh, and disappear.

THE DAY CARSON GOT SHOT

I'd just completed the DNR's gun safety course, meaning I was supposedly mature enough to handle firearms. This story will cause you to question that notion.

"Let's go shoot some squirrels," Carson Osbourne suggested, as if firing a rifle within the Duluth city limits wasn't illegal.

It was autumn. The birch were golden, the maples fiery, the aspen, just coming into glory.

"My dad's guns are locked up," Carson continued, bemoaning the fact that his father was wise enough, and knew his boys well enough, to take precautions.

"I can get my .22," Ricky said before adding, "but I don't have any bullets."

The proper term, I'd learned in gun safety, was "cartridges." A bullet is a projectile that erupts from a cartridge when the firing pin strikes the base of the cartridge igniting the gunpowder and causing an explosion which propels the bullet. Because I was the youngest kid present, I didn't correct Ricky's error.

"If we only had some bullets ..." Carson said aloud.

"I can get some," I offered.

There was a bandolier of .22 cartridges hanging in my bedroom closet.

"Then do it!" Carson said.

Shortly thereafter, we entered the Woods and followed Merritt Creek as it wound through its narrow valley. Ricky led the way. We'd loaded the rifle in the Osbournes' basement with my cartridges and then, with full knowledge we were in the wrong, set out to violate the law. The trail cut through forest, across an aspen-encroached-field, and ended at cliffs overlooking Skyline Parkway. Skyline is a two-lane ribbon of serpentine asphalt that provides awe-inspiring views of Duluth. As we walked, we plinked at rusty cans and shot at red squirrels and chipmunks stupid enough to chatter at us. We were careful: We didn't shoot towards home. When we arrived at the cliffs, we set up beer and booze and wine bottles left over from high schoolers' "hill parties" as targets and took turns plinking.

"This is boring," Carson finally said after we'd fired off most of the cartridges. "Let's head back."

Because Carson Osbourne was, as you learned from the pellet gun story, not a person to trifle with, Ricky and I complied. As I followed Carson down the trail, Ricky—still carrying the rifle—followed me. Somewhere during our ill-fated journey, my gun safety instruction kicked in.

I'm not supposed to be in front of the guy with the gun.

I stepped off the trail, let Ricky pass, and joined in behind him.

Crack.

The rifle discharged without warning.

"Goddamn it, Rick, you shot me!" Carson screamed, clutching the back of his leg.

I was too stunned to think or act.

Regaining his balance after tripping, Ricky looked at the .22 as if it was possessed. "I forgot to put the safety on," he mumbled, clicking the gun to "safe" as he spoke.

"Goddamn it, Rick you shot me!" Osbourne repeated, collapsing to the ground. "No. I think it's just a rock splinter from a ricochet," Carson added, tears streaming down his face. "Goddamit, Cigar, help me up!"

The kid was twice my size. He wasn't fat—just husky. I leaned down so he could use me for leverage. Carson winced as he regained his feet.

"No. Goddammit, Rick, you shot me," Carson muttered, holding the thigh of his injured leg—it's been so long, I can't recall which one. "Rick ..."

Carson was about to ask Ricky, who was bigger, older, and stronger than me, to help him limp home. But Ricky was nowhere to be found.

"Fuck! The little chicken-shit took off," Carson said. "Well, you're all I've got, Cigar."

As we staggered down the trail, Carson came up with what, in his mind, seemed to be a brilliant cover story. He had a bullet buried in his thigh or his ass. There was a hole in his blue jeans where the bullet had entered but there was no exit wound. He needed a doctor and we both knew we'd have to deal with Carson's dad. Which is why, as he limped along, Carson came up with a whopper of a tale.

"There were these guys, you see."

"Uh huh."

"They were on the ridge above us."

"Uh huh."

"One of them said, 'Hey, isn't that Doug Osbourne's kid?'"

I held my tongue.

"My dad deals with some very bad people, real assholes," Carson explained. "So these guys, they figure out it's me and they say, 'Let's get him.' That's when we heard the shot." He grimaced, took a deep breath, and continued limping. "One shot. Got that, Cigar?"

I nodded.

We arrived at Carson's house. I helped him through the sliding glass door into the basement, hoping against hope no one was home. Doug Osbourne heard the commotion, came downstairs, saw his son was hurt, and helped Carson up the stairs to the main level. After we entered the living room, Doug started asking questions and Carson started spinning lies. Doug—a skilled cross-examiner—dragged an equally false version of events from me in fits and starts and inconsistencies. After hearing our stories, Doug left to make phone calls. One was to Wilco Ambulance. Another was to the Duluth Police Department. I didn't know it at the time, but Doug also made a third call. I had no idea Carson's dad was on to us but given I had the empty bandolier tucked inside my jacket, when Doug left the living room, I figured it was my cue to book.

Between the time I left Carson and walked in the back door of my house, I ditched the bandolier in my shack; a lean-to where Eddie and I spent time sipping lemonade and studying the lingerie section of Sears catalogs we stole from our mothers. We also borrowed a book on how to sketch nudes from Eddie's mom (Liz was a terrific artist) to peruse in the quiet confines of our retreat. We even stole one of Liz's bras that we studied in the privacy of the shack, thereby satisfying whatever curious thoughts pre-teen boys have about their mother's underwear. On the day Carson Osbourne was shot, I tossed the bandolier into my hideout, confident I was getting away, with—well, not murder—but something close.

"What'd you put in the shack?" Dad's voice was even and calm as he confronted me at the back door.

"Nothin'."

Dad didn't ask twice. Doug Osbourne had called and alerted Dad to the "fishy" stories we'd told, after which Dad had watched me ditch the bandolier. After I entered the kitchen, Dad grabbed me by the scruff of the neck, opened the door, marched me to the shack, and shoved me inside. "Get it!"

We walked down Chambersburg to the Osbournes where a Duluth black-and-white, an unmarked squad, and an ambulance idled with emergency lights flashing. We arrived just as paramedics were sliding Carson, who was strapped to a gurney, into the ambulance. A plain clothes detective joined Carson before the crew shut the doors, hit the siren, and the ambulance sped away. Dad handed the bandolier to a second detective and I spilled the beans before a single question was posed. Uniformed officers drove me to Ricky's house in their squad car, knocked on the door, and were escorted by Ricky's sister—Carol—into Ricky's bedroom where they found my co-conspirator hiding under his bed.

I'm pretty sure Doug and Harry told the cops, despite the fact we hadn't committed a serious crime, to "Give them the works." This was before Duluth had a juvenile detention facility. Mom became an advocate for the Arrowhead Juvenile Center (AJC)— spending countless hours traveling the country touring detention facilities as a member of the steering committee promoting the construction of a "kid jail"—after Carson got shot. I think she did that charitable work to prevent me from spending my adolescence in adult jail. But when Ricky and I were brought in, "Give them the works" meant hauling two scared-shitless-kids to police headquarters to be photographed and fingerprinted like adults. This "scared straight" approach must've worked. While I don't claim sainthood, I never rode in the back of a squad car again.

A week later I was waiting for a city bus to take me to Lincoln Junior and encountered Carson Osbourne at the bus stop.

"Hey, Cigar," Carson said, approaching me on crutches, his wound having healed but, according to scuttlebutt, the bullet still lodged inside Carson; the projectile too close to his spine to be excised. "Why the hell did you cave?"

I was petrified that Carson was going to whack me with a crutch but he never made a move towards me.

"I had them all fooled," Carson explained as the bus pulled up. "The cops at the house, my dad, the detective in the ambulance, the nurses, the doctors; they all believed my story."

I was certain Carson was spinning another yarn but I held my tongue as the bus door swooshed open and Carson Osbourne hobbled aboard.

DUCKS ON A POND

"Those look like bluebills," Dad whispered.

"Where?"

"In the middle of the pond."

I narrowed my eyes. A knoll rose behind us, sheltering the pothole though there was no wind, no weather to speak of on that day. My eyes, far younger than my father's, took far longer to focus.

"I see 'em," I finally replied. There were a half-dozen or so dark objects bobbing on open water.

"Stay low. Take the dog with you and come in behind them," Dad whispered. "They'll likely fly towards me so I can get a shot."

I nodded. Cradling my Stevens twenty-gauge in my arms, I waded through thick brush surrounding the edge of the pond. My black Labrador—Deuce II—pranced in front of me, his heavy tail beating a cadence in anticipation of a retrieve.

I lowered my profile. Oily water oozed between my boots as I sank deeper and deeper in bog. The dog's weight was evenly distributed across his paws, allowing him to stay atop the marsh. I wasn't so lucky. Muck and water climbed up my chest waders until I was shin deep in goo.

The ducks couldn't follow my progress because reeds and marsh grass blocked their view. I stopped and looked back at Dad. He was standing in a thicket, his shotgun resting across his chest waiting for the ducks to take wing. Deuce panted, his slick black fur shining in the sunlight, his bright brown eyes staring at me, as if to ask: "Why are you so slow?"

"Let's go, boy," I urged, prompting the dog forward.

"Other," Dad yelled.

I looked towards the other shore—the far shore—of the pothole. Sweat trickled from beneath the brim of my baseball cap. Moisture leaked from my armpits. I stopped and removed the cap. Balancing in the muck, I wiped perspiration from my forehead with my jacket sleeve. My black rimmed athletic glasses, preposterously ugly but functional, clouded up. I wiped them clear with the edge of my T-shirt.

"Other," Dad yelled again.

I resituated my ballcap. My eyes strained. I didn't see anything unusual, anything noteworthy, on the far shore; nothing but row upon row of defiant trees accentuated by light. Luminous birch stood in stark contrast to the largely monochromatic forest.

"Other."

Deuce's square ears were on full alert. Mud dripped from the hem of my jacket. A patch of alder allowed me to close on the ducks without detection. I raised the Stevens in anticipation of the birds' hurried flight but they remained on the water. I lowered my shotgun and resumed creeping.

Dad continued to yell. Deuce quickened his pace. My heart pounded. My quarry paddled just out of range. As I emerged from cover, it was obvious I'd been discovered. My prey had been watching me from the moment I left my father's side and had given me a wide berth. I patted Deuce on the head. A smile crept across my lips and I wondered how many times Dad would retell the story about his oldest son being hoodwinked by a family of otters.

LOSING A DOG

There was talk early in my parents' marriage of buying a cabin on a local lake. That never happened even though once, when a woman who was part of my parents' "dinner club" died far too young from cancer—leaving behind a despondent husband, a couple of kids, and a small cottage on Rose Lake—Dad entertained making an offer on the place. He didn't and given his lack of carpentry and mechanical skills—traits vital to owning a cabin—Dad's declination was a sound decision.

Mom grew up spending summers at her family's resort—Buena Vista—on Bear Island Lake in northern St. Louis County. She knew her way around a bucket of minnows, docks, boats, and outboard motors. I'm pretty sure Mom wanted a lake place to re-create the best of her childhood; a timeless experience chronicled by Aunt Sukie in her memoir, *Back of Beyond*. Though circumstances never aligned to fulfill Mom's desire, she did, when she divorced Dad and married my stepdad Duane Tourville, end up building *three* homes on water. As I write this story, Mom lives in West Duluth—in a townhome on the edge of the Western Waterfront Trail that boasts a view of the St. Louis River. Suffice it to say, in the end Mom got what she wanted.

Northern lakes are part of my heritage. As an infant, I accompanied my parents on fishing trips before I could walk. There's a photo of me as a toddler in a wooden boat, life jacket pulled tight, looking wide-eyed in anticipation of adventure. I remember that, during one of those early fishing trips, we visited downtown Winnipeg where I was totally and completely enthralled by the city's rubber-tired electric buses; modern versions of trollies serving the Manitoban capital.

The first cabin Harry rented for an extended period, he did so with his law partner, Blake MacDonald. There was nothing rural or rustic in that cabin's clapboard-sided construction. The cottage was located on Big Lake outside Cloquet. I'm pretty sure Dad didn't rent the place for us kids. I was twelve, going on thirteen, when we spent the first two weeks of July on Big Lake. I was too young to pilot the boat we had at the time, a used eighteen-foot run-a-bout Harry bought from one of his poker playing pals. That boat was powered by a seventy-five-horse, two-stroke Mercury outboard that coughed and gurgled and sent plumes of blue smoke into the air. The Merc was too powerful and too temperamental for a kid to operate. With no boat available, my only option was to fish from a black, rubber innertube for sunfish; fish that were abundant in the weed beds clogging the bay in front of the cottage.

I've disclosed the second issue with the cabin on Big Lake. Not only was there no boat for me to tootle around in; the shoreline was weedy and the bottom was muck. If you ventured out beyond the sand the owners had trucked in to form a beach, you sank up to your knees in loon crap. Good fishing, yes. But horseshit for swimming.

The summer we vacationed on Big Lake, I was finally fitted with eyeglasses. The first time I dove off the dock, I did so with my glasses in place. There was no hope of retrieving them from the mud. It took Mom a week to get me new specs; an expense Dad was none too happy to fund.

The saving grace to the cabin on Big Lake was the fishing. I'd take my rod and reel, a box of nightcrawlers, a small plastic tackle box filled with hooks and bobbers and sinkers, put a board across an inner tube, place my worms and tackle on the board, and shove off. I'd catch sunfish and bluegills at will. Dad was always up for fish dinner and when he arrived after work, he cleaned panfish wearing his sports jacket, slacks, dress shoes, and a tie.

The following summer, Mom found a rental on Caribou Lake north of Duluth. That cabin was another clapboarded bungalow. It wasn't some nostalgic lake cottage; it was pretty much, except for the fact it didn't have a basement, like our house on Chambersburg right down to the wood-burning, brick fireplace used to warm the place at night.

Dad never took a day off from work during the week, which was disheartening. The tradeoff was that I had the use of Dad's ten-foot Lund duck boat outfitted with a ten-horse Evinrude Uncle Paul had given Dad. Unlike the time I spent on Big Lake fishing from an inner tube, I was able to explore the entirety of Caribou Lake by boat. I never wore a life jacket when I went out fishing for walleye, crappie, bluegills, sunnies, and perch; but I always, with one sad exception, had Deuce II with me.

I say "with one sad exception" because the memory of what I'm about to write is as clear today as it was fifty years ago. I was sixteen. Dad was, as I've pointed out, busy with his law practice, leaving Mom and I and Dave and Anne to enjoy the fruits of his labors without him. It was a sunny, warm weekday. I decided to fish a weed bed across the lake. I noticed a dog barking while I fished but didn't put two and two together. I'd left Deuce chained to a tree in the shade with a bowl of water within reach. It never dawned on me that the dog making the racket was mine. As I sipped cold Nesbitt's orange soda and munched on a Snickers bar, hauling in a sunfish or a bluegill every so often, putting keepers on a stringer, tossing the wee ones back, I didn't realize the barking had stopped. I weighed anchor, lifted the stringer into the boat, pulled the starter rope on the Evinrude, took a spin around the lake, and headed for the cabin.

"Where's Deuce," I asked Dave as I pulled up to the dock and noticed the dog wasn't on his chain.

My brother was playing with Tonka trucks in the sand. Dave was big for his age, a fair athlete (he made the majors in Little League that summer) but sensitive to loud noises and arguing, which, given our parents' dynamic, is likely the reason he continued to have intermittent nighttime "accidents" late into childhood.

"Dave?"

"Mom told me to put him in the car."

It was over eighty degrees. The car Mom was driving was a 1964 Pontiac Grand Prix. The coupe was black with a vinyl, burgundy interior.

"When?"

"Huh?"

"When did you put Deuce in the car?"

Dave's eyes grew wide. "Mom told me to ..."

"When Dave?"

"Maybe an hour ago."

"What the hell!"

I tore off the dock. The Grand Prix was parked in the open. There wasn't a cloud in the sky. I could see the car's four windows were cracked open. I heard women laughing inside the cabin and remembered Mom was having her garden club over for lunch, the likely reason why, with Deuce barking, she had Dave put him in the car. I opened the front passenger's side door of the Pontiac. "Goddamnit!"

I scooped the unconscious Labrador into my arms and ran towards the lake. Deuce's eyes were closed. He was breathing in shallow, raspy breaths that did not bode well as I waded into the water.

Mom walked onto the cabin's front porch. "What's wrong?"

I turned, my eyes wet, my arms holding the dog's head out of the cool waters of Caribou Lake and let Mom have it. "Goddamnit, Mom! What the hell were you thinking, putting a black dog in a black car in the middle of a hot day?"

"I told David to crack the windows."

"It's eighty degrees out. 'Cracking the windows' doesn't do a goddamn thing."

Mom shifted nervously on her feet. "Is he OK?"

"No, Mom: I think you killed my dog."

Deuce's eyes finally opened and his unsteady gaze seemed sad, distant, and resigned. When Dad arrived after work, he called a veterinarian and made an appointment for the following morning.

I slept on the living room couch with the dog on the floor next to me. I awoke at sunrise. Deuce's eyes remained unfocused. He'd peed on the floor; something he never did. I cleaned up the mess, dressed, and ate a bowl of Frosted Flakes. Dad, already dressed for work, sipped coffee at the kitchen table. Finished with breakfast, I carried Deuce to the Jeep and we drove to town. I whispered soothing words and petted Deuce's velvety, sable fur as he labored to breathe. One look at him and the vet confirmed what Dad and I already knew. There was nothing to do but end his suffering.

A few days after Deuce's demise, I ran the duck boat across the lake to bum around with pals from Lincoln Junior, Pete Hoch and Rory Johnson. Pete had a big, goofy looking Saint Bernard. I don't remember the dog's name. When we decided to take the Hoch family pontoon boat out for a spin, the dog insisted on coming with. We anchored the boat in the middle of Caribou Lake and Rory and I dove in. When Pete joined us, the Saint Bernard didn't take kindly to being left behind and cannonballed into the water.

"Your dog's drowning!" I yelled as the Saint Bernard thrashed wildly in the water.

Pete climbed onto the boat and tossed us a rope. Rory grabbed it, looped the line around the dog, and handed the loose end to Pete. Rory and I pushed against the dog's ass as Pete dragged the dog towards him. After a lot of grunting and swearing, Pete hauled the exhausted animal onto the boat's plywood deck.

I have a vivid memory of Rory and me treading water and pushing against the furry rear end of Pete's Saint Bernard in the middle of Caribou Lake. That episode stands out because three teenagers, working together, saved a dog.

TEACHERS

I've previously written about Miss Ness, my kindergarten teacher but I need to flesh out who and what she was. Miss Ness was a sweet, older woman, small in stature but strong of voice who commanded her charges with kindness and confidence. My memories of her are positive; even after feeling her wrath for doing something stupid (like surrounding Curtis with cardboard bricks) and spending time in a corner of her classroom for misbehaving.

I don't remember much about Mrs. Nelson, my first-grade teacher, which, in and of itself, is a positive, I guess. I mean, I didn't do anything bad enough or stupid enough to end up on her radar.

Mrs. Bard, you've learned, was the object of Tim Thorp's and my prurient (though innocent) attentions. She was very young and pretty with deep brown eyes and dark hair cut in the style of Mrs. Kennedy. She was thicker of torso and limb than Jackie but every bit as stunning. She was a gentle prodder of children who made us strive to attain our very best.

I won't spend time discussing Mr. Stevens. I've said enough about his maltreatment of Tom. My view on Mr. Stevens' handling of the cloakroom incident hasn't changed.

I looked up to my fourth-grade teacher, Mr. Ames. He was smart, handsome, energetic and even though he placed the mantle of future greatness on my shoulders like a heavy yoke, I loved the guy. Still do. My niece Amy had him years later for sixth grade and confirms that Mr. Ames' enthusiasm for teaching never wavered.

My fifth-grade teacher—Miss Johnson—was a spinster who challenged me to read books that were years beyond my ken and instilled in me the love of a long-forgotten novel I later read to my sons (and one I'll be reading to my grandkids), *The Little Lame Prince*. It's a touching story about a lonely little boy locked in a tower due to infirmity, likely the source of my affection for sad laments.

Then there was Mr. Childs. As I've described in another story, I started sixth grade unable to see or hear. I was in jeopardy of failing Mr. Childs' class at a time when I was being considered for Miss Hollingsworth's special class. Robert Childs was a rotund, smiling, gregarious single man who lived with his mother. Was he gay? I have no idea and I don't care. He was a gem of a public-school teacher and, quite frankly, I done him wrong.

Jan Erickson and I commuted to Lincoln Elementary to spend mornings under Miss Hollingsworth's tutelage. Afternoons, we were back at Piedmont learning math and science and art and music and participating in gym. Mr. Childs was my teacher at Piedmont for those subjects.

"That's very nice, Mark," Mr. Childs noted one day as I experimented with watercolors.

I'm not a great artist though I've always liked to draw and paint. Mom encouraged these talents, but they never developed beyond the rudimentary. Still, I kept at it, interspersing cartoon dudes and dudettes with high school and college notes. I doodled during law school lectures, which led to my being drafted by my boss at the Minnesota Office of Consumer Services to illustrate pamphlets. With no training, I became a paid cartoonist. Go figure. Point is: Mr. Childs saw something in what I was doing and I wanted to reward him for his support. Mom had one of my better paintings matted and framed. My intention was to give the painting to Mr. Childs. Unfortunately, something prompted me to give my masterpiece to Mr. Ames instead. Mr. Ames showed the watercolor to Mr. Childs and I noticed a change in Mr. Childs' attitude towards me after my betrayal.

At Lincoln Junior High we were introduced to the best and the worst of teaching. There were ancient instructors like Miss Hanson and Miss Gilmore and Miss Gleason and Miss Carroll; Miss Gleason being a favorite of mine despite her age because she taught geography. Miss Carroll was my eighth-grade English teacher and was so blind she didn't notice when Scott Bloom stood on a desk in the middle of class and made faces at her. She retired during the school year and her replacement, a petite, brown-eyed Italian spitfire from the Iron Range—Miss Infelise— was the bomb. She not only got the goofs and lollygaggers and beauty queens to toe the line; she coaxed them to do their best work. She's the one who challenged me—over the summer between eighth and ninth grades—to "do something productive." Her charge caused me to spend evenings at our rental cabin on Caribou Lake watching Merv Griffin and creating a children's picture book. I titled it (after appropriating the character from Gordy Mesedahl) *Emery Goes to Sea.* I wrote the text, Dad's legal secretary typed it up, and I added color illustrations. When I handed a fat three-ring binder to Miss Infelise at the beginning of ninth grade (she was my teacher for ninth-grade English as well), she was incredulous.

"You've got to be kidding me!"

Despite the woman's diminutive size, Miss Infelise could be formidable. I was tongue-tied.

"May I take it home and read it?"

I nodded.

Though Miss Infelise loved the book, she cut me no slack. When I ducked her class to work an extra shift selling ice cream over the lunch hour (a fund raiser for student council) she awarded me a "U" in conduct. Since I was a nearly straight "A" student (including an "A" in English) that "U" kept me off the honor roll. Whenever our paths cross as adults, I mention this incongruity. Judy just smiles and says, "And you deserved both."

The lunchroom at Lincoln was a case study in the pecking order of adolescents. You started out as a seventh grader hunkered down in a far corner, out of the scrutiny and the attention of older boys. If you were lucky, you gained respect and popularity, and by ninth grade you were entitled to sit with the jocks and other "cool" boys. Girls worked their way up the social ladder in similar fashion; their equally steep climb hopefully culminating in seating at tables populated by the very best-looking young ladies. By the beginning of my last year at the penitentiary for wayward boys, I was sitting with Lien and Thorp and Bloom and Peltoma and Carlson and Misura and Rikala and Tynjala and of course, Eddie, all of us casting sideways glances at Sue and Jody and Vicki and, yes, even Dee Dee, who remained an enigma to me. This same hierarchy was repeated in high school, though the journey to the "cool" tables was more taxing, and the wait, seemingly longer.

Industrial Arts was an eye-opener. Seventh-grade boys were required to take metals, leather working, woodworking, and plastics. Our teacher was Sidney Skinner, a bald, no nonsense bulldog of a man who scared the ever-loving-shit out of me.

Shop involved dangerous tools. Even the materials could be harmful to one's health. In metals class, we cut pieces of galvanized tin to make cheese graters and dust pans and other household items for our moms. Fabrication also involved soldering irons, the tips of which were heated to orange in gas ovens. When Mr. Skinner's back was turned, boys would rip brown paper towels from the dispenser, ignite them, and toss them into the air where fans would whisk the fireballs through vents suspended above our heads as part of a crude fireworks display. Then there were the tools we used to bend and shape and drill tin. If Sidney hadn't kept a watchful eye, one of us could have easily lost an eye or a finger or a hand.

Plastics shop was little better. We used power tools to cut and mold and join pieces of clear plexiglass into snow scrapers and letter openers. I wasn't much good at shop, garnering low "B's" for grades but the letter opener I was working on to give to Dad for Christmas was an exception to my industrial ineptitude.

"I'd like to make mine blue on one side, red on the other," I'd said to Mr. Skinner.

"Think you're up to it?"

"Yes."

"OK. I'll find you some colored plexi."

I worked on the design and the shaping and the polishing of that letter opener until I was confident I had a winner. I finished my project over seventh hour—a period when boys could come in and work on their own because only a handful of Catholics from St. Jean's (St. Jean's lacked shop facilities so it sent its boys, liberated and hellaciously free of nuns, to plague Lincoln) were working in the shop—and placed the finished letter opener in my drawer.

"What happened to your project?" Mr. Skinner asked when I approached him the next day empty-handed.

"Someone stole it."

I resisted the urge to accuse the Catholics. I had an inkling of who'd done me wrong but no proof so I kept my mouth shut.

Mr. Skinner nodded. "I saw it a few days' back. Pretty good work. I'll give you an "A" even though the finished piece isn't here for turn-in."

"Thanks."

The replacement letter opener I rushed to complete—so I'd have something to give Dad—was a piece of crap.

Mr. Skinner did not abide poor behavior. If you made the mistake of leaving your wood plane blade-down on your shop bench, you'd be in store for something like what took place between Mr. Skinner and Kenny Danielson.

Kenny was a high-spirited kid whose idea of a joke included egging on our bald teacher. One morning, not long after we'd all been told not to leave the blades of our planes in contact with the tops of the "brand new, very expensive shop benches," Kenny fashioned a plywood shield, affixed a handle, and hid the shield under his workbench. When Mr. Skinner—dressed in his every-day uniform; a white lab coat with deep pockets holding fist-sized pine blocks—noticed the blade of Danielson's plane in the offending position, he blew a gasket.

It was common for Mr. Skinner to reach into his pocket, palm a pine block, and with the flick of his wrist, wing the block underhand—like a softball hurler—towards a misbehaving student. Sometimes the block found its mark. More often than not, the kid ducked and the missile would smash into floor-to-ceiling windows overlooking Lincoln's playground. Mr. Skinner would sweep up broken glass, step up to the plywood bin, select a piece of wood, cut it to fit, and replace the window pane with plywood while cursing under his breath. On the day in question, Mr. Skinner finally met his match. When he launched a pine block at Kenny's head, the resourceful teen raised his shield.

"Hull shoots tops shelf," Kenny said—calling to mind the hardest shot in the NHL— "but Maniago makes the save!" Caesar Maniago was the starting goalie of our beloved home-state Minnesota North Stars. Every boy—hockey fan or not—knew who Kenny was channeling when he frustrated our teacher's aim. Mr. Skinner accepted defeat with muted silence: I think he respected Kenny's resourcefulness.

A braggart in shop didn't fare as well. Chuck Magnuson was a pal of Eddie's. I tolerated Chuck's self-aggrandizing only because Eddie hung out with the guy. Pretty girls liked Chuck's confidence, so being around him had its positives. But here's the thing about guys like Magnuson: Adults deduce they're full of shit. Chuck was pure bullshit and Mr. Skinner smelled it on the kid like a mother sniffing out a turd in a diaper.

Keeping order in shop class meant Suzie Smart, Mr. Skinner's pet name for the pine paddle he carried during woodworking. He had a similar plexiglass paddle for instilling order during plastics class. Thank God he never forged a similar instrument out of tin in metals or made a cat-o-nine-tails out of horsehide to enforce order during leatherworking!

Mr. Skinner wasn't shy about displaying his cudgels and, if need be, giving a disobedient boy a whack on the ass to remind him who was boss. One morning, boys stood at the door waiting for the bell to signal the end of class. Chuck Magnuson attempted to leave early and, as he grabbed the doorknob, he was lifted off the floor by the scruff of his neck.

"I'm sorry, Mr. Skinner," Magnuson whined. "I was just opening the door so everyone can get to their next class on time!"

Whack.

Suzie Smart connected. "Bullshit! You stay in class until I say otherwise!"

Whack.

Magnuson started to bawl.

Whack.

"Are we clear?" Mr. Skinner asked, his big hand holding fast to the kid's scrawny neck.

Magnuson nodded and wiped tears from his face with a shirtsleeve.

"Good," Mr. Skinner said, lowering Magnuson to the floor.

I had other notable teachers and recall other memorable incidents at Lincoln. There was also—in the seventh-grade math class taught by Mrs. Early—the death of a classmate to mourn. Dawn Johnson, Dawn's father, and another girl were staying at a hunting shack when all three were asphyxiated by a faulty LP gas refrigerator. Dawn was the first kid (other than my cousin Brice) I knew who died. It was an extremely sad and confusing time as I sat in math with Dawn's empty chair looming like a great question mark in front of me. We didn't mourn her death as a school. No grief counselors met with us or guided us through our confusion, sadness, and pain. The pit in our collective stomachs was never addressed and I can still see that sweet little girl's expressive, youthful smile over fifty years later.

There was also the death of Dennis Wright, a ruffian from the West End with a ready grin and a big heart, to deal with. Dennis was a pal of Doug Wait, the kid who helped me dispatch Danny Cummins. I knew Dennis but we weren't close. Dennis was found dead in Lincoln Park—a plastic bag wrapped around his head—after huffing oven cleaner. At the time, I had no understanding of addiction and didn't grasp the depths of this tragedy until years later when I met my future wife, René. René lived a few doors down from the Wrights. She was a good friend of Dennis' sister and knew the details. Again, there were no school-wide discussions of Dennis' passing and no interventions by school staff to help us understand or grieve.

Speaking of mortality: when I was little, maybe four or five years old, I remember sitting in the bathtub, holding my breath, and ducking underwater. I'd listen to the echo of my heart, not really appreciating life and death, simply marveling at the sound of my body at work. But then, around seven or eight years old—and I'm sure you all experienced this as well—something changed. It was like a switch got thrown. One moment I was clueless about my soul and the fact there's a spirit buried inside the body I listened to in the bathtub, and the next instant I was staring out my eyeholes cognizant of being a live, breathing personage. That weirdness was eventually followed by an all-encompassing fear of death. This realization of a limited lifespan manifested as nightly crying jags in the darkness of the bedroom I shared with my brother. I was twelve years old when the notion, the reality, that we're not here forever, hit home. The fact that Dawn Johnson died around that same time added certainty to my new-found understanding of the fleeting nature of life.

Eighth-grade boys were required to take wood shop and electricity. Both sections were taught by a guy who thought he was funny. Mr. Wahlberg's jokes were corny and, though he envisioned himself as "cool" and "with it," he was anything but. He was also a bit of a sadist. When students went from making pine corner shelves in wood shop (I think Mom still has the one I made) to learning about electricity, Mr. Wahlberg made it a point to engage us in "hands on" learning. He'd have the boys (girls weren't allowed to take shop) stand in a circle, hold hands, and the first and last guys in line would grasp leads connected to a hand-cranked DC generator. The circuit complete, Wahlberg would start cranking the generator's handle like he was churning butter. As the electrical current grew stronger and stronger, pain eventually caused the weakest link in the chain to let go.

We suspected Mr. Peterson—our eighth-grade drafting teacher—of keeping booze in a floor safe in his closet. I believed the rumors because I detected liquor wafting from him whenever he checked my work. But what's more memorable than Mr. Peterson's boozing were the antics of his students while his back was turned. Tim Beardsley, a Piedmont kid and a real cut-up whose mom ran a small eatery in the Piedmont Shopping Center, would, when Mr. Peterson wasn't paying attention, mimic our teacher's slow, cautious drawl, mumbling "Boys, boys, boys ... That's not how it's done!" Beardsley also conceived a prank involving the compasses we used for drafting. When Mr. Peterson's back was turned or when he slipped into the aforementioned closet to sample his favorite "mouthwash," Beardsley would launch his compass skyward until it stuck in the acoustical ceiling tile. Other boys would follow Tim's lead and eventually there'd be a dozen or more compasses hanging over us like miniature guillotines. Over time, gravity would win out and compasses would start raining from the ceiling. Thankfully, no one ended up visiting the school nurse with a compass stuck in his skull.

Doug Lien and I were in Mr. Francis' eighth-grade art class. Mr. Francis had the hots for Miss Infelise—or so we thought—because every day Mr. Francis sent a student to Miss Infelise's English class with a note. No one, to my knowledge, read the notes being ferried between the teachers, though we all believed something romantic was going on. Another oddity about Mr. Francis (besides the fact he spoke with a pronounced lisp) was that he brought his poodle to work. I'm not sure how he pulled it off but that dog was as much a part of art class as the students were. Mr. Francis didn't leave class to let Fifi do her business but enlisted kids to walk the dog. One afternoon that errand fell upon Doug Lien and me.

Lien had just finished a paper mâché project; a piggy bank with a twist. The bank had a trapdoor in its belly. Doug's plan was to carry the pig into a store, put the pig down atop a candy bar or a can of soda, close the trap door, and leave the store with stolen goods inside the pig. It was an untested approach to thievery that Lien decided to try out.

We walked up 24th Avenue West to Ann's Store with Fifi on a leash. Kids often disparaged the proprietor of a corner store by referring to her as "Dirty Ann." She appeared—to junior high kids—to be an unkept, blunt old woman unable to exercise patience for the gaggles of school children flooding her store to buy candy and soda and cigarettes. At a high school reunion, Sue—Ann's granddaughter—called me out for my unkindness towards her grandmother. Sue reminded me that Ann did much for the downtrodden in the neighborhood, even allowing folks to buy groceries on credit when times were tough. Because of this corrected history, from here on, it's "Ann."

We stopped at Ann's store, tied Fifi to a post, went inside and, knowing Lien was intent upon committing a crime, scoped things out. I don't think Doug actually used the pig to steal anything and when we came out of the store, Fifi was gone. We searched and searched for that damn dog until we had no choice but to return to class poodle-less. Frantic, Mr. Francis rushed the class outside to scour the neighborhood. Someone found FiFi wandering around Lincoln Park none-the-worse for her escape and Lien and I were never entrusted to walk her again.

I encountered the weirdest and least conventional of teachers in ninth grade. Mr. Waterhouse was a hippy who taught biology. Eddie tutored me in math but I was always solid in science. In eighth grade, I was selected to be in Mr. Bowker's accelerated physical science class, which resulted in my taking biology a year early.

My lab partner was a know-it-all girl who made biology a pain. We muddled through the year working side by side with no love lost between us.

One day, I was bringing a rack of glass test tubes back to our bench. I was carefully carrying the tray of breakables with both hands. As I passed Lien, he stuck his foot out and down I went. The noise was tremendous. Kids laughed at my mishap and while I was pissed at Lien, I had to hand it to him: He'd made a gutsy play.

Mr. Waterhouse's unique choices of transportation come to mind. The guy—a self-proclaimed environmentalist—

occasionally drove a Winnebago to school. The motorhome was boxy and huge and when he docked that monstrosity next to Lincoln, it took up half a block. In contrast, Mr. Waterhouse's daily ride was a Subaru; a car that made a Volkswagen Beetle look like a limousine. The Subaru's size made it a target for mischief. Mr. Waterhouse would often leave school at day's end to find boys had lifted his tiny car over the curb and onto the sidewalk. Relocations of the Subaru happened so frequently that Mr. Waterhouse started parking the car below his classroom windows to keep an eye on it.

Quirky as he may have been (he scared me off frozen pot pies by proclaiming food companies use only diseased chickens to make them), Mr. Waterhouse loved kids who embraced his Save-the-Earth philosophy. Being inspired by Uncle Willard's conservationism, I wrote an essay about the environment that was published in the *Duluth News Tribune*.

"Munger," Mr. Waterhouse said not long after the piece appeared, "come up here."

I left my less-than-beloved lab partner and made my way to the front of the class. "Yes, Mr. Waterhouse?"

"You wrote this?" he asked, pointing to a clipping on his desk.

I nodded.

"You get it, Munger. You really do!" He handed the neatly trimmed newsprint to me. "You read this aloud to the class, you'll earn an 'A' for the quarter. Can you do that?"

I was involved in speech with Mr. Nyquist so, hell yeah, I could read an essay to my fellow students. "When?"

"Now."

I stumbled through the ordeal, received an "A," and enjoyed the fleeting admiration of classmates. More importantly, my moment in the limelight convinced me there might be an audience for my writing beyond Subaru-driving hippies.

DEER HUNTING

It's known as the Liston Deer Camp. It was built by Don, Jerry, Pat, and Jim Liston shortly after WW II, constructed from wooden grain doors used in boxcars. The bunks that lined the back wall of the shack were built of identical grain doors supported by rough sawn 2x4s.

After Dad graduated from St. Paul College of Law and returned to Duluth, he was invited to join the deer camp along with Warren Nelson, Red Lundeen, and Les Pelander. At some point, Bob Scott was recruited to be camp cook, a role he accepted even though he didn't hunt.

It was a diverse cohort of young men who aged while cruising the scrub and the swamps and the glacial eskers surrounding forty acres of land leased from St. Louis County abutting Coolidge Creek. That tiny stream, free flowing, black from muskeg, and stocked with tiny brook trout that never took, defined the landscape. Over time, other shacks were built on adjacent county plots. There was a camp of guards from the Sandstone prison across the creek. The first camp on the trail leading into the Liston place was the Keppers' shack. The Davidsons were at the end of the line; where the rugged trail dead-ended.

On the far shore of Hart Lake, a brackish puddle fed by Coolidge Creek, the Privettes—guys related to my future wife—built their place. But the most sophisticated deer camp in the area was owned by Ted Hubert and his Duluth, Winnipeg, and Pacific (DWP) railroad buddies. Hugging the south shore of Hart Lake, the Hubert cabin was built of peeled and varnished tamarack logs. The interior of the Hubert place—in stark contrast to the primitive and dark and dingy interior of the Liston shack—was lighted by LP gas fixtures hung from the log rafters. The bunks were crafted from logs and the floor was constructed of planks matching the rest of the building. In the hierarchy of deer shacks, the Hubert camp stood at the pinnacle. It was built to last—which it has—surviving long after the original Liston shack and other hastily constructed, tar paper-covered buildings thrown up during the '40s, '50s, and '60s vanished.

Dad dragged dead deer behind the Skee Horse as part of camp lore. I recall slain bucks hanging from the rafters of our garage on Chambersburg, the eyes of the animals glassy and distant. The carcasses had been field dressed by Dad to remove guts with the hearts and livers saved, fried, and eaten at deer camp. The hanging carcasses awaited butchering at Wrazidlos', a chain of family-owned meat markets run by Dad's Polish drinking buddies. I don't recall being frightened or saddened by the inert animals swinging from ropes in our garage. I was simply hopeful that one day, I too would be part of deer camp.

When I was a pre-teen, Dad drove Mom and Dave and me to the deer shack to be part of a work party. Camp members had done the math. There would be scant room in the shack for their sons. The men gathered at the camp—a stack of grain doors "acquired" by Red Lundeen through his job on the waterfront at the ready—and removed the shack's rear wall. While the dads were busy with hammers and saws, boys and girls played tag and touch football in an adjacent field as our moms made lunch. The project was completed in a day. The addition, while sturdy and serviceable, was nothing like the studied craftsmanship that had gone into the building of the Hubert place.

Sons could hunt at the Liston camp after completing gun safety. Daughters were not invited. When Jimber Liston and I walked the woods and trails of the deer camp—I was fifteen, Jimber a year younger—our fathers carrying twelve-gauge shotguns, it being bird season and you just never know when a ruffed grouse or spruce grouse or a woodcock might burst from undergrowth. The September sun was high and bright. Jimber and I were on the cusp of joining a fraternity of hunters, guys who had spent more than twenty years stalking deer and erecting crude tree stands in a woodland choked with maturing aspens. Our fathers knew the land like the backs of their hands and their sojourns weren't limited to the confines of the Liston lease. A county lease simply gives the lease holder permission to erect a building. Having a county lease doesn't preclude others from using the land. Hunters from surrounding camps are free to hunt adjoining leases though, by unwritten accord, guys from neighboring camps try to stay out of each other's way.

In addition to their shotguns, Dad and Jim carried 2x4s. Jimber and I carried hammers, spikes, and saws. Our fathers built new deer stands of aspen and used the lumber as bracing. After the work was done, we sat on mossy ground eating sandwiches, munching apples, and enjoying Gurley's cookies. Jim sold and delivered Gurley's cookies to grocers so his cookies were omnipresent at deer camp and at the Scott fishing opener. As we ate and talked, a bleating sound floated across forest.

"What's that?" I asked.

"A fawn looking for its mother," Dad said.

"Sounds like a lamb."

"It does. Eat your sandwich."

I spent close to two decades walking the trails and cruising the swamps and forest surrounding Coolidge Creek. The one time I had a chance to bring down a trophy buck, I was sitting in a tree stand as Dad pushed deer towards me. It was a quiet, cold day with a trace of snow on the ground. I was bundled up, wearing Grandpa Jack's red hunting jacket and red wool pants, clutching his .25-35 lever-action Winchester in my mittened hands. I was sixteen years old and fast asleep.

Crack.

My eyes opened. Six deer paraded single file where Dad said they'd come through. My heart pounded. My breathing grew rapid. I had a classic case of "buck fever"; an onset of adrenaline so fierce and sudden my body shook like I'd emerged naked from an icy lake. I raised the Winchester, placed the peep sight on a magnificent buck, squeezed the trigger, and sent seven shots—every bullet in the gun—in the eight-pointer's direction.

"What happened?" Dad asked when he found me on the forest floor looking for evidence I'd hit the deer.

"They came through just like you said they would," I replied. "I didn't see them until they were almost gone."

"You shot seven times and you didn't hit one?" Dad had been pushing the deer so he knew he'd sent a posse of whitetails my way.

"I think I hit the buck," I said hopefully.

"Let's take a look."

Several birch trees bore evidence of my panic but no hair or blood or tissue was found.

I inherited a .30-30 Winchester saddle gun from Grandpa Jack when he gave up hunting with his brother Stutz and their nephews Jim and John Sale. I shot a few deer with that ancient lever-action but I never again experienced a herd of whitetail taunting me like I did on the day I peppered that birch tree with bullets.

Over the years, as the sons—John and Tim and Poncho Scott, Jimber and his cousin Jackie Liston, my brother and me, Dave Lundeen, and the Pelander boys—became part of the fabric of the hunt, the need for more space became apparent. That need led Jim Liston and Red Lundeen to enlist Dad in thievery.

As far as I know, the owner of the building we took was never consulted. There was no money paid, no permission granted for us to dismantle an old shack and haul it away. Our dads simply stole a building. There was also the added intrigue of having Harry, never the steadiest hand at pulling a trailer, tow the dismembered building across rural St. Louis County; the load far too heavy for the Jeep's towing capacity but the trailer—built of plate steel that could carry a Titan missile—up to the task. Not far into our clandestine mission, Dad driving, me sitting in the passenger seat, Red and Dave Lundeen and Jim and Jimber Liston following in Red's car, the load shifted, causing the trailer to jackknife. Once the dust settled, things were resituated, and we were back on the road.

A floor was built, the walls were set in place, a roof was added, tar paper was laid down, a coal stove ("liberated" from a DWP caboose) was installed, doors and windows were hung, and bunks were built. The episode took but a single Saturday, likely a record for the dismantling, transportation, and reconstruction of a stolen building.

Jimber, his cousin Jackie, Tim Scott, and I slept in the new bunkhouse safe from the farting and snoring of our fathers. We learned quickly to go easy on the coal. The stove was meant to heat a space twice the size of the new shack and, with only a few scoops of coal, burned so friggin' hot, it was like a Finnish sauna without the steam. The first year of the bunkhouse was also the year Jimber and Tim shot nice eight-point bucks, likely the only time the camp had two trophy deer hanging from the dressing board at the same time. Wandering all the way to the Jim Ready Trail—a journey of five miles one-way through forest, bog, and swamp—I saw plenty of deer poop and piss marks in the snow and buck rubs on trees but shot nothing. That was my deer hunting methodology. I'd grow restless, tired of watching chickadees flit about and red squirrels skitter through dead leaves or pine martens undulate across the forest floor. I'd unload the Winchester, lower it to the ground by a rope, climb out of my stand, untie the gun, reload it, and meander. I might encounter a doe or a fawn on my walkabouts, but given I didn't apply for doe permits, I never shot a doe hunting at the Liston camp. In fact, the only time I shot a deer hunting alongside Coolidge Creek, I was using Dad's over-under twenty-gauge with slugs and sitting in a stranger's stand.

I'd decided to quit deer hunting. Dad begged me to give it one more go. I relented and arrived in camp ill-prepared and, having given Grandpa Jack's Winchester to my brother, borrowed Dad's Ruger twenty-gauge loaded with slugs to hunt. A guy from the Davidson party came upon me after I killed a buck. I was kneeling next to the first decent deer I'd ever shot, trying to gut the six-pointer with a pocketknife. I'll spare you the details regarding my dustup with the guy. I've written about it elsewhere. But that verbal fracas, as well as the argument that occurred later that night when my old man got into it with Red during a "friendly" poker game, the dispute causing a bout of discord such that my brother Dave and Poncho (both deep in their cups) started crying, sent me over the edge. I stood up from the table, gathered my meager kit, said "That's it," exited the shack, fired up my Dodge Dakota, and drove home with the dead buck in the box of my pickup.

Years of heavy drinking, arguments over petty grievances, and hunting with hangovers took a toll. So too did the death of Jackie Liston at age seventeen. Jackie and two other Morgan Park kids crashed into a bridge abutment not far from their homes, the cause of their deaths clear in the alcohol content of their blood, the accident happening right before deer season, leaving Jackie's empty bunk as a stark reminder that life is random and fleeting and unfair.

This is not to say that when Dad came to my house in the middle of the night trying to get me to rescind my resignation from deer camp, I couldn't be moved. He banged on the door. I answered in my underwear, let Dad in, and stood in the kitchen while he made his pitch, but his impassioned plea didn't alter my decision.

To be clear, on the night it all blew to hell, Red Lundeen hadn't caused the ruckus. He and my brother and Poncho and I were playing poker when Dad said something untoward. What Harry said, I can't recall. But I know this: Red wasn't the instigator. He bears no direct fault for me quitting the deer camp that night, though Red's earlier actions <u>did</u> factor into my decision.

In years he didn't pull a doe permit, Red would shoot a doe and use another hunter's permit to cover his ass. Party hunting is OK if guys are willing to share their doe permits. That wasn't the situation. Red would get buck fever and shoot deer he wasn't supposed to shoot, including, at times, fawns the size of cocker spaniels. This "shoot first and ask questions later" mentality never sat well with me. Think about it. You're traipsing about in dense forest with a bunch of hungover guys carrying high-powered rifles. If you're not completely sure of what you're shooting at, you shouldn't pull the trigger.

Dad and I always hunted opening weekend. We'd drive to the shack on Friday night, claim bunks, roll out sleeping bags, eat dinner, watch UMD hockey on a tiny black- and-white television powered by a chord running to someone's truck battery, have a libation or two, and hit the hay. Saturday morning, we were up before dawn eating fried eggs and bacon and toast before making sandwiches to take into the woods as part of our bag lunches. The fathers always made plans to meet for lunch. They'd use descriptions of where to gather like "near the big rock" or by "Jerry's stand" or "where Warren shot his ten-pointer" that none of their sons could decipher because the surrounding woods had changed. Camp veterans used a language of place and distance that forest regeneration had rendered obsolete.

We'd hunt hard, and after dinner watch the second game of the UMD series, play cards, and drink until lights out. Sunday we'd repeat our routine with the exception that, if the Vikings were on, we'd wander back to camp to eat lunch and watch the game together. After the final whistle, we'd hunt, hoping upon hope that no one shot a deer. Pulling a two hundred pound buck out of a swamp at dusk was not something anyone looked forward to.

The Sunday I'm writing about, Dad and I left camp skunked. It was late afternoon when we pulled into the Island

Lake Inn, ordered cheeseburgers and drinks, and sat at the bar, watching football on TV. The phone rang and the bartender shouted, "Is Harry Munger here?"

Dad raised a hand.

"There's a call for you."

Dad accepted the phone from the barkeep.

The only telephone near the Liston Camp was located at the Privette shack across Hart Lake. I remember that piece of trivia because, one year, as I sipped beer and played poker in our shack, Ken Hubert—an old friend from Miss Hollingsworth's class—came looking for me. My wife René had called the Privette camp in a panic. René's a Privette; a second cousin to Jerry Privette, the patriarch of the camp bearing his name. Ken just happened to be at the Privette shack when René called so he drove over, found me, and gave me a ride to the Privette shack. It turned out that René and Matt—our oldest son—were throwing up and fighting the runs and René wanted me to come home.

"But I'll miss hunting."

My perspective didn't sit well with my wife. I patched things up by getting Mom to take Dylan—our second son—who was crawling through puddles of puke in his jammies.

The point of this sidelight is that the call Dad answered at the bar came from the Privette shack.

"Red's in trouble," Dad said after hanging up the phone.

"Why?"

"He shot a moose."

Dad dialed the DNR and informed Officer Gawboy that he was an attorney and that one of his clients had just shot a moose—though Dad didn't break attorney-client privilege and divulge the offender's name. Gawboy agreed to meet us at the carcass. We picked up Red and met the DNR officers on the Comstock Lake Road. The officers followed Dad's Jeep into darkening forest in an old Ford station wagon. As we bounced along, Dad quizzed Red. It was clear from Red's demeanor that he'd shot the moose in haste; the result of another bout of buck fever.

"Over there," Red said, pointing to the middle of clear-cut. "She's over there."

"What the hell?" Harry asked, ire obvious in his voice. "You mistook a thousand-pound moose on open ground for a deer? What the hell is wrong with you?"

Red hung his head. I felt sorry for the guy but sorrier for the dead moose. The track got rougher. The Ford had difficulty keeping up. When the Jeep rolled to a stop next to the bloated moose, we got out. Not wanting to bottom out their station wagon, the DNR guys parked a distance away. We waited for the officers and then walked with them in silence across open terrain. At the cow moose's final resting place, we stood in November's chill, new snow dusting the ground, the sun setting. Officer Gawboy glared at Red—a former high school football and hockey star, a guy my dad first met when they fought over a basketball at the Welsh Center in West Duluth. Though the Native American officer held his tongue, Gawboy's disdain made it clear he knew who'd committed the crime. As the officer removed a skinning knife from a sheath on his belt, bent over the animal, and began to gut the moose, a haunting sound—akin to the baying of a distressed heifer—drifted across empty land.

"Her calf," Gawboy said. "It won't make it through the winter," he added with disgust.

We used the Wagoneer and a chain Dad kept in the Jeep to drag the moose to the Ford. The Ford was pulling a trailer and there was a winch mounted on the trailer's tongue. Officer Gawboy yanked rope from the winch, looped it over the moose's head, cinched it, returned to the trailer, and began cranking. The calf continued to wail as its dead mother left a bloody trail across snow. Once the moose was secured, we went our separate ways.

Dad agreed to have a "bump" with Red. We drove to Duluth's East Hillside, parked in the street, and entered the Lundeen house. I sat in the kitchen sipping hot chocolate, trying to avoid spilling the beans to Carol—Red's wife—as Red and Dad talked in hushed tones and downed shots of whiskey in the living room.

The moose steaks Officer Gawboy dropped off at Dad's law office as a "thank you" were mighty tasty. But the memory of that moose calf bawling as Officer Gawboy gutted its mother left me with doubts; doubts that merged with other circumstances and led me to finally retire from the Liston Deer Camp.

MY VILLAGE

I've written about the adults who guided me but I feel I've given them short shrift.

Dad, as ornery and thin-skinned and absent from parenting as some of my stories make him seem, was always in my corner. He was tough, yes; hard to live with, for sure. But Dave and Anne and I always knew we could count on Harry Munger. It's just that having grown up supremely independent, Dad sought to control every aspect of his life, his marriage, and our behavior. There was no compromising with Harry, which, given Mom was just as stubborn in her own quietly, assertive way, led to trouble between them; trouble that simmered and then boiled over.

Mom was our protector from familial turmoil even though I later learned her over-spending had much to do with Dad's upset. She was in charge of the family budget, a task Harry finally figured out Mom was ill-suited for. Truth is, Dad wasn't much better with money. He had a tendency to waste hundreds—if not thousands—wagering on cards or dice and betting on sports. I never knew how much Dad won or lost. I just know he never hit it big and Mom constantly complained about his gambling being a source of economic distress.

Mom loved us and sheltered us and tried her best despite a tendency to spend the weekly family grocery allotment on frozen food and second-rate meat (including something called "mock chicken legs" made from discarded pig parts skewered on a stick). Dad, given the poverty he'd experienced growing up, was understandably egocentric. I'm not sure where Mom's stinginess emanated from. Her upbringing was not, so far as I'm aware, filled with the sort of economic dread Dad's origins included. Grandpa Jack worked steadily—first in the mines, and then in sales—with nary a pause in employment. Grandma Marie was Normal School educated, possessing a poet's heart and a love of nature, music, and the finer things in life despite being married to an immigrant whose education ended in eighth grade. Why it is that Mom clutches to things worn out and unneeded, I don't know.

What I <u>do</u> know is that, even in my early teens, when I loathed Dad, I knew he loved me. I also instinctually believed my untoward feelings about Dad would pass. They did. What followed was a decades-long truce that evolved into love. I'll write more about that one day since the scope of this memoir will end long before that moment of rapprochement occurred. But you should know: We came to an accord, that things got better between us.

I never doubted Mom's love. Not a once. I think my urge to protect her from Dad's ire when things went downhill—like when I stepped between them after Dad discovered Mom's affair with the doctor—was based upon the affection she expressed for me. She was also the one who started me down my writerly path by reading to me every night until I could read for myself. When I first took up a pen and wrote an epic story (*The Piratas and the Two Man,* i.e., *The Pirates and the Two Men*) in first grade, she encouraged me to keep at it. As I became a more proficient reader, Mom fed my appetite for fiction by buying Tom Swift science fiction serials for me to enjoy. The point is, whatever I have written here about her foibles and faults does not diminish the fact that she loves me and I love her.

Hillary Clinton wrote a book about villages raising children. That's certainly true in my case because older relatives, neighbors, and friends of my parents played an essential part in making me the man, for better or for worse, that I am.

Grandma Munger made sure I was fed and content when I was in her charge. She was a straightforward cook who ensured I got the first cookie hot out of the oven. Grandpa Harry was gone before we could get sufficiently acquainted, but I recall him being very patient and quiet. Grandpa was a simple man who lived a simple life. A gardener even if he wasn't much of a farmer, I toddled after him into his unkept vegetable garden to pick raspberries; a treat that remains a favorite summer snack when covered in sugar and doused with milk.

Grandpa Jack Kobe—the only one of my grandparents to immigrate to America—never talked about being from Slovenia, a tiny European enclave that became part of Tito's Yugoslavia. I think Grandpa Jack kept the past in the past because, as an Eisenhower Republican, he didn't want to be associated with a communist dictator. Mom said I had Austrian heritage (in addition to English, German, Scots, Irish, French, Welsh, Dutch—and I learned later through DNA testing, Norwegian), which in the strictest sense is true since Slovenia was part of the Austrian

Empire when Grandpa Jack emigrated. Despite Grandpa's reluctance to talk about his roots, he was a heck of a role model. He took me hunting and fishing, loaned me his double-barrel Savage .410 when I took gun safety, and made sure I attended innumerable Masonic holiday parties with him. I remember—after he married Nancy—riding in his Plymouth sedan to visit the Grants—friends of my grandparents. This was long before cars had seat belts. I didn't ride on the rear bench seat of Grandpa's car; I stretched out across the deck of the rear window and fell asleep. Talk about faith!

Grandpa Jack, more than anyone except Mom (who ferried me to and from sessions with innumerable merit badge counselors), had his chest burst with pride the night I walked across the well-worn wood floor of the Piedmont Community Center to become an Eagle Scout. Grandpa became a Scout leader in 1927—just before Mom was born—having finished a Scouting leadership course in hopes his first child would be a boy. He and Grandma Marie had two girls, so Grandpa's Boy Scout training was never used; a bit of family history I didn't learn until after he died.

It was also obvious how much Grandpa Jack's younger sister—Great Aunt Ann—and Grandpa's younger brother—Great Uncle Steve ("Stutz")—cared about family. They greeted us with open arms whenever Dad and Mom and the three Munger kids stopped by to visit. Ann and Stutz shared a two-story, white house in Aurora because Ann's husband, Big Jim Sale, died before I was born, leaving Ann to raise two sons—Jimmy and Johnny—on her own until Stutz moved in to help out. There was always potica (Slovenian pastry) and hot food on the table when we stopped to say hello.

Grandpa Jack's other sister, Mary, was a bit dour. Whereas Great Aunt Ann reveled in a good joke and playing penny poker and teasing her grandkids and her great nieces and nephews, Great Aunt Mary was somewhat cranky though never unkind. I hated it when Mom and Dad would have Mary stay at the house when they were gone. Though I was old enough to drive, Great Aunt Mary tried to enforce constraints upon me that were more appropriate for a toddler. I was much happier when Mom tagged her aunt through marriage, Lizette Barber, to watch over us. I could wander off and do whatever. Great Aunt Lizette was a hands-off sort of gal who didn't care what I was up to.

I didn't get to know Grandpa Jack's younger brother Joe until his later years. He looked a bit like Grandpa and the brothers shared a wry sense of humor. Great Uncle Joe had been a miner in the Ely underground iron mines, one of thousands of Slovenian Americans who worked on Minnesota's Iron Ranges. I only met Great Uncle Fred—Grandpa Jack's other brother—once or twice at Kobe Family Reunions. I didn't really get to know him before he passed away.

So many relatives played a part in my becoming a decent (I hope) human being, father, husband, citizen, and man. Grandpa Harry's sister, Great Aunt Margaret Munger Miller, though I didn't get to see her often (she lived on the old Munger farmstead in Otter Tail County) always remembered me at Christmas and on birthdays and other special occasions; sending me a few dollars from her salary as a schoolteacher; penning thoughtful notes about life and faith in cursive beautiful enough to be framed.

Grandma Munger's sister, Great Aunt Linda Zuehlsdorf Clambey, always welcomed us to her farm outside Fergus Falls. When Linda's son Kenny and his daughter Kathy and Dad and I would come back from fishing with a bucket of sunfish, Kenny's wife—Margaret—would clean them faster than any man and Great Aunt Linda would fry the fish for us.

During one visit to the Clambey farm, I remember disregarding Linda's admonition not to enter the pasture next to the barn. I was exploring the forbidden field when a bull came loping over a hill with his head down and his horns pointed in my general direction. I ran faster than I knew I could, ducked beneath the bottom strand of fence wire—the bull only a few steps behind—and collapsed. Aunt Linda found me, brushed me off, and hustled me to the farmhouse; the stays of her corset creaking with every heavy step, her house dress clinging to her ample body in the heat.

"I told you not to go fooling around the bull pasture," Great Aunt Linda admonished.

She made us lunch. I sipped cold milk and ate peanut butter and homemade raspberry jam on thick, freshly baked bread while Linda sought to calm my frazzled nerves.

Aunt Elsie Munger Winter, Dad's only sister, made sure that though she and her husband, Ernie, lived near the poverty line, every Christmas and birthday present I received from her was something special. She filled my toy box with Marx and Remco playsets; the Alamo, Cape Canaveral, Normandy Beach, the Mounties, and many more. When I was too old for toys, she'd stuff a plastic ice cream bucket full of Mexican wedding cakes—my favorite cookie—she baked for me every Christmas. Her husband Ernie—a soft-spoken WW II Veteran—was supportive and hired me to work at his service station despite my inability to comprehend automobiles.

Uncle Willard. What can I say? Over forty years as a Minnesota state representative. Built the service station that Ernie and Elsie ran. Constructed his own motel. Was the general contractor for his brick house on Indian Point. Hired me to work at the motel and on Indian Point. I met governors and senators and mayors and congressmen and a host of other folks—infamous and famous—over innumerable breakfasts at the Willard Motel Café.

There was always a hint of conflict between Willard and Dad. A seventeen-year gap in their ages caused Willard to assert age as advantage. As an example, loud disputes fomented like clockwork whenever Willard made stuffing for the Munger holiday turkey.

"You need more sage," Dad would say, watching Willard prepare a meal in the motel's kitchen.

"Nope. It's good," Willard would reply.

"And you need more onion."

"Harry, I've been cooking since you were in short pants," Willard would retort, his voice rising, his ire climbing, "I think I know how to make stuffing!"

Their arguments would inevitably turn to politics where, despite both men being Democrats, more sparks would fly. But just as the conflict between Dad and me was founded upon love, so too were the disagreements between Willard and Harry founded on a strong, deep, and abiding affection—thorny as it appeared—for each other.

My mother's only sibling, Sukie, made sure I was a cultured young man. She took me to movies and to concerts performed by the youth choir of her Lutheran church. I spent considerable time at her home in Benson, Minnesota when my parents were off doing other things, so I also bonded with her husband Paul, one of the best men I've ever known. Aunt Sukie didn't come to be married to Paul, a confirmed bachelor-farmer, pilot, outdoorsman, and scratch golfer right out of the gate. She first married Cliff, a guy who, while nice enough to me, beat the ever living shit out of my aunt. At eight years old, I watched in horror as Sukie collapsed in our kitchen in the throes of what looked to be an epileptic fit. In reality, my aunt's seizure was the physical manifestation of a nervous breakdown caused by domestic abuse. It was pretty scary stuff to see someone you love whisked away by ambulance when you're a little boy. She finally escaped her abuser (after her hospital stay, Sukie was taken in by Great Aunt Mary in a supreme act of familial love), found Paul, fell in love, moved to Benson, had two daughters, and nurtured a slew of grandkids and great grandkids all the while encouraging my interest in writing.

Paul Pederson was a fine mentor. When I stayed with Paul and Sukie in Benson (one of the most boring places in Minnesota) he took me golfing, let me plink gray and fox squirrels with a .22 at the Pederson family lake cottage, and brought me to the local grain elevator to observe how corn is graded. He was going to teach me to fly, his vocation being that of a flight instructor. I flew with him a few times. In fact, Eddie got to ride with us from Duluth to Virginia and back in one of Paul's airplanes. When I turned fifteen, Uncle Paul gave me a "how to fly" manual to get me started. Then he had a heart attack. Though he survived, Paul lost his license to fly, ending my chance to become a pilot.

Dad's oldest sibling, Uncle Bob (who was twenty years older than Dad and had moved off the Munger Farm before Dad was born) wasn't around much. But Bob and his wife Alma (I think she was spouse number three; Dad learned a lot about serial relationships from his eldest brother!) would occasionally visit Duluth. When my cousins Sheila and Shaun and Kevin were young, Dad and Uncle Bob took my brother Dave, Cousin Kevin, and me up the North Shore to fish brook trout on the Temperance River. We hiked alongside railroad tracks in waders until Dad found a path to the river. We fished away the day, catching trout after trout, a glorious introduction to my favorite kind of fishing.

One July, when Bob and Alma were in Duluth to visit, I piloted the three of us around Island Lake in a rented boat (Bob brought his own outboard) in search of walleye. The boat was a little twelve-footer. The wind was whipping and the waves were high so I beached the boat. We fished from shore, just Bob, Alma, and me casting for walleye and eating sandwiches and crisp apples and sipping cold bottled beer while shooting the breeze.

Other adult role models during my childhood, including neighbors such as Romayne and Joe Urie and Ed and Liz Salveson and Elwood and Pudge Ramfjord and Paul and Joy Vesterstein had a hand in raising me. Then too, Mom's and Dad's high school friends had a profound, positive influence on my upbringing. My parents' dinner club; the Listons, the Monsons, the Lundeens, the Nelsons, the Scotts, and the Tessiers; a crew that stayed together—partying and carrying on for over fifty years—consisted of solidly loyal, hard-working, hard-loving, and hard-living men and women; couples who befriended an impressionable, somewhat unorthodox young boy and helped him become a man.

GOD, FAITH, & MYSTERY

I was raised Episcopalian but always wanted to be Lutheran. Eddie was Lutheran. Many of the prettiest girls in Piedmont Heights were Lutheran. I attended Wednesday morning Bible study and vacation Bible school at Eddie's church, Christ Lutheran. It would have been logical for me to be Lutheran—the faith of my paternal side; or Roman Catholic—the faith Grandpa Jack left behind when he emigrated from Slovenia. But I was steeped in the Americanized branch of the English church because that was the brand of Christianity my maternal grandmother professed. Mom had the upper hand when it came to matters of the soul, and my parents—despite Dad's Lutheran upbringing—were married in St. Paul's, Duluth's largest Episcopal church. It's the church where I'd marry a Roman Catholic girl. It's also where my sister got hitched. Just so you don't get the wrong idea, my family didn't attend St. Paul's, a big stone and timber Tudor cathedral located in Duluth's posh East End. My family worshipped at a little mission church, Holy Apostles Episcopal, located at 57th Avenue West and Elinor Street in West Duluth. It's the church my maternal grandparents attended. It's the church Mom and Sukie grew up in. Given that history and Mom's no-nonsense approach to faith—her "this is what I believe so you will too" version of evangelism there wasn't much chance of Mom allowing me to turn Lutheran.

Though it's no longer a church, Holy Apostles remains a tidy little building covered in cedar shakes painted deep cocoa brown with white trim. During my childhood, the congregation scraped together enough money to remodel the front entrance and add storage space, a basement classroom, and an office. Given the small population of Episcopalians in Duluth (ours was the only Episcopal family in Piedmont Heights), Holy Apostles shared a priest with other congregations. The yoked churches (variously St. Andrew's on Park Point and Christ Church in Proctor and St. Andrew's in Cloquet) owned a rectory, a house where the priest and his family lived. Eventually, the rectory was sold and the priests who came to nourish the small, stagnant, yet faithful flock at Holy Apostles rented or owned their own homes.

Mrs. Minter was my first Sunday school teacher. She also taught kindergarten at Homecroft Elementary. She was a patient, kind lady. In second or third grade, Mom became my Sunday school teacher and was a solid instructor in terms of church history and the basics of the Old and New Testament, using workbooks to explain our faith. When I was in junior high, Mom also became the youth group director. When I entered high school, Mom's cousin, Lizette Grinden—Great Aunt Lizette Barber's only child—took over the reins of youth group. Cousin Lizette was supremely cool and good looking, having been selected "Miss Duluth" in the '50s. She's the one, along with her husband, John, a handsome, towering red-headed presence (a fighter pilot, and eventually the head of the Duluth Airport Authority) who suffered the unspeakable. It was their son Brice who, at age four, wandered out the back door of their Park Point bungalow and drowned. Lizette and John had four daughters after Brice passed away—all lovely girls—but their marriage eventually fractured, I suspect in part due to the strain of such a devastating loss.

The stodgy services held at Holy Apostles demanded patience whether we were engaged in Morning Prayer or Holy Communion. Communion—the sharing of Christ's body (thin communion wafers that tasted like Styrofoam) and blood (sweet, red wine)—was celebrated once a month. In the early days of my church attendance, women and girls wore veils. We knelt when praying, an exercise in endurance that I'm thankful now, as an old man and a Lutheran (I finally won!), I no longer experience. Though Dad sometimes attended worship with us, Dave, Anne, and I were in church every week wearing our best clothes. Mom always wore a skirt or a dress. When he showed, Dad wore a blazer and dress slacks and a necktie.

Many Sundays, we'd pick up the Peterson girls, daughters of our milk man, on the way to church. Mr. Peterson delivered milk to our house, carefully placing half-gallon bottles of cold skim milk in a small tin box on our back porch. How Mom convinced Mr. Peterson to let his girls attend Holy Apostles with us, I have no idea. The point is, when it comes to matters of the Episcopal faith, Mom is a persistent advocate!

Children were excused a few minutes into worship to head downstairs to the social hall where tables and chairs were set up and divided by chalkboards into classrooms for Sunday school. The kids were brought back upstairs during Holy Communion, lined up at the altar rail, knelt, and received Communion (if we were confirmed) or a blessing (if we weren't) before returning to class. The celebration of Christ's body and blood included accepting the wafer, eating it, and sipping from the chalice, the priest wiping the rim with a cloth napkin before the next person partook. Inside the dark, foreboding, high-ceilinged sanctuary the only color came from fluttering candlelight and multi-colored shields of the Apostles adorning a false wall behind the altar. Other than the candlelight and the shields, the church was stark, cold, aloof, and pretty darn scary.

Episcopalians are confused Christians; at least, that's my take on things. They aren't Catholic, though, with minor exceptions, they worship as such. And they aren't fully Protestant either, not having been part of the Reformation the way that Lutherans, Baptists, Methodists, Presbyterians, and other Protestant churches are. This schizophrenia of belief is best demonstrated by how Mom dealt with Good Friday; the mourning of Jesus' crucifixion.

We had Good Friday off from school. At noon on Good Friday, Mom would call us into the house. I might be on the front stoop of Eddie's playing toy soldiers. Or in the middle of a game of trench ball. Or playing tag. Didn't matter. I knew, when Mom called, it was time to go. Catholic kids, if they weren't going to Mass during the three hours of Jesus' crucifixion, stayed outside playing dolls or games or guns or riding their bikes and trikes. The Lutheran kids? I'm not sure they even knew what day it was! But the Munger kids, the only Episcopalians on the block, were summoned inside to ponder the ramifications of a thirty-something Jewish guy being tortured to death. Occasionally, Mom would dress us in our Sunday best and drive to St. Paul's to catch an hour or two of the Good Friday service held in the old cathedral. The experience was somber and disheartening. But the reward? Not a place in heaven but a sundae or a malt at Bridgeman's ice cream parlor once the service was over and the bells tolled thirty-three times; one peel for every year Christ lived on Earth. It was all mysterious and hard to understand. It was also ritual and our lives in faith as orchestrated by Mom. Dad—so far as I can recall—never attended Good Friday services with us.

When I was eight or nine, Peg Munger (no relation but married to the doctor who stitched up my eye) tried to turn me into an acolyte, the Episcopal version of an altar boy. The few times I stood at the front of the church in a stupid-looking white angel blouse and black skirt, I hated every damn minute of it. Though Mom was steadfast in her opposition to me joining the Christ Lutheran choir (Eddie had invited me), she yielded on the question of making a round peg fit into a square hole: She allowed me to quit being an acolyte.

Mom's cousin Lizette was a great role model. She made confirmation, which she structured around the Gospel of Mark, enjoyable. She was also hip in terms of dealing with teenagers; so much so, I was able to recruit my high school pal Dave Michelson, who'd fallen away from Catholicism after watching his mom suffer and die from brain cancer, to join our youth group. With Michelson and Cheryl Welsand, the Peterson girls (on occasion), the Edwards girls (also on occasion), Cheryl's brother Neil, Bob and Ron Silverness from Christ Church in Proctor, Mike Town, Scott Mork, the White kids, the Senerighis, and two Mormon gals Cheryl brought along just to make things interesting, we were a small-yet-vibrant crew that had a great deal of good, clean, Christian fun. We went to the Blacks' family cabin on Sand Lake for a summer retreat. We spent a weekend at Cass Lake Church Camp. We escaped summer boredom at the Environmental Learning Center in Isabella. We played ball hockey, skied, skated, and enjoyed great meals, prayer, and each other's company all in the name of Christ. Youth group was the highlight of my membership in a small, virtually unknown (amongst my fellow Piedomonters) branch of Christianity. And yet: I always wanted to be Lutheran. Mom wouldn't hear of it: I was confirmed an Episcopalian, married in the Episcopal Church, and remained faithful to Mom's vision of heaven until I achieved middle age.

During high school I experienced a moment of such clarity and vision and sanctimony that I swear was a visitation from the Almighty. I was going through a very difficult stretch where I had no girlfriend, my best friend (Eddie) had left me in the lurch, my face was broken out, and my parents were again in conflict. I was in my bedroom in our new house on Miller Creek. It was nighttime. I was despondent and sad and crying in my bed with Pelly—my brother's golden retriever—asleep at my feet.

It was then I felt His presence.

There was a glow in the room. A stark, white, light blinded and briefly frightened me before enveloping me in what I can only describe as all-encompassing Love. I did not see God's face. I did not touch Jesus. But in that moment—desperate and alone and afraid—I <u>knew</u> there was Someone, Something greater than myself in control of my life. It was an instant in time that I haven't tried to analyze any more deeply than this: I believed.

PHOTO GALLERY (I)

The Kobes
(Grandpa Jack is in the back row, second from left)

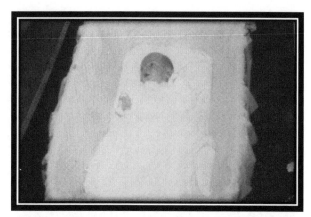

Twenty-seven Days Old: St. Paul, Minnesota

Baptism: St. Alban's Episcopal, Superior, Wisc.
Godparents Pauline and Jim Liston

November 1955

First Birthday
(Marie Kobe, Jack Kobe, Elsie Munger, Harry Munger, Sr)

Me and Dad

Success!
St. Paul, Minn. (1955)

Leech Lake, Minn. (1957)

Grandma and Grandpa Munger
and Me
(1958)

Me and Mom

Eddie and Me
2402 Chambersburg (1961)

Dad and Mom

Birthday Party (1960)
(I'm the lion)

Halloween (1960)

Missing the Ball

Labor Day Parade Viking (1962)

First Day of Kindergarten (September 1960)
(From Left: Dave Oman, me, Eddie, Karen Jentoft,
Bruce Patterson)

Kindergarten (1960)
(I'm in the third row, third from the right)

Miss Ness Retires
(1969)

The Mungers
(I'm in the first row, middle)

Eddie and Me
(The Yanks)

Me and Dave
(After the photo was taken, Dave sat on the truck!)

Mom, Me, Anne, and Dave
2402 Chambersburg (1966)

Lester River Brookies

Grandpa Jack
(Painting 2402 Chambersburg (1965))

Grandma Munger and Me (1960)

Dad with Betsie River Steelhead

The Munger Kids

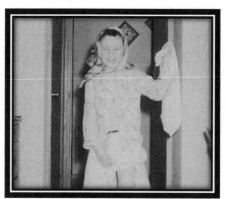

Cross Dresser (1964)

Hillbilly
Aunt Elsie holding Dave (1965)

Cousin Julie Pederson and The Munger Kids (1967)

Skyline Drive and the Ore Docks (1968)

The Woods and Merritt Creek

Miss Hollingsworth's "Special Class"
(I'm in the first row, third from right)

Basement Pelham Puppet Show with Eddie

Confirmation
Me, Dave, Anne, and the Grinden Girls

Telemark Ski Resort (1968)

Me and Deuce I

Mr. Childs and the Piedmont Police Boys
(I'm the last one on the right in the second row)

2402 Chambersburg: Big Snow in the Backyard

Me and Chief Red Fox
Wrazidlo's Meats

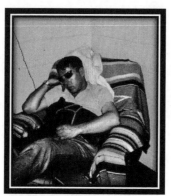

Dad and Deuce II

Me, Eddie, and Ed: Off to See King Olav
(Salvesons' House)

BOOK TWO: 2921 NORTH 22nd AVENUE WEST

We are here to help each other get through this thing, whatever it is.

—Mark Vonnegut—

BROTHERS

Water gurgles. Dave and I set up camp. An attenuated stream cascades across slippery rocks. The creek marks time in a way that humans only marginally understand. Quick, agile brook trout dart beneath roiling water. We don't have fishing rods with us. The trout are not in danger of ending up in a frying pan.

Stone towers above our tenting site. Here and there, grass has secured a foothold in the gabbro that forms this place. The ledge we've chosen to camp on is no more than eight feet wide. We call it a cliff. Really, it's just a shelf in the bedrock. We're only ten feet above the water. To a nine-year-old boy (Dave) and his fifteen-year-old brother (me), the ledge *is* a cliff.

When I was a little kid, this creek was foul. Someone got the bold idea to run a sewer line up to the airport so that human waste was no longer dumped into the stream. Funny how now, after decades of environmental activism, the suggestion of preventing sewage from being released into an urban creek harboring brook trout seems like such an obvious proposal.

By the time of our camp-out, the stream is pristine. We take the existence of native brook trout and clean water as a given. It doesn't dawn upon us that the creek could ever go back to the way it was.

I set up our two-person tent while Dave scours the forest for deadfall. The tent's green canvas has faded from sun. The mosquito netting is ripped but, because it's late August, mosquitoes don't pose a threat. The thin soil covering the ledge makes it difficult to anchor our temporary home. I don't worry: There's little wind and the overhang of the rock rising above us affords protection from weather.

Dave returns. He piles dry aspen and birch near the stone circle I've constructed to serve as a fire pit.

"Let's go for a swim," I suggest.

"Sure."

We strip to our underwear and thread our way to the creek. Rock defines the streambank. There is no beach. The water is only twelve or thirteen feet across. Earlier this summer, Scott Carlson and Dave Forsyth and I placed boulders across the creek to form a primitive dam. A pool formed behind our artificial wall but it's only waist deep. In reality, we're going wading, not swimming.

I take my time entering the creek. Once the water is over my groin, I extend my arms and hands to make sure I don't bash my face on a rock as I dive in. My brother is just learning to swim and is more cautious.

"Come on you baby," I jeer. "It's not that cold."

"I'm coming."

The sky is overcast and threatens rain as we splash each other and laugh. Our voices careen off the rocky walls shrouding our secluded paradise. We are less than a quarter-mile from our neighborhood; a neighborhood brimming with homes, families, and traffic. Despite our proximity to civilization, we hear nothing but our own squeals of delight.

"Time to get out," I say, feeling the need to make a fire and cook the hotdogs we've brought along for supper.

Water pours off us as we emerge from the creek in our wet jockey shorts.

"Here's something to dry off with."

Dave, the minimalist in our family, accepts my offer of a towel in silence. I watch as he pats water off his smooth skin. He enters the tent, removes his wet briefs, finds dry underwear, and dresses. I stand in the chilling air, the day fading to dusk, and remove my soaked underwear. I slip on dry briefs. My Wranglers are less cooperative: The trousers bunch up at my knees where moisture remains.

I wonder why I'm so at peace with my brother here, in the shadow of the bluff, and so angry with him when we're at home. I don't mean to say cruel things or pick on him. But whenever my parents are gone and leave me in charge I go after him. He's a good kid. He doesn't tattle. Maybe he should. I don't understand why I act this way. Maybe it's because my parents don't get along. Maybe it's because I'm small for my age and I'm always getting bullied at school. Maybe I feel the need to retaliate and he's just the unlucky target of my rage. Or maybe I'm just a jerk. Thankfully, no trace of this part of me intrudes as we camp alongside Miller Creek.

Fire crackles. Sparks, drawn towards the night sky by a draft emanating in the valley, spiral upward. We roast Elliot's wieners on sticks, the skins of the hot dogs blackened by flame, before sliding them into buns. We cover the wieners with catsup and mustard, drink grape Kool-Aid from tin camping cups, and talk sparingly as salt from Old Dutch onion and garlic potato chips clings to our lips.

A pair of resident mallards flies past. Diminutive tree frogs sing.

"This is neat," I observe.

"I'm going to sleep," Dave announces, his words slow and tired.

"Make sure you leave room for me."

I watch my brother unzip the tent fly and climb in. Flashlight glow frames Dave in silhouette as he undresses and slides into his sleeping bag. I stir the fire and add another log. The light in the tent goes out. My brother is soon snoring.

There is no moon. The stars are absent. A tinge of fear graces me as I look around our modest camp. After the last log turns to embers, I douse the fire, climb into the tent, undress, slide into my sleeping bag, and wonder how Dave will measure this day against all of the other days we've shared.

FOOTBALL

You've already read about my parents' close-knit group of lifelong Denfeld friends. Some of the men in the group were high school football stars. That's where the idea of trying out for the Denfeld High School B-team likely originated. No: That's only partially true. Other factors prompted me, at five foot six and just over a hundred pounds, to try out. Dad had also been vertically challenged in high school. But he matured enough to put on the pads for UMD, so Dad's football playing legacy probably had something to do with my decision. But the final piece of the puzzle as to why I chose to play football? Eddie made me do it.

During sophomore orientation, the B-team coaches—Bergy and Jake—made a pitch for boys to join the team. Eddie and I sat in the auditorium listening as the coaches implored us to give football a try. At Eddie's suggestion, we signed up. I stuck with it throughout high school. Eddie quit football after our sophomore year.

When we showed up for practice, the first order of business was selecting equipment. Steve Zanko—who'd been a pretty good varsity player—was killed in a car accident shortly after graduation but his name was still taped to the front of his old helmet. It was the only serviceable helmet left so it's the one I wore. That helmet was so big, if an opposing player grabbed the face mask, it spun on my head like a top.

Given I was the smallest kid on the team, I didn't see much action. That didn't stop my coaches, a Mutt and Jeff combo—Bergy was tall, lean, and wore athletic glasses and Jake was short, squat, and pudgy—from having fun at my expense. Kent Seaman towered over me but wasn't an asshole or a jerk, which was a good thing since our coaches found great humor in pitting me—a puny, barely pubescent kid—against Kent in "squares." Squares is a drill where two players lay on their backs, the top of their helmets nearly touching. One player has a football placed under his helmet and when the whistle blows, the guy playing the running back flips over, grabs the ball, and tries to make it past the defender. I'd spring up, grab the ball, and take off. Sometimes, I out-maneuvered the big guy. Other times, Kent crushed me like a bug. It was a different story when Kent was the ball carrier and I was the defender. My quickness allowed me to latch onto Kent, but I was little more than an ineffectual human leech attached to the big guy's leg as he dragged me across the turf.

We were playing at Duluth Cathedral. Greg Granmoe was our starting strong safety. This story is one of two I'm going share here regarding Jake and Bergy. Nice guys, sure. Well-intentioned, no doubt. But as coaches, they were putzes.

Greg went to tackle a Hilltopper. The players met helmet to helmet. The running back seemed OK but Greg was woozy and needed help finding our bench. Back then dealing with a suspected concussion didn't include taking the kid out of the game, having him examined by a physician, and clearing protocol. In 1970 when confronted by a disoriented player, a coach would pull out an ammonia ampule, break it open, place it under the player's nose, and, after checking to see if the player could tell two fingers from three, send the kid back onto the field. That's what Jake and Bergy did with Granmoe. He passed inspection and was back in the game as if nothing had happened. On the bus ride back to Denfeld, Granmoe kept insisting we were driving to Cathedral to play the game we'd already lost. It got worse. When Mom drove us home, she asked Greg for directions to his house. The befuddled kid couldn't remember where he lived. Despite his altered state, Greg was back at practice the next afternoon.

Thinking about Greg's concussion reminds me of another story. We'll get back to Denfeld football shortly but I think you'll like this diversion.

Dad asked me, when I was a junior and on the Denfeld varsity, to help him coach my brother's Junior League football team. Piedmont didn't have a team so kids in our neighborhood played for Duluth Heights. Dave was a big, brawny sixth grader who started both ways on the line. We were playing a team from the West End, kids who would eventually become my brother's teammates in high school. While on defense, Dave stopped the West End fullback with a nice tackle but, when the scrum cleared, you could tell Dave was injured.

"My shoulder hurts," he said when he got back to our bench.

"Shake it off," Dad replied.

We got the ball back and Dad sent Dave back onto the field to play offensive guard. I could tell the kid was hurting because his arm (I can't recall which one) was hanging from his shoulder like a wet towel. He lasted one play before he returned to the bench crying.

"What's wrong?" Dad asked.

"My shoulder hurts," Dave said between tears.

Dad took one look at Dave's arm and shook his head. "Mark, drive him to St. Mary's. He needs an x-ray."

I did as I was told. Problem was, because I was just a kid myself, the ER nurses pretty much ignored me until Dad made his way to the hospital. When he got there, Dad insisted that an ER doc examine Dave. An x-ray confirmed this truth: Dad had sent his youngest son back into the game with a broken collarbone.

A nearly identical instance of Bergy and Jake's coaching prowess took place on our home field, Public Schools Stadium (PSS), the field shared by all of Duluth's public high schools. I wasn't in uniform. In fact—other than playing a few minutes at a scrimmage in Hermantown (where a brawl broke out and the contest was called) and getting in for a few minutes at the Cathedral game—I didn't take the field again until my junior year.

At PSS our star running back—Dan Dillan—went down like a ton of bricks. I was in the stands with Eddie and other benchwarmers watching as Jake and Bergy evaluated Dan's injury. You could hear what they were saying, including speculation that, "It looks like a minor shoulder separation. I think we can pop it back in place." That's when assistant varsity coach (and later head coach) Marv Heikkinen stood up in the stands, vaulted the railing, ran onto the field, and stopped the nefarious coaching duo dead in its tracks.

"He's got a broken collarbone," Coach Heikkinen said. "Don't yank on his arm!"

Thankfully, Bergy and Jake followed Marv's advice. Dan went off to the doctor, and was, like my little brother, diagnosed with fracture. Though Dan's football season was finished, at least he wasn't rendered a cripple.

My junior season was complicated by the fact I'd been elected treasurer of Pyramid, Denfeld's student council. Jan Erickson—that nerdy girl from Piedmont who attended special class with me—was elected secretary. It was heady stuff, being elevated to a position of importance as an underclassman but there were a couple of things that detracted from me basking in the glow of celebrity.

My main duty as treasurer was to run the concession stand during home football games. Even though I rarely saw action, because I dressed for all home games, I had to recruit Jan to manage concessions. Then there was this: Tom Stolen—the debate coach—was after me to give up my gridiron career for, in his words, "something more suitable for a boy of your size and stature." Meaning, forego the opportunity to sit on the bench during games and gawk at cheerleaders. I demurred, full in the knowledge that Mr. Stolen was likely right but steadfastly wanting to prove him and every other detractor wrong.

August in Duluth can be hot. After a morning practice in swelter, a senior I'd just gotten to know, a big, strong kid who should have been the starting tight end but ended up quitting before the season started—Kerry Lee—came up with an offer I couldn't refuse.

"Let's get some inner tubes and float down Keene's Creek."

Kerry made his proposal after we'd showered and were eating our bag lunches in the shade of Denfeld's iconic clock tower.

"But won't Coach know?"

"He won't miss us," Lee insisted.

We ducked afternoon practice, drove to Lee's house, grabbed inner tubes, inflated them, and hauled them upstream. Keene's Creek was overflowing from rain. The water was turbid and cold and one hell of a respite from being beaten to the ground by ornery guys in pads.

Dave Griffin was a new teacher at Denfeld. I loved Griff. He made eleventh grade social studies come alive. But one afternoon, I told him I had to leave class early for a football game and he was incredulous.

"You play football?" Griff asked in a tone that suggested he thought I was trying to con him.

"Yup."

"What p-p-position?" he said through an omnipresent stutter.

"Defensive end."

Griff eyed my less-than-imposing stature. "You're j-j-joking, right?"

I shook my head.

"OK, then. D-d-d-on't get hurt."

I knew that there was little chance of my incurring injury: I wasn't even dressing for the game. Coach Heikkinen was letting me tag along on the bus trip to International Falls because, despite being undersized and slow, I worked my ass off.

A few weeks earlier, Coach had me play defensive end during practice. The scout team I was assigned to consisted of misfits and underachievers and wannabes whose sole purpose was to mimic the defense of that week's opponent. We were going up against the starting offensive unit, which included a rotation of Doug Lien (also a junior) and a senior, Brian Christiansen (nicknamed "Sugar" because he was diabetic) at quarterback. Before the center hiked the ball, I made up my mind I wasn't going to give the quarterbacks any free plays.

I lined up opposite a senior nicknamed "Tug". Tug was a nasty player, one who, if memory serves me right, got the team involved in a riot during the homecoming game with Duluth Central. Central's star running back Ted McKnight—an African American kid of such speed and talent he'd spend time in the NFL with the Chiefs and the Raiders—took exception to remarks made by someone on our team. There was a rumor floating around that it had been Tug who said untoward things about McKnight and other Central players of color. I don't know for sure how the beef started. I do remember the clock ran throughout the melee, the end result being a Denfeld loss. In any event, I saw my time on the scout team as a chance to impress Coach Heikkinen.

The first time I stepped across the line of scrimmage, Tug leveled me with a forearm to the chin.

"Come at me like that again, Pussy Boy," Tug hissed as he stood over me, the play concluded, my head throbbing, "and you won't get back up. This is fuckin' practice, not a game."

The next play I again came at Tug at full speed. But when Tug tried his patented forearm-to-the-face move, I spun on my heels, got past him, and leveled Lien.

"Munger!" Coach Heikkinen yelled. "Go easy on the quarterback."

I nodded but, having bested Tug, felt pretty damn good about myself. For the next half-hour, every time the whistle blew and I stepped across the line, Tug was waiting for me. I never got past him again, though I never quit trying. Not when Tug stood over me. Not when he hissed further warnings. Not when I had nothing left to give. I thought no one had noticed what I'd gone through. I was wrong. Paul Lund, a big, strapping kid I met as a sophomore and who became a good friend, noticed me sitting in the locker room, tears still flowing long after practice was over.

"What's wrong?"

Embarrassed, I shook my head and said nothing. I stripped down, took my shower, dressed in my street clothes, and waited outside for Mom to pick me up.

I only played in a couple games my junior year. I didn't letter. But during another practice where the starters weren't putting out much effort Coach Heikkinen blew his whistle, called everyone together, and pointed at me.

"If the rest of you had half the guts Munger has, we'd be winning football games instead of losing them."

That was it. That was the one jewel I was gifted by Coach. It felt good to be recognized, if not for ability, then for heart. That was the highpoint. Bobby Douglas and Tug and few other seniors taunting me in the locker room after practice, forcing me to my knees, and ordering me to lick the mud off Douglas' cleats was the low point. Thankfully, before lips touched leather, Ernie Conito and Ed Larrivy—also seniors—intervened.

"That's not funny, Bobby," Ernie said. "Munger, get the hell off the floor," he added, pulling me up by the collar of my sweatshirt. "Leave the kid alone," Ernie added, nodding to me, sending me on my way.

"What's the deal?" Larrivy asked, watching me walk towards my locker. "You guys have nothing better to do than pick on little kids?"

Two other stories from my junior year on the football team need telling. The first involves senior punter Tom Walczinski. Tom was a gregarious guy—friendly even to benchwarmers—who contracted spinal meningitis. With Tom out, Bruce Patterson—the reserve punter—took over. Patterson, who has long legs and is athletic, boomed the ball during practices, making everyone wonder why he wasn't the starting punter. We were going into a game with Cloquet, a team led by a big running back who was likely to give our defense fits. As we knelt on the hardwood of the Denfeld gym floor, Coach Heikkinen leading us in the Lord's Prayer, at the end of the meditation, someone shouted, "Let's win this one for Tommy!"

Patterson's first punt went straight up in the air and landed ten yards from scrimmage. That misfire was an omen: There were no fairytale moments for the Hunters that night. My *Oracle*, the school yearbook, confirms we lost 41-6.

The second story involves foreign exchange student Edgar Herrera. Edgar—who hailed from South America—lived with the Kirby family during the school year. Though Edgar lacked a clue as to how to play American football, being a soccer player, he could kick the shit out of a ball. In practice, Edgar split the uprights from forty-five yards with room to spare and sailed kickoffs into the end zone. It didn't take a genius to figure out what his role on the team would be.

Our first home game at PSS, Coach Heikkinen figured Herrera was ready to handle the kicking chores. But whether it was the lights or the crowd or the adrenaline or whether Edgar's success on the practice field was an anomaly, his first kickoff dribbled off the tee and landed a few yards past the waiting Morgan Park Wildcats. His second kickoff wasn't much better. After that, while he dressed for every game, I don't remember Edgar kicking again.

It's funny how a nasty incident can stick in your mind against a backdrop of happy memories. I always thought that the players I idolized had no clue what I'd gone through the afternoon Tug beat me silly. Turns out, at least one guy had been paying attention.

When my first novel, *The Legacy* was published, Debbie Dillan—Dan's older sister—an attractive, smart girl two years ahead of us at Denfeld showed up at a book signing to buy a copy for her brother. I haven't seen Dan since high school. He lives somewhere in Pennsylvania. I signed a copy for my classmate figuring he may or may not read it. I'd never known Dan to be anything other than an athlete, so I figured the novel was destined to become a dust collector on a shelf.

I was wrong about that. Dan not only read the book: He wrote me a letter praising my writing. That wasn't the half of it. In his letter, Dan recalled the day Tug reduced me to tears and kindly echoed Coach Heikkinen's view that I'd been "one tough, little kid".

A letter from a classmate forty years later made it all seem worthwhile.

WHITEWATER

Miller Creek defined my life from ninth grade through college. When my family moved to the house on the creek, I'd already experienced Merritt Creek—the small rivulet located near our first house on Chambersburg Avenue. But unlike Merritt Creek, Miller Creek is an actual trout stream; a place where native brookies survive and propagate. Years ago, the DNR annually planted German browns in Miller in the hopes those non-native trout would provide an additional fishery. When kids found out the DNR had stocked the creek, the browns were fished out in a week. I never caught a planted brown from the waters flowing past my house. Maybe that just proves I'm a slow learner. Or a poor fisherman.

I invited—with Mom's permission—fifty to sixty ninth graders to a party I threw at the new house shortly after we moved in. Nearly every name I've listed in prior stories received an invitation. I left Scott Carlson, a kid I'd known forever and someone I'd spent considerable time with, off the list. The slight was unintentional but hurtful all the same.

The summer we moved to North 22nd Avenue West Scott, Dave Forsyth, and I built two dams across Miller Creek. I've already detailed the dam we built to create a swimming hole. The second dam was built in front of my new house with a wholly different purpose in mind. When that dam was finished, we reached between stones and caught nearly a hundred sleek, colorful brook trout by hand. We placed those fish in a bucket and "planted" them behind our second dam. The thinking was that the trout would stay put and be easy to catch. Yeah, right.

"You forgot to invite my cousin Scott," Rod Peltoma said after I'd handed out invitations to the big party.

"I'm pretty sure I gave him one."

"Nope. He's really hurt."

"I'll take care of it."

I handed Scott an invitation the next day.

We're talking about ninth-grade boys and girls eating pizza and snacks, drinking sodas, and listening to live music (Wildflower—a band consisting of Jeff Tynjala, Steve Cordes, Rod Peltoma, and Evan Wingness—played in the basement utility

262

room) all without direct supervision. Barb and a few other moms were upstairs—making sure we had plenty of food and soda—but didn't keep close tabs on things. Maybe they should have.

"Dee Dee's in the closet with Brooks," a girl told me as I put out another pizza.

I remember thinking, *So what?* When the comely, dark-haired, brown-eyed girl opened the door leading to the crawl space beneath the stairs, readjusting her hair and her clothing as she emerged, Brooks—looking sheepish and rumpled and in need of oxygen—following close behind, I stilled the urge to ask questions. It wasn't any of my business what had gone on in the dark.

"Sven Larson's passed out across the creek," somebody told me after Bruce and Dee Dee resurfaced.

I sent Eddie to investigate.

"He's zonked out under some trees," Eddie reported, "but seems fine."

I left Sven where he'd crashed. I have no idea how he made it home but I was—as a Boy Scout and somewhat prudish kid—not going to invite a drunken ninth-grader into my parents' home.

Fast forward to my last day of school at Lincoln. Miller Creek flows past the back door of the house, tumbles down the hill, crosses beneath Piedmont Avenue, becomes Lincoln Creek and meanders through Lincoln Park before emptying into St. Louis Bay. Lincoln Park and its namesake stream are a stone's throw from my old junior high. Which is why on the last day of ninth grade I decided to dig up nightcrawlers, rig my fly rod with a hook and split shot, slip into chest waders, and fish my way to school.

It was a cloudless morning. I had that silvery slip of urban fishery all to myself as I negotiated mossy rocks and deadfall and cast towards trouty spots. When I arrived at the pavilion across from Lincoln Junior (having caught and released a handful of small brookies) I left the streambed, walked across the street, entered the school, found my locker, took off my fishing garb, and went to class.

After my last exam, I retrieved my waders from my locker and pulled them over my jeans, slipped on my fishing vest, pocketed the padlock that held my secrets safe, grabbed my fly rod and worms, closed the locker, and headed out. As I passed the office where Mr. Card and his staff were busy with paperwork, I pulled a party popper—a paper contraption with a wee bit of gun powder inside that explodes when tossed on the ground—out of my waders and hurled it against the hardwood floor.

Pow!

Confetti exploded.

Pow!

I slammed another popper onto the floor and kept walking.

Pow! Pow! Pow!

Mr. Card scurried into the hallway but was too late to catch me.

Dad had a yellow rubber life raft he bought just before we took his eighteen-foot run-a-bout from Grand Portage across twenty-plus miles of open water to Isle Royale National Park. Mom wouldn't get in Dad's run-a-bout, the boat packed to the gunwales with food and supplies for a week's stay. She also refused to allow Dave to ride with us. Mom, Dave, and Grandma Munger rode the *Wenonah*—a commercial ferry—to and from the island. That's where the life raft came in: Dad bought it as a precaution. It wasn't inflated. There was no room for an inflated raft in Dad's boat. What good an uninflated life raft would be if we ran into trouble in the middle of Lake Superior, I haven't a clue.

I was intrigued by tales of whitewater rafting on the Colorado and the Green and the Snake and the Flathead, fiercely flowing Western rivers where experienced guides took tourist-filled inflatables down dangerous rapids with impunity. But I didn't live out West: I lived in Piedmont Heights and the only water close at hand was Miller Creek.

I finally found courage the spring of my sophomore year at Denfeld to give whitewater rafting a try. Miller Creek was raging from melt and rain; brown and frothy and swift in its course. On a Saturday morning in mid-April, snow still covering the ground, the creek in flood, I inflated the raft, donned a winter jacket and stocking hat, put on an orange life preserver, and hauled the raft across our snowy backyard.

I stood at the edge of rushing water trying to decide if I was ready to risk life and limb for adventure. After brief reflection, I slipped the raft into the current, climbed in, and pushed off.

Over the course of the next week, I made a half-dozen runs down the creek in that inflatable; bouncing off boulders, hitting my ass on rocks, and being doused with cocoa-colored water. The rush was everything I'd hoped for. I had an absolute ball and never suffered harm. The raft was less fortunate. On my last voyage, the inflatable slammed into a rock, ripped open, and lost its air. After wading ashore, I carried the limp, heavy, rubber skeleton of Dad's raft home over my shoulder.

A few weeks later Dad asked me how his life raft came to ruination. I pled ignorance and despite Dad's expertise in questioning folks, he let it go.

THE LAST GAME

I was a senior. Standing on an aluminum stepladder, the rungs spattered with maroon and gold paint, I held a strand of crepe paper in my right hand and taped it to the ceiling of the first-floor hallway, the hallway leading to the Denfeld auditorium. At the other end of the roll of paper another senior, a girl, stood on another ladder.

My classmate was short, athletic, and cute. She was also a cheerleader. She was one of the reasons I decided, as a skinny puke of a sophomore, to forgo debate and try my hand at football. I knew I'd never amount to much on the gridiron. I realized early on that I'd likely ride the pine. Didn't matter. I'd gain the satisfaction of being part of a team. I'd be one of the players who, the day before a big game, got his locker fancied up by the pretty girls. I knew going in that was about the best I could expect and it was a bargain I was willing to make.

Perched on the ladder, I watched Betty, her femininity so agonizingly wondrous and mysterious at the same time. It was Thursday, the day before the big homecoming game against Central.

Back in the '40s, '50s, and into the late '60s, the Duluth Denfeld—Duluth Central game was billed as the biggest game of the year. Central was touted as our rival. By the time I was in high school, that was no longer true. Duluth East had taken on the role of Denfeld's antagonist. Denfeld kids believed East students were born to wealth. This perception made the "Cake Eaters" a far better foil than the rough and tumble kids from Central. Central was too much like Denfeld; kids largely from blue-collar homes, with an occasional poor or well-off kid thrown in for good measure. The kids from Central were more like kindred spirits than rivals.

Denfeld had defeated East the Friday before. Miracle of miracles, I'd actually been called upon to play when the contest was in doubt.

"You're starting on the suicide squad," Coach Heikkinen had said. "Don't let me down."

I lined up as the last defender on the right side during kickoffs. Standing under the bright lights of PSS, a wave of unrelenting pride came over me.

Dad never got to do this!

Although my father was a sports fanatic, a benchwarmer on the UMD Bulldogs football team, and played considerable fastpitch softball as an adult, he was too small and too slow to play high school anything. As I think about it, much of why I stuck with football in high school had to do with the fact that it was something Dad never did.

The summer between my junior and senior years, the starting quarterback—Doug Lien—invited me to captains' practices. That hadn't happened my junior year so I figured good things were in the offing. But when I showed up on the practice field at Denfeld, having driven in from the family's summer rental on Caribou Lake, my fantasy of being the target of Lien's passes was shattered.

Dave Langley hadn't played football during our first two years at Denfeld but was recruited to play our senior season. A speedster, Dave ended up starting at wide receiver and safety. Slow as mud, I spent my time working with Tommy Hill, the third string quarterback, and then—when Coach Heikkinen realized how good a running back Tommy was—catching passes from Doug's sophomore brother, Mike. Both Liens went on to play college ball and both threw nice spirals, but Mike had such force behind his throws, he could bruise your chest if you weren't careful. Before Tommy Hill was elevated on the depth chart, a highlight of my brief time catching passes from him was doing a simple slant route in front of Langley, catching the ball, making a move, and taking it to the house despite the fact Langley ran a sub-eleven hundred-yard dash. Didn't matter to anyone but me (and maybe Tommy Hill) that I'd burned the fastest guy on the team but it felt damn good.

After finishing wicked two-a-days, we'd pack our cars with sweaty players and make the short jaunt up Highway 53 to the Auto Club on Pike Lake. In changing rooms adjacent to the beach, we'd strip down to our bathing suits, clamber across hot sand, and dive in. But the refreshing embrace of Pike Lake after a day of sweating on the practice field wasn't the Auto Club's main attraction. The place was filled with bikini-clad Proctor and Hermantown girls in all shapes and sizes, a sight that warmed a young man's heart and sent one's imagination a-wondering.

The whistle had blown. The ball had been launched. My spikes churned furiously against damp grass as I ran towards the East return man. Marko was his name. He was the coach's kid. He stood motionless under a moonless October night, caught the ball, and took off. A wave of defenders forced him towards me. I wrapped my skinny arms around Marko's waist and held on long enough for other Hunters to topple him to the turf. Later in the game, I repeated my success: I sealed the edge, dove at Marko's feet, wrapped my arms around his ankles, and took him down.

Heady from success, I looked forward to the homecoming game against Central when all the seniors would be introduced under the lights. My home finale would be bittersweet: I knew that, even though I'd grown some (to 5'8" and 140 pounds), my days as a football player would end with high school graduation.

I want to explain something about a guy who was a role model to all of us in the Class of '73. His name is Russ Stover—like the candy baron—reportedly a distant relation. Russ was born with a condition that rendered him about half the size of an ordinary person and wheelchair-bound, though to label Russ "disabled" or "handicapped" would be more than a mere injustice: It would be untrue.

The way Russ tells it is, after having been mainstreamed at West Junior, when there were rumblings he'd be sent to a "special" school for students with disabilities instead of attending Denfeld, Russ' mom stepped in and told the school board, "No way in hell! My son will be mainstreamed or I'll sue your pants off." Brave woman, for sure, though Russ' attendance at Denfeld did create one small issue.

Denfeld is a three-story building, which—at the time—had no elevator, meaning Russ had to be carried up and down stairs to class. That problem was easily solved: Linemen from the football team and close friends like Donny Anderson hoisted Russ and his wheelchair into the air and carried him—like an Asian potentate—to his classes. Russ went on to have a successful career in the construction business and serve on the Duluth City Council all because he had a mother who wouldn't accept folks telling her, "That's how it has to be."

"I'm gonna start all the seniors against Central," Coach Heikkinen had said following our win against East. "We'll see what you can do."

I knew this meant I'd get another chance on the suicide squad. As I hung decorations, I cast a wistful glance in Betty's direction. If I wanted to make an impression, I'd have to make the most of the few seconds each kickoff occupied. Those moments would be mine; mine to give it my all in front of parents, siblings, friends, and Betty.

Late autumn's cold lingered in the vinyl seat of the Jeep. It was after 11:00 p.m. I needed sleep: I had a big day ahead of me. It was a fitful night. A slight catch in my throat, the result of a cold, intensified. When I awoke on game day, my mind was disoriented. Chills wracked my body. The cold had exploded into a full-blown case of strep throat. That was my annual autumn course as a child. Strep barred my enjoyment of two of the three "Red and Black" celebrations at Lincoln Junior High. I'd missed Maroon and Gold Day my sophomore year at Denfeld with the same malady. I was healthy for homecoming my junior year when I stood on the sideline in freezing rain and watched the Denfeld-Central game deteriorate into a fistfight.

It was my last year of high school, my last home game, and I was delirious and shivering. I willed myself to take a shower. I pulled on my underwear, jeans, socks and game jersey: No. 86. I really wanted No. 88 (Allen Page's number with the Vikings) but Paul—a two-way starter—picked No. 88. Exhausted, I fell onto my rumpled bedspread, wearing a number I didn't want, struck down by an illness I couldn't best.

I fantasized about getting out of bed and making it to a class, any class so I could suit up for the game. In reality, I barely made it to the bathroom to cool my sweat-soaked face with a damp washcloth.

That night, I listened to the broadcast of the game on a clock-radio sitting on the nightstand next to my bed. I heard Assistant Principal Michaels, the PSS announcer, introduce the Denfeld seniors. I wasn't mentioned. Despite my disappointment, I smiled when the Hunters took the game from the Trojans.

A week later, I walked across the Denfeld auditorium stage during a pep rally at which the senior football players were introduced to the student body one last time. Coach Heikkinen said nice things about each of us, mentioning something about me being undersized in stature but oversized in heart. That night I watched the Denfeld Hunters flail against a bigger, faster, more athletic Cloquet Lumberjack team. A blizzard raged as I stood on the sideline in a raggedy maroon and gold raincoat. My jersey remained unstained, my meager talents unused. I never got the call, never stepped on the field as the Lumberjacks rolled over the Hunters.

GIRLS

It's not like Mom didn't express love. Or that Dad, in his own gruff way, didn't evince affection. They did and in Mom's case, still does. Dad passed recently, years after we'd come to rapprochement. To say that I grew up in a loveless household isn't true. Which makes my craving for love as a child and as an adolescent all the more puzzling. Two things are certain about my quest for romantic love as an adjunct to the familial love I was blessed to receive. First, I was destined, fated, as it were, to be an unrealistic romantic. And second, I had a steadfast desire to be a hero; to be the cowboy at the end of the Western who saves the damsel tied to the railroad tracks.

A memory. I'm sitting in the living room of Grandma Munger's dusty house in Riverside. It's the middle of the day and her old black-and-white console television set is on. A movie, perhaps *For Whom the Bell Tolls* with Gary Cooper in the lead as the hero, the guy who gives up his life to save the gal he loves—a not uncommon theme in old movies—is playing. I'm fixated on the love scenes and I'm only in kindergarten. I know nothing of sex or the physical connections of adulthood. I only *think* I know something about love as I watch the movie.

I build a fort out of a chair, the couch, and an afghan, crawl under the makeshift canopy and pretend an enemy bullet has found its mark. I need medical attention. A beautiful nurse cares for me. We fall in love. I survive. A happy ending ensues. Come to think of it, maybe I was watching *Farewell to Arms.* Doesn't matter. You get the gist.

That scene from my childhood pretty much summarizes how I viewed girls growing up. My mother, an idealist trapped in a marriage that turned loveless, encouraged surrounding the connections—between men and women, and between boys and girls—with the milky gauze of unattainable love. I don't recall Dad ever being overtly affectionate towards Mom; not even when I was very small and they were still young. I don't remember surprising them with their lips locked in a passionate kiss, or hearing evidence of lovemaking from their bedroom, or seeing Dad ogle

Mom the way that I still—after forty-plus years of marriage—ogle my wife.

My take is, that desperate not to be left behind by their high school friends (seven couples that gathered for dinner parties and trips throughout my father's life; Mom was later replaced in the group by my stepmother, Kay, a blow that seemed unduly cruel) my parents started dating, *maybe* fell in love, and married. Back in the '50s, the expectation was that you started a family soon after getting hitched. Which is where I came into the picture. When Mom couldn't carry any more babies, Dave and Anne arrived. It's very likely Dave—and probably Anne—were added to the mix to save a marriage. If that was the plan, it didn't work.

All of this history, especially the mythology of my parents' group of friends—Denfeld athletes and girlfriends-turned wives—had a huge impact on me. I started life curious about girls in a very specific way, and I was looking to marry from my very first proposal to Cheryl Williams in first grade. Kind of cute, right? Or if you're the little girl or the teenager in bloom or the college coed I was chasing, maybe a tad creepy. But that's the foundation of where I was coming from and it made things difficult. For me. For the girls. Truth is, I should've been looking to replace Eddie with a female companion, not seeking some idolized version of womanhood. But while negotiating the contradictions and uncertainties of adolescence, I had the onset of puberty to contend with.

Cheri Urie, the youngest of the Urie kids, is a year older than me. She's the one I played doctor with when we were very young. She's also the one who showed me—in a picture book her mom bought her—the differences between boys and girls. There were colored drawings of testicles and ovaries and sperm and eggs in that children's book, all of which made no sense whatsoever to two kids under the age of eight. I pretty much forgot what I'd discovered in Cheri Urie's bedroom until the summer she grew boobs.

I'm not exaggerating. One day, my friend from across the street was a flat-chested little girl. The next day, Cheri and Carla Tessier were sunbathing on beach towels in the Urie backyard in bikinis; both girls suddenly needing tops for their bathing suits.

My first "date" was with Nancy, a pretty, happy-go-lucky neighbor girl whose father, Al, saved my neck when I got the Jeep stuck in the middle of Miller Creek. I took Nancy to a basketball game and a dance in seventh grade. She's sweet and all and is married to a guy who's a good friend. But the truth is, even at thirteen, I figured out we didn't have a romantic connection. Friends, yes, but that's where it ended.

Other junior high girls touched my heart. The prettiest lass in seventh grade, Sue, a sleek, long haired brunette, was "dating" (whatever that means at thirteen) Bruce Brooks. You remember him, right? The skating wiz. One day, Sue was standing outside Lincoln Junior waiting for a ride home. She lived on Skyline Drive and was either an Upper West Ender or a Piedmonter depending upon one's point of view but was so stunning, such designations meant nothing. She was crying when I walked up to her—timid, shy, and awed by her beauty—and asked her what was wrong.

"Bruce and I broke up."

"Oh."

"I'm thinking about walking home."

"Oh."

Eventually Sue's not-so-subtle hint sunk in.

"Want some company?"

"That would be nice."

We talked about non-serious stuff as we walked through Lincoln Park. I left Sue on her front porch. I was so high up in the clouds, I don't remember the rest of the long walk home. But that was it: Sue and Bruce got back together and she and I remained friends.

Jody, another fetching girl and a cheerleader (I forgot to mention that Sue was a cheerleader as well) caught my eye but the interest wasn't mutual. Getting to know Jody brought me into contact with Vicky, a smart, perpetually cheerful girl who, for all of eighth and ninth grade, pulled at my heart strings. Did I divulge that Vicky was also a cheerleader? Well, she was. But she was spoken for. Doug Lien, the best athlete at Lincoln, a guy who looked the part out of central casting and who could hit jump shots with deadly accuracy and throw a football a mile, was her beau. I was no competition for that handsome, Scandinavian, fully-developed, intelligent icon of maleness. Didn't faze me: I hung around Vicky hoping she and Doug would break up and I'd become the shoulder for her to cry on. That never happened before Vicky's family left Duluth. I attended her going-away party a few weeks after we matriculated from Lincoln. Doug was there but I was stunned when Vicky asked <u>me</u> to walk her home. We sat on her front porch in the dark, talking about her family's upcoming move to Alexandria, Virginia. We wrote letters to each other throughout high school and into college. Our correspondence continued when I joined the USMC Platoon Leadership Corps in Quantico, Virginia. Despite being in close proximity to the supposed girl of my dreams, we didn't meet up when I had liberty in D.C. A year after my stint at Quantico, Vicky wrote she was coming to Duluth to visit. She called me when she got to town and we made plans to meet up at the Shack Bar in Superior. I was pretty nervous—given the passage of time— as I sat at the bar, waiting for Vicky to show. She never did.

Maturation complicated things. I'll spare you the details of the changes a boy goes through because most of you either went through them or witnessed them first hand from the other side of the gender divide. I'll say this: The six weeks of faith-based sex education classes I completed at church and the ridiculous filmstrips we watched in junior high and senior high health classes in no way prepared me for the urgency to procreate that comes from the onset of male puberty. Whether I was a typical boy or just inordinately horny, I have no idea. But damn, what a curse puberty was! By ninth grade there were oodles and oodles of lovely, pretty, now-developed girls, wearing mini-skirts or very tight jeans or hot pants wandering the hallways, sitting next to me in class, or standing across the gym waiting to be asked to dance at school dances. I'm pretty sure that, except for one or two turns around the parquet with Michelle, an exotic Italian girl I didn't know well but who asked me to be her escort for the ninth-grade formal dance, I never danced a single dance with a girl in junior high. I was just too damn scared—given every female at Lincoln was taller than me—to ask. I was pretty much like Raj from *The Big Bang Theory*; completely tongue-tied in the company of pretty girls.

I never kissed a girl—apart from a quick press of the lips with Sandy Sletten while playing "Spin the Bottle" in eighth grade at a party at Lynn Northey's house, a group of ten of us, five boys, five girls, listening to tunes and drinking sodas and eating pizza in Lynn's basement—until I was a junior at Denfeld. That's when

Suzie Lind grabbed hold of me, pressed me to her chest, and proceeded to explore my mouth with her tongue. The arousal from that kiss, well, it was damn embarrassing; something Suzie noted and smiled at. But other than that ambush French kiss, I was totally inexperienced.

As a teen, I was fond of finding the steamy parts in novels like *The Godfather* and *Beyond the Valley of the Dolls;* books Mom was reading (was she reading them for the same reasons I was?). I'll spare you the details of such fictional encounters other than to say that my brother, who slept on the bottom bunk until we moved into the new house, grew annoyed with me.

"Why is the bed shaking?"

"I'm just rocking myself to sleep."

Given Dave was six years younger, he had no clue. I think, since he's a father of a fully-grown son and twice-married, he's figured it out by now. But then? The lie stuck, at least until we moved and began sleeping in separate bedrooms. Did Mom know? I think so. Dad? He wasn't around enough to notice what the hell I was up to, much less zero in on my late-night shenanigans.

I said before I was role modeling Mom when it came to love. Mom got that from Grandma Marie whose view of the world—all puppy dogs and rainbows and unicorns—Mom emulates. As a result, I was—and still am—an incurable romantic.

It was tough sledding for a short, immature, unathletic kid going from the top of the heap—a ninth grader at Lincoln—to starting over again at Denfeld as a sophomore. I don't remember any real connections with girls my first year at Denfeld. The party I referenced earlier, where Suzie Lind nearly choked me to death with her tongue, took place my junior year. Sophomore year, I attended a school dance or two only to stand across the gym from female classmates, too shy to make a move.

Sometime during my junior year, the drinking age in Wisconsin—a stone's throw from Denfeld—changed to eighteen. Minnesota would adopt an eighteen-year-old drinking age the summer of 1973; the year I graduated. Some bright light—having watched eighteen-year-old boys die in Vietnam—felt it imperative to give high schoolers the chance to screw up their lives with alcohol and got the legal drinking age changed. What this meant for Denfeld kids, and I'm not only talking about the greasers or

275

the stoners or the dropouts here but the entirety of the school, was that alcohol became readily accessible.

I began to approach girls I found attractive with a libation or two under my belt though nothing nefarious happened. That first French kiss with Suzie? Alcohol fueled, for sure, but harmless. And, for the most part, after Eddie and I were caught during our first night "out on the town", retrieved by Dad and deposited in side-by-side bunks in my bedroom with a curt, "You boys sleep it off and I'll call Dave's father", I stayed away from booze during athletic seasons. I lettered as a sophomore in skiing, one of only a handful of tenth-graders entitled to wear a letter jacket, which I thought would give me an advantage with girls. It didn't.

The other momentous change in my life was that after failing my over-the-road test at least twice (maybe it was three times) I became a licensed driver. The day after I passed the test, I bugged Mom to let me drive to school, a big ask since we only had two cars and three drivers in the house. Mom relented and I ended up giving Nancy and her friend Bonnie a ride home in the family Jeep Wagoneer. I was pulled over half a block from Denfeld by Officer Al Butler—the only Black cop in Duluth.

"You rolled through a stoplight," Officer Butler said, looking at the paper copy of my driver's test I handed him.

"Sorry, Officer."

"You just passed your test?"

"Yes, Officer."

He looked at me. "You Harry's kid?"

I nodded.

Butler returned my paperwork, nodded at the girls—Nancy in the front passenger's seat, Bonnie behind her—and said: "Slow down, pay attention, and say hello to your dad."

I'm pretty sure, had I asked either girl riding in my car for a date (which I was too scared to do) they would've taken a flier.

I tried to make connections with girls at parties thrown by senior members of A Capella Choir. Like I said before, I'd started life with a beautiful soprano voice. As I entered a prolonged and agonizing period of puberty, my voice changed and not for the better. By high school, my vocal range was stuck somewhere between a tenor and a baritone. The point here is that within choir there was a lot of dating. I felt left out, especially since the one girl in A Cappella who mattered, Patty—a slender senior with a killer smile—didn't know I existed. I fell for Patty but she had a boyfriend who was a senior and a star athlete. I was barely tall enough to kiss Patty comfortably and was a deep reserve on the football team.

One afternoon Mom asked me to pick up groceries from Piggly Wiggly. It was a sunny day in late May. I decided to pedal my Schwinn Varsity five-speed to the store. I'd used chore and allowance money to buy the Varsity. I'd added curved handlebars, a generator-powered headlight, and a racing seat to make the Varsity look like a ten-speed Collegiate; the top of the line in terms of Schwinns.

I picked up Mom's items from Piggly Wiggly and coasted down Hoover Street. Passing Scott Carlson's house, I realized I was going too fast. I was carrying a brown paper bag filled with groceries in my left arm. When I squeezed the right brake lever, nothing happened. The pads were so worn they couldn't slow the bike and I realized this truth: *I'm not gonna make the turn!*

I awoke at the bottom of Hoover Street to someone poking me with a stick.

"You OK, Son?" a disembodied voice asked.

It took a minute for me to piece together what had happened. I was laid out in the ditch with my Schwinn off to one side and Mom's groceries scattered to the four winds.

"You OK?" the voice, that of an old man, asked again.

I nodded. My eyes focused. The guy who'd been talking to me wandered off. I stood up and collected the bike and the groceries. Mom wasn't around when I got home. I put away the salvaged food, found a wrench, straightened the bike's front wheel, and went downstairs to shower. After toweling off, I bandaged a nasty gash on my chest, took some aspirin, and got dressed. Eddie picked me up in his Plymouth Valiant: I wasn't going to let a bike accident cause me to miss any party Patty might attend.

When spring came and the snow melted and hormones percolated, it was tradition for Denfeld kids to flock to a rocky outcropping above Skyline Drive for "hill parties." There was always a bonfire raging and beer and hard booze and Boone's Farm wine flowing at such impromptu gatherings.

"What happened to you?" Patty asked, standing before a raging bonfire with a libation in her hand.

It was awkward—given I wanted to impress the girl—to reveal the truth but I opted for honesty. "Bike accident," I mumbled.

"What're ya doing here?" Patty asked, sisterly concern obvious in her voice. "And <u>what</u> did you do to your chest?" she added, pointing to blood seeping through my T-shirt.

"It's nothing."

"Doesn't look like nothing."

That was the moment a brave boy, a boy who knew how to talk to girls, would've stepped up to the plate and said something meaningful. But before the words came to me, Patty's boyfriend appeared, and the conversation was over.

I encountered Patty years later in the Detroit airport. She was married, working as a flight attendant, and had her kids in tow. She hadn't aged a bit and was as sweet and open and unattainable as she'd been in high school. We shared a brief conversation, hugged, and said goodbye. I didn't tell Patty that—a week after the hill party—Mom noticed my face was off kilter and dragged me to the Duluth Clinic where Dr. Leek determined my nose was broken. I checked into Miller-Dwan Hospital and was put under. Doc Leek smacked my face with a mallet and torqued my deviated septum back into place. I saw no purpose in burdening Patty with such details when we reminisced many years later.

Sex was certainly on my mind in high school; especially after Eddie and I borrowed the family station wagon and enjoyed Angie Dickenson's breasts, which she proudly displayed during *Pretty Maids All in a Row*, a film we took in at the Skyline Drive-In. When we arrived at the outdoor theater in Hermantown, off-duty cops checking cars (it was buck night; you paid a buck a head to get in) confiscated our booze. We weren't miffed. We had a reserve supply hidden under the spare tire. The protagonist in the movie, a male teacher stalking cheerleaders (and eventually, a very naked Ms. Dickenson) was played by Rock Hudson. At the time, we had no idea Rock was batting from the other side of the plate as he portrayed a serial rapist and killer.

As Eddie and I lusted after Angie Dickenson from the hood of the Salveson Family Vista Cruiser, things turned to shit.

We were using the windshield as a backrest and when I shifted my weight to get comfortable, the glass cracked.

"What the hell did you do?"

I turned my head to discover a spiderweb interrupting the windshield. "Must have been a rock ding that expanded when I leaned back."

Speculating as to the cause of the damage didn't make it any easier to tell Ed Salveson his car needed a new windshield.

I dated sparingly in high school. Kim—a girl I'd known since Piedmont Elementary—and I went out a couple of times when she was a sophomore and I was junior. Predictably, I didn't have the guts to ask Kim for a date: I used an intermediary.

Leanne was a smart, engaging, sophomore who—had I thought things through—I should've asked out. But she was so self-assured, such a leap of faith seemed implausible. We became friends—despite my being nervous about her looks and poise—when Dave Griffin, our social studies teacher selected Leanne and me to represent Denfeld at a Mock United Nations conclave held at Duluth Central.

I picked Leanne up at her house in West Duluth in the Jeep and dropped her off later that night, which is when she remarked that I was "a nice guy" and should be dating. She asked who I might be interested in. I was stumped. While I'd longed to connect with a young lady, dating scared the ever-loving-shit out of me. As Leanne persisted, Kim—a pert, funny, smart, and energetic sophomore—came to mind. Leanne made the inquiry and Kim said "Sure."

I remember knocking on the front door of Kim's house, entering the living room to pick her up for our first date, and chatting with her dad. Kim's older brother, Craig—and her younger brother Chris—were members of Troop 67, meaning their dad—Dale—occasionally attended Scout outings. Even though I knew Dale, meeting him formally as the father of the girl I was taking out to dinner and a Three Dog Night concert made me shake like a leaf. I got through the first date. We had a second date where I managed to get the Wagoneer stuck in a snowbank when leaving Morgan Park High School after a basketball game. We got unstuck. I got Kim home. Though things seemed to go well, I stopped asking Kim out because I didn't know what I wanted in a relationship.

The first time I touched a human breast, the experience nearly killed me. Amy was a sophomore I met at a party. Nothing happened that evening. But Amy was so elfishly pretty and seemingly open and available, I figured I'd ask her out. Which I did, the night I puked on Principal Samskar's shoes (more on that little incident to follow). True to form, I needed to be three sheets to the wind to approach a girl. Amy was in band, playing rousers during a basketball game in the balcony of the Denfeld gym when I staggered in, sat down beside her, and asked her out.

"Wanna go to a movie?"

"With a group of people?"

"No. Just you and me an' dinner and a movie."

Amy took full measure of me and shrugged. "Why not."

Terry Maust, one of the only guys shorter than me in the Class of '73, drove. We picked up Terry's date and Amy, ate pizza at Shakey's, and sat through *Poseidon Adventure*. After the movie Terry parked in front of Amy's house and necked with his girlfriend while I walked Amy to her front door where we kissed fleetingly before she disappeared inside her house.

Riding around in the Wagoneer with Amy after another date, I parked on Skyline Drive. We found each other across the Jeep's vinyl front seat. The heater struggled to warm the car as our lips met and our mouths opened. I was thankful Suzie Lind had taught me how to French because Amy was a very good kisser. Things progressed. My hand slipped beneath Amy's jacket, under her sweater, and inside her bra. But like Hermie, the kid from a book I had not yet read but would come to love in *so* many ways, I experienced the unexpected. When my fingers found Amy's nipple, I began to shudder.

"What's wrong with you?"

"Nothing."

"You're shaking like you're having a seizure," Amy whispered, gently removing my hand, adjusting her bra and her sweater, and creating distance. "I think it's time I went home."

That was it. Well, almost. At a party at Vicky Stauber's house during my first year in college, Amy now a junior in high school, we ended up under a quilt on the couch in the basement. Mouths opened. Tongues explored and I loosened the snaps of Amy's body suit.

"Do you want me to take off my clothes?"

It was at that moment, overheated and nearly ready to do something that might be beautiful—but also might be life altering—when those sex-ed classes at Holy Apostles Episcopal Church popped into my brain.

"No," I said, rolling over so Amy could resituate things. "No."

I never asked a girl to the sophomore formal dance or to prom my junior year and no girl asked me to the couple's dance—a gala to which girls asked boys—while I attended Denfeld. Feeling like I was missing out on the high school experience, I searched for a girl to ask to senior prom. The big day was approaching and I was getting more and more desperate. Nostalgia regarding my parents' tight-knit group of friends had warped my sense of what going to prom meant. Most couples in my parents' dinner club connected in high school. Shortly after graduation, there were weddings and jobs and babies and houses. I figured that's how it went, the transition from high school to adulthood. But to get there, you had to take a girl to prom.

Betty had been in a steady relationship. Sometime during senior year, she and her boyfriend broke up. We were friendly but not close. She was small of stature but possessed a winning smile and was very smart. In her cheerleading outfit, she showed off her athleticism and her legs. What wasn't to like? Still, a cheerleader, as I'd learned in junior high, was likely beyond my reach. I confided in Heather, a girl I met working on the *Criterion*—the school newspaper where I was the sports editor and she was a reporter. Heather and I spent a lot of time together and I trusted her judgment. She tried to find me a prom date but every girl I had an interest in—including Kim—was spoken for. Desperate, I asked Betty if I could walk her home from school. She looked puzzled. We weren't close and the only class we had together was first hour chemistry with Fog Hanson. To my surprise, Betty acquiesced. During our walk, I asked her to prom. She turned me down flat. I'm pretty sure Betty said "No" because she was still hurting from her breakup. I accepted her declination as God's message: *This prom's not for you.*

Later that summer, Betty and I went on a couple of dates. I was too intimidated to be myself and I'm pretty sure she sensed my uneasiness. When I left her on her porch after dinner at the Jade Fountain and watching *The Life and Times of Judge Roy*

Bean at the West Theater, Betty pecking my cheek with dry lips, and a whispered "Thanks, it was great" as the coda to our brief interlude, that was that.

Except.

There is one last snippet to our story.

Two things happened—actually, three—*before* we dated. Betty was named Queen of Honor Court; meaning she was the titular head of Denfeld's senior scholars. Unfortunately, after her election, it came to light that Betty had been arrested for shoplifting and had to relinquish her crown. Those are the first two events of note: Betty being elected queen and Betty being dethroned.

Prom night, I showed up on Betty's back porch holding a brown paper grocery bag.

"What's this?" Betty asked after answering my knock on the door.

She was wearing sweats—her outfit a far cry from what she would've worn to a formal dance—as I stood in the gloaming.

"Our prom," I replied, extending the bag.

Betty accepted the sack, looked inside, smiled, and invited me in. I sat down at the kitchen table while Betty found two glasses and a corkscrew. She removed a bottle from the bag, unscrewed the cork, and filled the glasses with wine. We sat— sheepish and awkward—toasting the end of high school. Though we drained the bottle, we left our prom dinner—a can of Spaghetti O's—unopened at the bottom of the bag.

HEATHER

She didn't deserve the maltreatment. For forty-plus years I've regretted my actions; my level of animus and rancor so unspeakable, only my wife knows the depths of my regret. It's sort of odd, now that I think about it, that the woman I ultimately married and love so dearly is the only person in whom I've confided the totality of my sins. I've told no one else; not a priest, not a pastor, not a counselor, not a therapist, not a friend beyond my wife.

We met working on the *Criterion,* the monthly newspaper chronicling the news of Denfeld. I was a senior and the sports editor and she was a junior and a reporter. Working side-by-side, we became friends, so much so that when I wanted to take a girl to prom, I asked Heather—not as my date but as my intermediary. Within a few weeks, Heather had exhausted all potential candidates. I never, despite being friends with her and despite thinking she was pretty swell, thought to ask Heather to prom.

When we finally did something together unrelated to the *Criterion*, it was Heather who approached me.

"Do you have a bike?" she asked one day, my ego bruised from yet another rejection, likely Betty's shaking of her head "no" when I asked her to prom.

"Yup. A five-speed."

"Wanna go for a ride?"

"Sure."

This is the thing about the year or so Heather and I could have—but never did—date: I remained a noncommittal jerk. She was a kind-hearted girl discovering her sexuality. I was an immature idiot who was so hormonally confused and misguided as to how men and women come to affection, I missed the opportunity to learn how to become a loving, giving human being.

After that first bike ride, we started hanging out and things heated up. Heather was the first girl I touched intimately until we were both breathless. How it all transpired remains a bit of a mystery.

The truth of the matter is that, behind my adoration for Heather's young and supple body, there was disdain. Not for her—

though that's how my self-depreciation manifested—but for myself. Here I was, an Eagle Scout, a seemingly bright, intelligent boy on the cusp of graduating from high school when we began our explorations and I didn't have a clue.

Oh, there were moments, like when we sat in the front seat of the Wagoneer on a grassy track behind Vo Tech, surrounded by forest overlooking Miller Creek, early summer rain pounding the Jeep's roof in cadence to our labored breathing, when I thought I might be falling in love. But as we teetered near giving in to lust, I knew I was too immature, too young, to be a father, the natural consequence of where we were headed. She was not on the pill. I was unprepared (too embarrassed to buy condoms from the local Rexall pharmacy) and didn't want to play reproductive lottery. So we stopped.

Like I said, I don't remember actually going out on a date—me showing up at Heather's house, introducing myself to her parents and walking out arm in arm to a movie or dinner. Our relationship, if that's what it can be called, was based upon mutual admiration for each other's intellect and an understanding that we didn't have a clue about love.

I gave Heather a Bread album; the soft, sophomoric tones of that band perfectly suited for her innately positive view of life. She gave me a book of poetry and wrote extensively in my senior yearbook; scrawling a word or two atop each page as gentle reminders of the travails and joys (however fleeting or weird) we shared.

Heather was also my first muse. Because of her praise for my writing, I began (far too early, it turns out) to craft a memoir about growing up in Piedmont Heights. She read the first draft and urged me to keep putting pen to paper.

We continued exploring our sexuality when Heather babysat for neighbors and when I worked nights at the Willard Motel. I could have asked her to join me in my uncle's bedroom and put it all to rest. But there was the issue of Grandma Munger living next door, interrupting us by wandering in unannounced to ask, "Do you two need anything"? Then, there was the risk—very real and likely certain—of procreation; a reality stopping me short of culminating my desire.

I convinced Heather to be part of the cast of a silent movie Dave Michelson, John McLoughlin, and I were putting together. We also attended an "end of the year party" held at a log cabin owned by Shane Anderson's folks, though we didn't go as a couple. She noted my arrival, scowled, sought distance, and ended up in the cabin's loft with Wayne. I took exception to Heather's apparent betrayal and bellowed something untoward. Her face appeared above a railing in the loft. She wasn't wearing her glasses (which clued me in on what was happening) so I launched my beer mug at her. The mug hit a beam and shattered. A shard of glass cut Heather's cheek, causing a scar. Inexplicably, after that incident, we resumed spending time together.

"There's gonna be a party on graduation night," I said. "You wanna go?"

"Sure, but you'll have to ask my dad."

I didn't have access to the Jeep. I was riding to graduation with my folks and attending the party—a bonfire and drunken gala held at a gravel pit in Solway Township—with Steve Cordes. "OK," I said, as Heather and I sat outside Denfeld, the spring sun pulling testosterone and estrogen from places deep within.

After listening to the keynote speaker at commencement—Minnesota Governor Wendy Anderson (Dad had convinced him to speak)—tell us how pleased he was to be at "Den-Field," and checking in with Heather's parents, we drove to the party with Steve and his girlfriend-of-the-moment. In front of a bonfire, surrounded by other drunken teenagers, we fumbled around in a sleeping bag until it started raining. I'd promised Heather's parents I'd have her home by midnight. The rain began around nine, so we packed it in, both of us drenched, our attempts at satisfaction as dismal as the weather, and headed for another party at Gary Edward's house.

In Gary's basement, I came to a decision. *This needs to end*, I told myself as a dozen teenagers drank themselves blind.

"Mark, it's time to go," Heather said.

I was pissed off. Not at Heather. At myself. The thing about self-loathing is that it's expressed as meanness and unkindness towards those you love. Love? Maybe that's too strong a word for the tortured waltz we'd engaged in. No, that's unkind. I think there was love in what we shared. But I was so upset with myself, so unable to sort out my feelings, I couldn't grasp the positives in our tortured relationship.

"Steve, you goin' home?"

"Just leaving," Cordes said.

"Can you give Heather a lift?"

"Sure."

I don't remember Heather's reaction to my deserting her. She knew Steve and likely trusted him to get her back to Piedmont Heights in one piece. But I'd made a promise to her parents, a promise I was breaking. I'm pretty sure that, even though she didn't say the words, Heather was thinking: *You bastard.*

I spent the night in Gary's basement. Gary was gone when I woke up with a splitting headache. I had no ride to Piedmont. I couldn't find my shoes. I located the wet sleeping bag that had been the shelter of our disappointment, draped the soggy thing over my shoulder, and started walking home. Halfway up 40th Avenue West, Mike Schiltz—a classmate who later became a Duluth cop—picked me up. I was in my own bed, sound asleep, by four that afternoon. I never found my shoes.

That wasn't the end of our sad, little dance. A few weeks later, the house was deserted, we were messing around in my bedroom, and I knew things had to end. Or, I should say, I wanted them, for whatever reason, to end. Being a coward, I couldn't say the words aloud.

"I wrote you something," I said after Heather told me we couldn't go any farther because she was beginning her period.

"Really?"

God, I remember the sparkle in her eyes, diffuse late afternoon light shining through the windows, the reddish highlights of her hair illumined by the fading sun. *I'm an asshole,* I thought. I reached up, retrieved an envelope, and handed it to her. She began to open it. "No, save it for later!"

Heather looked at me with sad eyes. "You're not breaking up with me are you?"

I didn't want to deal with reality. I was ill-equipped to console her and wanted no part of trying to explain myself. "Oh no," I lied. "It's just that I want you to read it in private."

"OK."

Heather had asked me to go to the couple's dance the following February—during her senior year. I'd agreed, even though—like I said—no girl ever asked me to the couples' dance while I attended Denfeld. But Heather asked me to take her and

I'd said yes. Now, with an unkind, handwritten dismissal, I'd broken her. Not just her heart but the all of her by handing her that damnable letter and sending her out the door in the throes of her monthly. I think, in retrospect, "asshole" comes far short of describing the person I was at that moment.

Despite my unkind dismissal, Heather and I reconnected later that summer at a log cabin my buddies and I built on the Tynjala Farm. It wasn't really a party; just a gathering of young folks to drink beer and sauna in the old Finnish bathhouse Wayne and I had restored. On the walk from the cabin to the sauna, Heather gave me a look that said, "I forgive you." We ended up sprawled on a beach towel under a sweltering August sun, clothes akimbo, wanting everything but consummating nothing. After taking sauna, we went our separate ways.

Later that fall, we finally slept together but not in the way you might think. We were at Val's place for a party. After drinking too much, Heather and I found an empty bed in an upstairs bedroom, talked long into the night, and fell asleep, fully clothed, spooning beneath a quilt. Before we nodded off, Heather worked up the courage to ask me whether I was still taking her to the couple's dance. I reassured her I was. A few weeks later, one of Heather's friends reminded me of that commitment. Like Saint Peter, I denied making any such promise. I broke my vow to take Heather to the couple's dance just like I broke everything else between us.

Heather didn't let me ruin her senior year. She went to the couple's dance with Dave Michelson—who was between girlfriends. Heather even offered to pay for the evening but Dave, always the gentleman, wouldn't hear of it.

I'm told they had a wonderful time.

QUEGLEYS

I'm not an actor. I may have talents but acting is not one of them.
When my archrival Dee Dee was cast as the lead in a play at
Piedmont Elementary School, I wanted in. But I'm terrible—
despite a Harry-like memory—at memorizing lines or lyrics or
poetry. So the director of the play (Miss Johnson, my fifth-grade
teacher) came up with idea of me being a mimic: I'd play the twin
brother of another character and simply repeat his lines. I did fine
when the play was performed in Piedmont Elementary's dingy
basement auditorium. But up until a fateful day in electronics class
(the spring of my senior year at Denfeld) that mimicry—other than
a bit role in Miss Hollingsworth's rendition of *The Wizard of Oz*
in sixth-grade special class (fittingly, I played a Munchkin)—was the
only acting I'd attempted.

"We're gonna make a movie," John McLoughlin said.

I don't remember what John was building. I know I was
trying to put together a microphone mixer. My project took shape
out of spare parts our teacher, Mr. Broman, had access to through
his work as a pilot with the Minnesota National Guard. Colonel
Broman scavenged gizmos to save us from having to wander up to
Radio Shack and spend our hard-earned cash. He also had a
fantastic collection of model airplanes hanging in his classroom;
fighters and bombers he'd put together and painted over the
years. He was a neat guy who went on to command the Air Guard
in Duluth, ultimately retiring as a Brigadier General.

"Really," I replied, my attention not on John but on my
project.

McLoughlin wasn't my partner. My bench partner was a
fellow football player and all-around good guy, Glen Merrier.
Glen was listening in as John described what he was getting at.

"It's called *Day of the Quegleys.*"

"Quegleys?"

"Washburn came up with the idea. He created three
brothers, identical triplets, all dressed alike. Conjured them while
doodling in physics class."

I nodded and kept tinkering.

"Michelson and I will play two of the Quegleys. We want
you to be the third."

I'll stop right there to say this: Other than the fact that McLoughlin and I both wore John Lennon-style wire rimmed glasses, we didn't look anything alike. And Michelson? He bears no resemblance to either one of us. Instead of pointing out the obvious, I kept tinkering with the mic mixer that would—even though it never worked—garner me a "B."

"We're going with three brothers who aren't identical. Matt—that's Dave; Tom—that's me; and Jebediah—that'd be your part."

I agreed to be a Quegley but changed my character's name to "Jedford" in honor of Jed Clampett of the *Beverly Hillbillies.* My character was, like Mr. Clampett, a mountain man. John's Tom was the gunslinger, à la Richard Boone's Paladin in *Have Gun Will Travel.* Dave's Matt was a rancher, a dead ringer for Chuck Connors' character in *The Rifle Man.*

The storyline and plot was all McLoughlin. John was a genius. A big man who would have been a starting offensive tackle his senior year but for the cancer that took one of his kidneys, John had the same inclinations and instincts as other big men of the stage and screen: Jackie Gleason, Jonathan Winters, John Goodman, and John Candy. It's a shame John never left Duluth for the Twin Cities or Hollywood. He acted in local theater, played guitar in cover bands, made commercials, and produced regional sports programming for ESPN but never made the big time. John McLoughlin should've become a household name. He didn't before he passed away (succumbing to a bad heart not long after pre-reading this memoir; his final gift to me), and that's a shame.

To shoot a movie you need more than three guys willing to act silly: You also need a plot. The storyline was pretty simple. Bad guys take over Denfeld. The Quegleys are summoned to save the school. That's it in a nutshell.

Depicting a mountain man, I wore a mink coat I'd purchased for fifty cents at a church rummage sale, a coonskin hat, leather leggings, ripped-up jeans, and carried an antique shotgun. Dave dressed the part of a rancher and carried a Winchester .30-30, a bowie knife, and a revolver. John was decked out in gunfighter togs with toy six-guns riding in holsters strapped to his hips. The firearms Dave and I carried were real but unloaded. Other folks in the movie, from Principal Wayne

Samskar, to Sheriff Bill (Denfeld's bouncer), to the sheriff's deputies (Mike Town, Glen Merrier, Gordy Mesedahl, and Russ Stover) also carried real (but unloaded) firearms. Extras—the girls track squad and members of the football team who ended up battling the Quegleys inside and outside the school—used wooden prop guns left over from a long-disbanded junior ROTC drill team.

McLoughlin convinced Coach Heikkinen to loan us the football team's Super 8 camera. Since none of us had extra cash, buying film was an issue. Glen agreed to loan us just shy of forty bucks for film. How did we repay Merrier for his kindness? His financial assistance is noted in the movie's end credits, though he's listed as "Gwen"—not Glen—another bow to McLoughlin's warped sense of propriety. By the spring of my senior year, we had the cast, the plot, the film, and the camera so we wandered off to make a silent movie.

John was masterful at getting folks, including the school principal, teachers, Sheriff Bill, and assorted students to act stupid for no pay. My only contribution to casting was to enlist Heather to appear in the film.

Featuring other students in the film made us beloved. Further adoration came when we sold tickets. Screenings were scheduled for every hour of the school day. Smart kids bought seven tickets (at a dime apiece) to secure their release from an entire day of classes. The kids who bought a days' worth of tickets saw the film once and vamoosed. Dumb kids bought a ticket, watched the flick, and went back to class. We sold enough tickets to pay Glen back with money left over to splurge on Totino's frozen pizza and Buckhorn premium lager beer to celebrate our cinematic triumph.

I was a poor choice to portray Jed Quegley. I was pretty sure guys with actual talent (Bruce Cusick and Tim Swanson and Mike Town come to mind) would have been a better fit. But I did as my buddies asked, finished the film, and proceeded to graduate from Denfeld full in the knowledge that my brief moment in the spotlight was over.

Plans change. During his senior year at Denfeld, John enrolled in a college film course, got his hands on a 16mm camera, found some old film stock, and began working on the script for *Where There's Quegleys, There's Hope.*

A car zooms past a sign reading "Proctor Atomic Test Site." Garbage is tossed from the car. Special effects (a railroad flare) make it look like the garbage is transformed into ... wait for it ... the Bagman, an evil monster in the tradition of the Blob or the Creature from the Black Lagoon or a host of other scary dudes children of the 1950s and early '60s grew up watching menace civilization. The outfit John wore as the Bagman was classic McLoughlin. He scrounged around in my parents' garage and found a pair of old flight pants, a yellow rain slicker, a plastic attaché, a distressed baseball mitt, a leather work glove, and a can of air freshener. He cut eyeholes in a brown paper grocery bag, plopped it on his head, slid floppy, black galoshes over his tenners, and a monster was born!

The plot involved the Bagman terrorizing Duluth and called for scenes to be shot at Jay Cooke State Park, inside Dad's law office, at Holy Apostles Episcopal Church, in Lincoln Park, around West Duluth, inside a Bridgeman's ice cream parlor, at Enger Tower, and on the roof of the KDAL television studio.

The plot of the second film is simple. The Quegleys are summoned by a resistance group to rid the Zenith City of the Bagman, who is, with the help of that aerosol can, turning innocent Duluthians into Bag People. Dad, sister Anne, brother Dave, and a host of John's classmates formed the cast; an ambitious undertaking that remains my favorite Quegley movie.

Despite me being an ass, Heather agreed to play multiple roles in the sequel. She appears as a Bag Person in a scene shot in the Holy Apostles church office and, looking fetching in a bikini and wearing a bag over her head, she also appears sitting astride the diving board of an outdoor swimming pool while the Bagman lounges about and plans his next caper.

One of the stars of the film is Carol, Scott Mork's girlfriend at the time. John made Carol's character a tragic focal point. It's a silent movie so we don't get to hear Carol's screams as she's taken captive by the Bagman, tied up, and placed on a railroad track. Carol—who disliked me intensely due to my betrayal of Heather—is masterful in her role. Tightly bound with rope as she lays across steel rails, her exaggerated kicking and screaming and flailing as a Duluth, Missabe, and Iron Range (DM&IR) locomotive speeds towards her is the best scene in the movie.

By the time the second film was completed, Michelson and I were in college; meaning we weren't free to wander around Denfeld during the premier. John got permission from Mr. Samskar allowing us back in school to show the movie in the same classroom we'd shown *Day of the Quegleys.* As graduates, Dave and I were no longer bound by rules. After a morning of projecting our masterpiece, the three of us spent the noon hour at Dave's apartment. That wouldn't have been so bad if it had been just Dave and me getting plastered. But we lured John into helping us drain a quart of Finlandia over ice. When the Quegleys returned to Denfeld after lunch, John was in no shape to project a movie. I don't know who we found to step in but the three of us sat in the back of the classroom, giggling to high heavens as the film rolled; confident we'd created a classic. According to public sentiment, we hadn't. Though I loved the Bagman concept—our audience, who expected another movie centered on Denfeld—was lukewarm to *Where There's Quegleys, There's Hope.*

John's younger brother, Tim, had been one of the Fung-Yu monks (don't ask) in the second film and convinced John that his class (the class of '75) deserved a movie. Given John was attending college to become a filmmaker, director, and producer you would've expected him to build upon the experimentation of *Where There's Quegleys, There's Hope.* But there would be no expansion of the crazed lunacy of the Bagman; no branching out from Denfeld in terms of setting or theme or plot when the third Quegley movie was filmed. Instead, John satirized *The Godfather.*

The Godfather is played by Tim McLoughlin's classmate, Scott Maida. In a reversal of roles, the school principal—Mr. Samskar—is the hero; the guy who calls upon the Quegleys to save the school. The third film relies heavily on Denfeld's varsity athletes for muscle: Dave Stano, Al Potvien, and Bob McKercher being memorable in their roles as Mafioso. Gunfights and fistfights and skullduggery—all sanctioned by school administrators—were again filmed inside Denfeld. When the movie wrapped, we showed *Quegley* on the big screen in the Denfeld auditorium because Mr. Samskar had finally figured out our selling-tickets-to-skip-class-scam. The change in venue was fine with us since Pyramid (the school's student council) funded our third and final film. Pyramid made a profit thanks to brisk sales at the box office, but I don't remember the Quegleys getting a cut, meaning Michelson, McLoughlin, and I didn't repeat our noontime tippling.

Though the acting in *Quegley* is high quality camp, because *Quegley* was really just a rehashing of the "bad guys take over the school theme" of *Day of The Quegleys,* and because it lacked the brazenness of the Bagman concept, *Quegley,* is my least favorite of the three films.

That's the sum and substance of my acting career. Though Dave and John went on to star in a Duluth Playhouse production of *The Odd Couple*, I never acted again. I think that's a good thing for the world having re-watched the Quegley films while writing this essay.

RUNNING AWAY

It started the first summer I lived in Piedmont. I've already recounted how, when my propensity for dashing from our house on Chambersburg brought me to the precipice of death-by-drowning, Mom harnessed me to the back porch. As I grew older—maybe I wasn't willing to sacrifice time with friends to engage in an obligatory half-hour piano practice or didn't want to miss seeing a movie because I had to finish trimming the lawn—I'd take off. Most times, I'd wind up across the street talking things over with Romayne Urie, the lady who cared for me while Mom worked and the person I deemed to be "the Boss of the Neighborhood." Despite the fact Mrs. Urie no longer took care of me (Mom quit her job at the Duluth Clinic when Brother Dave came along) hers was a sympathetic ear. I didn't stay long at the Urie house. After listening to my tale of woe, Romayne would telephone Mom and Mom would wander up the hill, collect her wayward son, and shepherd me home.

Sometimes, I ran as far as Jeffery Heights, a development built on the east side of the St. Lawrence parking lot. I didn't know many kids in Jeffery Heights despite the fact it was only a block away. It was as if the church parking lot was an imaginary border preventing interaction with kids from the other neighborhood. Additionally, I was mad at the developer of Jeffery Heights, the creation of which ruined the one and only true pond within walking distance. There was still the pollywog pond next to the Osbournes' house where we scooped tadpoles in the spring. But that was nothing compared to the Thoreauesque pool located a stone's throw from my backyard. Eddie and I thought (with no proof whatsoever) there were fish in that pond, fish we tried to catch by drilling holes through the ice and offering minnows left over from Dad's ice fishing excursions. We didn't catch anything because the pond was less than five feet deep. Beyond omnipresent frogs, toads, salamanders, tadpoles, and assorted ugly bugs, that pond couldn't sustain larger lifeforms. But it was our pond, one that the developer who built Jeffery Heights had no business draining. In any event, upset with Mom, I'd run towards Jeffery Heights seeking solace.

On occasion, Eddie would also get into it with his ever-patient mom or taciturn father. After experiencing one such parental dustup Eddie and I got the bright idea—we were around ten or so—to run away together.

"We'll show 'em," I said, packing a knapsack with cans of pop, sandwiches, and apples. "I've got enough food here to last a few days."

Eddie and I were sitting in the shack we'd built behind the white picket fence that demarcated the end of the Salvesons' backyard and the beginning of the St. Lawrence Memorial Forest.

"We're gonna need more than a couple of sandwiches," Eddie lamented.

Inside the musty, overheated confines of our sanctuary—the glass windows Grandpa Jack had given me functioning not only as the shack's roof but as a greenhouse—we pondered issues of no money and limited food.

"What about your dad's garden?"

"Whatdaya mean?"

"It looks like the beans and peas and carrots are ready."

"Hey, that could work!"

Ed Salveson wasn't happy when, a few hours later, all the food and pop in my knapsack gone, our attempt to run away from our chores and obligations thwarted by reality, we showed up at the back door of the Salveson home.

"Who pulled up my vegetables?" Ed asked sternly, puffing on his omnipresent pipe.

I shivered in fear. Eddie's dad wasn't a big man, but he was a commanding presence. His military bearing made him seem indefatigable as the two of us stood mute, evidence of our crime obvious since we'd left ample shoeprints across the black soil of Ed's garden.

"I did," Eddie lied, saving my skin. "It was all my idea."

After we moved to the house on Miller Creek, increasing marital discord between Mom and Dad made me want to find a safer, quieter, saner place to live. And once I passed my driver's test and Mom and I were forced to share the Jeep—Dad having traded the Grand Prix in for a new Pontiac Grand Ville—there was even more conflict. The arguments Mom and I had—me wanting to take the Jeep to Denfeld or to visit friends or to work at the

Willard Motel; Mom needing it to run errands, buy groceries, make a tennis match, or meet friends—finally came to a head.

"I've had it!" I said, slamming my fist on the kitchen counter. "You never let me use the car. I can't live here anymore."

"Mark, be reasonable. We only have two cars. Your father needs one for work and I have things to do." Mom stopped, tried to assert calm, and added, "We need to learn to share."

"Bullshit," I said, storming out the door. "You having the Jeep seventy-five percent of the time isn't sharing!"

I jumped on my five-speed—maybe ten bucks in my wallet—and started pedaling. I was girl-less, without a date for senior prom, and upset with my lot in life. I rode over the Arrowhead Bridge (the toll taker didn't ask for money since I was on a bike) into Wisconsin, biked through Superior, and headed east on U.S. Highway No. 2. Near South Range, the day starting to wane, the sun slipping toward the horizon, I stopped, found a pay phone, and called Heather.

"If I make it back to the West End, can you give me a ride up the hill?"

She paused. "I'll have to ask Dad for the car."

"I'd appreciate it."

Heather asked. Her dad said "yes." I biked back to Duluth in the dark. Heather met me with the car at the bottom of 24th Avenue West. I crammed my bike into the trunk, tied the lid down with twine, and Heather drove me home.

There were times when alcohol didn't seem to answer the questions I was asking myself. My attempts at dating were dismal. My ability to woo a girl and nurture friendship into love was laughable. Sitting with buddies in a bar, I'd start feeling sorry for myself and an unrelenting urge to vamoose would demand my attention. Without so much as a "so long" to my pals, I'd vanish. Friends took to calling such disappearances "Munger Mirages."

The most extreme case of a Munger Mirage occurred on a below-zero night. I was at the Yellow Submarine (Yellow Sub) Night Club on Tower Avenue in Superior with Wayne and Shane and Eddie. A live band was playing covers on the saloon's raggedy stage. Drinking piss warm beer in the middle of winter with a bunch of guys, even guys you like, is far less appealing than it might sound. Good and buzzed, my friends off playing pool, I decided I'd had enough feminine rejection for one night and slipped out the back door.

It's eight miles from the Yellow Sub to the house on Miller Creek. Over the Arrowhead Bridge and up 40th Avenue West to Skyline Drive. Over Skyline to Piedmont Avenue. Up Piedmont to Chambersburg. Right on Chambersburg for five blocks and right on Leonard for another four. Left on North 22nd to the house. I walked home that night in below zero weather wearing no gloves and no hat and with only my Denfeld letter jacket for protection.

"You could've frozen to death," Eddie said the next morning when he called to make sure I made it home.

"Maybe."

"Don't do it again."

I didn't.

HUNTING THE ORE DOCKS

The river spreads out beneath the Bong Bridge. A flat plain of decaying ice extends from Minnesota to the wooded Wisconsin shore looming through the windshield of my wife's Rogue. I'm headed to Appleton to say goodbye to a friend. My wife sits in the Nissan's front passenger seat, Warren Zevon playing softly in the background, rubber humming against concrete. I'm thinking about Pat "Poof" Pufall. We met at Denfeld playing B-team football. As the engine purrs, I muse that as long as I've known Pat, I've known Vicky, Pat's wife, even longer. Vicky Stauber Pufall and I were raised in Piedmont Heights. Poof lived in West Duluth and, given that he grew up a stone's throw from the St. Louis River and the fat, grain-fed green-headed mallards that claim the marshes and seasonal ponds of the St. Louis as their home, you would've thought he knew something about duck hunting.

Autumn of my freshman year at UMD, Rick Washburn—who lived near Poof—discovered that the cattailed ponds behind the Elliot meat processing plant (in the shadow of the titanic DM&IR ore docks) were favored by ducks gathering for migration. Hunting the Superior side of the St. Louis River, provided one stays a safe distance from businesses and dwellings and provided one possesses a Wisconsin license and a duck stamp, was and is perfectly legal. But Rick and I were college guys working minimum wage jobs. We weren't about to buy a Wisconsin non-resident license and duck stamp on the off-chance we might shoot a mallard or two in the Badger State. No, in the time-honored tradition of Dad and his West Duluth buddies, we chose to hunt the Minnesota side of the river, which meant running afoul of the law. Rick and I weren't stupid. We bought Minnesota licenses and duck stamps, making us *eligible* to hunt in Minnesota. But there was—and still is—a pesky Duluth city ordinance that prohibits the discharge of firearms *within* the City of Duluth. So, while Rick and I could legally hunt ducks in *Minnesota*, we couldn't legally hunt ducks in *Duluth*.

The Washburn house was home to Mr. and Mrs. Washburn and their six kids. Rick was the oldest. On the mornings Rick and I were going to hunt, Mrs. Washburn would make us a hot breakfast and the three of us—Rick's mom, Rick, and I—would sit at an enormous table in the Washburn kitchen eating, talking, and sipping hot coffee as darkness cloaked the still-slumbering neighborhood. Rick's mom never asked us where we were hunting, though, if she'd asked, we would've told her: "Behind Elliot's" and she would've accepted that. Being the mother of five sons and a daughter, Mrs. Washburn wasn't about to get excited if one of her kids violated a seldom-enforced city ordinance. There were bigger things—such as how to keep five boys in hockey skates on a railroader's salary—to worry about than fretting over whether an over-zealous Duluth cop would ticket her eldest son for hunting inside the city limits. Tradition held that, so long as no one complained, the cops looked the other way. Mrs. Washburn understood this unwritten rule.

You're impatiently asking, "Ya, but what does this have to do with Poof?"

I'm getting to that.

After Rick and I fortified ourselves with Mrs. Washburn's breakfast, we'd drive to the Bay and set up decoys in shallow water. Behind the meat packing plant, a point interrupts the St. Louis River on its methodical descent to Lake Superior. Men working the ore docks would notice us and yell out, "How's it goin'?" as we hunkered down and waited for sunrise. No one questioned our right to hunt the Minnesota side of the river. It wasn't that big a deal. Hiding in bulrushes, decoys bobbing on riffles, we'd shoot mallards or teal or woodies drawn to our floating ruse, watch my brother's golden retriever—Pelly—retrieve ducks, reclaim our decoys, tromp back to the gravel parking lot, pack up the Wagoneer, and drop off dead birds for Rick's mom to clean before heading to class. Rick would leave his shotgun at home. I'd store Grandpa Jack's Model '97 Winchester pump in a well-worn gun case in the Jeep parked in the UMD parking lot. A different time; a different world.

Playing poker at Poof's, the topic of duck hunting came up. "I'm going tomorrow morning with Washburn," I said. I'd hunted grouse with Pat and knew he wasn't much of a shot. But he seemed so hell-bent-for-leather to accompany us, I couldn't say "no." The next morning, Poof joined Rick and me and Rick's mom for breakfast.

November wind whipped St. Louis Bay to a frenzy. I plodded through cold, bronze-colored water in chest waders, anchoring decoys to the river's silty bottom. "You stay in the blind," I told Poof when I returned to shore, my friend standing behind cover. "Rick and I'll walk the point. Hopefully, we'll jump a few mallards. They might swing towards you. Stay low. Pop up and shoot as they drop down to land. The dog'll do the rest."

"Got it."

I left Poof—his breath curling in the bracingly crisp, early morning air, the barrel of his sixteen-gauge pump reflecting the newly risen sun, with Pelly by his side—and waded through marsh grass. Coots scattered. A pair of wood ducks, the male resplendent in color, rose out of range, caught the wind, and scuttled towards Wisconsin. On the other side of the point, Rick's twelve-gauge barked. I kept moving and jumped a great blue heron. The heron took flight, looking more like a prehistoric dinosaur than a bird, its long wings slowly lifting its slight body off the water. Sunlight caught the heron's narrow head as it turned towards the point where Poof was hiding.

Oh oh.

Poof's sixteen-gauge coughed. Once. Twice. Three times. I moved as quickly as my waders would allow. When I arrived at the blind, Poof was standing, gun at parade rest, Pelly by his side, admiring the heron's retreat.

"Biggest damn goose I've ever seen," Poof said. "Too bad I missed."

Charged with giving the eulogy at Pat's memorial service, I'll have some things to say about my friend. But the story of the heron that got away is not a story I'll share with folks gathered in Appleton, Wisconsin.

MEMORIAL DAY

We were camped on an island on Omega Lake inside the BWCA. Larry Paasch and I were working a shallows between the island and a rocky islet choked with cedars. It was early morning. A pale, blue sky stretched uninterrupted to Canada. Larry and I sat at opposite ends of a dented aluminum canoe. The other guys in our group were still asleep.

I learned to canoe in Scouts but took a brief hiatus from wilderness until Dave Michelson planned a trip into the BWCA near the end of our senior year at Denfeld. After creating a menu and shopping for food, Michelson, Rick Washburn, Tim Johnson, Tommy Denison and I borrowed two canoes, packed camping gear and supplies into my Jeep, and headed north.

The trip wasn't a disaster. We didn't capsize trying to navigate roaring rapids in overloaded canoes. No bears stormed into our camp to steal food. No one was hurt, though a couple of incidents stand out.

When trying to get cold, clear, water for cooking, Washburn lost the outer pot to Dad's cook kit. The rope Rick was using to pull the pot up from the depths broke or the knot let loose. Knowing how pissed Dad would be that I'd ruined his cook kit by losing the pot that held the contraption together, I whined incessantly about Washburn's neglect until the poor guy stripped to his birthday suit and dove into the frigid lake. Johnson also stripped, dove in, and tried to salvage the pot. We could see the shiny pot resting between boulders but no one could withstand the near-freezing water long enough to grab it. Attempts to snag the pot with a treble-hooked lure went for naught. We gave up trying to recover the cookware. Funny thing is: After arriving home and putting my gear away, Dad never noticed the pot was missing.

With five guys and two canoes, Michelson and I ended up with Tommy as a duffer. That would have been fine except, true to form, Tommy was drunker than a skunk as we fought whitecaps crossing open water. As we paddled, Tommy insisted on digging in the food pack for a snack, thrashing about without consideration for the delicate balance needed to keep a canoe upright. Eventually he found something to eat and fell asleep with his head pillowed by a Duluth Pack.

We mistakenly crossed into Ontario and entered the Quetico Wilderness with Washburn holding a dime bag. Given the remoteness of the place and the lack of drug-sniffing dogs, we snuck in and out of the Queen's domain without incident.

We only had the one car for the five of us, our canoes, and all our crap. Dad gifted me the Wagoneer as my graduation present and had it repainted by one of his clients. True to form when dealing with Dad's drinking buddies, the paint job lasted about as long as a case of beer. And though the Wagoneer made it to the BWCA just fine, on our way home, the Jeep's transmission went to shit.

"It won't shift into drive."

"Downshift into low, then upshift and see if it will kick in," Tommy suggested.

Didn't work. The automatic transmission wouldn't shift higher than second gear. Our two-hour trip back to Duluth became a four-hour slog. There wasn't a problem with our pokey pace until we left Highway 169 and turned onto U.S. Highway 53. It was the Monday of Memorial weekend. Everyone who'd driven from the Twin Cities and Duluth to vacation in God's country was heading home. At the time, U.S. 53 was a two-lane highway. The Wagoneer's turtle-like crawl caused traffic to build up behind us. A dozen cars and trucks full of impatient, pissed off vacationers followed the Jeep on its southward odyssey. Horns honked. Middle fingers thrust in the air as vehicles roared by us when it was safe to pass. Pulling into Virginia for gas, I'd had enough.

"You wanna drive?" I asked Michelson.

"Sure."

Back on the road, Washburn and I hunkered down in the Jeep's cargo area, leaned against Duluth Packs, talked about life, and ignored the assholes honking their horns and shaking their fists as we calmly smoked the rest of Rick's weed.

"Coffee tastes good," I said reverently, trying not to scare fish as I sipped from a tin cup and admired the wilderness surrounding Omega Lake.

"Ssshhh," Larry murmured. "I've got one nibbling."

"Ya, right."

302

"Just a little bit more ..." Larry said, "... got 'em!"

Larry's line dove under the canoe.

"Northern," I said.

"No kidding."

My pal dropped a thrashing, angry two-pound pike into the Grumman, opened his tackle box, searched, and found a stringer. In short order, the fish was tethered to the canoe.

"Now that's how you catch fish!" Larry said, tossing me a cigar and pulling a second stogie out of his tackle box.

I struck a farmer's match against my jean zipper, lit the cigar, inhaled pungent smoke, and retrieved my Daredevil.

A loon paddled into view.

"Loon," Larry whispered.

"I see him," I said. "Got one!" I exclaimed as the hooked fish sought refuge under the canoe. "Another northern."

"Don't let it break your line," Larry instructed. "We need it for fish soup."

The pike fought hard, but the steel leader held firm. I reeled the fish in and leaned over the canoe's gunwale to grab it. As I reached for the fish, my eyeglasses slid off my nose, fell into the water, and waltzed towards the lake's rocky bottom.

"Crap."

"What?"

"I just lost my glasses."

"How'd you manage to do that?"

"They fell off."

"Can you see them? Maybe you can snag them with that Daredevil."

"Ya, right."

The loon drifted closer and laughed before diving.

I landed the northern, unhooked it, tossed it in the bottom of the canoe, and returned to fishing. Larry added my fish to the stringer. Without glasses, I'm nearly blind. I had to squint to make out the most obvious details of the landscape. Behind us, the Canadian Shield rose from the lake to undergird our campsite. Haggard cedars capped primitive stone. Smoke curled from the firepit. A breeze carried the aroma of sizzling bacon.

"The boys are up," Larry said.

Crack.

"Did you hear that?"

"Nope."

"Something's on the rock pile," I whispered.

"Sure, Mark."

"There's something on that little island!" I implored.

I stared hard into the scraggly trees capping the islet. As if being filmed by a severely intoxicated wildlife photographer, a blurry form emerged from the cedars and entered the water. I squinted harder. The canoe drifted. Another object— larger still and black—exited the tree line and waded into the lake.

"Larry ..."

"Holy Moses," Larry whispered. "It's a cow moose and her calf!" Larry put down his rod, picked up his paddle, and backed up the canoe.

I wish I could tell you how magnificent the moose looked swimming a stone's throw away from my seat in the canoe. I wish I could describe the fine, morning mist that coated their fur as they crossed the bay, or how their large eyes reinforced the link between God and His creation. But I can't. All I saw were two enormous blobs swimming the tannin-stained waters of Omega Lake.

THE CABIN

Kids in Piedmont Heights built forts and shacks, sanctuaries from scrutiny. Our dads didn't build elaborate refuges for us. I don't remember a single playhouse constructed under the head of a father's hammer. But I remember plenty of rickety structures cobbled together by boys and girls, most of which couldn't withstand rain and snow; the best of which lasted a winter or two.

I've already told you about the tree forts older boys in our neighborhood built, spending hour after hour chopping down aspen trees for bracing, nailing timbers to tree trunks with sixteen-penny spikes, using plywood lifted from Mr. Huseby's piles of concrete forms to create floors and roofs for those elevated palaces. Well-heeled boys would hand over chore and allowance money for tar paper and roofing nails at the local Coast to Coast to keep out weather.

Carolyn Granley had a shack behind her house, a place where she and her girlfriends played; a place where her younger brother Ronny—who loved to eat raw onions to the point of offense—and Eddie and I would sneak into and marvel at the clothes stored for dress-up including those ugly blue singlets girls were once required to wear during gym class. Our explorations were innocent. We were too young to form deviant thoughts. Carolyn's was the only girls' shack or clubhouse I can remember beyond the temporary lean-tos the older girls built as part of their ill-fated day camp.

Eddie and I built a shack behind Ed Salveson's vegetable garden. Grandpa Jack saved some old double-hung windows he'd removed from his house on Vermillion Road. Eddie and I thought the windows would make for a great roof. We didn't have a clue about caulking and those repurposed windows leaked like sieves. But when it wasn't raining, we'd open the plywood door, crawl into the low-slung, A-frame shack, and study bra and panty ads in Sears and JC Penney catalogs lifted from home. We were maybe ten, eleven. Far too young to understand the mysteries of the female body.

I've already told you about the shack I built a year or so after the one behind Eddie's house collapsed, the one where I tried to hide the bandolier after Carson Osbourne was shot. I stored all manner of contraband in that shanty, including—as I got a bit older, *Playboys*—along with cigarettes and matches and assorted other treasures. I didn't experiment with alcohol as a kid. I only knew of one boy in elementary school who did; he nearly died after chugging a pint of his father's whiskey in fifth grade. The kid had to have his stomach pumped and missed a week of school. His experience scared the shit out of me.

Later, I built a crude shack of unpeeled aspen logs behind our new house on Miller Creek. I scored plywood from a nearby construction site for the roof and floor. Grandpa Jack contributed an old wooden door and a window. Despite the place being a dry repository for my dogeared copies of *Playboy* (and that "new kid on the block" in terms of skin mags—*Penthouse*), given the land surrounding the place was low lying and marshy, biting flies and mosquitoes were omnipresent. I spent a night or two in the shack by the creek but that was the extent of my interest in the place.

Speaking of porn, the first photographs of naked women I ever saw were black and white; grainy images found inside a skin magazine I discovered in a snowbank next to the Lincoln Park skating rink. The pages were soddened and mildewy but enough clarity remained to discern detail.

There were also a few times that Mark Kirby, Eddie, and I dove into the back of Mr. Kirby's garbage truck in search of *Playboys* unaware that if Mark's dad got in the cab and pressed the wrong button, we'd be squished. Even to a pubescent boy, the qualitative difference between *Playboy* and the tawdry skin mag I found in Lincoln Park was obvious. Still, upon discovering such treasures, all we did was look. My pals and I weren't about to act out that scene from *Angela's Ashes,* the one where Frank and his mates wank off in unison.

The most troubling incident concerning naked pictures involved a pastor's son. I was in the Lincoln Junior High boys' locker room after gym class getting dressed when Hugh Spencer pulled an envelope out of his jacket pocket.

"Wanna see something?"

"What?"

"Dad got one of those new Polaroid cameras, you know, the ones that develop instantly."

"We have one too," I said. Harry and his law partner, Blake, had purchased a Polaroid to take photos of people's injuries and crunched cars as part of their PI practice.

"I used it to take naked pictures of my sister!"

Another kid in the locker room chimed in. "Of your sister? She's like what, four years old?"

"Five."

"That's gross," I said. "You're one sick bastard!"

No one looked at Hugh's pictures. Even hormonally-challenged teenaged boys knew a pervert when they met one.

I first heard about the Farm in Miss Hollingsworth's special class. The Farm was described by Jeff Tynjala (whose parents owned the place) and Wayne Rikala (who Jeff invited to spend time at the old Finnish farmstead) as a haven for boys to do things they couldn't do in town. Like drive an old car across a rocky, shrub-choked hayfield free from cops and the danger of being sent to AJC.

"We're building a cabin," Jeff said towards the end of our sophomore year at Denfeld. "We could use another guy."

"Where?"

"The Farm."

"By Whiteface?"

Jeff nodded.

I was in.

The project started the spring of our sophomore year with a five-man crew consisting of Jeff, Wayne, Eddie, Paul, and me. Building the Cabin was backbreaking work. Not only did the project require heavy, physical labor but hordes of mosquitoes and flies attacked exposed flesh and made us miserable. When I joined the effort, the Cabin's floor and waist-high walls of freshly peeled aspen were in place. The walls and roof weren't completed so we pitched the Salveson family tent inside the cabin's shell for shelter.

Most weekends we'd head north—in my Jeep Wagoneer or Wayne's Mustang or Eddie's "White Mouse" (an ancient Plymouth Valiant Eddie shared with his sister, Diane) or in the very cool Volvo 1800 coupe Paul inherited from an older brother—to work on the place.

"What'll we do for a roof?" I asked.

"We need plywood. And roofing paper," Wayne, who would later spend his professional life as a civil engineer, said.

307

Since the project was financed by a guy who worked nights as a handyman at a motel (Wayne), a kid who worked part time at a local television station (Jeff), and three guys who were pretty much penniless (Paul, Eddie, and me), we couldn't afford to buy plywood. Tar paper and roofing nails? Sure. But not plywood.

"Where we gonna get that?" I asked.

Wayne is a West End guy and very resourceful. "Freeway project. Plenty of plywood not far from my house."

"Steal plywood from the federal government? I don't know …"

"Your Jeep is the only car big enough to carry it," Wayne said, stating the obvious.

After we stacked stolen plywood in the back of my Jeep, the leaf springs, well, they no longer had any. Spring, I mean. Jeff and I headed north in a Wagoneer packed to capacity with Jeff lying across the plywood because the passenger seat was filled with gear. Along the way, a friendly township constable stopped us for a "chat" because I was doing forty-two miles-per-hour in a forty-mile-per-hour zone. No ticket was issued, and after satisfying the cop's curiosity, we were back on the road.

While Jeff and I were sweating bullets, hoping against hope the inquisitive part-time cop wouldn't ask where we got the plywood, Wayne was at the LakeAire Motel securing cardboard to the top of his '68 Mustang. His ingenuity was boundless. We couldn't afford insulation and needed something to keep out winter's chill. "Cardboard will work," Wayne had declared, "as long as we sheet the inside of the cabin with plastic."

"What about fire?" Jeff had asked.

A valid point. The old farmhouse—a quarter mile away—had no telephone. The possibility of fire destroying the Cabin was very real because we were installing a Torrid Windsor pot-bellied stove to heat the joint.

"Sheet metal."

"Huh?" Jeff asked.

"We hang sheet metal behind the stove. That way, the heat's reflected into the room," Wayne said.

The Cabin became a haven. We'd wander up on Friday evenings, cars packed with canned goods, drinking water, coolers filled with meat, eggs, and milk, and cases of cheap beer. We'd stay through late Sunday afternoon, always lamenting the drive home.

The place amassed a collection of castoff utensils and dishware and pots and pans along with glassware stolen from taverns. We slept on bunks built out of boxcar doors retrieved from the Liston Deer Camp. We added a fold-out couch as extra sleeping space. We lugged sleeping bags, food, clothes, and booze from cars parked outside the woodlot during the summer or in from the main road in winter, light the Coleman lantern and the wood stove, lust after unattainable girls, eat, drink, play poker, and try to figure out why we were all still virgins.

The place was a treasure trove of soft porn—including *Penthouse Forum* from which we read "true" stories about threesomes and bondage and women who just couldn't get enough of it—*Playboy, Penthouse, Hustler,* and some torrid XXX novels Paul was especially fond of.

Despite his quirky nature, Mom always thought Paul should become a man of the cloth. He never voiced an affinity for a pastoral vocation despite forming a close bond with his Lutheran minister, Dave Eckman, who coached Paul, Eddie, Wayne, and me on softball and basketball teams sponsored by Elim Lutheran and joined us for late-night poker games in the basement of my parents' house. Whether it was his affection for racy novels or some other reason, Paul never followed up on Mom's vocational suggestion.

Paul eventually found the girl of his dreams. Sandy, a compact, spritely cheerleader from Morgan Park inexplicably said "yes" when Paul asked her out. They became an item, would eventually marry and later divorce (the reasons are theirs, so I'll leave it to them to share the details), but while they were a couple, Paul asked me to go on a double date. He wanted me to escort his South American cousin to dinner and a movie. I agreed, expecting to interact with an exotic, lithe, Hispanic girl. When we met at Paul's house, it was immediately clear that my date was taller than me and shared Paul's sturdy Swedish conformation; attributes that doomed the evening. It was the one and only blind date I ever agreed to.

The front wall of the Cabin had an opening meant for a window that never got installed. Instead of glass, we cut screen and stapled it to a frame to allow exterior light and fresh air into the room whenever the heavy plywood sheet (hung on hinges) serving as a portal was open. A pine table and folding chairs provided seating and a place to eat meals. A white porcelain sink hung on the wall outside the *faux* window. A plastic bucket beneath the sink caught wastewater. Wayne donated a steel barrel with a spigot to store water for washing dishes and ourselves. A two-burner Coleman stove served as our range. Occasionally, we'd heat soup or beans on the Torrid Windsor woodstove or cook hotdogs, steaks, or burgers outside on a charcoal grill though most meals were cooked on the Coleman. After eating, we'd heat water on the gas stove, pour it into a porcelain dishpan, add cold water and dish soap, scrub away, rinse with hot water, and let the dishes air dry. Coolers full of food and cases of beer were stored on the porch and often froze in winter. Frozen Buckhorn was affectionately known as "Bog" and when thawed, was a treasure never wasted.

You read what a bastard I was to Heather. I'm sad to report that my insensitivity—no, that's too kind a term for my actions—my cruelty did not end when we parted company.

"She looks just like Heather," Wayne said, handing me a *Playboy* one cold, winter's evening as we sipped Buckhorn from stolen glassware.

"Damn," I admitted. "She is a dead ringer for Heather Sundquist!"

I tore the centerfold out of the magazine and tacked it to the wall.

Maybe I'll write more about the religion I invented. Maybe not. But for now, what you need to know is that, as part of this new "faith" (The Six Divine Truths of Bungo Jen) a few of us pretended to see the Light. None of us believed the garbage I concocted about Bungo Jen—the cactus messiah/god of Mongolia—but somewhere along the way, Dave Michelson loaned me his DeMolay Grand Inquisitor's robe to wear as a Bungo Jen monk while he paraded around in a Tai Quan Do outfit as a sergeant-at-arms. Heather—still pissed at me for standing her up—sewed monk robes for Wayne and Shane from brown wool blankets (think Friar Tuck and you've got it) but refused my request for a robe. Heather's handiwork was superb: My pals were so proud of their new duds they wore them on many "festive" occasions.

Followers of a new creed are subject to ridicule and derision (just ask the Mormons) so I came up with—as the founder of the faith—a desire to arm myself. I handcrafted a battle ax and a spear for protection. Those artifacts weren't suitable for my bedroom at home so I hung the weapons next to that freakishly familiar pinup and Wayne dubbed the entire display "Heather's Wall."

Other adornment could be found inside and outside the Cabin. A hand-painted sign declaring "Repent or Perish: Prepare to Meet Thy God"; a beauty parlor placard stolen from Biwabik; a purloined bit of tin announcing the Cabin as a "Fallout Shelter"; a stop sign and a realtor's "For Sale" sign lifted from Cloquet; and a "No Parking" sign designating the spot where we parked our cars—all added zeitgeist.

One wintry evening, Wayne, Eddie, and I were in Virginia looking for more signs to steal when we became separated. Wayne and Eddie thought I'd walked onto Silver Lake, fallen through the ice, and drowned. Panicked, they asked a clerk at a convenience store if he'd seen me. The guy was a dick so Wayne slipped into the restroom and ensured the toilet would overflow. Wayne's prank, which resulted in a flood, caused a young female employee to get excited, prompting my pal to drunkenly declare: "I'm a handyman. I can fix anything!" The repair was made and moments later I came face to face with my buddies, which is when Wayne confessed his toilet sabotage.

With so many folks visiting the Cabin, we needed more space. I approached the original crew about removing the flat roof and adding a loft but no one seemed interested. Wayne was deep into his engineering studies at UMD. Jeff was working at Erie Mining. Eddie was gone, having enlisted in the Air Force. Paul was too busy trying to get laid to be of use. Undeterred, I enlisted Larry, Poof, and other friends to help. The loft addition was completed during the summer between my freshman and sophomore years at UMD.

My dedication to task was driven by a series of back-to-the-land epistles. I devoured all of the *Foxfire* series before shelving the books next to our treasured nudie magazines and Paul's racy novels. When I'd get bored or weary or tired of fighting bugs, including the time a wasp hive fell out of a tree, lodged in the neck of my sweatshirt, and caused so many stings I had to lie down to overcome nausea, I'd drive to Aurora to say "hi" to Great Aunt Ann and Great Uncle Stutz. Stutz would chirp excitedly as he greeted me at the front door, "Annie, it's Markie!", hug me like a small Slovenian bear, and usher me through the doorway saying "Markie, Markie—come in and have a beer!" Ann would cook me a hot meal and once, noticing how worn out and filthy and smelly I was from working at the Cabin, she insisted I "take a good, long soak" and stay the night. She drew me a hot bath and put fresh sheets on the bed in her extra bedroom where I slept like the dead.

When the loft was finished, I suggested adding even more space.

"Go for it," Jeff said.

I again enlisted Larry and Poof and others to construct a kitchen/dining room wing. By the time we'd laid down the plywood floor, cut and peeled enough aspen logs to raise the walls waist-high, I'd fallen in love and was on the cusp of graduating from UMD. Time for working on the Cabin evaporated and the kitchen addition was never completed.

One autumn night, we arrived at the Farm in a borrowed Chev LUV pickup. Poof was driving and I was riding shotgun. Larry, Mike, and John McLoughlin were hunkered down in the topper when the LUV was pulled over by DNR Officer Gawboy (the same guy who dealt with Red's moose) and his partner. Gawboy made the stop because, as the little truck pulled off the main road and bounced across uneven pasture, the officer was certain the LUV's occupants were shining deer. Gawboy activated his siren and lights and stopped us in the middle of the hayfield. Poof and I were as sober as nuns. The guys in the topper? They were drunk and started whooping and hollering while the officer questioned Poof and me.

"Where you boys headed?"

"To a cabin across the field."

Gawboy studied Poof by flashlight. "Cabin?" I don't know of any cabin out here."

"We built it in high school," I offered, hopeful Gawboy didn't recognize me.

"Mind if I check inside the topper?"

Pat nodded. The officer walked to the back of the LUV. Even after talking to the drunks and ensuring our shotguns were unloaded and cased (we were going grouse hunting in the morning), Gawboy remained unconvinced.

"Mind if we follow you?"

Poof nodded. "Not a problem."

The vehicles stopped outside the woodlot in front of the "No Parking" sign. We poured out of the LUV. Gawboy and his partner exited the Ford. The seven of us stood shoulder to shoulder considering a crude log building illuminated by headlights.

"Well I'll be damned ..."

My brother's golden retriever, Pelly (nicknamed "Pelke the Finnish Wonder Dog because you wondered what he'd do next) and I were headed north to hunt grouse. I was hauling plywood for the kitchen addition in the Jeep and just south of Whiteface, we both needed a piss break. I stopped on the shoulder of Highway 4, let the dog out, and stood in the ditch doing my business. Pelly was off leash and across the road when a northbound pickup truck came upon us. The dog, who never quite figured out cars, trotted out in front of the truck, was hit broadside, flipped into the air, landed on his back, and was most certainly dead.

"I'm so sorry," the guy, a decent fellow for stopping, said as he helped me pull a sheet of plywood out of the Jeep to use as a stretcher. "Never even saw him."

"Not your fault," I said, trying to fight back tears.

What you need to understand about Pelly is that he wasn't just a dog: He was a buddy who attended stag parties and drank beer from Frisbees to the point of canine intoxication. He took sauna at the Scott Cabin during the fishing opener and stole meat off neighborhood grills, proudly prancing home while displaying his ill-gotten gains. To see him hit like that, well, it did a number on me.

Before we could cross the road with the plywood, the dog shook off the effects of the collision, rose from the asphalt, walked over to us, stood beside me, and nuzzled my hand with his wet nose.

The boys decided to play softball one afternoon in the hayfield next to the Cabin. We had a softball and gloves but no bat. With one swing of the ax, I solved <u>that</u> problem. Using an unpeeled balsam limb as the bat, we played ball across stubble and rocks and unmown hay—five or six guys a side—the teams led by "Wampum" Rikala (coach of the Markum Midgets) and "Boom Boom" Tynjala (coach of the Palo Payloaders). I smacked the ball and ran shirtless around makeshift bases—the straps of my blue and white bib

313

overalls digging into sunburn—wearing leather work boots and trying to stretch a single into a double. I don't know if I was out or safe, but I do remember the laughter, the unbridled joy of guys drinking beer and playing ball under an intense summer sun in a dormant field of an old Finnish farm.

There's a movie—taken with Paul's father's Super 8 camera—of a monk party, a feast held in honor of Bungo Jen, at the Cabin. I have that footage, transferred to DVD, but haven't watched it in years. It likely shows guys higher than a kite on weed and cheap whiskey engaging in a weird yet harmless devotion to an imagined god. Maybe this is the place to explain how Bungo Jen came to be.

I took German II my junior year at Denfeld. Wayne and Jeff were also in the class. Manfred Bayer, our teacher, was from Germany. In a bow to a popular Saturday morning cartoon, we addressed him as "Hair Bear." In response to a question asked by our teacher, one of the dimmer bulbs in German II piped up and displayed ignorance.

"Isn't that one of the *six* commandments?" the kid asked.

His stupidity caused Wayne to mutter, "I think he means the Six Divine Truths of Bungo Jen."

A few weeks later I found myself in trouble with Mr. Griffin for gabbing with Poof while Griff lectured. As punishment, Griff required me to write a two thousand word essay on any subject I chose. Wayne's remark came to mind, so I wrote *five* thousand words detailing the origins of Bungo Jen, the imagined cactus messiah/god of Mongolia. Griff enjoyed my essay so much he read it aloud in class.

Another incident involving Hair Bear deserves mention. Given how gullible Mr. Bayer was, guys in German II (the girls were better behaved) hid beneath desks or in the cloak closet to screw up his daily attendance count. Once the tally was completed, guys would pop up from beneath desks or open the closet door and yell, "I'm here!". Remembering Gordy Mesedahl's junior high choir antics, I thought I'd emulate Gordy's disappearing act. Thing is, at Lincoln, Gordy was four feet above the sidewalk standing on a window ledge. I was two stories above Denfeld's parking lot when I decided to perch like a pigeon outside Hair Bear's classroom. Standing on a ten-inch-wide concrete platform and tempting death, I smiled and waved at the burnouts and druggies and smokers congregating around Denfeld's chimney, and all was right with the world until Gary Doty showed up.

Doty was the school bouncer in charge of patrolling Denfeld's parking lot. When he came around the chimney—an imposing figure who'd played football at UMD—Doty scattered deadbeats before him like Moses parting the Red Sea to find me precariously balanced on the ledge.

"Munger, what the hell are you doing?"

I don't know why I said what I said but I thought my response was pretty damn funny. "Don't come any closer, Mr. Doty. I'm pretty depressed and I might jump!"

Doty ran inside the school. I pounded on the window and Wayne drew open the curtains.

"Herr Munger," Mr. Bayer said calmly, "please join the class."

Wayne let me in but before I could take my seat, Doty stormed in, grabbed me by the neck, and hustled me off for a very unpleasant meeting with Denfeld's principal.

Eddie's younger brother Jerry showed up at the Cabin one evening unannounced. Eddie was at Air Force basic training in Texas but had told Jerry the Cabin was open to his use. Mike and I and Larry and Poof were playing poker when we heard a commotion outside. It was night, dark as ebony, and twenty below zero. We were hunkered down, getting ready to enjoy the juicy steaks Officer Gawboy had given Dad after Red shot the moose. We'd brought potatoes and carrots and onions to go along with the steaks—which we were going to fry up on the Coleman stove—and had a cooler full of other food to see us through the weekend.

When they stumbled in from the cold, Jerry and his pals were surprised to find the place occupied. We'd already laid out our sleeping bags in the loft, which meant the uninvited guests— who'd waded through snow in street shoes, summer jackets, and blue jeans without hats and gloves—had to find places to crash. The fold-out couch was the only available bed. The newcomers had brought a single can of Dinty Moore Stew to eat. No bread. No milk. No juice. No eggs or bacon or cereal for breakfast. While we ate like kings, the intruders split their can of stew. After dinner, Jerry and his pals cracked open beers, dried their wet shoes and socks in front of the woodstove, smoked weed, and watched us play poker.

The interlopers were gone at first light.

Jeff set up an interview for me with Erie Mining. Summer positions in the mines were primo jobs for college guys. Taconite mines paid top dollar to utilize the strong backs of young men for hard labor. You could make enough cash working over a summer to fund a year at UMD. I was nervous about the interview and started drinking. Dave Michelson and John McLoughlin and Mike Town were staying with me at the Cabin for the weekend. I'm not sure how we came up with the idea that, since I was too toasted to attend an interview, John—who was sober—would take my place. We drove from the Cabin to Hoyt Lakes. John sauntered into the mine's office pretending he was me and sat for the interview. Despite McLoughlin's best efforts, "Mark Munger" didn't get hired.

When the snow was deep we left our cars—including the four-wheel-drive Jeep—on the main road and hiked to the Cabin. In the spring and summer and fall, the old hayfield could be deceptive. You'd think the ground was dry and firm and before you knew it, you were stuck. That's what happened to Tim Scott and me when I drove Dad's Suburban to the Farm to show Tim the place. After burying the SUV, we walked to a nearby farmhouse and enlisted a neighbor's help. The guy fired up his John Deere, drove to the Farm, hooked a logging chain to the sunken Chevy, and pulled it out of the mud.

This getting-stuck-thing is a trait I inherited from Harry. When Dad bought his first Wagoneer and drove to Saskatchewan to chase geese and sharptail partridge with his buddies, he did something similar. Given his new Jeep had four-wheel-drive, Dad was undeterred when a sign on a desolate stretch of the Queen's Highway warned "Road Closed." The Jeep ended up buried up to its frame. Dad walked to the nearest farm and paid a guy to come to his rescue. The farmer's tractor promptly sank. Workers rebuilding the road witnessed the episode and decided to help. The first dozer joined the Jeep and the tractor in the muck. It took the biggest bulldozer on the project to retrieve the Jeep, the tractor, and the small dozer while Dad and his pals stood around like characters from that Green Day song about idiotic Americans.

Another time, Mike, Larry, and I decided to grouse hunt near Shane's cabin. After traversing passable gravel roads in the

Jeep, I headed down a trail that kept getting swampier and swampier.

"What'dya think?" I asked, stopping before a very wet spot.

"I dunno." Mike said.

"If we go fast enough, I think we can clear it," I said.

"I dunno." Larry said.

Halfway through the quagmire, the pink Princess telephone I had sitting on the console of the Wagoneer fell onto the floor. I took my eyes off the trail, took my foot off the gas, picked up the phone's receiver, put it in its cradle, and promptly buried the Jeep.

"Really?" Mike asked. "You stop in the middle of a swamp to put a fake phone back on the hook?"

We cut down trees. We scavenged boards from an abandoned shack. We placed the logs and lumber in front of and behind the tires in hopes of gaining traction, but the Wagoneer wouldn't budge.

"The highway isn't far," I suggested. "It'll be light for another hour."

Hitchhiking, Shane's half-brother Harry Brock saw us, stopped, and picked us up. Harry didn't know us from Adam. It was pure chance or a response to prayer that he stopped, learned we were pals of Shane's, and gave us a ride. When we arrived at the Anderson cabin, Shane wasn't around but his parents fed us dinner and put us up for the night. In the morning, Harry returned in his International Scout and we headed out. He was amazed at how far back in the toolies I'd managed to drive. The trail was so tortured, the Scout broke a leaf spring on the way in. Undaunted, we found the Wagoneer, Harry hooked a tow chain to the Jeep and the Scout pulled the Wagoneer out of the swamp. A few days later, I sent Harry Brock fifty bucks. I was likely a little short given the fact he'd busted a leaf spring saving my ass. But I was a college student; it was the best I could do. The pink phone? It stayed in the Jeep until I sold the car.

Somewhere along the way, Larry Paasch came into ownership of two motorcycles, small in size and Japanese in origin, which he brought to the Cabin. After tinkering with the bikes, Larry managed, despite the fact both cycles lacked starters, to get one going by charging the battery, turning the key, running full bore across the farm's uncut pasture, hopping on the bike, and popping the clutch.

I don't remember how long Larry's innovative approach to motorcycle maintenance kept that cycle operable. But we had a blast zooming across the Tynjala hay field on the bike. On occasion, we even drove on local roads. I remember being three-sheets-to-the-wind on Buckhorn premium lager beer, sans shirt and wearing only cut-off jeans and tennis shoes, flying over gravel to Weiberg's store on that little Japanese motorcycle to buy beef jerky, chips, and cold soda. Though Larry supplied a helmet as a nod to safety, the bike gave up the ghost long before any of us wore it.

At some point, Wayne and I decided the Cabin needed a sauna, but we had no stove and no money to buy one. Randy Skoglund—another Denfeld guy—and I were hunting the Wasoose Road near the Farm, hoping to pot a ruffed grouse or two when we stumbled upon disaster. A single-wide trailer had been leveled by an LP gas explosion. Bits and pieces of twisted metal and furniture and other debris were strewn across the woods. In the middle of all that destruction stood an intact sauna stove.

"Lookie what we found," Randy said.

Randy knew Wayne and I were planning to restore the Farm's sauna; a fine piece of Finnish carpentry that had fallen into disrepair. But there were two issues with the old bathhouse. First, it was home to a big, fat woodchuck that needed evicting. And second, it didn't have a stove.

"Looks like we've solved our stove problem," I said.

The thing weighed a ton. It took supreme effort to hoist the stove into the back of Randy's Ford pick-up and an equal amount of grunting and swearing and sweating to resituate it in the sauna. Once the stove was in place, Wayne and I patched holes in the floor and walls, dispatched the woodchuck, connected stove pipe, filled the stove's hopper with stones, and rebuilt the sauna's benches. Louie Tynjala—Jeff's dad—was staying at the Farm during the sauna project. He worked at Erie Mining and stayed with Jeff (who'd purchased a small house in Aurora) or at the Farm to avoid commuting from Duluth to Hoyt Lakes. Louie—who was on night shift—took exception to our hammering and sawing and cursing and beer drinking.

"I'm trying to sleep!" Jeff's dad yelled from the cement stoop of the farmhouse clad only in a T-shirt and boxers, his bald head shining in the late afternoon sun. "Knock it off!"

Wayne and I were unwilling to the test the mettle of the patriarch of the Tynjala clan and retreated to the Cabin.

Wait: That label isn't quite accurate. The <u>real</u> patriarch of the Tynjala clan was Louie's dad, George. I first met Grandpa Tynjala when he showed up during the construction of the Cabin.

"Boys, that's never going to work," Grandpa said as he leaned against the fender of his pickup. "A Finn would dovetail those corners. And aspen? Who uses aspen?"

Grandpa George was right and he was wrong. His quip about aspen was valid. Pine or tamarack, straight and true would have been better choices. But all the good trees had been harvested from the land years ago, leaving only second-growth aspen as a source for logs.

I don't remember how often the sauna got used. I already wrote about having Heather and her girlfriends up for a visit. I also fired up the sauna a few times after deer and grouse hunting; washing the dirt and grime of the woods from my body with soap and hot water as logs in the purloined stove crackled, water sizzled on the rocks, and steam rose towards the dark, sacred space's only window. I remember sitting in heat, contemplating what it must have been like to be a pioneering Finn in northeastern Minnesota when the Farm was built. I felt gratitude to the Tynjala family for providing a sanctuary where I could ruminate and consider my tortured path from adolescence to adulthood.

Grandpa Tynjala—his own Finnish bathhouse in need of a stove—eventually claimed the sauna stove Randy and I had stolen. Work, school, and romance interfered with visiting the Cabin and over time, Grandpa Tynjala's prophecy was fulfilled. With no one attending to the place, the roof collapsed from the accumulated weight of winter. The Torrid Windsor, furniture, mattresses, dishes, pots and pans, utensils, stolen glasses and pitchers and signs, skin mags, racy novels, weaponry, and a beloved centerfold were buried beneath a heap of tar paper, plywood, logs, and snow.

PUKING ON THE PRINCIPAL

You read the title of this story correctly. Before I explain what happened at a high school dance, I need to set the stage.

I first tried alpine skiing when I was seven years old. My folks bought me a pair of wooden skis with bear-trap bindings; the kind where you wear thick wool socks and rubber galoshes, tuck the toes of the boots into the bindings, and pull spring-loaded bindings over the heels of the overshoes. There was no safety release if you fell and no safety strap to prevent a run-away ski if one came off.

I tried out my new skis in the Uries' backyard. I didn't have a clue how to stop or turn, which is why my very first run ended with me piling into a birch tree. I didn't get hurt, but I managed to crack a ski. I remember Dad being upset that I'd busted half my Christmas present. But Dad's anger was short-lived when a neighbor—ski jumper Elwood Ramfjord, the father of the four Ramfjord girls—screwed a metal plate onto the face of the ski, repairing the fracture. I don't remember how much I skied on those Sears catalog skis after Elwood's repair. I do remember Elwood recruiting his nephew Mike Urie—a decent though accident prone ski jumper—to take me under his wing. Mike would drive us to Chester Bowl, two sets of jumping skis crammed inside his car, the Beach Boys or the Ventures or Bobby Vee playing on the AM radio. I started out on Rabbit Ears, the smallest of the three jumps at Chester Park. Rabbit Ears wasn't like the two "real" jumps, Little and Big Chester, both of which featured multi-storied wooden scaffolds with steep stairs leading to platforms where skiers strapped on skis and launched into the abyss.

After I survived Rabbit Ears, Mike convinced me to carry my borrowed skis—the bottoms waxed for speed—up the ominous stairs of Little Chester. From great height overlooking Chester Creek, I pondered death. One look at the evil lip defining the end of the jump and I retreated down the staircase, never to jump again.

I grew out of my Sears catalog skis and started using ancient wooden skis, skis made by my Slovenian immigrant great grandfather—a smithy in the mines. Great Grandpa Ivan Kobe's homemade skis were too long for me but that didn't deter my ardor. I skied a hill behind our house and side-stepped up the slope after each trip. Those runs were straight schusses: The skis had no metal edges to facilitate turns. Their saving grace was that the heels of my boots were unencumbered, allowing me to cross-country ski to and from the hill.

My introduction to *real* alpine skiing came after Mom—in her thirties—started taking lessons at Mont du Lac, a local, family-run ski hill. Mom isn't a natural athlete. Plus she's left handed, which made it difficult for her to master sports, though she became—through diligent effort—a decent tennis player. With lessons and time, she also turned into a stylish alpine skier. She never skied fast and never conquered black diamond runs. But she became adept and capable on slopes from Idaho to France to Yugoslavia; places she and Dad and my stepfather Duane visited. Mom skied well into her late-seventies, until she took a spill at Bridger Bowl in Montana and cracked her pelvis. She healed up and gave it another go but yielded to age just before her eightieth birthday. The point of this is that Mom was the one who drove me to Mont du Lac where I learned to ski using Aunt Susanne's equipment. Sukie's skis were too long and her boots too large and I spent a lot of time on the bunny hill teaching myself to snowplow. I became competent enough to use the T-bar, a tortuous lift requiring skiers to shove a metal pole between their legs; the pole being spring loaded and attached to a cable that pulls skiers to the top of the hill. I fell a lot; both on the T-bar and while making runs. Still, the feeling of freedom that came from successfully navigating Mont du Lac captivated me.

My first set of alpine skis were used Head Giant Slaloms. Back in the '60s, there was a serious rivalry between the two ski shops in town. Ski Hut, owned by Wes Neustal; and the Continental Ski Shop, owned by Estonian immigrant (and neighbor) Paul Vesterstein. The Ski Hut sold Harts, which I never owned. The Continental sold Heads, which my entire family skied on. Dad was never graceful or pretty on skis. Rudy Monson—Harry's high school pal and a tremendous athlete—once remarked that Dad looked like a "beer barrel on two staves" zooming down the hill.

When I was twelve we took a family ski trip to Snowmass, Colorado. My folks signed me up for a week of ski lessons with a

Norwegian named Per. I was the only kid in my group. Those lessons were meant to accomplish two things. First, they freed up Mom and Dad from having to ski with me. Second, my parents really wanted me to learn from someone who knew the sport inside and out. Per was that guy and by the end of the week, I was an expert.

Before that trip to Snowmass, I'd tried my hand at ski racing. Over an eight-year stint with the Duluth Alpine Club (DAC), I earned a few medals and trophies that have long since been sent to the dumpster. I first raced when I was ten, snowplowing my way to third place. That near-victory, and the fact Dad bought me those used Head GS skis, fueled a desire to compete. I attended one or two DAC ski camps but those sessions didn't advance my skills. I was too cautious: I never had Cindy Nelson's or Lindsey Vonn's hell-bent-for-leather courage. I was timid and slow and, well, just plain ordinary as a ski racer. That wasn't an impediment because few Piedmont or West End or West Duluth kids skied. My early introduction to alpine skiing gave me a leg up when I joined the Lincoln ski team and later, earned varsity letters at Denfeld. I was the only kid at Lincoln—and one of a handful at Denfeld—competent enough to successfully navigate a slalom course.

In high school, I had a succession of coaches. The pay for coaching a minor sport like skiing was mere pennies. Which is likely why my first high school ski coach, Marv Johnson, a nice guy and my homeroom teacher, never held a single practice. We skied on our own, showed up at meets, and got our asses kicked by other schools. If you competed in four meets, you earned your athletic letter, which I did my sophomore year. Same thing my junior year when another teacher took over the coaching reins.

Sometime during our junior year, Gordy Mesedahl—a pretty good cross-country skier and alpine racer—and I became determined to improve. As a result, Gordy and I cut down aspen saplings, removed the branches, and set up an attenuated alpine course on a steep grade behind Piedmont Elementary known as "Suicide Hill." Suicide is a wicked pitch where neighborhood kids defied death on toboggans, sleds, and flying saucers. I'm pretty sure no one—before Gordy and I set up our course—had ever skied the hill. Our practices on Suicide were old school. We'd side-step back to the top of the hill after each run. Gordy and I decided that, even though neither of us was going to make the Olympics, we wanted to bring honor to Denfeld despite our coach lacking motivation. On the Hunter team bus after the last meet of the year, Gordy and I hatched a plan. Every boy on the team signed our petition and our lackluster coach was either sacked or resigned (I forget which) resulting in an art teacher, Mr. Salmela, being installed as the ski coach.

Coach Salmela was a welcome change. The fall of my senior year, he called a team meeting to make it clear that boys and girls under his tutelage would receive *real* coaching. You caught that, eh? Because of Title IX, girls joined the Denfeld Ski Team. When we began our dry land training, running up 40th Avenue West, across Skyline, down Highland, and back to Denfeld, there were young ladies in the mix; a nice change of scenery! Coach also had us play pick-up basketball during open gym to build stamina. By the time snow fell and Mont du Lac opened for the season, I was in good shape.

We never took home the gold as a team but our collective performance got us noticed. I was skiing with such confidence that Coach approached me during a meet at Giant's Ridge and asked me to fill in on the cross-country squad even though, other than tooling around the woods surrounding our house on cross-country skis Dad bought to get in shape, I hadn't done much skinny skiing.

"Sure," I said. "But I don't have skis."

Tom Nowak, a neighbor from Piedmont, a sophomore, and the best cross-country skier on the team, was standing next to me when Coach made his pitch.

"We've got extra skis and boots in the van," Tom interjected.

Jerry Nowak—Tom's dad and the guy who helped develop the Piedmont Ski Trails—retrieved the extra equipment and waxed the skis for me. I finished sixty-ninth out of eighty-five skiers; performing well enough for Coach to approach me with another request.

"I need a jumper."

Mike Shopa, our team's only ski jumper that day, chimed in. "You can use my skis."

I remembered back to the day I stood at the top of Little Chester and quit ski jumping. "No way in hell."

Coach Salmela let it drop.

I skied well enough my senior season, as did sophomore Ron Carlberg, to receive mention on Marsh Nelson's television show. Marsh—a local sports icon—was interviewing the Cloquet ski coach when the guy mentioned Ron and me as "contenders" at the upcoming state meet. Having gone from skiing through aspen poles on Suicide Hill to being mentioned on television was pretty heady stuff.

The day of the state meet was cold. The February sky stood open and cloudless above Mont du Lac. Dad had finally realized I was serious about racing and he'd sprung for new boots, poles, bindings, and flashy orange and black Kastle GS skis. As I stood at the top of the hill, blue and red flags of the gates flapping in the breeze, dressed in warmups and waiting to take my first run, I felt like I had a decent chance to make my mark (no pun intended!).

Dad watched from the middle of the course. As I passed him, I was skiing the best run of my life. It wasn't that I suddenly grew a pair and became reckless. It was the course. The slight wind and the sun and the plethora of racers had iced up the line such that many of the better skiers fell. I skied steady and true and ended up in the top twenty; something no Denfeld racer had done since Ron's older brother Chuck raced years before. But—and in such stories, there's always a "but"—I still had one more run to make.

Coach was ecstatic when he found me in the chalet.

"Keep it up, Munger!"

I sipped cocoa and nodded. "I'll try my best."

Coach Salmela smiled and slapped me on the back. "You do that."

Things went to shit during my second run. As I hit the flats—near where Dad was standing—a race official stepped onto the course to adjust a gate. I pulled out of my turn and came to a near standstill. When I got to the bottom of the hill, days behind the leaders because of the idiot's interference, I was furious. Fortunately, other officials had seen the guy's transgression and I was given another run.

My third time down the hill I missed a gate. I'd had a good top section, keeping up just enough speed but being cautious of the ruts and ice, to maintain my top-twenty standing. That all changed when I lost an edge, missed a gate, stopped, and muttered "Fuck!" The curse was loud enough for the Cloquet coach, the guy who'd praised me on television and who was monitoring that section of the course, to hear. I was toast anyway but he made sure the scorers knew I'd violated state high school rules by dropping the F-bomb. I was not only beaten by the hill: I was disqualified.

That night, there was a varsity basketball game in the Denfeld gym with a dance to follow. I was depressed. The booze Gordy Mesedahl and Terry Maust and I shared as we sat in Terry's car waiting to go into the gym to watch the game seemed to be just the ticket. I drank from Terry's thermos until the world seemed tolerable. Terry snuck the thermos into the gym in his jacket. The band was in the balcony where I knew Amy, a pretty sophomore blond I had my eye on, would be playing her flute. I made an ass of myself by asking Amy out. Inexplicably, she said "yes." After the game was over, Gordy and Terry and I made our way to the auditorium. We took off our shoes (dances at Denfeld were "sock hops"), left our jackets on chairs, and joined the dance. I was feeling pretty good, what with the liquor buzz and Amy saying "yes" and all and should have known my limit. But between dances, away from the watchful gaze of Officer Butler (who was providing security) and the scrutiny of teachers and staff and parents acting as chaperones, I found Terry's jacket and polished off the booze. That's when the room began to spin, and I knew I was toast. Sitting in the auditorium, my head hanging between my knees, I heard a familiar voice.

"Have you seen Mark Munger?"

"No."

Principal Samskar left. I figured he thought I was someone else and moved on. He had over a thousand students to remember so that seemed logical. I was wrong. While I tried not to vomit, Samskar was searching for Officer Butler. Butler found me and escorted me to a room across the hallway from the auditorium. He said something about how disappointed my parents would be. Scott Mork—a guy I've known forever—got wind of my situation and showed up. Mr. Samskar reappeared while Mork was making a pitch to Officer Butler.

"I can give him a ride home."

Scott's suggestion seemed to strike a chord with the cop. Unfortunately, my stomach turned. Puking on the principal's shoes ended any chance of leniency. Mr. Samskar pushed a trash can towards me with a vomit-covered shoe. As I emptied the rest of my stomach into the garbage can, the principal grabbed a paper towel, wiped off his Florsheim's, and went to call my parents.

JOBS

My inability to obtain a driver's license was an issue. I failed the "on- the-road" portion of the test multiple times. I'm not, at least in my opinion, a stupid person. Why I also failed the written permit test, I have no idea. Nerves? Maybe. Or cocky self-assuredness such that I didn't need to study the handbook I was given in ninth-grade social studies by Mr. Nyquist? That's more likely.

I took driver's ed at Old Central High School in downtown Duluth. That may have been part of the issue. Driver's ed was supposed to be broken into three parts; computer simulation; in-the-parking-lot practice with an instructor; and a behind-the-wheel segment spent piloting a driver's ed car on public roadways with an instructor in the passenger's seat and another student in the back seat as an observer. Mom was late signing me up for driver's ed, which meant I couldn't take the course at Denfeld.

Driver's ed crammed a couple dozen would-be drivers into a converted single-wide mobile home filled with illuminated dashboards and steering wheels and pedals. You had the option of trying to run simulations with an automatic or a manual transmission. I chose the stick shift and promptly stalled out. Given my stubborn streak, I wouldn't give up trying to master a manual transmission even though I was wasting precious practice time. My real troubles began when we were expected to go from the simulator straight to the on-the-road driving. The class at Central eliminated driving through cones because the school's antiquated parking lot didn't have space for a course. Timid and worried after being defeated by the simulator, I was thrown into highway driving with little understanding of how to operate an automobile.

I passed driver's ed, passed the written permit test on the second try, and attained my instructor's permit. Which meant I had time to practice between my fifteenth birthday and turning sixteen. I had visions of being a celebrity—a sophomore who pulled into the Denfeld parking lot in his very own car. That vision was flawed in a number of ways.

First, I needed practice. Given what you know about my relationship with Harry, there was no way I could drive with him. Mom was my co-pilot and that led to a lifelong issue. Mom is a two-footed driver. Most folks use their right foot for both the accelerator and the brake. Not Barbara. She uses her right foot on the accelerator <u>and</u> her left foot on the brake. Consequently, that's what I do to this day. Some argue hovering your left foot over the brake pedal wears out the pads. That's not true but it's out there. Despite this flaw, Mom has abundant patience and even though I was a scared, herky-jerky driver, she never yelled or screamed or chastised me as we toodled down the road. Dad would've made me stop the car and walk home given his short fuse. Mom was the better choice despite her two-footed ways.

The next hiccup in my plan was the fact that once I turned sixteen and sat behind the wheel for my road test, I was a miserable failure. Whether I flunked the on-the-road test two or three times doesn't matter. What's significant is that each time I failed, a state trooper gave me a lecture about practicing and not returning for a re-test until I was ready. This drumbeat of "practice makes perfect" had the opposite effect: I stopped practicing altogether.

Which brings me to the title of this story. When I turned sixteen, my dad's only sister, Aunt Elsie, asked me if I wanted a job at the Western Oil service station she and her husband, Ernie, managed in West Duluth. I said yes. The distance between our house and the station was a long way by bike and required, unless Mom or Dad picked me up, pushing my five-speed up a very steep hill to get home. I began work as a gas jockey after the snow melted and hung it up in June. I didn't mind the work; pumping gas, checking oil and tire pressures, cleaning windshields and mirrors, taking cash, making change, and talking to folks. That was all fine. But with Mom's busy social schedule and Dad's law practice, I found myself pushing my Schwinn up 24th Avenue West way too many times.

I was scheduled to work the Saturday of the Minnesota fishing opener but had Sunday off. I hadn't missed an opener at the Scott Cabin since eighth grade and dearly wanted to make it to Whiteface Lake for Saturday night steaks, the celebrated Smear contest, and the comradery. Fishing was and is always secondary at the opener. Dad and Dave would already be at the cabin, so I caught a ride with Eddie Nelson—one of the other kids who fished the opener at the Scott cabin—because he also had to work. When Nelson showed up at Ernie's Western service station in his rumbling, growling Dodge Super Bee, I knew I needed to pass my driver's test! Even after Nelson scared the shit out of me by hitting speeds of over a hundred miles an hour on County Highway 4 before defying death on the gravel road leading to the cabin—my life passing before my eyes, Black Sabbath's *Paranoid* blasting from the eight-track, the Dodge hurtling over uneven class five—I yearned to drive. That was all well and good, wishing a thing. By June, I was tired of asking for rides home. I told Aunt Elsie I couldn't work at the station anymore and that was that.

I eventually passed my behind-the-wheel test. It happened on a snowy, December day. I took the examination in the Wagoneer. The trooper sitting next to me seemed to be doing everything he could to help me out.

"Parallel park between those cones."

There were two orange traffic cones set up on a steep hill in Proctor. Snow was falling and the road was slippery.

I gulped, nodded, signaled, and started to park but the car's tires were so bald, the Wagoneer wouldn't move.

"Slick, eh?"

I nodded.

"This car has four-wheel-drive, right?"

I nodded again.

"There's no rule against using whatever equipment the car has on it."

I may have been a nervous wreck—a trembling piece of adolescent flesh about to fail my driver's test again—but I'm no dummy. I slid the silver shift lever on the carpeted floor into four-wheel-drive, eased the Jeep into the appointed space, and passed the test.

Having a license didn't mean I had wheels. I had to share the Jeep with Mom. Dad drove the black Pontiac Grand Prix most days, though, on occasion, I was allowed to drive the Batmobile. Despite conflicts at home involving vehicles, getting a license allowed me to accept a job working for Uncle Willard.

Willard hired me to work at his motel and his Indian Point property; a former resort on the St. Louis River located behind the motel. Willard had purchased the decaying resort for a song. The resort's main house was caving in on its foundation. An adjacent chicken coop was also failing. Assorted guest cabins and sheds were in similar states of disrepair. But the seven acres Willard and his second wife Francis acquired were—once the St. Louis River was cleaned up due to Willard's environmentalism—priceless and became the site of a lovely brick home.

Working for Uncle Willard meant mowing the lawn at the motel and on Indian Point. Willard had a small Panzer garden tractor with a five-foot mower deck. Driving that rig, a contraption manufactured in the '40s, wasn't prestigious but the Panzer got the job done. I spent sultry summer days repainting rooms at the motel or mowing the lawn or tilling Willard's big vegetable garden with a cantankerous front tine tiller. I demurred when Willard tried to get me to don a beekeeper's suit and tend his hives. Despite my balking at becoming a beekeeper, my uncle was a good boss. The pay was four bucks an hour, damn fair when you consider Willard's motel rooms rented for ten to sixteen dollars a night. But Uncle Willard had one grating flaw. He was so disorganized, he nearly drove his OCD nephew to the looney bin. Here's an example of what I mean.

"Mark, I want you to paint Unit No. 8," Uncle Willard said.

I retrieved brushes, paint, and a drop cloth and got to it. While I was painting, Willard stopped by and said, "Good work. When you're done here, go help Baker on the Point. There's a pile of railroad ties that need moving."

I nodded and returned to painting. Willard wandered off, maybe to buy something at the local hardware store or more paint at Andren's. When Willard came back a few hours later, he appeared to be hot and bothered. He'd been down on Indian Point inspecting whatever he had Ray Baker—another Denfeld kid—doing and seemed upset.

"How come those ties aren't moved?" Willard growled.

I bit my lip, wanting to keep the job and make my uncle happy. Without irony or sarcasm, I answered, "I thought you wanted this room painted."

My uncle shook his head. "I want those ties moved!"

Ray and I moved the ties, which led to another discussion.

"Why are those ties on the lawn?" Willard asked.

Ray and I looked at each other, sweat pouring down our cheeks, our lean, adolescent bodies tanned and weeping water like rain. We'd just spent several hours moving over a hundred railroad ties—castoffs Willard got from the DWP Railroad for a buck apiece—to the location Willard had designated.

"You told us to put them there," I said.

"I did not. I want them over here," Willard said, pointing to the very place the ties had come from, "right next to the garden so I can use them as fenceposts. Move them back."

We did.

The spring of my senior year, Willard hired me to be the night man at the motel while he and his second wife, Francis, stayed in St. Paul during the legislative session. The pay was ten bucks a night and free dinner and all the soda I could drink. I slept in Willard's and Francis's apartment behind the restaurant's kitchen. Angie, the cook, made me whatever I wanted to eat. It was pretty simple fare: burgers, grilled cheese, omelets, Denvers, Salisbury steak. Greasy spoon stuff. Heather would stop by and we'd end up necking and carrying on in Willard's apartment until Grandma Munger caught on. Grandma, who'd sold her house in Riverside, lived in a tiny kitchenette next to the motel's café and would drop by unannounced, which imbued my time with Heather with a certain element of danger. Grandma's constant interruptions were one drawback to the night job. Another was that, even though very few tourists checked into the motel after I came on duty, I was routinely aroused from sleep. A buzzer would go off. I'd get out of bed, slip on my clothes, stumble out to the front desk, and check DWP crew members into their rooms. The railroaders came in from I' Falls, and I had to make sure they had a place to sleep. I was up again at seven in the morning and riding my Schwinn—or if I was lucky, driving the Jeep—to chemistry class, my first class of the day my senior year at Denfeld. Most mornings in Fog Hanson's chemistry class it was all I could do to keep my eyes open.

My job with Willard lasted until the legislative session ended. After being cut loose from the motel, I was looking for work. With my freshman year at UMD looming. Dad came up with a way for me to make money for tuition.

"I got you an interview with the DM&IR", he said, likely reminiscing about his own brief time working on a track gang for the railroad to make money for college.

"OK."

I did alright during the interview and went to the physical with the railroad's in-house physician, old Doc Barker. He took one look at the x-rays of my low back, noted I had a defect in a facet joint near the beltline (the likely cause of intermittent, severe pain), and nixed me as a railroader. Whether congenital, caused by my fall from a cliff above Skyline as a member of the Adventure Club, or the result of flying off my Schwinn and landing in a ditch at the bottom of Hoover Street, my back was toast and I wasn't going to follow Harry's footsteps and work for the railroad.

Thanks to Dad's connections, I _did_ find work as a night watchman at Great Lakes Storage's warehouse and grain terminal in Superior. As part of that gig, I also spent time as a stevedore at the company's dock in Duluth. Being a stevedore meant moving cargo from ships into the company's Duluth warehouse. I loved the stevedore work: It was my first and only union position. Being a good Democrat, I was happy as a little boy playing in mud to carry a union card.

My boss at Great Lakes—Dobs Nelson—was a short, rotund, cranky guy who looked and sounded like William Conrad (of _Cannon_ fame). Maybe that's pejorative towards Mr. Conrad. I mean, so far as I know, Bill Conrad wasn't a crook.

When on duty as the night watchman in Superior, I'd walk the fenced yard checking for anything out of the ordinary, stopping at intervals to insert a key in timeclocks. By inserting the key, the clocks kept running. If you failed to insert the key, the clocks would stop and Dobs would know you were sleeping instead of watching.

As I walked around the cavernous indoor grain storage facility, piles of wheat and corn stored out of the weather, the place crawled with rats. There was an eeriness about working alone on the silent waterfront, flashlight in hand, every moment expecting the worst. Nothing bad ever happened. But it was scary walking my post all night long with rats skittering underfoot.

Around the same time, Wayne and Shane and Eddie and Paul and I took up rat hunting. Our midnight misadventures involving grain-fed Norwegian rats played out on the Duluth waterfront.

After Shane got off his shift as a cook at Anton's, we'd pile into cars and head for the docks. Parking next to silently spooky grain elevators, we'd pull hockey sticks from the trunks of our cars and aim the vehicles' headlights at piles of rotting grain to illuminate swarms of ugly rats. We'd club our prey, sometimes killing two or three dozen in a night. If other Denfeld guys were rat hunting, we'd line up our "kill" on the hoods of their cars to advertise our machismo.

One wintery night, a rat turned on Eddie and scurried up the leg of his Levi's. He was wearing long johns and was able to knock the bejabbers out of his leg with his hockey stick, killing the rat before it bit him. None of us lifted a hand to help our buddy. We all stood around, watching Eddie's panicked dance, laughing hysterically at his misfortune.

Every so often we'd kick up a rooster pheasant while rat hunting, the birds far north of their native range but content to fatten up on the smorgasbord of spilled grain. After freeze up, we'd also encounter snowy owls, big white birds down from Canada that migrated south to feast on rats. Once the elevators realized leaving rotting grain on the ground was the cause of their rodent infestation, the elevators laced the grain with poison, causing owls to die from eating toxic prey. We came across any number of fluffy, white birds of prey frozen stiff, killed by human stupidity. Eventually, the elevators cleaned up the grain, which reduced the rat population and the need for poison. That change saved countless owls, though it also eliminated rat hunting as a late-night pursuit for drunken college guys.

A Greek ship was waiting to be loaded. The crew was off ship, looking for female companionship. As the night watchman, I was supposed to scrutinize sailors when they returned and only allow authorized personnel into the fenced yard. A car horn woke me from my nap. I grabbed my flashlight and went to the front gate. A taxi idled on the other side of fencing. Two burly Greek sailors accompanied by two women—presumably, from their too-big-hair and too-short-skirts and their garish make-up, ladies of the evening—stood in hot, humid night air waiting for me to open the gate.

"Yes?"

"We go back ship," one of the Greeks said, clearly tipsy from a night spent cruising Superior bars.

"No girls."

The other sailor—much bigger than me—tried to argue. "No, no. It's fine. Captain say OK."

I shook my head. "Can't let the girls in. That's the rule." Both sailors frowned.

"It's OK," the smaller Greek said through a slur. "Like Ari say, Captain let us do all time."

"Not tonight, Boys. Sorry: No girls."

The Greeks shrugged their shoulders and kissed their companions goodnight before putting them in the cab. I opened the gate and let the sailors into the yard. The Greeks didn't complain or curse or threaten me as they stumbled back to their ship.

"Take a tractor and a trailer to the coal dock in West Duluth. There's some dunnage I want you to bring back," Dobs Nelson said to Steve, my work partner for the day.

I had no clue how to drive a big rig. Steve, despite not having a Class A license, did. We bumped across the wooden deck of the old Arrowhead Bridge in the semi, selecting that route to avoid cops who might want to ask Steve about his driving credentials. The toll booth was closed so we didn't stop. We made the trip to Duluth without incident, found the lumber Dobs wanted, and started loading the trailer.

"You know this dunnage is supposed to be burned, right?" Steve asked.

"Really?"

"The Coast Guard would fry Dobs' ass if they knew what he was doing."

I had no interest in going to prison for violating U.S. Maritime Law. I'm pretty sure Steve was of a similar mind. Yet, we'd been told to do a job and we did it; at least until a pickup truck roared onto the coal dock and a guy jumped out to holler at us.

"What in the hell do you two think you're doing?"

Steve straightened up. I looked out from the back of the trailer. The guy yelling was in his thirties; big, brawny, and enraged.

"Dobs Nelson told us to come and get this wood," Steve responded.

"Fucking Nelson, that no good sonofabitch!" The guy glared. "I'm calling the cops. You two are stealing my wood!" He pulled the keys from the Ford's ignition and stormed into a single-wide serving as the dock office.

"What the ..." Steve said. "I'm not going to jail for that fat bastard. Help me unhitch the trailer and we'll get the hell out of here."

Police sirens wailed in the distance as the trailer-less-tractor retreated to Superior.

I worked that evening as the night watchman. The phone in the guard shack rang around ten.

"Great Lakes Storage."

"Who is this?" a male voice asked.

I recognized the caller as the angry guy whose dunnage we'd nearly stolen. "The night watchman."

"You tell that goddamned Dobs Nelson the Duluth Police have tagged his trailer and his ass is <u>mine</u>!" the guy said before hanging up.

Dobs called a few minutes later. The cops had already interviewed him. He asked me to explain what had happened. I gave him the CliffsNotes version.

"You left my trailer in Minnesota? You two are just about the stupidest clucks in the henhouse!" Dobbs paused. "Christ, what a mess," he added before hanging up.

The next morning, I told Dad I'd had enough. I never went back to Great Lakes Storage. I never talked to Steve, Dobs, or the pissed off guy from the coal dock again. Though I was short on cash for college, it didn't matter. I was going to college. I wasn't going to jail.

THE TRIAL

I stopped drinking. First off, before we get too deep into this tale, I want you to understand something: I wasn't a total drunk in high school. Obviously, I wasn't a prude. I had my moments. But unlike some guys, guys who couldn't abide by the rules that forbade the consumption of alcohol or smoking weed or using tobacco while participating in school athletics, I toed the line. Though I spent many weekends at the Cabin during football season, I stayed sober. During ski season, I avoided booze; at least until I puked on Mr. Samskar.

March of our senior year, Eddie and Jeff and Shane and I decided to take in the Minnesota State High School Basketball Tournament in Minneapolis. There wasn't a lot of planning behind our decision, though one thing was certain: We weren't going to the tournament to cheer on the Hunters.

Denfeld's roundballers (including Eddie and Wayne) were supposed to be part of something special. After football season was over and Doug Lien and Dan Dillan shed their cleats and pads for sneakers and shorts, some Twin Cities sports pundit predicted the 1972-1973 Denfeld Hunters Boys' Basketball Team would be the state champion. The team garnered a number one ranking right out of the gate. Talk about being overly optimistic! As the sports editor of our school newspaper, I witnessed some great individual performances during the season, many of them by our 6' 10" center, Donny Brandt. Brandt was tall, gangly, and moody but made up for his shortcomings with great touch and a marvelous jump shot. Thing is, as Eddie related, and as Donny confirmed when we were out riding around in Eddie's Valiant, the big guy, despite being on the radars of several colleges, hated the game. Brandt saw himself as the head freak in a freak show; a freak show he wanted no part of. As the season wound down it wasn't a surprise that the Hunters went only as far as Donny's thin arms and narrow chest could carry them. Which wasn't, despite predictions, to state.

I ended up staying at the Minneapolis Holiday Inn with my buddies. How I convinced my father it'd be a good idea for me to go to the tourney, I have no idea. Dad gave me his blessing, full in the knowledge that most of what happened at the state hockey and basketball tournaments, no parent wanted to know. As I packed some Swisher Sweets—cigars I intended to smoke to curb my desire to drink—my clothes, and a couple of twenties in my wallet, I was pretty sure I could manage three or four days in Minneapolis without getting arrested.

We never took in a game. We watched the tournament on the television in our room or on TVs in rooms occupied by friends. The partying was non-stop. There were plenty of junior and senior girls from Denfeld to chase. Of course, I didn't make any such connection. Most of the girls were spoken for or were out of my league. Three of us: Jeff, Shane, and I were nerds. Eddie? He was blond-headed, handsome, and in love with Susie. Why he decided to leave his girlfriend in Duluth, I have no idea. After two nights of partying, Eddie grew tired of it all. Same thing for Jeff and Shane. I wasn't ready to give up. I figured that maybe, just maybe, I'd catch the eye of a pretty young thing. My pals checked out, piled into Shane's Cadillac, and headed north. I stayed even though I had no hotel room, no ride home, and was down to my last ten bucks.

I'd vowed to stay away from booze during the tournament and I was as good as my word. Sober as a nun, I ended up spending two nights in Sue Ettinger's bathtub—the best bed I could find—a blanket and a pillow my only bow to comfort, the shower curtain closed for privacy. I got sick of smoking cigars and gave them away. I hung out with Mark "Lizard" Morris, a buddy from Miss Hollingsworth's special class and a starting forward on the ill-fated Hunter basketball team. We connected with Sue's boyfriend and eventual husband—Billy—a guy who married up, but who—when all is said and done—did Sue right. I bummed a few bucks off Lizard for meals. And though I never found a girl to connect with, my time in Minneapolis was a positive experience. Attending the tournament also provided me with temporary respite from dwelling on stupid choices I'd made.

"Mr. Munger," Principal Samskar said after knocking on the door to Mr. Broman's electronics shop a few weeks after the state basketball tournament, "a word, please."

I followed the principal into the hallway. He shut the door behind us.

"I have some bad news."

I was clueless.

"Because of your little escapade, you'll face repercussions."

Shit.

"Technically, the ski season wasn't over when you showed up intoxicated at a school dance. As a consequence, you'll lose your skiing letter."

"That seems fair," I mumbled.

"And I'm afraid you'll also forfeit your football letter."

That one stung. I'd worked three years, had the shit kicked out of me, all in hopes of lettering.

"There's more." A brief pause. "You'll be dismissed from honor court as well," Mr. Samskar said with assured finality.

My name had been published in the *Criterion* as a member of honor court, which meant Samskar's pronouncement would cause me no end of embarrassment. The principal sent me back to class to reflect upon the destruction I'd wrought on my name, reputation, and legacy.

I pondered my misfortune riding home on the bus. *The skiing letter, I get. The football letter? Makes no sense. The puking incident happened months after football was over.* I took a breath, looked out the window, watched newly-leafed trees lining 24th Avenue West zoom by, and bit my lip. *And kicking me off honor court—after announcing to the world I'd made the cut— seems like an attempt to humiliate me.*

I had no interest in law as a career. But I knew, from Scouts and church and life and lessons taught by my parents and other mentors there are right and wrong ways of doing things. Simply put, what the school was proposing felt wrong. When I got home I explained it all to Dad.

"That's not fair," he said, Windsor-water in hand as we sat at the kitchen table, night falling, mosquitoes buzzing and Miller Creek gurgling, the windows open to their screens. "Isn't there a procedure for this?"

I shook my head. I'd looked into it with Mr. Donofrio, my guidance counselor. "The school has no written process covering student discipline."

Dad sipped his drink. "You <u>should</u> lose your skiing letter," he said without sympathy, "but the football letter and Honor Court are different."

I nodded.

"We need to schedule a sit-down with Samskar."

Wayne Samskar wasn't a harsh man. When a scared senior and his pit bull, trial lawyer father made an appointment to see him, he had no problem with a face-to-face. Samskar listened as Dad laid out my case. Harry argued that the school was being unduly punitive by publishing my name as an honor court member only to exclude me. Dad also postulated that taking away my football letter was unnecessarily cruel.

"What do you suggest?"

"It's Mark's fight."

Mr. Samskar looked at me.

"A jury of teachers should decide, about the football letter and honor court, I mean. I accept that my skiing letter is gone. But the other things, I think teachers should decide."

Mr. Samskar studied me. "How do we pick this 'jury'?"

I shrugged. Dad didn't interject.

"I'll let you select five faculty members to hear the matter," the principal finally said after much thought. "Any five."

Years later—after working as a trial lawyer and judge—I'd learn that selecting a jury has nothing to do with empaneling fairness. Jury selection is about stacking the deck in your favor. A good trial lawyer would've scanned the roster of teachers and picked folks sympathetic to his or her cause. But I was years away from the courtroom that April afternoon. I figured my duty was to be fair; to me, to the school, to the process, and to Principal Samskar. Without consulting Dad, I listed off five names: "Coach Heikkinen, Mr. Broman, Miss Cohen, Miss Endrizzi, and Mr. Griffin."

The three men were compassionate guys. Coach Heikkinen had watched me work my ass off in football and in his political science class. His influence still has a positive effect on my life. Mr. Broman had been my electronics teacher, was a colonel in the Air Guard, and is a straight shooter. Griff loved me; loved my fondness for social studies and my quirky sense of humor. But here's where my naivete clouded my judgment: The two women I named were no-nonsense-gals unlikely to cut a drunk any slack. Sure, Miss Cohen respected my talent and named me the sports editor of the *Criterion* but she was a stern, nearly humorless taskmaster. I wasn't holding out hope she'd see things my way. Miss Endrizzi?

In sophomore English, Jean Endrizzi required students to select a poem and read it aloud in class. Though I love reading, I'm only an occasional poetry fan. I had no clue what I should read. Instead of finding a poem that moved me, I wrote my own. I copied the style and rhythm of Poe's "The Raven" and titled my effort "The Changer" (you can read it at the end of this memoir). When I read my work aloud in Miss Endrizzi's class, I attributed it to a dead Irishman no one had ever heard of. Jean Endrizzi was so taken by the thing, she gave me an "A." I later worked with Miss Endrizzi on school committees. In a nutshell, Jean Endrizzi liked me, liked that I loved literature. But she was also straightlaced. I had no reason to think she'd be in my corner when it came to my showing up blitzed at a school dance.

A problem surfaced. Griff wasn't available for the hearing. Mr. Samskar asked me to choose an alternate. I nominated the varsity basketball coach, Tom Stone, who'd been my sociology teacher. Coach Stone liked and respected me as I liked and respected him. He agreed to serve.

The "trial" was held in an empty classroom. Harry was there but didn't say a word. It was up to me to convince the jury I deserved mercy, that I should keep my football letter and remain on honor court. I made my pitch. Dad and I left the room while the teachers deliberated. I was expecting a three to two vote, the three men in favor of leniency, the two women voting against me. I was wrong. Five to zero, the jury ruled that the school, by having no written policy, had no business taking away my hard-earned achievements for one misstep. The teachers went out of their way to chastise the administration for allowing my name to be published in the *Criterion*—and having me participate in honor court practices—before dropping the ax.

Despite my acquittal, my name became synonymous with screwing up. When Dave Michelson was called into the office by Assistant Principal Michaels for a "chat" about Dave's role in senior skip day—a drunken celebration on Wisconsin Point that left a public beach littered with cans and bottles—Michelson was told, in no uncertain terms: "You don't want to be like Munger and lose your scholarships. You need to clean up the mess you made." What Mr. Michaels said was true. In addition to losing my skiing letter, I'd lost an academic scholarship. Mr. Michaels' admonition must have hit home because Dave organized a group of Denfeld seniors to ride the Hunter bus to Wisconsin Point to pick up trash. Michelson's act of penance got him out of the dog house.

During a nighttime program to honor seniors, I sat with other honor court members on folding chairs on the Denfeld auditorium stage. An administrator read the names of the inductees aloud to an audience of parents, siblings, teachers, students, staff, and guests. Each student stood in turn as his or her name was called. Every single name was called. Every last one.

Except mine.

A classmate patted the sleeve of my sport coat and I rose to claim my rightful place amongst my peers. As applause echoed in the auditorium, I scanned the crowd for friendly faces and realized this truth: My parents weren't in attendance.

UMD

Questions arose during my tempestuous senior year at Denfeld, questions such as "Where will I go to college?" and "Who will pay for it?" The answers were simple: "UMD" and "Me." I had less than three hundred dollars to my name in the form of United States Savings Bonds, securities that cost eighteen bucks to buy in elementary school and were worth twenty-five dollars at maturity. You purchased the bonds from your teachers—one twenty-five cent stamp at a time—until you filled up a little book with stamps and turned the book into the post office for a bond. My parents traded in a handful of books filled with stamps for bonds on my behalf—the full extent of any parental financing of my higher education.

I barely had enough money to enroll. Tuition at UMD was two hundred and thirty-two dollars per quarter (health care premium and activities fees included). Dreams of going elsewhere died when they collided with financial reality. Plus, I'd only taken the ACT and not the more prestigious SAT—the entrance exam required by private colleges—so I was limited to state schools. Then there was this: Why live away from family and friends, cast out amongst strangers, foregoing all the fun that awaited me in Duluth?

I was trapped in a science classroom at UMD on a stifling August afternoon with twenty other nervous nellies. We were attending freshman orientation; all of us expectant and filled with anxiety. A big guy with an impressive blond afro sat at a desk next to me as we filled out "wish lists" of the courses we hoped to take. My form was filled with a first-year history offering, a journalism class, intro to political science, and freshman composition. The big guy's dance card included engineering graphics, chemistry, physics, and calculus; courses aimed at attaining an engineering degree.

"Where you from?"

The guy smiled, his eyes glinting behind black-framed glasses. "Morgan Park."

I sniggered. Morgan Park was one of Duluth's four public high schools and served kids from predominantly working class families living in Duluth's far-western neighborhoods. "Kids from Morgan Park don't go into engineering," I teased.

He smiled again. "This one does."

His name was Russ Ditman. We became fast friends. He was in my wedding, the only non-Denfeld guy to stand up for me. He died of cancer awhile back. Big Russ had the most potential of anyone I've known but was content to be an ordinary Joe, a bartender, dad, husband, and terrific slow-pitch softball player.

I started college car-pooling with two Piedmont guys, Gordy Mesedahl and Mark Kirby. There were still three drivers in my house—Dad, Mom, and me—with only a Pontiac Grand Ville (the Batmobile had finally died) and the Jeep available for our use. Dad drove the Grand Ville so Mom and I argued over who got to use the Jeep. This intrafamilial conflict made me an unreliable member of the carpool and eventually, the whole notion of taking turns driving to school fell apart.

I tried biking to campus but there were too many hills to arrive at UMD on time and without body odor. I was still girl-less and showing up smelling randy for class was certain to continue that. Instead of biking, I conned rides with friends, begged Mom for the car, and somehow got my ass to class.

I managed a B-minus average my first quarter. My pals in engineering fared far worse. Eddie fell the hardest and, after two quarters, pulled the plug and enlisted in the Air Force.

With my background on the *Criterion* and my declared major being journalism, I joined the staff of the campus newspaper—*The UMD Statesman*—and wrote a couple of articles and drew a couple of cartoons accepted for publication, though the highlight of working at the *Statesman* had nothing to do with writing.

After putting the paper to bed, two pals from Denfeld also working on the *Statesman*—Dean, who'd been in Miss Hollingsworth's special class, and Ron, who later became a professional journalist—smuggled a quart of Southern Comfort into The Pit. The Pit was a subterranean hangout; a place for UMD students to sit, talk, relax, play cards or foosball or pool or air hockey or primitive electronic games (Bi-plane and Space Invaders come to mind) between classes. Easily diverted students missed class because they were having too much fun in The Pit. I was pretty good about playing a game or two of Smear between lectures and making class. When Kenny Hubert and I relaxed upstairs of The Pit in the Kirby Lounge watching *The Gong Show, All My Children,* or *Happy Days* re-runs, we managed to break away from such mesmerizing entertainment and get to class on time.

The Pit was the perfect place to drink in school and I proceeded to get plastered with Dean and Ron, the three of us sipping bourbon straight from the bottle beneath the stairs. Tuned up on Confederate booze, I decided to steal a table but didn't get far with heavy furniture on my back. One of the student employees saw me and gave chase. I dropped the table, but as drunk as I was, the guy easily caught me. Paul, who was walking to his car, saw my plight, intervened, and explained, "He really didn't mean it" to the irate employee. Thanks to Paul's quick action, I avoided seeing the inside of the St. Louis County Jail.

Speaking of jail, one of our favorite college hangouts was the Venture Night Club near Pike Lake. One summer evening, I showed up at the Venture with Wayne and Shane, the place's allure being live music and a ton of high school and college girls ready to party. I'm pretty sure I never danced more than a dance or two at the Venture but at least I gave it, pardon this—the good old college try! The night in question, Shane and I had prearranged Shane's murder. I approached my pal on the crowded dance floor, pulled out a revolver, and screamed: "Anderson you asshole! You're dancing with my woman!" Three shots rang out and Shane collapsed to the floor. It was a great gag—using a starter's pistol to fake a homicide. But the bouncer, a muscular guy I graduated with—Craig Lanthier—knew me, knew Shane, and knew a false narrative when he heard one. Like the scene from *It's a Wonderful Life* where Nick the bartender tosses Clarence and George into a snowbank, we found ourselves outside the Venture, admonished by Lanthier to "Never pull that shit again!"

Another time five or six guys were drinking at Michelson's apartment. Having ingested sufficient liquid courage to approach girls, we piled into Al the Finlander's Toyota and pulled away from the curb ... right onto the tree-filled median of 59th Avenue West. Rather than return to the roadway, Al drove down on the grassy median until he found pavement. Things were depressing in terms of girls and all at the Venture so I drank. A lot. By the time we were ready to head home, I decided to steal a chair. We crammed a piece-of-crap plastic chair and a gaggle of drunks into Al's Toyota. Then, on the way home, Rick Washburn—who was riding with us—spied a dead fox on the highway. Al stopped the car, Washburn grabbed the dead critter and tossed it in the trunk. "It'll make a nice mount," was all the explanation needed.

The next morning, Mom woke me up to answer the phone. I stumbled into the utility room and picked up the receiver.

"Mr. Munger," a very serious voice said.

"Yes."

"This is Deputy Swartz of the St. Louis County Sheriff's Office."

Fuck.

"Yes?"

"We understand you took some property from the Venture last night. The owner won't press charges if you bring the stolen item back."

Think. Think.

"I've never been to the Venture in my life!"

The voice on the other end of the line tittered like a schoolgirl. Then Michelson was on the phone: "Gotcha!"

"Asshole," I mumbled, slamming down the receiver.

Months later, I was with Eddie and Paul at a Superior bar when I decided to vamoose. My pals were distracted and as I booked, I decided a wrought iron bar stool would make a nice addition to my bedroom. I went out the back door lugging a fifty-pound piece of iron and wood, the bartender screaming, "Hey, dumb shit, bring back my chair!" In the alley, I spotted a fire escape, pulled the stairs down (just like in the movies), and climbed up to the roof with the stool. From height, I heard sirens and saw police cruisers headed my way. I knew I wasn't going to make it out of there with the barstool so I left it on the roof. I don't remember how I got home.

Like I've written, I was never much of a brawler, though a couple of dustups I was involved in while attending UMD come to mind.

Eddie and I were playing H-O-R-S-E at his house, taking turns making trick shots and avoiding a puddle next to the driveway in hopes of keeping the ball clean. My old nemesis Pat Osbourne showed up and started to talk shit. Not to Eddie, who'd grown to six-four and weighed over two hundred. To me. What Osbourne didn't factor into things was that I'd also grown, had been hitting the weights, and had nearly a decade of pent-up rage seething inside me. I took a shot at the basket, missed, and the ball landed at Osbourne's feet. Pat intentionally dragged the ball through the mud before throwing it at me. I was wearing a white T-shirt and because I didn't expect the ball, I ended up with mud all over my clean shirt. Before Osbourne knew what hit him, he was on the ground and I was on top of him, punching him in the face. I might've killed the jerk but Eddie pulled me off.

"What the fuck, you psycho!" Osbourne screamed, rubbing his jaw. "You need some serious mental help!"

I wanted to give my childhood tormentor more but Eddie planted himself between us.

"I think you'd better leave," Eddie said. "I'm not sure I can stop him if he goes after you again."

The one-time bully glared at me, realized his reign of terror was over, and sulked away. That was the last time I ever saw Patrick Osbourne.

The fall of my freshman year at UMD, Poof and I were wearing Denfeld letter jackets and exiting PSS after the Denfeld-Central football game. Poof said something to a kid wearing Central colors and the next thing I knew, the kid was punching me! I'm not sure why that happened but I'm certain of one thing: Poof—who'd instigated the fracas—vanished. Though the Central kid had a good six inches on me, I was able to get inside his reach, grab hold of his jacket, and drag him to the ground where I used my weight as advantage. I was pretty much giving the Central guy his comeuppance when a hand grabbed my collar and yanked me off my opponent. "Let go, Poof!" I screamed. But it wasn't Pat who'd somehow grown a pair. It was Dad's buddy—former Detroit Tiger, Larry "Lunga" Tessier—who broke up the fight and sent me on my way.

"Get out of here before the cops come," Lunga warned sternly.

I complied. Poof? He found me just as I was climbing into the Jeep. I never figured out where he'd run off to or why the Central kid thought I, not Poof, deserved to be punched.

Another time, Poof and I were at the Yellow Sub playing pool with a guy Pat knew from work. For whatever reason, Poof's pal decided to pick at me. The more glasses of warm tap beer the guy drank, the more obnoxious he became. Finally, I'd had enough. "Let's get out of here," I said, pulling on my letter jacket and heading for the door. Unfortunately, the guy with the mouth staggered after us. I ignored his blathering until he grabbed me from behind. I was pretty sure he intended to sucker punch me but that didn't happen. I wasn't the guy who ended up on his ass in the middle of Tower Avenue.

I resisted pot during high school, even though I had friends who loved the stuff, smoked it regularly, and didn't seem to move on (à la *Reefer Madness*) to more potent drugs. It wasn't like I stayed away from pot because I was scared straight. I just wasn't a smoker and taking a drag off a pipe or from a bong or off a joint was foreign to me.

Not long after the Southern Comfort incident I found myself in Dean's car in front of Hardee's. A joint came my way. I'm pretty sure the guys were expecting me to pass it on without taking a toke. For whatever reason, I gave in, sucked hard, held the acrid smoke, and *then* handed the joint to Paul. It took a bit for the weird, hazy grip of marijuana to manifest. But by the time I sat down in my next class (which happened to be Intro to Psychology), I was zonked. The prof—a guy I'd once found dry and boring—was suddenly so damn funny, I nearly peed my pants giggling in the back row of the lecture hall.

After finishing a quarter of UMD's journalism curriculum, I became disenchanted with the notion of working as a newspaper reporter if and when I finally graduated and found a "real" job. The pay was for shit. And, whereas I've always loved creative writing, newspapers don't generally reward whimsy. I switched to a double major in political science and history with an eye towards becoming a teacher. That path lasted a quarter or two and then, frustrated with the teaching program at UMD, I plowed ahead with a BA in liberal arts with no thought as to what the hell good a social studies degree would do me in the real world.

Maybe a few got-their-shit-together college kids choose a career path and stick to their guns. With one or two exceptions, none of my friends followed that example. We were all—in life, love, school, and vocation—adrift, searching for answers. I was, however, pretty sure about one thing: I didn't want to be a manual laborer for the rest of my life.

After I left that pile of dunnage on a coal dock in West Duluth, I found a part-time job at a lumber, door, and millwork warehouse in the West End. Scot Graf Lumber had been a waterfront icon since the1890s; at one time employing hundreds of men making building products from lumber floated down the St. Louis River from logging camps north of Duluth. By the time I saw the job posting at UMD, there wasn't much left of Scot Graf. Which is why, after ghosting around that empty monument to a long-departed age—being paid for twenty hours of work a week while barely keeping busy for ten—my boss, a drunk named Billy, sent me packing. Since I was paying my own way through UMD, I wasn't happy to be let go. But what really got my dander up was that while I was cast to the wind, Cade—a ginger-haired asshole hired the same day as me—kept working.

Paul found me a job with the City of Duluth as a caretaker at Peterson Arena. Peterson was a natural ice hockey facility located next to the ore docks in West Duluth. Years later, the place burned to the ground. But when I worked there, Peterson was fairly new. In early December, Paul and I installed wooden hockey boards so we could make ice. Because there was no refrigeration, we had to wait until temps inside the arena were below freezing to flood. We swapped weeks, one week on, one week off. Our duties were supposed to include sweeping the ice with a derelict Ford lawn tractor with a brush mounted on its front end. The tractor was an illusion. Its engine was fried, meaning the ice had to be swept by hand. For games involving younger teams—Mites, Squirts, Pee Wees, and Bantams—it was easy to get parents and coaches to sweep. The Senior B's? Those guys (and it was all guys; no girls played organized hockey back then) were jerks. Senior B games—games between high school guys who weren't good enough to make varsity or recent graduates who were seeking to reclaim their glory days—routinely ended in fights. Once brawling broke out, the refs would chase players and coaches off the rink leaving me to sweep the ice by myself. After I finished sweeping, I'd flood, close up, drive home, and hit the hay, sometimes after two in the morning.

Working at Peterson had positives beyond earning a paycheck. While teams played or practiced, I had nothing to do. Having learned my lesson about college coursework, I brought my textbooks to Peterson and spent time sitting on the busted tractor, highlighter in hand, reading and underlining. Then there were the boot hockey games Paul and I organized. We played after the last "real" game of the night. We banned booze, making it plain to the guys we invited that the City of Duluth frowned on drinking on city property. We also made sure our pals understood that, in return for playing, they'd have to help sweep and flood. I'd developed a serviceable wrist shot playing boot hockey on Hutchinson Road and was a good bet to be an early pick when we chose up sides. I think the fact I could actually see, having traded my regular glasses for black-framed, rubberized athletic specs everyone with poor eyesight—including professional athletes— wore, occasioned my transformation from non-athlete to sought- after draft choice.

A fondness for music was where my excess cash—what little I had—went. Music has always been a huge part of my life. When I was a child, Mom bought me a crystal radio kit. That tiny receiver relied upon piezoelectric principles (a crystal magically creates electrical current) and was my introduction to rock and roll. My parents listened to folk music and show tunes. Though they came of age in the 1950s, Harry and Barb had no affinity for Buddy Holly or Roy Orbison or Elvis. When I hooked up the crystal receiver's ground wire to the radiator in my bedroom, turned it on, tuned in to WEBC AM to listen to Top 40 hits, I was in heaven. Later on, I used allowance and chore money to upgrade. Dad took me to Mel's TV in Duluth's East End where I plunked down a hundred bucks on a Panasonic stereo AM/FM radio and cassette player. The unit operated on either AC or DC and came with an adapter to plug into a car's cigarette lighter. Given the Jeep's radio was only AM, it was a godsend to prop up the Panasonic on the back seat, connect it to the lighter, and tool around listening to rock and roll.

Before my job at Peterson ended, I amassed enough savings to wander up to Team Electronics and purchase a cassette deck, stereo receiver, and Advent speakers. I later added a turntable I received as a premium from the RCA Record and Tape Club; one of those outfits you joined to get a shitload of music for a penny on the promise you'd buy albums or cassettes or eight-tracks through the mail at inflated prices. I'd get nearly-free tunes (as many as a dozen cassettes for a penny), order the recordings mandated by the agreement, cancel my membership, and re-join the club to start the cycle all over again. At one point, I belonged to RCA, Columbia, and the Record Club of America at the same time, though I should have ordered vinyl because after a few plays, cassettes went to shit.

Thanks to the job at Peterson, I also earned enough to pay for my tuition, fees, and books at UMD. But once the ice went out, I was again looking for work. Which is when Dave Michelson convinced me to join him in a couple of endeavors. Understand this about Dave: He's always been a role model for me in terms of intellect. When he suggested I attend summer school at UMD, given I had nothing else to do other than stain the trim on my folks' house, I accepted Dave's challenge. I ended up taking two political science courses and garnering "A's."

About staining the house. I used oil-based stain, plenty of which ended up on my bare skin. You need turpentine to remove oil-based stain. I was planning on taking a bath to scrub the shit off but knew soap and water wouldn't do the trick. My solution? Pour a few caps of turpentine into the bath water and climb in. The fire that ripped through my nether regions when I sat down in the tub made me recall—as I danced a frantic jig and grabbed a towel— trying to turn off a light switch with my tongue!

The other suggestion Michelson made was to accompany him to the Marine Corps recruiting office to check out the Platoon Leaders Course (PLC). I'll share details about the time I spent in Quantico, Virginia with you later on. For now, all you need to know is that while I filled out the paperwork and turned it in to the recruiter, Dave never followed through. He didn't trick me or anything. He was genuinely interested in a career as a Marine Corps JAG Officer. Me? I hadn't thought about life after college and had steered clear of law as a vocational choice. But Dave's suggestion seemed like something to explore. In the end, I did my six-plus weeks at Quantico, survived, collected my pay, and came back to UMD for my sophomore year, my head shaved, my body lean and tan and well-muscled.

When the money from my PLC stint ran out, I went back to the job board at UMD and found a position that fit my skills and interests. I ended up in a General Cleaning jumpsuit buffing the floors of First American National Bank in downtown Duluth. That's where I met Mike, a guy from Chicago. I buffed terrazzo and Mike vacuumed carpeting. We got one fifteen-minute break per shift to shoot the shit. I liked Mike. He was a smart guy, a college graduate who couldn't see himself wearing a suit or working in a lab (he had a BS in chemistry from the University of Chicago—or so he said) who ended up in Duluth chasing love.

Getting to and from the General Cleaning job proved a challenge. Until I bought a Chrysler 300 from Shane, I shared the Jeep with Mom, which meant I rarely had a car. When the weather was decent, I'd hop on my Schwinn and bike to work. I'd hit speeds of over forty miles an hour zooming down Piedmont Avenue. The rush I got from passing cars and trucks and buses, gliding in and out of traffic with impunity (no Duluth cop was gonna waste time stopping a college kid on a bike wearing a custodian's uniform) was a true runner's high. When work was over, I'd stand in front of the bank with my Schwinn, board a city bus, pay the driver, and lean the bike against an empty seat for the ride home. I stayed at General Cleaning for a year. I was proud of my work ethic, even going so far as to wear the tan jumpsuit displaying the General Cleaning logo into Mr. J's—a college hangout bar. Maybe I wore that stupid outfit into a bar filled with UMD football and hockey players in hopes of starting a brawl. That never happened though I learned, despite the oft-repeated premise that girls love guys in uniform, a janitorial jumpsuit is not a chick magnet.

I maintained my grades at UMD, having finally figured out a balance of fun, work, studying, and going to class that kept me on course to graduate and I wasn't one of the assholes who sat on the window ledge outside the UMD bookstore and rated female students aloud (on a scale from one to ten). I might have been a jerk to Heather but I learned from my sins. I kept my head down, did my work, played intramural sports, and took a phy ed class every quarter to stay in shape.

Those gym classes brought me in close contact with my future wife's friend, Eleanor. I could never figure that girl out even after I took three tennis classes just to see what might happen. Playing singles or doubles against or with Eleanor, I tried to connect but she wasn't interested.

By the time René and I were an item, I was looking toward the future. I started thinking about options and, despite my disinterest in the work Dad did—especially the personal injury aspects of his practice—law school appeared to be my only viable option. I knew there wasn't much out there for a college grad with a BA in political science and history, so I started taking practice versions of the Law School Admissions Test (LSAT). Based upon the results from those practice exams, I was limited to lower-tier schools. I wasn't a dullard: I'd eventually graduate from college with honors but taking those practice tests unnerved me. Even so, a guy can dream and I started considering law schools in the mountains (where I could ski) or Florida (where I could hit the beach).

Throughout it all, I kept up my friendships with my high school pals and guys like Big Russ I met at UMD. We spent a lot of time drinking and trying to figure things out, far less time smoking the occasional doobie, all-the-while avoiding serious trouble.

One night, Russ and I were settled in the basement rec room of my folks' house with a case of beer and munchies. Celebrated Minnesota boxer Duane Bobick (38-0 as a pro) was fighting rugged ex-Marine Kenny Norton. The winner would be entitled to fight an aging Muhammad Ali for the heavyweight title of the world. Russ and I planned to watch the bout while polishing off our case of brew. We cracked open beers, took our first sips, and the damn fight was over! Norton hit Bobick with one punch and the Minnesotan crumpled like his jaw was made of paper mâché. The fight ended in less than a minute, leaving Russ and me with nothing to watch on television. Consequently, we pulled up stakes and drove to Superior in Ditman's car.

I tried to go beer for beer with my buddy who, at six-four and two-twenty-five, had a lot more tolerance for alcohol than I did. Sometime during our evening at the Yellow Sub, while Russ made a play for a girl he knew and I felt the room spinning, I wandered outside and passed out next to a dumpster. Happenstance intervened in the form of John McLoughlin and Mike Town finding me asleep in the alley. They didn't know I was with Russ when they loaded me into John's T-bird and drove me home. I had some explaining to do when Big Russ called me the next morning.

Eddie was dating Susie. They weren't engaged but getting close. We'd been at Mr. J's drinking and Eddie was my ride home. He was driving the White Mouse. On the way home from J's, the car's floor loaded with stolen pitchers and glasses, our route took us up 27th Avenue West. Cherries came on behind us. Eddie pulled over and opened the driver's door with the unintended result that some of the stolen glasses were liberated.

"You realize you don't have your headlights on," Officer Butler said.

"No, Officer, I didn't know that."

"You boys been drinking?"

"Yes, Officer, we have."

Butler studied the glassware littering the roadway. "Looks like you boys've had a good time tonight," he said, ignoring the likelihood he'd not only caught a drunk driver but a couple of thieves.

Unable to hear what was being said, I rolled down the window and yelled: "HEY EDDIE, WHAT THE FUCK IS GOING ON?"

My timing couldn't have been worse. A door of a nearby house opened. Three people—mother, father, and daughter—exited the bungalow to stand on the back porch in their pajamas.

"Hey, isn't that Dave?", a familiar female voice asked.

Eddie's girlfriend and her parents were our audience. Standing in cold, winter air, Officer Butler made a charitable decision. Since Eddie was only a few blocks from home, he let us off the hook with a stern admonition: "Turn on your headlights and drive straight home. If I see this car on the road again, you're going to jail."

We did as we were told.

Eddie had a thing about headlights. We were driving on I-35 near 40th Avenue West when once again, cherries came on behind us. This time it was a no-nonsense Minnesota State Trooper who pulled the Valiant over.

Eddie was behind the wheel. I was in the front passenger seat. Dave Michelson, Wayne, and Tommy Denison were in the back seat. We'd just come from Mr. J's and were again loaded to the gills with stolen pitchers and beer glasses. Michelson's dad and stepmom were gone from Duluth for an extended period of time, leaving Dave the upstairs of their duplex to live in. We'd stolen

353

the glassware to accessorize Dave's apartment. When Eddie opened the front door to talk to the trooper, some of our ill-gotten gains spilled out and made a racket.

The trooper ignored the glassware and took Eddie aside for sobriety testing, which is when I heard this exchange: "You know you were driving without your headlights on, don't you?"

I looked at Dave and Wayne and Tommy in the back seat. Dave and Wayne were awake but Tommy was zonked.

"The Adios Option?" I asked, opening my door.

Michelson followed my lead. We noted the patrolman was wearing a traditional trooper's hat and started humming "Smokey the Bear" as we exited the car. Rikala stayed put to restrain the now-awakened Tommy who wanted to climb out of Eddie's car and "kick the trooper's ass." Free of the White Mouse, Michelson and I broke into a sprint while yelling "Run away, run away," in a warped-yet-timeless homage to Monte Python's *Holy Grail.* We soon found ourselves thigh deep in snow between the freeway and Continental Crystal's, the food supplier Poof drove truck for. Clinking sounds—made by stolen glasses hidden in our jackets—echoed across the night with every labored step.

"Weren't there five of you?" we heard the trooper ask Eddie.

"Yessir."

A spotlight followed Dave and me as we trudged through deep snow. Exhausted, we ducked inside an empty delivery truck to hide. Though Eddie wasn't arrested, he received another ticket for driving without headlights. Once the coast was clear, Dave and I walked to Frankie's Pizza where Dean and Randy worked the late-night shift. Randy got off early, comped Dave and me a couple of pizzas, and gave us a lift. Our pals were waiting for us in the White Mouse when Randy pulled up in front of Michelson's place.

Despite the free pies, Eddie wasn't happy.

A PARTY ON BRIGHTON BEACH

When I learned that Eddie was enlisting in the Air Force, I figured the least I could do was throw him a party. I approached Shane, who was still working at Anton's Supper Club as a cook, about buying prime rib to barbeque. Shane said he could get a roast and side dishes at cost. I proceeded to plan the event and bought a few cases of beer to share with guests along with a pint of Everclear for my own bemusement.

Given Eddie was departing for basic training at Lackland Air Base in Texas the end of May, I scheduled his party for mid-month. Eddie was leaving Susie in Duluth pending his completion of basic training, AIT, and—eventually—their wedding. I made it plain no one was to bring gifts but allowed myself an exemption from that prohibition. I thought and thought and thought about what sort of present would do our friendship justice. Then it dawned on me.

I found an old canvas duffle in the garage—a sack Dad used to store duck decoys—that I imagined into a pair of impenetrable panties. I cut strands of barbed wire and sewed them into the waistline and along the leg openings of the stiff undies to function as a barrier against wandering hands. The exclamation point was an oversized, rusty, padlock I added to the contraption. I wove musty rope through the canvas to serve as a belt and secured it with the lock. The resulting crude chastity belt wasn't functional as a deterrent to lust, but the overall affect appeared—to my warped eye—masterful.

The day of the party was sunny, cool, and windy. The ice had just gone out, meaning the temperature of Lake Superior was just north of freezing. Shane arrived at Brighton Beach with the food. We built a fire in the park pavilion's stone fireplace. I removed coolers filled with beer and ice from my car and the chef and I shared shots of Everclear while the prime rib cooked. I laid out potato salad, Cole slaw, condiments, paper plates, plastic beer cups, and plastic utensils on a picnic table. Becky, a girl I'd eventually get to know more intimately, Becky's friends, and the usual suspects showed up. Heather—who was a friend of Susie's—came despite me having stood her up for the Denfeld couple's dance. Shortly after the guest of honor arrived, Shane pronounced the roast was done. Which it wasn't. Regardless, we ate and drank, and then the big moment, the moment I was waiting for, arrived.

"I've got something for you, Susie," I said through alcohol-thickened lips.

"You said no gifts!" Paul admonished.

"It's handmade, 'specially for Susie!" I continued undaunted.

I gave the bride-to-be her present. Eddie frowned. Susie tore at the wrapping paper. She discovered my "gift" and an instruction manual (complete with diagrams) as to how to wear the godawful thing inside a cardboard box.

"Thanks, I guess," Susie said. "But I'm not too sure about the barbed wire ..."

After downing the rest of the Everclear, Shane and I got into an argument and ended up wrestling in a mud puddle before wading into Lake Superior. Heather approached me as I stood fully clothed and thigh deep in frigid water. She tried to say something conciliatory. I took exception to her intrusion, picked up a rock, and threw it at her. I missed. She continued trying to reason with me over the roar of the surf. I threw another rock and missed again before someone finally moved Heather out of range. Other than one brief, encounter during the filming of the second Quegley movie, Eddie's farewell gathering was the last time I ever saw Heather Sundquist.

As the party wound down, I stood in declining light, soaked to the skin, my French beret askew on my head, my clothes sodden and muddy. Wayne saw my plight and offered to fire up the sauna at the LakeAire Motel where he worked. Kenny and Shane and I took him up on the offer.

I started going off the rails at the LakeAire that can only be ascribed to being tuned up on grain alcohol. Sitting naked as jaybirds in the sauna (Wayne, Shane, Kenny, and me all proud graduates of Miss Hollingsworth's special class) I got the bright idea that, rather than piss in the john, to piss on the stove. The smell was hideous. Then, inspired by stories of Gary streaking football games, Kenny and I exited the sauna and ran naked through the motel parking lot. Motorists passing by on London Road honked encouragement, obliging Kenny and me to take a second lap in our birthday suits.

I was driving a hot little yellow-and-black Olds two-door hatchback Dad was leasing (the Jeep was in the shop). My mind addled, I left the sauna, grabbed my wet clothes, declined Kenny's offer of a ride home, opened the driver's side door of the rental car, slid behind the wheel, started it, and drove through Duluth buck-ass naked.

When I got home, I found all the doors were locked. Standing in the altogether, shivering in chilly night air, I knew better than to wake Dad. I walked into the backyard, found a window ajar, and pulled on the sash. The window wouldn't budge. I put my weight into it and broke the crank, which allowed me to pry the window open. As luck would have it, the window led to my bedroom. I removed the screen, slid through the opening, replaced the screen, threw on a pair of briefs, crawled beneath the covers, and fell asleep.

I was not a pretty sight in the morning. Neither was the window. Mom kept my break-in a secret though I had to pay Mr. Crooks—Mom's handyman—to repair the damage.

The chastity belt? Susie ditched it somewhere between Brighton Beach and her parents' house.

EDDIE GETS HITCHED

He was, for the better part of two decades, my on-again, off-again wingman. Sure, we had our moments. Like when he grew tired of my immaturity. In our early teens, Eddie became interested in cigarettes and girls while I was still playing with army men. We separated whenever Eddie found someone cooler to hang with. Chuck Magnusson, a guy Eddie became enamored with but a guy I had a hard time being around, comes to mind. Through it all we remained, at least to my thinking, as close as brothers. That was true even after Eddie wandered off to the Air Force, married Susie, moved to Texas, returned home to begin his career as a firefighter, bought houses, had kids—a son and a daughter—and settled down. We've since grown apart. We've not been separated by a personal or ethical rift but by political estrangement. Maybe we can patch up our friendship and get back to being brothers. Maybe not. But for nearly sixty years, that's what I thought of when I thought of David "Eddie" Salveson: *Brother.*

"I'd like you to be in my wedding," Eddie said when he was home on leave. He'd managed, after breaking his leg, to finish basic training and AIT. Before enlisting he'd made his pitch to Susie Berghult, a vivacious little thing and the product of a romance between an American serviceman and an English war bride, and Susie had said "yes".

Hell, yeah, I thought. *I'll be your best man, Eddie.*

"You'll be a groomsman along with Wayne," he added. "Paul's gonna be the best man."

I have to be truthful here. I mean, this entire exercise in writing down things remembered is to try and get at the core, the truth, of where I came from and who I am. Eddie's relationship with Paul, while pretty solid and pretty deep, was only four years old. Ours was a friendship, a comradery of nearly two decades' duration. As kids, we'd grown up one house away from each other and saw each other nearly every day. I thought there was no other possibility, in terms of who Eddie would ask to be his best man, than me. I was wrong about that and it hurt like hell.

"That's great," I lied.

If Eddie detected disappointment in my voice, he never let on. I've never talked to him about this perceived slight. Maybe he knows; maybe he doesn't. In any event, I stood up in the sanctuary of Elim Lutheran Church for my buddy. But before the wedding, a simple affair that ended with a reception in the basement of the Berghult home, there was the matter of a stag party to consider.

I'd been part of one other stag party. When Dave Michelson got engaged to his girlfriend, Debbie, he asked me to be a groomsman and I accepted. Dave also asked me to find a place to have his bachelor's party. I suggested the Liston Deer Camp. The shack was pretty primitive. It had no running water, no electricity, and sat in the middle of nowhere. Regardless, it was free and open to my use so that's where Michelson's stag party was held.

Given the deer camp didn't have electricity, the place lacked one essential element for hosting a successful stag party. With no power, there was no way to project nudie films on the shack's primitive walls. Add to this deficiency a foolish attempt to swim in Hart Lake (full of leeches with a bottom made of loon shit) in our underwear; and the fact we brought along enough liquor for an army, well, Michelson's stag wasn't the gala Dave envisioned. Still, we had fun playing cards and eating and bullshitting and getting blasted, though the lack of porn did put a damper on things.

We held Eddie's bachelor's party at Jeff Tynjala's house in Aurora. Jeff's place was a safe choice given Aurora has no city cops. Shane, still cooking his way through college, brought the food. Trouble was, Shane was once again too blitzed to oversee the prime rib we were supposed eat for dinner, meaning the roast was raw and still kicking when we sat down to eat.

Unlike Michelson's stag, we had plenty of old-fashioned porn to watch at Eddie's shindig. Jeff's lecherous cousin brought skin flicks to project on an old sheet hanging in the basement. After watching a movie or two, the plots contrived, the women undesirable, the men endowed beyond normal humanity, most of us had seen enough and wandered upstairs to drink and play cards. Not Paul: He watched the flicks over and over and over again until Jeff's cousin took his precious horde of deviance home.

Wayne and I were asleep on cots in the basement when all hell broke loose. There was banging and hollering and stomping; a disturbance that made no sense. We had no idea, as we lay in the dark, what the hell was happening until Eddie, skinnier than he'd been before basic training but still every bit of six-four and ornery, tromped down the stairs, yelling "Wake up, wake up!" at the top of his lungs wearing only his tidy whities as he whipped a leather belt through the air like some crazed lion tamer.

"Shut the fuck up."

Whack.

The belt whizzed past my head and struck the cement floor. I don't think Eddie was trying to hurt me: He was just trying to get my attention.

"Eddie, go back to bed," Wayne mumbled. "It's three o'clock in the morning."

"Wake up! Wake up! "

Whack.

I threw off my sleeping bag, grabbed a mop resting against the cinder block wall, and hit Eddie over the head with the mop's wooden handle in an attempt to slow the big fella down. Wayne grabbed hold of the momentarily stunned groom-to-be, wrestled away the belt, and the two of us dragged Eddie upstairs.

"What the hell?" the very drunk and agitated Airman said as we forced him into the living room. "It's my party and you assholes need to wake up!"

I kept a firm grip on Eddie while Wayne opened the front door. Jeff's house had no front porch. There was nothing between the living room's warmth and winter's cold.

"What the fuck!"

In the blink of an eye, Eddie was airborne; his lean, lanky, and nearly naked body soaring through bone numbing air.

"You guys are assholes!", Eddie screamed, standing in his skivvies in a snowbank. "I'm walking home," he muttered, wading through thigh-deep drifts until he reached the plowed driveway. "Fuck you!"

After fumbling around in his underwear for a bit, Eddie knocked on the back door, apologized, was let back in the house, and went to bed.

I've often wondered if I tossed Eddie into that snowbank in retaliation for his decision to make Paul his best man. I'd like to think that wasn't the case but I can't be sure.

DICK NIXON'S SIX-WEEK WONDER MARINE

It was all Dave Michelson's fault. It's that simple—how I ended up crawling through the Virginia mud.

"Hey," Dave said as we sat around in the upstairs lounge of UMD's Kirby Student Center watching *National Lampoon's Lemmings* on TV. We were between classes, waiting for Dr. Peterson's statistics, a course I took because Michelson had talked me into taking micro and macro econ. I got solid B's in both. But stats? When I sat in front of that Wang terminal, one of the only computers available on the UMD campus in 1974, each desk having a keyboard linked to the mainframe, I was flabbergasted.

This isn't going to end well.

Despite Michelson's belief I could handle the math and inputting needed to get through statistics, I was done after two weeks. I went to the registrar's office and pulled the plug. I didn't touch another computer until I worked as a law clerk for the Robins Law Firm seven years later when I used Westlaw to research legal issues. But the point of this snapshot of my relationship with Dave isn't that I sucked at math or computers; it's that I often followed Dave's lead. That's how I ended up crawling on my belly at Camp Upshire at the United States Marine Corps Officers' Candidate School in Quantico, Virginia. Dave's innocent "Hey" was a prelude for what came next.

"I'm thinking about joining the PLC," he said. "Got nothing else going this summer and since I'm looking at law as a career, becoming a Marine JAG officer doesn't sound too bad."

"OK."

"I'm gonna stop by the recruiter's office," Dave added, handing me a brochure.

Six weeks of boot camp. Paid training. Back to college. A monthly stipend after signing a contract. The next summer, six more weeks of boot camp followed by additional training. Commissioned as a second lieutenant in the United States Marine Corps. A six-year obligation after college; full-time, full tilt.

Until Dave proposed his Big Idea, I'd never considered joining the military. After Humphrey tanked and the nation elected a liar to the White House (the war did not end "soon" as Nixon had promised), I'd marched with others through downtown Duluth protesting the Vietnam War. With a lottery number of fifty-two (the draft had been suspended but eighteen-year-old males still had to register), I was primed to become Canadian. When Dave floated the idea of becoming a Marine, the notion took me by surprise. Michelson was hell-bent-for-leather to attend law school. I wasn't interested: I'd watched Dad work long hours to cultivate clients and prepare for trial. Additionally, the law held no intellectual attraction for me. But what did? I spent one quarter as a journalism major before deciding to become a social studies teacher, a diversion that lasted the blink of an eye. The one thing I was certain of, as Dave talked about the money, the training, the rigors, the camaraderie of becoming a Marine, was that I still didn't have a girlfriend. And that truth weighed heavily on my mind as we sat in Kirby and watched nonsense on television.

I'd never considered the armed forces as an option, but with no savings in the bank and no prospects for a summer job, Dave's pitch made sense. Just as I'd agreed to become a Quegley, attend summer school, and take college econ classes when I had zero interest in the subject, I followed Michelson to the recruiting office, listened to the sergeant, took the paperwork home, completed it, and turned it in.

"You turn in your application?" I asked a few weeks later.

Dave shook his head. "Change of plans."

"I thought you were interested in the JAG."

"I was. But now I'm not. Still going to law school. Gonna also get my MBA; just not joining the Marines."

I'd planned on the two of us training together. There I was, sitting in Dave's apartment, the paperwork that would take me away from friends and family filled out and submitted, charged with making up my own mind.

What the hell? They'll pay me to get in shape. I can decide what I want to do about staying in or getting out when I come back.

Poof drove me to the airport. I left Duluth on July 14, 1974 and flew home on August 25th. Between the time I told Michelson I was going and when I left, I started running. I was inspired to push myself when I found out that Carl Nelson—a former Scout in my troop and someone who had trouble keeping off the pounds—was also going to Quantico. Carl boasted that his three-mile time was under twenty-two minutes. For a pudgy kid, that was impressive: The last thing I wanted was to be bested by a fat guy.

Even though I was only in uniform for six weeks, wearing Vietnam-era green utility fatigues and black leather combat boots for every drill (the exception being that Physical Training (PT) was done in gym shorts, T-shirts, and running shoes), the experience built character. Wearing helmet liners painted silver identifying us as "Chrome Domes"—Officer Candidates—we were targets for abuse from anyone in a uniform. When our platoon sergeants addressed us, it was always "Candidate" followed by our last name. We weren't "sirs"; that would happen if we became commissioned officers. The way "Candidate" rolled off our sergeants' tongues, sort of hissed out like you'd expect a snake to talk—if snakes could talk—you could tell we weren't gonna be cut any slack just because we might one day give orders.

PT testing gauged how many sit-ups you could do in two minutes, the number of pull-ups you were able to correctly complete, and your time in the three-mile run. Sit-ups were easy: I maxed the test every time it was given. Pull-ups were a different story. The best I could do was fourteen. That was the max, and I achieved that magic number only once, on my last PT test just before I was sent home. The three-mile run was where things got interesting.

Our platoon commander, a captain who'd served in 'Nam, loved running. He'd once competed in the 10,000-meter event at the Pan American Games. While other platoons lollygagged through their morning runs, our captain put the pedal to the metal. Instead of three miles, we ran five. When we did our twenty-five-mile forced march with full packs while lugging M-14s (all the M-16s were being used by "real" Marines), our captain's fevered pace caused sweat to pour off us like heavy spring rain.

Arriving at Quantico by luxury coach (after flying into D.C.) was pretty much the last time we were afforded reasonable transportation. We marched everywhere. If we needed a ride from our unairconditioned Quonset huts (think Gomer Pyle) to a distant location on base, we were transported in cattle cars—big semi-tractors pulling livestock trailers—the sort of thing used to haul steers to slaughter. We were crammed together in those cattle cars, Candidates standing upright and grasping steel handles or holding onto each other for dear life, as the tractors and the trailers careened through camp.

We spent hour after hour on the parade deck learning how to march and pivot and turn and execute the manual of arms with unloaded M-14s. When the mercury topped ninety-five with humidity to match, we were restricted to barracks where floor fans provided slight relief. A black flag flying outside the commander's office forbade any physical activity until conditions improved.

To prevent cramps that dropped big men—like Candidate Tuttle, a guy who played nose tackle for a West Virginia college—salt tablet dispensers were mounted next to every exit in the mess hall. Printed warnings on the dispensers cautioning us against over-consuming salt were universally ignored. We gobbled salt tabs by the handfuls in hopes of avoiding Tuttle's fate: No one wanted to spend time in the infirmary.

I wasn't happy with my first three-mile run: 21:56. Carl Nelson could run the three-mile in under twenty-two and I didn't want to be bested by a "fat body," the term applied at check-in to guys who looked like Nelson. When I stepped off the bus from D.C., I was relegated to the fat body platoon until an officer, who just happened to be walking by, saw me standing with the fatties and barked: "Sergeant, get that Candidate into a regular platoon and get yourself some fucking eyeglasses!"

I worked my ass off on the confidence course, climbing wooden walls, dancing through tires and making like my old junior high nickname, "Monkey Munger," when I reached the climbing rope at the end of the course. I also upped my game from eight pull-ups to ten to twelve, finally hitting the max of fourteen, which wasn't much of a feat since an Italian guy from St. Louis managed forty-five pull-ups before our platoon sergeant made him stop.

We also spent time on a wooden balance beam, football helmets secured to our shaved heads by chin straps, smashing and smacking and jabbing each other with padded sticks ("pugils") until one of the combatants was knocked off the beam. Having grown up fighting for my life at Lincoln Junior, I wasn't afraid of being hit in the head by a giant Q-tip and I managed to hold my own. When our African American sergeant with a thick drawl pronounced the surname of a set of identical twins—the Gaskin brothers—I thought he was saying "Beau Gaskins," as if he was referring to one Candidate. He was actually addressing both brothers, "Both Gaskins." I gave "Both Gaskins" plenty on the balance beam but I never beat either one. They were the best of the best at pugil combat given their square shoulders, low center of gravity, and innate Alabama toughness.

My time in the three-mile run steadily improved until, as we approached Field Day—where platoons battled for the title of "Most Fit"—I'd bested eighteen minutes. Carl Nelson? His three-mile time regressed. That wasn't the worst of it: Carl was unable to complete the confidence course. The last task before the climbing rope was grasping an overhead bar and doing a flip—a simple gymnastics move. Nelson couldn't master that requirement, just like he was never able to complete the rope climb.

When it came time to select Candidates to compete in various events for Field Day, my lieutenant had me slotted for the confidence course. But my sergeant made a pitch for me to join our platoon's three-mile team. The other guys selected—one from North Carolina and one from California—were both college runners.

"Really?" my lieutenant asked, eyeballing me.

Even after losing weight (going from 185 to 160 over the course of five weeks) I didn't possess the physique of a cross-country man.

"He hit 17:55 and I think he can, with a little incentive, go faster. He's the best we have for the number three slot," my sergeant said.

"Candidate, I had you down for the confidence course. I'll give you the choice of which event you want to enter."

I gulped, looked at the ground, and said: "Run, Sir."

"Very well. Just don't fuck it up."

I finished fourth behind the kid from North Carolina—who ran a sub-fifteen three—and the dude from California who bested sixteen minutes and some guy from another platoon who nosed me out at the finish line. My time—18:20—wasn't my personal best but was far better than my first timed runs. And that wasn't the end of my improvement. According to a notebook page I saved in my scrapbook that lists my progress in terms of PT testing at Upshire, by the time I was ready to go home, I'd run a

17:23 three-mile! Don't take my word for it: I found a letter from Eddie Spinella—a New York City kid whose greatest goal in life wasn't to be a Marine but to work as a garbageman in Queens—in the same scrapbook. His words, as he wished me well after we'd left Quantico: *I hope you're ... in good shape ... Can you still rip off a 17-minute 3-mile?* The answer to that question—forty-five years and fifty pounds later—would be "No!"

I drew liberty in D.C. where I stayed at a fancy hotel, toured the Smithsonian, visited Arlington Cemetery, and watched the Marine Corps' Silent Drill Team perform. While on leave, I tried to get in touch with Vicky, my ninth-grade heartthrob who'd moved to Arlington, Virginia the summer before high school. I called Vicky and left a message with her mom but Vicky never called me back.

"You're gonna want to see this," our assistant platoon sergeant said after we'd made it back to Upshire from leave. "The president is about to speak."

I wasn't concerned that Nixon was going to toss the U.S. back into the Vietnam fire even though I was, technically, on active duty. By August of 1974, the U.S. was pretty much done with the war. But I was curious why our sergeant had called us into the lounge to watch a fibbing Quaker address the nation on live television. I'm certain all the Candidates in the room were stunned when our Commander in Chief announced his resignation. It was August 9, 1974; one week before I flew home.

I truly enjoyed the physical challenges of Upshire. Though a northern boy—not at all accustomed to high temps and humidity—I managed to make it through the "Junior" session of PLC training unscathed. But when I returned to Duluth, my ass far skinnier, my hair much shorter, my body lean with muscle, I had a decision to make.

Do I take the monthly stipend and sign up for the Senior PLC course, meaning I'm committing myself to six years in the Corps? Or do I opt out and take an honorable discharge?

Memories of training on the parade deck, where two hundred Candidates thrust M-14s with fixed bayonets towards Heaven, haunted me. Why? Some of the guys shouted pejorative slurs about Asians as we drilled. Insults—affixed to people I didn't know and had no reason to hate—didn't sit well with me. Another piece of evidence against me taking the monthly stipend and returning to Quantico for the Senior PLC Course concerned the adage *Once a Marine, always a Marine.*

I pictured my future self sitting behind a gray, steel, utilitarian desk in a JAG office studying legal papers when my commanding officer enters and says: "Munger: Grab your .45 and your kit. We're at war."

A vision of leading Marines up a hill in some godforsaken place—out of shape from years of desk duty, gasping for breath, my heart beating like it's going to burst—was all it took to convince me that money isn't everything.

THE OLD 300

Picture this. I'm twenty years old. My mom and I are fighting over the '67 Wagoneer Dad gifted me as a high school graduation present. The Jeep, despite Dad's attempted generosity, is really a family car. Dad drives his new, two-door Pontiac Grand Ville to and from work, which means Mom and I share the Jeep. Mom's schedule dictates I rarely drive the Jeep. Me being the eldest—six years older than my brother Dave, eleven years older than my sister Anne—I don't share very well. Ditto for Mom. So, when the daily ruckus over who's going to drive the rattling, wheezing, cantankerous Jeep gets to be too much, I decide to buy my own wheels. Problem is, I'm working as a janitor at General Cleaning making four bucks an hour and paying my own way through UMD. I don't have extra cash to spend on a car. That's how I end up with a broken down, rust-afflicted 1963 Chrysler 300, the best car I can afford.

Even though I'm not a native son—I was born in St. Paul and moved to Duluth before kindergarten—my formative years were spent here, in the hilliest town east of San Francisco. Having attended Piedmont Elementary, Lincoln Junior, Denfeld High, and UMD, I consider myself a Duluthian. Like others who share that label, I learned at an early age to negotiate Duluth's steeps regardless of weather. I had to parallel park on a hill in a blizzard to pass my driver's test. Those of you who hail from more geographically sedate places, well, be honest: You don't brave driving *to* or *in* Duluth when there's snow in the forecast. Non-Duluthians just don't buy that locals can safely navigate the town's perilous streets in winter. And yet, I'm living proof that we do.

I bought the 300 from Shane. He managed to amass a small fortune before he started UMD, and part of his wealth was automotive. Before his twenty-first birthday, Shane owned two Caddies, a vintage '50s Plymouth (nicknamed "The Bob"), and the 300. He wanted fifty bucks for the Chrysler. I got it for half-price, complete with a busted power steering pump, an inoperable driver's door, suspect brakes, and four bald tires.

A Saturday in January. I'm intent on making a beer run across the Arrowhead Bridge between Duluth and Superior before meeting up with Larry. The drinking age is eighteen. In Superior, just across the St. Louis River from Duluth, you can buy a case of Buckhorn Premium Lager for less than three dollars and get sixty-five cents back when you return the bottles. I'm headed down Piedmont Avenue in the Chrysler, thoughts of cold beer on my mind though I haven't had a lick of anything stronger than milk to drink before driving.

The road conditions are snowy but manageable even for a rear-wheel-drive iron sled with bad tires. But as the hill steepens towards the Big Lake, as I get closer to Five Corners—a messy intersection that disappeared when the MDOT gave us Mondale Drive—the snow turns to rain, which, because it's below freezing, becomes ice. As I approach the stop sign at Five corners, I tap the brakes. Nothing. I glance to the left and to the right. No other cars are around as I slide onto 24th Avenue West. I take my foot off the gas. Doesn't matter; gravity pulls the car downhill. I pump the brakes. Nothing. The old sedan, the heater roaring to keep the windshield clear of ice, the broken springs objecting at every pothole, picks up speed. At 10th Street, I try the brakes again and the car does a one-eighty. I'm now looking uphill; back towards where I came from, and the Chrysler isn't slowing down. The only saving grace to my situation is that there's no one else on the road. The Chrysler leaps and plunges like a bucking bronco as it enters and exits plateaus of intersecting streets. I'm wearing a seat belt but I'm pretty sure it won't do me a lick of good if the Chrysler collides with a semi-truck at the bottom of the hill.

In my youth it was common for truckers to take shortcuts to grain elevators located on Duluth's waterfront. Every year local television stations ran clips documenting the destruction wrought by runaway tractor-trailers full of corn or wheat or oats that lost their brakes on Duluth's hills and ended up in the living rooms of unsuspecting citizens.

That's gonna be me, I think, my gloved hands gripping a steering wheel that offers no solace. *I'll end up crashing into Wayne's front porch.*

At the intersection of 24th Avenue West and 6th Street, I brake again and a rear tire catches pavement. The Chrysler whips around to face downhill. The car continues to slide until I slam the passenger-side front tire into the curb and stop next to Lincoln Junior.

The following summer, I give the Chrysler away. That winter, a snowstorm buries Duluth. Even with places to go and people to see, I have my pride. I don't borrow the Jeep from Mom despite the fact it has four-wheel drive. Instead, I carry my skis to the top of Piedmont Avenue, slide my boots into the bindings, secure safety straps, and push off. I glide towards Lake Superior—making occasional turns to control my speed—until there's no more hill. On the flats, I pole and skate my way to West Duluth. I arrive at a familiar front yard. Larry—dressed in a snowmobile suit and helmet—is sitting on the seat of an idling Ski-Doo waiting for me. I unhook the safety straps of the skis, release the bindings, hop on the rumbling machine, and wrap my arms around Larry as he hits the gas. The Ski-Doo floats past drift-encased cars. We roar onto the Arrowhead Bridge, hell-bent-for-leather to make it to Superior to buy beer. We pass the bridge's empty tollbooth without slowing, though I'm pretty sure Larry wouldn't have stopped to pay the toll even if the tollbooth had been manned.

ASHTABULA

No, not Ohio.

Ashtabula was an apartment building located across the street from St. Mary's Hospital in Duluth. Now it's a parking lot. Back in 1976 it was home to nurses and assorted miscreants.

Dad and I, having done battle about this or that, finally had it out. I knew that Mike from General Cleaning was looking for a roommate to share his apartment in the Ashtabula Building. Mike's place boasted a huge kitchen, dining room, a fireplaced living room (the fireplace hadn't worked in ages), a full bath and two extra bedrooms. I'd been to the apartment for dinner with co-workers from General Cleaning, liked what I saw, and after Dad and I exchanged words, took Mike up on his offer. I conned Larry and Poof and John Benson (Poof's brother-in-law) into moving my crap from Piedmont Heights to the lower East Hillside. In addition to my bed, a dresser, and a desk, I also brought Dad's weight set; the one Mom bought Dad so he could become Charles Atlas (or Charles Bronson). The weights went in my new bedroom with my furniture, stereo, albums and cassettes, textbooks, a handful of paperbacks, and clothes. Since the building had no elevator, we carried my worldy possessions up five flights of stairs.

Mike was easy to get along with. The only rule he enforced was that I pay my share of the rent on time. The lease was in Mike's name. The phone was in Mike's name. The water was in Mike's name. The gas was in Mike's name. I don't remember signing anything saying I was living there. As far as I knew, the landlord had no idea about my arrangement with Mike. My share of the rent was one hundred and thirty-five dollars a month. I was pretty sure I couldn't afford the place and that was without factoring in expenses related to the Jeep. But I wanted to give living independently a try.

Dad bought himself a new Chev Suburban. Mom was driving the Pontiac Grand Ville. With the Jeep freed up for my use, I gave the Chrysler 300 to Tommy Denison. Tommy's Ford had crapped out on the Arrowhead Bridge after a night of drinking in Superior. I was driving Tommy's Fairlane—because Tommy was too loaded to get behind the wheel—when the car's transmission gave up the ghost in the middle of the old bridge. I felt responsible for the guy's troubles so I transferred the 300's title to Tommy and drove the Jeep when I could afford gas.

Mike liked to smoke pot and I wasn't above joining in. It was while smoking weed and drinking beer in the living room of our apartment that Mike introduced me to his favorite musicians. High on my roommate's list of musical saints was The Band. Mike had all of The Band's best stuff including *Big Pink* and made sure I understood the group's importance to Minnesota's beloved native son, Bob Dylan. He also possessed every Steve Goodman album ever pressed. We'd smoke and sip and listen reverently to the master singer/songwriter/storyteller—Mike's kindred Chicagoan—and I was bowled over by Goodman's talent. I fell head-over-heels in love with "The Ballad of Penny Evans," an a Capella lament. Even today, nearly fifty years after first hearing that song, Goodman's take on love, war, and loss remains seminal. It was an "aha!" moment in my life brought to my attention by my stoned yet very wise roomie.

Friends visited Ashtabula. Nearly everyone you've met in these stories (except Eddie and Susie who were married and living in San Antonio) showed up at the apartment, and with so many folks stopping by, I figured we should throw a party. In preparation for the bash, I conned Big Russ into helping me lug cases of beer and grocery bags of munchies up those five flights of stairs.

A few weeks before the party, Russ and I made a play for two cute lasses enrolled in St. Luke's Hospital's three-year registered nurse program. We broke the girls out of their dorm after curfew. I was partial to Stephanie, a gregarious, smart, shapely, and—should this surprise you—ex-cheerleader from the Twin Cities while Russ was courting Diane, a tall, laconic Lutheran farm girl from some Podunk town on the Minnesota-Iowa border. Our first and only double date with the girls ended in disaster. When Stephanie, who'd been a hockey cheerleader (did I mention that already?), hinted we should accompany the girls on a moonlight skate at a local ice rink, Russ and I should have suggested bowling. Or ping pong. Or a movie. Or parking on Skyline Drive. But we went along, tripping and falling and deflating our egos until the girls had seen enough. It was sort of funny that Diane ended up—at the party Mike and I threw—on the arm of my pal, Scott Mork. I was OK with that even though after Diane lost interest in Russ, she hinted she "wouldn't mind me asking her out." I didn't date Diane mainly because she reminded me a lot of Heather and I figured I'd end up staring at fatherhood if we ever hooked up.

The problem with having a party at Ashtabula was that the front door was always locked and the building had no intercom. My solution? I took a brass Christmas bell from childhood, attached string to it, ran the string through an open window, and hung a "Ring to Enter Mark's Party" sign by the front door.

My future wife showed up at the party as Gary's date. Gary had quite a reputation. He'd knocked up the same Montana girl twice, all the while lamenting what shitty luck he had. He attended college in Bozeman where he built a legacy as a streaker, though, so far as I know, he never got caught running through the MSU football stadium in the altogether. The night of the party, I noticed the girl Gary was dating; someone I'd been introduced to at the Yellow Sub. I hadn't thought much of Gary's girlfriend when we met in a dimly lighted bar. But in the brighter lighting of my apartment, where René's big, brown eyes and intriguing aspect came into focus, it was a different story. I found her attractive but because René was with Gary, she was off limits, meaning I looked elsewhere for companionship.

Rhonda—a shapely Proctor girl—was sitting on the front room carpeting smoking dope with Mike. I knew her from UMD but hadn't said much more than "Hey" when we passed each other in crowded hallways.

"Need anything?" I asked.

"Another beer," Rhonda said, smiling.

I brought her a beer, we talked, and she asked to see my album collection. We retreated to my bedroom and sat down on my bed. Rhonda picked up *Four Way Street*, and studied the album cover while enchanting me with hints of pot and perfume and woman.

"Did you sleep with her?" Mike asked, after the party was over and we were cleaning up the mess.

We'd had so many folks attend our gala—and things got so loud—the next-door tenant called the building manager. The guy called Mike and told him to "keep it down." That wasn't the end of it. When the building owner found out what I'd done—

374

hanging a bell on a string outside the building—the letter Mike received made it clear: *No more parties!*

I shook my head.

"Are you crazy?" Mike asked. "She was hot! I made my play and she shut me down. But you, she liked. What the hell's wrong with you?"

I knew, within a minute of Rhonda rising from my bed and looking back at me from the doorway, her eyes expectant yet dismissive, I'd blown my chance. When I saw her a few days later at UMD, Rhonda was surrounded by guys: guys who were savvier and more upfront about what they wanted than I was. Still, I tried talking to her, but those conversations went nowhere. After the quarter ended, she left UMD, and I never saw her again.

The Jeep became an issue. It got eight miles to the gallon. Granted, gas was only fifty cents a gallon, but even with cheap fuel, I found myself falling behind. Rent took half my monthly income, food another third, which left little money for tuition, books, and gas. Though it was winter and a couple miles to campus, I tried walking to school. That sucked. City buses served UMD, but I missed as many buses as I made. I ended up using the Jeep more than I should have, though the cost of gasoline wasn't the main problem with driving the Jeep.

Ashtabula didn't have a parking lot. On-street parking was limited. Tired from long days at school and working nights, I circled the block in the Wagoneer in hopes of finding a parking space before giving up and parking in the lot of an adjacent mortuary. The funeral home's signage was clear: "No Parking" but I was desperate, and the illegally parked Jeep was towed multiple times. I borrowed cash from Jeff to retrieve my car from impound but the cumulative cost of repeated tows emptied my savings account.

I might have to move home, I thought, though it took more than mere poverty for me to ask Dad's forgiveness.

I returned to the apartment one afternoon to find Mike making out with a girl on the couch. I'm no saint. I dated a high school sophomore when I was a senior and experienced intimacies with her that, today, would have me labeled a felon. I wasn't about to judge Mike if he fell for a slightly younger woman. But the girl smoking weed and swapping spit with my roommate was—at best—fifteen. Despite lustful hormones routinely clouding my judgment, I knew right from wrong. I nodded to Mike and the girl, went into my bedroom, and started to pack.

SEX, DRUGS, & ROCK AND ROLL

She wasn't a beauty but I knew—because I'd seen inside her purse at Eddie's going-away party—she was on the pill. That clandestine bit of knowledge and the fact I was three sheets to the wind sitting with Becky (the girl in question), two of her friends and Wayne and Shane at a table in the Yellow Sub, led me to lose my virginity in the front seat of Becky Tedisco's Ford.

We French kissed in front of my buddies, who tittered at the prospect of me getting naked with a girl who could out arm-wrestle me. I didn't give two shits for Wayne's and Shane's opinion of the choice I made that night. I wanted to get it over with and that's exactly what transpired: I finally figured out a way, at nineteen years old, to lose my virginity.

It wasn't love and it wasn't pretty but at least it was consensual. I did what needed doing, whispered "thanks," kissed Becky on the cheek, dressed, opened the passenger's side door, and went back to being a jerk.

That was it. No emotional connection, no great orgasmic union of man and woman like I'd read about in my mom's trashy novels or had been told takes place by the "experts" writing in *Penthouse Forum*. I did what guys have been doing for thousands of years, Becky was left disappointed, and that was the end of it. Other than passing what seemed to be another obligatory milestone on the way from the "cradle to the crypt" (thanks, Steve Goodman, for that imagery), there wasn't anything remarkable or special or earth-shattering about the fifteen minutes I spent with Becky Tedisco on that hot summer's night behind a Superior bar. I'd always wanted to be Hermie, the protagonist from *The Summer of '42*. Maybe if I'd lost my virginity—as Hermie did—to a war widow who looked like Jennifer O'Neil instead of a plain-looking, big-boned Italian girl from Oliver, Wisconsin, something deeper and more memorable might have transpired. But I wasn't Hermie. When it came to girls I was more like Oscy—Hermie's crass and uncouth buddy—than the romantic and overly sentimental Hermie. That was my role—being Oscy—and I played it well.

Months later, I found myself in the back seat of the Jeep after Dave Tynjala's (Jeff's younger brother's) wedding. The

377

wedding and reception were held on the Iron Range and I was staying the night in a cheap motel with Wayne. Wayne was back at the motel so I couldn't bring the brunette bridesmaid I'd connected with to our room. No way was I giving Wayne a free show. When the girl—whose name I don't remember—and I got interested in each other over brandy-cokes at the wedding reception and I suggested we visit my car, she was all in.

The Wagoneer's windows fogged. Things happened according to schedule until visions of changing diapers, working in the mines, and marrying an Eveleth girl I'd just met flashed through my mind. I stopped, dressed in a hurry, apologized, kissed the nameless girl on the cheek, and went back to the reception.

The following summer, I was hoodwinked by Michelson into joining the Marines. Though I was certain losing my virginity in Becky's Ford was a one and done event, Becky and I ended up back at it in the front seat of her Ford in the parking lot of the Mayor's Brass Rail in Superior. I tried to make amends for my dismal first performance and despite my inexperience, things seemed to work out. When we were done, fully clothed, and talking, I told Becky I was leaving for basic training. She asked me to write her. Despite having no affection for the girl—Becky Tedisco being only a means to an end—I said I would. Uncharacteristically, I followed through with my promise and Becky wrote back. Those letters were the end of any connection—carnal or otherwise—between us.

One bitterly cold December day, Michelson and I came up with the bright idea to have a party in honor of Comet Kohoutek. That far-distant bit of space debris was acclaimed to be the real deal; supposed to put on a show as impressive as Halley's as it approached Earth on its once every 75,000-year orbit. It seemed like a marvelous idea to celebrate the arrival of a wandering cosmic visitor. Evangelical pundits were predicting the end of the world so we figured, *What the hell?* We gathered up a couple dozen kids and drove to Shane's cabin for a monk party, invoking Bungo Jen as the comet's patron saint. Wayne and Shane donned the scratchy, wool robes Heather had sewn for them. I wore Michelson's Grand Inquisitor's outfit (he was a big wig in DeMolay and just happened to have a Grand Inquisitor's

378

robe hanging in his closet). Dave wore his white karate *gi* as the event's sergeant-at-arms.

By the time we got to Shane's cabin, the Buckhorn we'd stowed in the trunk of Michelson's Mustang had frozen solid. Shane started a fire in the cabin's stone fireplace but after an hour of coaxing flames, the cabin wouldn't warm.

"It's fuckin' cold. We need to move," I complained.

"My place," Michelson replied. "We can take the party to my apartment."

On the way to Duluth, we stopped in Pike Lake for gas. Dave fueled his baby blue Mustang wearing his *gi* as I shivered by his side in the Inquisitor's outfit. Wayne and Shane entered the station in their monk robes to buy munchies. I have no idea what folks inside the store thought of it all.

Franny, Dave's girlfriend-of-the-moment, showed up at the apartment with Lori, a girl I'd met a time or two. Lori was cute, possessing cat-like, muted, emerald eyes and a wry smile. By the time Franny and Lori made their way to the great Comet Kohoutek Party, I was tossing my cookies and making such a racket in the bathroom that Lori took pity on me, wandered into the lavatory, held my head, and washed my face with a wet washcloth. When I finally stopped barfing, Lori left to give me privacy. I resurfaced; my breath sour from puke, my head pounding like I'd gone ten rounds with famed UMD alum and professional boxer Scotty LeDoux.

"Got any aspirin?" I asked Dave, who was standing with Franny and Lori in the kitchen, Totino's frozen pizzas baking in the oven.

"All out."

I was fighting a godawful headache; the residual of too much Wild Turkey chased by cheap, bottom-of-the-Hamm's-vat Buckhorn beer.

"I've got some Midol in my purse," Lori offered.

I'll be honest: Even in my debilitated state, I thought I might, given the empathy Lori had shown, have a shot. I had no game plan. I didn't know if she was interested. But when Lori mentioned Midol, I felt things slipping away.

Shit.

I had no guideposts, other than one brief, sad exchange with Heather before I sent her packing, as to what a woman goes through when menstruating. Mom didn't have periods: She had a hysterectomy shortly after I was born. I was out of the house by the time my sister encountered puberty. Standing in Michelson's kitchen as Lori offered me Midol seemed to signal she was off limits. Lori found the medicine, pulled out three pills, and handed them to me. I located a relatively (this was a bachelor pad, after all) clean glass, filled it from the tap, swallowed the Midol, and chased them with water.

"I think I'll take a walk to clear my head," I said, placing the glass in the sink.

"Mind if I come with? Lori asked, her opaque eyes shining with intensity.

"That'd be great."

We walked up 59th with our gazes fixed on the sky despite the glow of streetlamps and light leaking from houses. Staring heavenward was for naught: Kohoutek remained a bust.

"I'm getting cold," Lori said.

I put my arm around Lori and escorted her back to Dave's.

The party was raging. John, the downstairs tenant, wasn't home and his apartment was dark. Upstairs, lights glared and the stereo thumped out late '60s and early '70s rock classics as young men and women danced and drank and kissed and flirted. I stayed away from alcohol. Lori nursed a beer. We went out on the second-floor porch overlooking the backyard. It was twenty-five below. We scrutinized the inky void above Duluth in hopes of glimpsing glory.

"What a farce," I said.

"I'm cold."

"Me too."

We kissed. She opened her mouth. I took that as an invitation.

Lori was a petite woman with a wonderful ass. We were in Dave's bedroom, on the floor, a sleeping bag covering us, snuggled into the rug, fully undressed, our fingers and mouths and bodies seeking and yearning. Given the signals Lori was putting out, I was pretty sure we'd be terrific together despite the fact that Dave and Franny were in Dave's bed, just a few feet from us, where things also seemed to be progressing.

But, like Kohoutek losing its orbit and colliding with Earth, it all came crashing down.

Honk.

"It's my brother," Franny said, sitting up in bed, pecking Dave on the cheek as she wiggled into her bra, pulled down her sweater, found her jacket, put on her shoes, and stood over us. "You coming?"

No, I thought, *but we're close.*

Lori sat up, found her underwear, dressed, kissed me hard—a hint of regret behind the gesture—and smiled. "Sorry about that. Maybe another time," she whispered as she grabbed her parka and left.

Naked and breathless and confused under the sleeping bag, I muttered: "He honked and they were gone ..."

Dave met Debbie. I stood up at their wedding. Despite being loaded at the reception, and despite there being a plethora of pretty, single, women in attendance, I didn't get laid. It wasn't until a year later that I found satisfaction with one of Debbie's bridesmaids.

First though, you probably want to know if Lori and I ever reconnected? Nope. I mean, I saw her a few times in crowded college hangouts after "He honked and they were gone." But that was it. Our brief moment under the hesitant light of an infantile comet wasn't replicated.

The occasion was Dave and Debbie's going away party. Dave had been accepted into both the University of Minnesota's MBA program and the U's law school so my buddy and his new wife were moving to the Twin Cities. Debbie, a legal secretary, was the breadwinner. Dave always insisted—in his analytical way—that dating someone with a nice body was OK but marrying a woman with "income potential"—well, that was the best a guy could hope for. Dave and Debbie were leaving the following morning, packing up the antiques Dave's dad and stepmom had given Dave to furnish the apartment, Dave's cameras and darkroom equipment, his weight set, his stereo and speakers and turntable and albums, and all Dave's and Deb's other worldly possessions for the move. Tommy Denison, and another of Dave's pals, Andy Swenson, and I were staying the night, getting up at dawn, loading Dave's Mustang and the Swenson family farm truck (an antique in its own right with an open bed and a canvas tarp to cover grain, or—in this case—Dave's and Debbie's shit) and helping the newlyweds move on the promise of free pizza and beer.

It just so happened that one of Debbie's bridesmaids was at the going-away party. Dave's apartment only had one functional bedroom—the second bedroom served as Dave's darkroom—so John, the downstairs tenant (who was again away for the weekend) gave Dave permission to use his pad.

I don't remember her name. Sounds familiar, right? The bridesmaid and I got naked in John's queen-sized bed. I remember thinking, as things got serious, *Shit, I don't have a condom.* I wasn't worried about STDs. The girl in question was a homespun young woman with an ample body and a refreshingly candid outlook on life. I was worried—from all those sex education lectures I'd attended at Holy Apostles—about making a baby. But passion being passion, I tossed caution to the wind.

The next morning my nameless partner nudged me and suggested an encore. Not wanting to risk fatherhood a second time, I declined, got up, dressed, leaned over, kissed her forehead, and headed upstairs. When I arrived at the landing outside Dave's apartment, a panel opened above my head to reveal Andy Swenson's smiling face.

"How's it goin'?" Andy asked from the attic.

"Fine."

"Saw you with that bridesmaid."

I nodded.

"You left with her?"

I nodded again.

"You spend the night with her?"

My face flushed and I nodded again.

"What's her name?"

I shrugged, opened the door, and escaped into Dave's apartment. As we loaded the car and the truck, the bridesmaid made her way upstairs to say goodbye to Debbie and Dave but I didn't interact with her before she left.

The drive to the Cities was a shit storm. Andy's farm truck barely made it up Thompson Hill on I-35. We stopped in Hinckley for gas and Tommy disappeared. Here's the thing about Tommy back then: If there was liquor within reach, he'd drain the bottle. Andy and I screwed up our most important assignment, which was to keep Tommy sober until we unloaded in Minneapolis. While Andy and I fueled the truck, Tommy snuck off to the municipal liquor store, bought himself a pint of rock gut, and guzzled it. Thankfully, the booze just made him sleepy.

Somewhere between Hinckley and North Branch, the sky, which had been open and blue, clouded over. A thunderstorm moved in. The tarp protecting Dave's and Debbie's possessions ripped in the wind and the downpour soaked everything.

The title of this story alludes to drugs. That's pretty much bullshit. I mean, other than smoking a little weed, that's about all that happened. The one time pot became an issue, Wayne, Shane, Jeff, and I showed up in the Twin Cities to party with Michelson at his sister's place. Wayne and Shane had downed the better part of a quart of whiskey. Jeff, Dave, and I were relatively straight when one of the guys living at the apartment hauled out a thirty-gallon Hefty bag full of marijuana for us to enjoy. Unfortunately, the combination of weed and whiskey had a deleterious effect on Wayne and Shane and they became convinced Dave's sister (or the roommate) had laced the pot with LSD.

Jeff and Dave and I laughed when our pals verbalized their paranoia. Our disrespect caused Wayne and Shane to insist on being driven to Wayne's brother's house across town. I made fun of my two delusional buddies on the way to Jeff's car, Wayne took exception to my teasing, and we ended up rolling around on the ground engaged in our first and only fight. Michelson separated us and Jeff drove the paranoids to Wayne's brother's place. Because of my chiding, Wayne refused to talk to me for months. Since we shared a locker at UMD, his Finnish *sisu* made for some interesting non-verbal interaction until we reconciled.

If you're expecting some Hunter S. Thompson revelation about coke or acid or heroin-fueled episodes, I'm sorry to disappoint. I was, at best, an occasional pot smoker. I bought marijuana maybe twice in my life. Once, before a concert at the Duluth Entertainment Convention Center (DECC) headlined by Wishbone Ash—with an up-and-coming outfit, whose hit single "Dream On," was climbing the charts (I caught Aerosmith *before* Steve Tyler was famous)—I bought a dime bag. I then proceeded—with John McLoughlin and Kenny—to smoke the entire stash in

John's '61 classic T-bird before the Turner Brothers took the stage.

John was proud of that T-bird. McLoughlin, who'd been dumped by his girlfriend at his hospital bedside after having a cancerous kidney removed while still in high school, was smitten with Michelle. I was out driving around in the Chrysler 300 (before I gave it to Tommy), three sheets to the wind, trying to make it up 59th Avenue West to Michelson's place because Dave had beer and you can never, at nineteen years old, drink too much beer. It was winter. The road was slick and the Chrysler couldn't climb the hill. I figured my best course of action was to slam the car in reverse, back down 59th, and try again. As the 300 roared backwards down the hill, John turned onto 59th from West 8th in his refurbished T-bird. You see where this is headed, right? On John's very first date with his future wife, I slammed the ass end of my rust bucket into the grill of John's classic car. I paid John three hundred bucks to repair and repaint the front of the T-bird, though I'm pretty sure the car was never the same. I have no idea what Michelle thought of the encounter.

There was one night when collective genius, enhanced by Dad's Windsor, shone through. McLoughlin, Town, and I were hanging out at my house on Miller Creek. By then, we were all in college and confident of our intellects.

"Your old man have anything around here to drink?" John asked as we watched something inane, likely *The Rockford Files*, my favorite television program.

Rockford was a show I watched many Friday evenings in the basement of the Tynjala house on West 5th before Jeff bought his house in Aurora. Jeff, I, and his ornery, older brother Paul would sit in the near dark, order the youngest Tynjala (Jon) to fetch us beers, and watch intently as James Garner solved crimes. Paul was ornery in the sense he'd sometimes wander in on poker games taking place in the dining room of the house, survey neatly stacked poker chips in front of Jeff's buddies, remark "I hate piles", and knock the piles into disarray. That said, the three of us often shared the comradery of being girl-less, dateless, and stuck in the Tynjala rec room on a Friday night.

"Check in the bar," I replied, pointing towards an old Hoosier cabinet housing my parents' booze.

McLoughlin did as suggested and came back to the couch carrying a quart of Windsor Canadian and three glasses. "Look what I found."

I grabbed an ice bucket from the Hoosier, wandered into the utility room, opened the fridge, and filled the bucket with ice.

Mike smiled when I returned. "Harry's whiskey on the rocks. What could be better?"

In the process of draining the bottle, we grew more and more reflective as to why three young, eligible, bright, and decent looking young men were stuck in my parents' basement on a Friday night. It wasn't long before we were writing an editorial to the *Duluth News Tribune* bemoaning what a shithole Duluth was. As we collaborated, our post-adolescent vitriol poured onto a yellow legal pad.

"Good to go?" I said once we'd memorialized our tirade.

"Mail it in," John said.

"We've got it down pat," Mike added.

The next morning, I heard John yell, "What the hell?" from my bedroom.

Since my parents and siblings were gone, I'd slept in Dave's room. Hearing John's expletive, I got up and wandered down the hallway in my skivvies. I opened the door to find Pelly and John on the bottom bunk. The dog was on top of John, licking my pal's face with considerable affection.

"Get this fucking dog off me," John bemoaned.

"But he likes you," Mike gleefully observed from the top bunk.

The essay we'd written? It never got mailed.

When Jeff Tynjala and Evan Wingness and Steve Cordes and Wayne Johnson and Mike Schiltz formed a band in high school (the band was originally called "Wildflower" after a song Tynjala wrote and I penned lyrics to but morphed into "Lusitania" just before the band broke up), I signed on as an unpaid roadie. I figured that lugging amps and speakers with Bruce Berg—gaining free admission to dances in return for labor—would be a prelude to meeting girls but that didn't happen.

Just after graduation, Steve and I spent a night on Park Point watching unattached young women flit across golden sand like unencumbered fireflies. Sitting around a bonfire drinking beer, waves lapping the shoreline, the loneliness of near-adulthood seemed crushing and perpetual as the sun's red orb rose over the amazingly serene lake. We never connected with those girls on the beach.

But what I did gain from my experience as a roadie with the band was a love for all things Buffalo Springfield and Neil Young and Stephen Stills and CSN and CSNY-related. The long laments Young penned in the late '60s and early '70s—"Down by the River," "Southern Man," and a host of other jammers—were my friends' stock in trade. I fell in love with that music. I also admired my buddies' don't-give-a-flying-fuck attitude. I know, I know, I'm off topic again. Relax. We'll get back on track shortly.

Our senior year—Johnson and Cordes—honored Denfeld's homecoming celebration in unique fashion. Two motorcycles decorated in maroon and gold crepe paper—the two riders' identities concealed by helmets and face shields—rumbled up the school's back stairs, through an open door, and roared into Denfeld. The mystery pair zoomed past the cafeteria; by Principal Samskar's office; past the main entrance; down another flight of stairs; by the auditorium; out an open Tower Entrance door; and down two flights of stairs into the parking lot. Principal Samskar chased the clandestine intruders out the door but lost them in a sea of parked cars; the riders' identities forever unknown to the powers that be.

During high school and college, I reveled in live shows at the Duluth Arena Auditorium (DECC), including *Jesus Christ Superstar*. I bought the album and played it over and repeatedly until I could sing the entire rock opera word for word. There were other concerts I managed to take in; all of which I attended relatively straight and sober. Edgar Winter. Ricky Derringer. Leslie West. Fog Hat. Nazareth. The James Gang. Three Dog Night. Brownsville Station. Commander Cody. Joe Vitale. Kansas. I wasn't able, like Kenny, to score tickets to really *big* shows like Clapton or Elton or Dylan or The Band or The Dead or ELP. I pretty much confined my concert-going to the DECC with one noteworthy exception; a trek to Northrup Auditorium in Minneapolis to see Todd Rundgren's Utopia.

I managed to beg the Grand Ville from Dad for the trip. Roaring down I-35—the sedan's four hundred and fifty-five cubic inches purring under the hood as the speedometer touched one hundred, pot smoke billowing from open windows in a Cheech and Chong moment, the car's cassette deck belting out Mountain's "Mississippi Queen"—McLoughlin and Washburn and I had us a time. When John tried to light up *during* the concert, a campus cop made sure he understood the rules: "No smoking indoors." No tickets were handed out. No one was arrested. It was all, with the exception of the mind-numbing volume of Rundgren's music, very civilized.

Dropping acid? That happened only once and not by choice. After returning from Quantico, I hosted a gathering at my parents' house attended by many of the folks, including Gary, populating this memoir.

"Feel anything yet?" Gary asked as we listened to music in the rec room as guys and gals talked quietly or necked or whatever.

"How's that?"

"I put a hit of acid in your beer."

I looked at the half-empty bottle in my hand.

"You should be feeling something 'bout now," Gary added.

I didn't. It was the only time I supposedly dropped acid and, for whatever reason, I experienced no Timothy Leary moment.

REBORN ON THE FOURTH OF JULY

"Let's spend the fourth fishing," Larry suggested. "There's a nice campsite on Fish Lake."

I was in, as were Larry's older brother Rick and Larry's best friend, Steve. But we had a problem: How to get from the boat landing to the island? I'd busted Dad's eighteen-foot Larson inboard/outboard any number of times. Dad wasn't about to let me take his pride and joy for a drunken weekend on a shallow, rock-infested lake.

How about the Lund?

With the ten-horse Evinrude on Dad's duck boat, it hauled. I knew Dad wouldn't object to me using the Lund and the Evinrude. They were just collecting dust. But the boat only had one seat, with room for a second guy to sit on a cooler. Given there were four of us, we'd have to make multiple trips across the lake.

I was off work from General Cleaning and Larry and Rick and Steve had three-day weekends as well. Steve borrowed the Hansen family canvas tent and I brought a Coleman two-burner stove and lantern from home. We loaded food, clothing, fishing rods and tackle, and sleeping bags into the Lund and ferried the four of us and our gear across Fish Lake.

Planning the weekend, Larry and I made an executive decision: We bought only bad beer. We filled coolers with ice and the nastiest brands we could find: Hauenstein, Fox Deluxe, Northern, and Pfeiffer. In retrospect, that was a stupid idea. Cheap beer is drinkable on a hot day if it's ice cold. But with the mercury hitting ninety over the holiday weekend, when all the ice in our coolers melted, we were "forced" to drink lukewarm, skunky beer.

A thunderstorm rolled in after we made camp. Steve's tent collapsed in the downpour and despite our best efforts to raise the center pole, we ended up hunkered down under wet canvas, our sleeping bags soaked, the four of us shivering until the weather relented.

The morning of Independence Day, we dried out our wet clothes and sleeping bags, cooked eggs and bacon, drank Tang, and sipped hot coffee. Later, while fishing from shore, I caught a couple of nice walleye. Not wanting to clean the fish near the campsite, I got the bright idea to fillet them on a boulder in the lake.

"Hey, isn't that young man naked?"

Fish Lake's shoreline is crowded with seasonal cabins and year-round homes. Given it was the busiest weekend of the summer, folks were out and about boating, floating, fishing, and enjoying the holiday. The elderly woman who spied me cleaning fish on a rock in the altogether got more than she bargained for.

"Goddamnit, he is!"

I waved my fillet knife in greeting and saw the old man, his hand on the tiller of a small outboard, scowl in response.

"Duck, Mildred, and I'll take off!" he yelled, coaxing speed from the ancient Merc to whisk his beloved away from perdition.

That night Larry and I ran the Lund back to the landing to retrieve Gary. Fish Lake is generally calm but can turn wicked. Years later, five Apostolic Lutheran boys would overload their own little boat and lose a battle with an angry Fish Lake during a thunderstorm. Three of those Laestadian kids would drown because they weren't wearing lifejackets. Larry and I—both Eagle Scouts—had life jackets with us in the Lund but weren't wearing them. Like those ill-fated boys, drowning was the furthest thing from our minds as we raced across the lake, no lights on the boat with only the moon showing us the way.

I don't remember much about Gary's time on the island. Besides being a little full of himself, an aspect of his persona that he balanced by being perpetually unsure, Gary wasn't a bad guy. Immature and narcissistic, yes; but not an irredeemable soul.

A year later—1976—the fourth of July fell on America's two-hundredth birthday. Someone decided Denfeld should hold an all-class reunion during the nation's bicentennial celebration. The reunion was a big production that included mailings to every graduating class. I'm not sure why I signed up for all the hoopla. Most of the kids from my class whom I considered friends lived in or around Duluth, working fulltime or going to UMD or UWS or Vo Tech or Scholastica. I saw former classmates I wanted to see on a regular basis. Why I forked over money for events I wasn't going to attend, I can't explain.

Over the course of the weekend, Larry and Rick and Steve and I decided to drink two hundred beers for two hundred years in celebration of America's historic birthday. We started our quest at a Denfeld-sponsored picnic at Spirit Mountain—a new ski hill owned by the City of Duluth overlooking St. Louis Bay. We were working our way towards our lofty goal when we began wrestling, a caper that ended with all four of us rolling topsy-turvy down the ski hill. No one got hurt and, with more beers waiting in the trunk of Larry's Vega, we left Spirit Mountain in search of further amusement.

René and Dode Komalainen (Larry's girlfriend and eventual wife) and other Denfeld alum met us on Park Point where we swam in Lake Superior's frigid waters and drank more beer. In the evening Larry, Dode, and I attended a Class of '73 reunion dance. Cock-sure and self-important, I showed up in my standard anti-establishment uniform; blue-striped bibs, a maroon beret, shirtless, and wearing sandals. I don't remember who I talked to or who I hung out with but I know I went home alone.

The next morning was America's bicentennial birthday. I managed, despite a prodigious hangover, to force myself out of bed to meet up with Larry and Rick and Steve. After opening a bottle of Schlitz and sampling the hair of the dog, I set about helping my pals polish off the rest of those two hundred beers, thereby ensuring my legacy as a patriot.

LOVE

I didn't immediately fall in love with the woman I married. It wasn't like some sappy romantic movie where I saw her and she saw me across a crowded dance floor, sparks flew, and the rest is history.

That's not it at all.

I'd been infatuated with other girls, maybe even Heather, though our relationship was so toxic, I'm not sure what my true feelings for her were. Here's what I learned from my brief, weird connection to Heather Sundquist: I valued brains, more than a perfect body or a portrait-worthy face. Heather had that—smarts—in spades. Maybe, when it was all said and done, my time with her revealed this truth: Whomever I ended up with would have to be passionate, for sure, but would also have to be smart. I wasn't into dumb women who make their mark in the world based upon their looks but who can't string an intelligent sentence together. Minnesota singer/songwriter Jonathan Rundman has a great song about this very thing:

Listen to me boys
And learn important things,
Benefit from wisdom
That experience brings.

I will be specific
I will be direct
When you look for love,
Look for intellect.

You know that smart girls
Shine like laser light
'Cuz they're so sharp
And they're so bright.
I'll tell you
Smart girls know the human heart
Because love is science
And love is art.

My first interaction with René Kathleen Privette was innocuous. As I said, Gary introduced me to René in the dark recesses of the Yellow Sub. She was nineteen, a year out of Denfeld where she'd been a classmate of Amy's; a sophomore when Gary and I were seniors. I'd met her older sister Diane—a chatty, tall, long-limbed girl when we shared homerooms at Lincoln and Denfeld—but Diane was someone I never said more than "hello" to in passing. Upon encountering René at the Yellow Sub, we exchanged pleasantries and I was underwhelmed. I could tell she had a nice figure. But her overall personage didn't strike me as exceptional. I certainly didn't perceive the depth of her intellect from one, brief meeting. Besides: I didn't want to get too friendly with her. I figured—given Gary's reputation—René would fade from view, becoming just another of Gary's romantic casualties.

I'd known Gary a long time. He'd been in Miss Hollingsworth's special class so I appreciated that he was precocious and inscrutable. I was reminded of this truth on a number of occasions, including a discussion held when driving back from a Denfeld varsity basketball game. Dad allowed me to borrow the Jeep for my first long-distance road trip. I drove Jeff (who didn't have a driver's license) to a game in Hibbing. Gary ended up riding back to Duluth with us. He'd been the team's student manager but got into it with Coach Stone. The argument led to Gary being canned or quitting—I don't recall exactly which. On the way home, Jeff and I got an earful as to how much more Gary knew about basketball than Coach Stone. That conversation was but a small sampling of Gary's belief in his own superiority.

Gary had enough credits to skip the last quarter of our senior year at Denfeld and embark upon an exodus across America. He put out his best Jack Kerouac vibe, proclaiming he would, as the brilliant writer he ascribed to be, craft an epic tale of life on the road. At the time, I hadn't read Kerouac. I have now so I get the allusion. I don't know if Gary journaled his hitchhiking experience. I do know he never published a narrative about his walkabout.

After my first encounter with René, I was convinced she was little more than Gary's temporary sidekick. And as I spent more time with Gary and René, sometimes with René's friend

Eleanor as part of the mix, I recognized aspects to Gary's and René's relationship that mimicked my own behavior towards Heather.

I was riding in the back of René's white Vega station wagon, Eleanor sitting platonically on the seat next to me. Gary was driving and René was in the front passenger seat when Gary asked for a cigarette.

"I'm all out," René replied.

"What the fuck?"

Gary started verbally abusing René in a way that didn't convey respect. After a brief argument, Gary stopped the car, René got out of the Vega, entered a convenience store, bought a pack of smokes, returned, and handed a cigarette to Gary. It was René who dug in her purse, found the cash, and paid for Gary's smokes. The guy never had any money. He needed cigarettes but it was René who bought him a pack with her own, hard-earned cash after being harangued.

I pretty much stayed on the outskirts of their relationship, whatever its merits or issues, while trying to cultivate—at least in my mind—a connection with Eleanor; a connection that never materialized.

"I'm gonna be at basic training," Gary said one night. Gary, René, and I were driving around Duluth in my Jeep looking to steal wooden fish crates to use as bookshelves in my apartment. I was driving. Gary was in the front passenger's seat and René was in the back seat. "I want you to keep an eye on René while I'm gone."

"Sure."

Without hearing from the woman involved, I made a pact to watch over René while Gary wandered off to become a warrior.

Things changed. I'll leave it to my wife to tell you what happened. My guess is that René heard plenty from Gary about his intellect, his talents, and his plans but saw precious little action backing up any of his bullshit. Here's what I *do* know: I didn't violate my friend's trust; I didn't start up with that brown-eyed, West End, Catholic girl.

Since we were both attending UMD, we began sharing rides to school. René did the brunt of the driving in her white, manual transmission Vega station wagon. That car was René's pride and joy until Gary totaled it while home on leave, requiring her to buy a used, black and yellow Datsun B-210 Honey Bee as a replacement. She bought both cars herself, with no help from her parents, using money she earned as a salesclerk at the Ward's store in the Miller Hill Mall.

Sometime after Gary went back to his military training, René started dating Jim, a motorcycle-driving, ice-hockey-playing, hard-drinking, fun-loving Proctor guy. I was the odd man out, trying like hell not to look like an idiot, as they became an item. I'm not sure how long they dated. I do know that René's parents— Don and Merc—couldn't stand Gary and were relieved when the short-statured, blond-headed ball of energy from Proctor started courting their daughter. René's parents knew who I was from engaging in small talk with me on the rare occasions I picked up René for school in my Jeep. As Jim and René grew closer and I hung around the edges of their burgeoning relationship, I suspect Merc took René aside and said something like: "What are you doing? You can't string Mark along like that."

I witnessed one such exchange when I showed up at the Privette house to go on a bike ride with René. I pulled my Schwinn out of the Wagoneer, leaned it against a cement block retaining wall, and walked up the sidewalk in the backyard. René was pushing her ten-speed towards me dressed in shorts and a tank top. She was braless, a circumstance that caught my eye and drew her mother's attention.

"René!" Merc called out from the porch.

René turned around. While Merc didn't say it aloud, I was able to read her lips: *You ... don't ... have ... a ... bra ... on!*

My future wife smiled and said, "It's fine, Mom."

Though René was pretty clear we were biking to Canal Park as friends, I hadn't gotten the memo. I'd made sandwiches and brought along a bottle of red wine and plastic cups in a rucksack. At twenty-one years old, you don't bring a bottle of decent wine (the kind with a cork, no less) on a bike ride with an attractive girl if you're just "friends." I'm fairly certain, once I spread a blanket on the grass, pulled out lunch, and opened the wine bottle, René knew what was up. We ate, drank wine (me more than her) talked, laughed, walked to the end of the pier, stood beside the lighthouse, and took in Lake Superior's beauty. Though something had changed in the way I felt about René, nothing, so far as I could tell, had changed in her view of things. She was done with Gary. She was dating Jim. We drove to school together. I shared the tennis court and biked and even canoed with René and her girlfriends. But those weren't dates; they were simply outings between friends.

What made things so damn hard was that, despite my initial blasé reaction to René, over months of riding together to school, hanging out in the same group of guys and gals, coupled with my growing appreciation for René's intellect, heart, and yes, her body, it wasn't long into Gary's absence and Jim's intrusion that I was smitten—totally and absolutely in love. I don't think—in fact I know—René didn't have a clue. She was nineteen, dating a fun-loving guy everyone liked and had no inkling of my feelings. I'm certain this was the case because, just as we arrived at the Privette home on our bikes, Jim roared up Third Street on his motorcycle to pick René up for a date.

A funny thing happened while I stood in the shadows. We were at Caribou Lake. I'm pretty sure there were other folks with us but all I remember is René, her younger brother Virn, and me being at the public landing. I'll say this: That girl looked fetching in a bikini. Virn and I were on shore, beers in hand, shooting the shit, when René exited the water. Her two-piece suit had a strapless top; the cups held in place by curvature or hope or gravity. From what transpired, I know it wasn't a lack of curves that caused mischief with her bikini. And there was no shortage of hope on my part that René would come around. So that leaves only gravity as an explanation for why, when René stepped out of the lake, Virn and I were treated to a *Playboy* moment: The top of René's suit had slipped to her waist, embarrassing René but putting a big smile on my face.

To keep an eye on things, I chummed around with Jim and his Proctor buddies, dragging Larry with as my wingman. Larry's girlfriend, Dode, and Jeri—a co-worker of both Dode and René at Ward's—were part of the mix. Since René was otherwise occupied, when friends invited me to a Fleetwood Mac concert at Parade Stadium in Minneapolis (the Mac's first album with Stevie Nicks was blowing away the charts), I asked Jeri to accompany me. She said "sure" but like most of my interactions with women, things got all balled up. When I pulled up in front of Jeri's house to pick her up in Dad's Suburban, Jeri was under the mistaken impression we'd be driving down to the Cities, go to the concert, and drive back that evening.

"Ah, no. We're staying over at Rick's and Steve's and driving back tomorrow," I said as Jeri's mom watched her daughter climb into the front passenger seat of the Suburban.

"Oh?"

I noticed a catch in Jeri's voice. "Is that alright?" I asked.

"Mom," Jeri yelled through the window, "we're staying the night."

"OK, Dear. Be safe," Jeri's mom replied.

That wasn't the end of our miscommunication. Jeri had no idea I considered the trip a date. She figured it out when, after she insisted on paying for her ticket, I demurred, saying "My treat." That's when Jeri's brow furrowed and she likely thought, *Oh shit: I'm staying overnight in the Cities with a guy I hardly know!*

Despite a deluge dousing Jeff Beck (the opening act), the rest of the concert was great. When the Mac took the stage, the sun peeked through the clouds, and all was right with the world. That feel-good moment didn't carry over to my date with Jeri. Once she encountered Steve at his apartment I could tell—watching Jeri and the curly-haired leprechaun interact—I was toast. Jeri and Steve connected, dated, and got hitched. I even stood up at their wedding. They have two kids, a great life, and remain together forty-plus years after our first and only date tanked.

Hanging out with Jim and his Proctor pals, Larry and I found ourselves at a toga party doing our very best *Animal House* impersonations inside a motorhome stocked with Falstaff beer. After drinking to instill nerve, we ran around inside the DECC in togas during a UMD hockey game to the delight of the crowd and the annoyance of security. It grated on me, pulled at my jealous manhood, to pretend Jim was my buddy. I didn't hate the guy. I really <u>did</u> like him. But he was <u>the</u> competition; <u>the</u> guy standing between me and love. To have to sit back and watch Jim woo René tortured my heart and disenchanted my soul.

What could be more gut-wrenching than René inviting me to tag along as she and Jim spent time together at the Thomas Shows? Every summer, the carnival sets up in the DECC parking lot. The Thomas Show features rides, games of chance, and the traditional foods of a Midwestern fair; cheese curds and pronto pups and cotton candy and caramel corn and the like. Why I accepted René's invitation to walk around the fair with Jim and her, I have no idea. I guess I fell in line because I didn't want to disappoint the object of my undeclared affection.

We were standing in front of a booth where you toss balls at an impossibly small target to win prizes. Jim hit the bullseye with all three baseballs, won a ginormous blue Hippo, and proudly handed it to René.

Shit.

You know my feelings about God, right? I mean, I'm a believer, though my faith—like that discussed in the Gospel of Mark—is akin to a tiny seed. What happened next, well, despite the fragility of my belief, leads me to conclude there is a God. It's not like I prayed for Jim to die or be rendered a quad in a motorcycle accident or anything nefarious. I'm pretty certain that, despite my despair after the Thomas Show fiasco, I never stooped *that* low. But God heard something. Maybe Merc prayed for her daughter to stop toying with me. Or maybe I uttered a fleeting, tenuous plea for divine intervention. Whatever the case, something momentous and unexpected happened to change the dynamics of our relationship.

"Jim's going to Alaska," René revealed as we sat in her Datsun. We were parked on Skyline Drive, just shooting the shit, when she dropped her bombshell. "His dad's sending him away to work on a fishing boat."

"Why?"

"Jim's not stupid but he pretty much partied away his freshman year. His father isn't happy."

I nodded, letting René tell her story.

"Truth is: Jim's dad isn't all that keen on us."

The moment was ripe for confession. But instead of opening my mouth and my heart, I balked. "I'm sorry; sorry Jim has to go to Alaska," I lied. "He's a good guy."

She nodded. "He is."

"But ...," and here's where I finally found some self-respect, "... I can't say I'm sorry to see him go."

That's as close to a declaration of love as I was able to mumble sitting in the late summer sun in René's black-and-yellow

Honey Bee. Despite the temerity of my reply, from the way things turned out, I'm pretty sure René got the message.

TALKING

I went to work for Wickstrom and Nevin building houses on a four, sometimes five, man crew. Larry got me the job. Maybe he felt I needed something more challenging than working as a janitor. Or maybe he thought I could earn more money working for Bruce Wickstrom and Tom Nevin, the owners of the company, than I made buffing floors for General Cleaning.

I liked both Bruce and Tom ("Nevie"). They were easy-going guys who loved a good joke and were as fair with me as the day is long. Coming from a household where Dad didn't engage in home repair, my prowess with tools was dubious. The bosses learned early on not to trust me to make precision cuts with a skill saw. Instead, they used me as a grunt. I carried sheetrock and plywood—once moving six sheets of half-inch plywood (approximately three hundred pounds) Larry stacked on my back—across the job site, up a plank, and into the house we were building. I also had no trouble carrying a bundle of shingles on each shoulder up a ladder and onto a roof. Such stunts are likely *a* reason—along with childhood accidents already related—I ended up having a low back fusion before I turned forty. But I loved the work, loved the comradery, and reveled in the tales told and the laughter shared over beers and pre-mixed cocktails (Bruce didn't drink beer) at the end of a workday.

We built garages and homes in Saginaw, Hermantown, Duluth, and Cotton. After a day of shoveling and carrying and toting and fetching at the Cotton homesite, Larry and I slipped Dad's Lund duck boat into the tannin-stained water of the Whiteface River and drifted downstream with the current. We drank cold Hamm's beer from cans and caught walleye after walleye and life was pretty damn good, though both of us were disconcerted to see the Cotton landfill encroaching upon the Whiteface as the river wound through wilderness. Why the powers that be allowed a landfill to spill into a pristine walleye fishery, I have no idea. Though Larry and I were young men with much to learn, as Eagle Scouts we knew—floating past a riverbank overflowing with trash into a waterway desecrated by hatched appliances—we were witnessing a very distressing thing.

Larry was the only smoker at W&N. He left his cigs in his jacket while working. It was easy pickings for Nevie to pluck Larry's smokes from a pocket, climb a ladder, and painstakingly staple individual cigarettes to a truss. Larry also once made the mistake of leaving his cooler unattended. When he opened the Coleman to grab lunch, it was empty. After a brief search, we found Larry's baloney and cheese sandwiches air-nailed to a wall.

We were working on a new house, rolling out sod, when Larry became inspired: Why not sod the roof of the garage and place Nevie's lawn mower (he lived right across the street) on the roof? Lord, did we catch it! Not from Bruce and Nevie; they thought our prank was funny. We caught holy hell from the homeowner when he showed up at the jobsite to find rolls of sod and a battered lawn mower sitting on the roof of his new garage.

Before Gary came back from basic training and totaled René's Vega wagon, Larry and I and Rick and Steve set about replacing the engine in Larry's Vega coupe. Larry found a used engine at Chesney's junkyard, bought it, loaded it into the back of Bruce's pickup, and hauled it home. With the encouragement of two cases of beer, some stern warnings from Shirley—Larry's and Rick's mom—that the tripod we'd built out of aspen logs wasn't safe, and the assistance of René (we used her Vega as a template), we dropped the used engine in Larry's car. After some minor adjustments by Dick—Larry's neighbor and the owner of a transmission shop—we tooled around Duluth in the refurbished coupe. Installing the Vega's hood was the only thing left to accomplish.

Occasionally, Bruce's son would join our four-man crew. He was a teenager, not very energetic, and lacked common sense. While I crawled around an attic where it was a hundred and ten degrees, the kid's only job was to keep the hopper of a blower full of insulation. If you operate a blower without insulation, it sends shit everywhere. I was sweating like a pimp in a police raid when the kid disappeared and let the hopper run dry. While I was cussing and wiping fiberglass from my mouth and eyes and nose, Larry was working in the basement. We later met for lunch and burst out laughing: Nevie had used leftover paint and a piece of plywood to craft a sign proclaiming that Larry's hoodless Vega was for sale for "$50.00 or Best Offer." Larry's phone number was prominently displayed and Larry's mom received quite a few calls about the car. That same week, Nevie took his wife to the Cities, leaving his kids at home with his mother-in-law—an immigrant who spoke broken English. Larry and I were doing last minute touch-ups on the new house. That was Nevie's mistake, leaving the two of us working unsupervised a stone's throw from his front door. Imagine the confusion Nevie's mother-in-law experienced when folks rang the doorbell of the Nevin home and asked if the place was really in foreclosure and available for "$500.00: Cash Only" as our crude billboard proclaimed.

Gary was stationed in Okinawa. Jim was stuck on a fishing trawler in the Bering Sea. I figured it was time to make something of my luck. From the first time I met René to our first date, I'm thinking maybe a year passed. During that time, as we shared rides to and from UMD, she and I talked. I knew after Gary and René visited me at Ashtabula she was studying art at UMD. I really didn't understand the depths of René's creativity until we started carpooling. Snippets of her talent were revealed as our friendship blossomed. She encouraged me to take an art class at UMD. I'm a fair cartoonist but I'm no artist. René helped me through that class by giving me tips that earned me a passing grade.

Sometime after Jim got his ass shipped off to Alaska, René called me. She was crying. She and her dad had been in an argument. She'd said something Don took exception to and while trying to slap René's face, he inadvertently punched her, causing a swollen lip and a black eye. I picked René up at her house and we drove to the Robin Hood restaurant in the Mall. We ordered drinks and talked and I felt like a knight in shining armor or a brave soldier from a Hemingway novel.

Later that summer, René and Jeri showed up at a job site in West Duluth while the W&N crew was pouring a concrete slab for a new garage. The girls were on their way to Thunder Bay, Ontario to buy Canadian jeans.

"Sounds like fun," I said, standing next to a wheelbarrow and leaning on a No. 2 shovel as we talked.

Tom and Larry were troweling concrete. Bruce was using a gasoline-powered vibrator to shift cement into place. I could tell that my co-workers were giddy about having two pretty girls show up at a job site. I also knew there'd be hell to pay once René and Jeri left.

"See you when you get back?"

René, who was wearing those damned white painter's pants—the ones that really showed off her figure—nodded.

"Drive safe," I said.

She nodded again.

I leaned the shovel against the wheelbarrow and walked across the driveway. René was standing outside her Honey Bee when I hugged her. She smiled, created distance, got in the car, backed down the alley, shifted into first, and drove away.

"Interesting," Nevie said. "Very interesting."

"He's had the hots for her for a year," Larry chimed in. "Says they're just 'friends.' Says all they do is 'talk'."

Bruce smiled. "So that's what they call it these days, eh? 'Talking'?"

My time with W&N ended in early September. I found a custodial position at the Montgomery Ward store in the Miller Hill Mall. I got an interview through Mom's cousin, Lizette Grinden, who was a department manager at Ward's. Funny thing about that job: René just happened to work behind the Ward's candy counter.

I was hired by a drunk named Loren. Because my shift included weeknights and weekends and Loren worked weekdays, I was essentially my own boss. It was pretty simple stuff: emptying trash cans, keeping the floors free of water and snow and dirt, cleaning nastiness in the men and women's bathrooms, mopping the always dirty floor of the Ward's automotive building, cleaning up messes in the Buffeteria (the store's restaurant), and such. Occasionally, I'd get called to the warehouse to help the guys in receiving load a mattress or a couch or another large item onto a delivery truck. My connection to the receiving guys nearly got me fired.

Nate and his partner in crime, Orson, had a habit—when unloading wrench and screwdriver sets—of diverting tools into the trunks of their cars. The receiving guys also liked to smoke pot during breaks. I joined them a time or two but found it too hard to concentrate on work while stoned. But smoking pot on the job wasn't why I almost got fired. I was nearly canned because I'd witnessed my pals' thievery, was called into the office, and refused to squeal. Ultimately, the head honcho didn't fire me. He just acted on his suspicions and dealt with Nate and Orson in due course.

My first date with René happened just before I left W&N. Poof asked Larry, John Benson, Jeff, and me to stand up for him when he married my old Piedmont friend, Vicky Stauber. I asked René to be my escort. She said "yes," wore a salmon dress, and was stunning. After the wedding mass (Catholic and way too long) and the reception, we went back to Poof's house to party. René had to work the next day and left early. I was smitten but also drunk and needy so I fooled around with one of the bridesmaids in an empty bedroom. Nothing scandalous happened. My heart wasn't in it. There was only one girl for me and it wasn't the one looking at me with expectant eyes from a borrowed bed.

I asked René out on a second date. She again said "yes." We went to the Chinese Lantern, Duluth's iconic Asian restaurant. René had sprained her ankle and was on crutches. Despite her affliction, we had a great time. Emboldened, I asked her to spend Labor Day weekend in the Twin Cities. A group of mutual friends was attending the Minnesota State Fair and had invited me to tag along. René again said "Sure."

On a mattress in the spare bedroom in Rick's and Steve's apartment, we shared our first real kiss and our first flirtation with love. But whether it was my history with Heather—where I'd become intimate with a wonderful girl with no real understanding of what I wanted—or some weird notion of gallantry spawned by my mother's romanticism, or an infantile devotion to sagas of heroes saving damsels in distress (wasn't I saving René from Gary or from Jim or from her father?), as we snuggled and explored, I looked into those bright, shiny, bigger-than-life brown eyes and said, "No. Not like this. I want to make love to you for the very first time in a big brass bed."

After we married, we bought that brass bed. By then, we'd made love—incredible, delicious, ravenous, spiritual love—many times. I once believed our consummated passion was proof I'd rescued René from whatever demons or dragons sought to devour her.

In truth, it was René who rescued me.

THE END

PHOTO GALLERY (II)

Miller Creek

Mired!
Dad getting helpful advice from Rudy Monson.

Ninth-grade Lincolnaires
I'm the shortest dude in this picture!

The Munger Kids and Deuce II

Lincoln Ice Cream Salesmen
Gotta love the shirt!

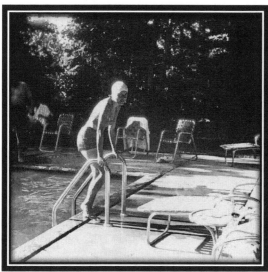

Mom at Smitty's Super Club
(Solon Springs, WI)

Lincoln Viking Basketball Team
(I'm in the second row, third from the left)

Lincoln Student Council Executive Board
Again, I'm the shortest one in the picture ...

Me, Kirk Vesterstein, Dr. Mark Neustal, Potter Neustal,
and Scott Vesterstein (Snowmass, Colo. 1970)

Summer Rental on Caribou Lake (1970)
(Kirk Vesterstein, Scott Vesterstein, Me, Dave)

Lincoln Ski Team
(I'm in the first row, second from right)

Dad, Me, and Mom: Eagle Scout Ceremony (1971)

Lincoln Speech Team
(I'm the first one on the left in the first row)

Camp Jamar

Denfeld Ski Team (1971-72)
(I'm the middle guy in the first row)

Snowmass, Colo. (1972)

Denfeld High Ski Team (1972-73)
(With girls on the team, I dressed formally for the occasion)

Skiers Visit Spirit Mountain Site
(I'm the middle student)

The Jeep and Pelly at the Cabin

The Cabin Before the Loft

The Quegleys

Where There's Quegleys, There's Hope
(Poster by the Author (1974))

A Cappella
(Partial photo: Dode is in the middle of the second row)

Waiting for the Bus to Piedmont
(Vicky Stauber's wearing the white boots; I'm next to her)

Anne in Costume as a Bag Person for
Where There's Quegleys, There's Hope

Varsity Football Squad **ROW 1:** G.King, S.LaFlamme, P.Conole, S.Carlson, D.Lien, S.Pafulsi, D.Dillan, T.Hill, R.Tahl, **ROW 2:** L.Anderson, J.Jacobson, D.Wrazidlo, B.Johnson, S.Bloom, P.Pafall, J.Gunderson, M.Town. **ROW 3:** Coach Marv Heiskinen, M.Lien, R.Peltoma, B.Hansen, B.Patterson, M.Munger, D.Langley, S.Burns, J.McLoughlin, M.Donahoe, Coach Joe Deschin. **ROW 4:** G.Merriet, T. Swanson, D.Larsen, P.Lund, T.Luczak, B.Buffalo, D.Stono, G.Federsen, **ROW 5:** P.McLeod, A.Potvein, D.Larsen, L.Anders, S.Leslin, R.Johnson, G.Vittorio, K.Skinman, T.Buttsik, C.Hagberg.

The Handwriting? Heather's Endearment ...

ABOVE Mari Baker, Shane Anderson and Kathy Menz correct copy while BELOW Mark Munger prepares a sports report.

School, community and area activities were investigated and reported by students of the Denfeld Criterion. Ten issues produced during the year were distributed free to all students.

Replacing the traditional editor-in-chief this year were four page editors. These were: Kathy Menz-news, Shane Anderson-editorial, Mari Baker-feature, and Mark Munger-sports. Each of these senior editors held responsibility for his page, while the rest of the staff contributed with special assignments. Page editors attended the Minnesota High School Press Association convention in Minneapolis in the fall, and some also contributed articles to the Duluth Budgeteer and Duluth Herald and News Tribune. Production adviser for the Criterion was Goldie Cohen. Dale Strand was business adviser.

Denfeld *Criterion* Editors
(The endearments are again Heather's)

BWCA (1973)

418

Denfeld Honor Court (partial photo)
(I'm in the first row, last one on the right)

"My name is Edith Ann, and that's the truth!"

Roni

419

The Cabin after Adding the Loft

AGE CHAMPIONS — Elim Lutheran captured the cham-
nship of the first annual Boy's Club basketball tournament
week. Team members are, from left, Front row: Jim
nson, Wayne Rikala, co-captain; Jeff Johnson, Dave

Salveson, co-captain, and Mark Munger. Back Row: Dr
man, coach; Carl Steffen, Greg Anderson and Cliff Okail
(Staff photo.)

Elim Lutheran Basketball Team (1974)
(I'm the last one on the right in the first row)

After My Bath at Eddie's Going Away Party

What Everclear Does to a Guy

John McLoughlin, BWCA (1975)

Larry and Poof, BWCA (1975)

Omega Lake, BWCA (1975)

The Life of a Bungo Jen Monk is Lonely

The Barbarian

The Feast of Bungo Jen

The Cabin in Winter

The Farm

425

Tuttle Assumes the Position
Camp Upshire Rifle Range (1974)
(I'm in the second row, first on the right)

Home from Upshire

Six-Week Wonder Marine

Pelly and the Author at the Cabin

Eddie's Stag: No-Hands Drinking

Eddie's Stag: The Quegleys Conduct Research

Eddie at His Stag

The Sauna

Jeff Doing His Best Take on *Deliverance*

Wampum Rikala at Bat

2921 North 22nd Avenue West

Big Russ and Pelly

Susie and Eddie

Fishing the Knife River (1975)

Me and 'Nay (1976)

Like Bono Says: *Love Rescued Me ...*

The Changer

(In Memory of Jean Endrizzi)

A man who tries to fight with his world
Is a man whose mind is totally unfurled.
For things have been for ages of time
Like the thump of a drum or the search of a mind.

Ringing
Resounding
Despairingly real.
Silent
Then thunderous
As a gallows appeal.

Pity poor changer
And optimistic rearranger
Your efforts will end when you're dead.
To accomplish a task
In a die that is cast
Is something the world will dread.

Ideas and theories
Have long to take hold
In a world that is ageless
Yet seemingly old.
The man who wants change
Who tries to rearrange
Will be forgotten
His tributes untold.

A man of dreams and silver-lined skies
Will end up a dust pile the day he dies.

Like the tick of a church clock
Or the sound of a locked door
The Changer be remembered
Nevermore.

For things have been for ages of time
Like the wind overhead or the birds up to climb.

Ringing
Resounding
Despairingly real.
Silent
Then courageous
Like a martyr's last meal.

Prayer of the Creek

(For Harry Leonard Munger)

You first walked beside me when you were a child. I remember your small feet dangling in my pools, scampering over my grassy banks, sliding uncontrollably across my mossy rocks. You were only six years old. I have been since the retreat of the last ice age.

I was dirty then. My water was fouled. There were few frogs, fewer fish. I was near death. But I remember how enthralled you were with my swiftly churning rapids, my noisy falls. You loved me then but I was too tired, too damaged to return your love properly.

After that first visit, I knew I was in your mind. I felt you thinking about me, felt a child's heart searching for me whenever the four walls of the classroom closed in around you.

From a distance, I watched your gangly limbs form muscle. I saw acne creep across your brow. As you aged and came more frequently to visit, you cast worms into my waters; you sat in shade provided by cedars lining my grassy banks and dreamed of a day when you could live beside me.

Then, miracle of miracles, someone stopped the sewage flowing into my waters; someone determined that the health of the children who fished my ripples and waded my rapids meant something. Within a few short years, I was clean. I flowed sweet and pure. Trout flourished. By happenstance, you came to live within a stone's throw of my dancing path.

Through adolescence, I drew you and your friends to play ball hockey upon my tortured ice. In summer, your passion for trout found you drawing fish with your bare hands from beneath my stones. But, like the men who built the great cities of America, like the pioneers who carved their farms from prairie, you were not satisfied with my nature.

In front of your new house, you loosened boulders and rocks from my ancient bed and piled them across my course, damming my current until the water rose. With shovel and bucket, you scooped gravel from my shoals and filled in the cracks and crevasses of the dam to confine my power. You caught luminescent trout by the dozens under the rocks and released them into your private pond. Naively, you intended they should remain there to be your private stock and treasure.

It was then that I became not only your friend but also your teacher. You learned that, though you are man, you cannot own me, you cannot possess my bounty, you cannot control me. Late summer rains doubled my idyllic pace. A crest of water dislodged your dam. When the torrent subsided, only a few large boulders—rocks too large for me to move—remained. A hundred years ago, your dam may have held. Because of progress, it did not.

For you see, men continued to harm me. Upstream, where my pace was less rapid and my course meandered, men had covered my floodplains with asphalt. Greed destroyed marshlands birthing cool waters. Men built upon soggy earth—built stores to feed commerce. It was the dogged overbuilding of my floodplain, not God's rain, which caused the flood to come with such sudden fury. You knew this. You heard others cry out but you remained mute.

Through high school and college, you continued to love me, to visit me, to ski my snowy shoulders, and walk narrow trails traversing my valley though your ears did not hear my pleas and your eyes did not see my loss. Slowly, ever so slowly, you stopped hearing and seeing me at all. Your walks became infrequent. You did not introduce me to your children with the same affection and reverence you and I had been introduced. You lost your wide-eyed innocence and left me to defend myself.

I am virtually alone now. My old friends have grown up and forgotten me. My waters no longer run clean and cold. Salt washes into my arteries from ten thousand blacktopped parking spaces. In summer's heat, my rocks sprout green slime. The frogs and salamanders have vanished.

You try—when you come home to visit—to grasp the delicately decorated flanks of brook trout hiding amongst my stones but there are few fish left to touch.

I hear politicians and moneymen talk about more buildings, more asphalt. I cry out to them to explain my worth but they do not hear me.

As spring approaches and another construction season looms, I long for you to look at me with the awe and wonder of a six-year-old boy on his first visit to Miller Creek. For in that wondrous gaze was my salvation. I pray that you see me that way again. Before it is too late. Before I am no more.

About the Author

Mark Munger, a former trial attorney and District Court Judge, is a lifelong resident of Northeastern Minnesota. Mark and his wife, René, live on the banks of the wild and scenic Cloquet River north of Duluth. When not writing and editing, Mark enjoys hunting, fishing, skiing, and reading excellent stories.

Other Works by the Author

The Legacy
(ISBN 0972005080 and eBook in all formats)

Set against the backdrop of WWII Yugoslavia and present-day Minnesota, this debut novel combines elements of military history, romance, thriller, and mystery. Rated 3 and 1/2 daggers out of 4 by *The Mystery Review Quarterly*.

Ordinary Lives
(ISBN 97809792717517 and eBook in all formats)

Creative fiction from one of Northern Minnesota's newest writers, these stories touch upon all elements of the human condition and leave the reader asking for more.

Pigs, a Trial Lawyer's Story
(ISBN 097200503x and eBook in all formats)

A story of a young trial attorney, a giant corporation, marital infidelity, moral conflict, and choices made, *Pigs* takes place against the backdrop of Western Minnesota's beautiful Smoky Hills. This tale is being compared by reviewers to Grisham's best.

Suomalaiset: People of the Marsh
(ISBN 0972005064 and eBook in all formats)

A dockworker is found hanging from a rope in a city park. How is his death tied to the turbulence of the times? A masterful novel of compelling history and emotion, *Suomalaiset* has been hailed by reviewers as a "must read."

Esther's Race
(ISBN 9780972005098 and eBook in all formats)

The story of an African American registered nurse who confronts race, religion, and tragedy in her quest for love, this novel is set against the stark and vivid beauty of Wisconsin's Apostle Islands, the pastoral landscape of Central Iowa, and the steel and glass of Minneapolis. A great read soon to be a favorite of book clubs across America.

Mr. Environment: The Willard Munger Story
(ISBN 9780979217524: Trade paperback only)

A detailed and moving biography of Minnesota's leading environmental champion and longest serving member of the Minnesota House of Representatives, *Mr. Environment* is destined to become a book every Minnesotan has on his or her bookshelf.

Black Water: Stories from the Cloquet River
(ISBN 9780979217548 and eBook in all formats)

Essays about ordinary and extraordinary events in the life of an American family living in the wilds of northeastern Minnesota, these tales first appeared separately in two volumes, *River Stories* and *Doc the Bunny*. Re-edited and compiled into one volume, these are stories to read on the deer stand, at the campsite, or late at night for peace of mind.

Laman's River
(ISBN 9780979217531 and eBook in all formats)

A beautiful newspaper reporter is found bound, gagged, and dead. A Duluth judge conceals secrets that may end her career. A reclusive community of religious zealots seeks to protect its view of the hereafter by unleashing an avenging angel upon the world. Mormons. Murder. Minnesota. Montana. Reprising two of your favorite characters from *The Legacy*, Deb Slater and Herb Whitefeather. Buy it now in print or on all major eBook platforms!

Sukulaiset: The Kindred
(ISBN 9780979217562 and eBook in all formats)

The long-awaited sequel to Suomalaiset: People of the Marsh, Mark Munger's epic novel of Finnish immigration to the United States and Canada, *Sukulaiset* portrays the journey of Elin Gustafson from the shores of Lake Superior to the shores of Lake Onega in the Soviet Republic of Karelia during the Great Depression. The story unfolds during Stalin's reign of terror and depicts the interwoven lives of Elin, her daughter Alexis, an American logger, and two Estonians wrapped up in the brutal conflict between Nazi Germany and Communist Russia. A page-turning historical novel of epic proportions.

Boomtown
(ISBN 978-0979217593 and eBook in all formats)

An explosion rocks the site of a new copper/nickel mine in northeastern Minnesota. Two young workers are dead. The Lindahl family turns to trial attorney Dee Dee Hernesman for justice. A shadowy eco-terrorist lurks in the background as Hernesman and Sheriff Deb Slater investigate the tragedy. Are the deaths the result of accident or murder? Equal parts legal thriller and literary fiction, this novel reprises many characters from Munger's prior novels. A page turner of a tale.

Kotimaa: Homeland
(ISBN 978-1-7324434-0-2 and eBook in all formats)

Wondering why Anders Alhomäki, the protagonist in *Suomalaiset* left Finland as a young man? How does the historic migration of Finns from Nordic Europe tie into the present-day immigration of Muslim refugees to Finland? Is a terrorist's threat on the cusp of Finland's centennial real or imagined? Part historical novel, part contemporary thriller, this book is the culmination of more than fourteen years' research. The final chapter in Munger's Finnish trilogy, *Kotimaa* is certain to challenge and entertain!

Kulkuri (Vagabond) and Other Short Stories
(ISBN 978-1-7324434-1-9 and Kindle eBook)

Mark's second collection of short fiction includes award-winning stories and the new novella, "The Angle," as well as a handful of other, brand new gems. Tales from Minnesota to Estonia to Hawaii will engage and enlighten and entertain readers who love short-form fiction.

Visit us at:
www.cloquetriverpress.com
Shop at our online store!

SmileTrain

Changing The World One Smile At A Time.

10% of all gross sales of CRP books are donated by CRP to SmileTrain in hopes of helping children born with cleft lips and palates across the world. Learn more about SmileTrain at http://www.smiletrain.org/.

Made in the USA
Columbia, SC
16 September 2021